China's Strategic Multilateralism

China sometimes plays a leadership role in addressing global challenges, but at other times it free-rides or even spoils efforts at cooperation. When will rising powers like China help to build and maintain international regimes that sustain cooperation on important issues, and when will they play less constructive roles? This study argues that the strategic setting of a particular issue area has a strong influence on whether and how a rising power will contribute to global governance. Two strategic variables are especially important: the balance of outside options that the rising power and established powers face, and whether contributions by the rising power are viewed as indispensable to regime success. Case studies of China's approach to security in Central Asia, nuclear proliferation, global financial governance, and climate change illustrate the logic of the theory, which has implications for contemporary issues such as China's growing role in development finance.

Scott L. Kastner is Professor of Government and Politics, University of Maryland, College Park. He is the author of *Political Conflict and Economic Interdependence across the Taiwan Strait and Beyond* (2009), and his articles have appeared in journals such as *International Security, Journal of Conflict Resolution*, and *International Studies Quarterly.*

Margaret M. Pearson is Professor of Government and Politics, University of Maryland, College Park. Her publications include the books *Joint Ventures in the People's Republic of China* (1991) and *China's New Business Elite: The Political Results of Economic Reform* (1997), as well as articles in *World Politics, The China Journal*, and *Public Administration Review*.

Chad Rector is Associate Professor of Politics at Marymount University in Arlington, Virginia. He is the author of *Federations: Political Dynamics of Cooperation* (2009), as well as articles in *Security Studies, International Studies Quarterly*, and *Pacific Focus*.

China's Strategic Multilateralism

Investing in Global Governance

SCOTT L. KASTNER
University of Maryland

MARGARET M. PEARSON
University of Maryland

CHAD RECTOR
Marymount University

CAMBRIDGE
UNIVERSITY PRESS

University Printing House, Cambridge CB2 8BS, United Kingdom

One Liberty Plaza, 20th Floor, New York, NY 10006, USA

477 Williamstown Road, Port Melbourne, VIC 3207, Australia

314–321, 3rd Floor, Plot 3, Splendor Forum, Jasola District Centre, New Delhi – 110025, India

79 Anson Road, #06-04/06, Singapore 079906

Cambridge University Press is part of the University of Cambridge.

It furthers the University's mission by disseminating knowledge in the pursuit of education, learning, and research at the highest international levels of excellence.

www.cambridge.org
Information on this title: www.cambridge.org/9781108429504
DOI: 10.1017/9781108695725

First published 2019

Printed in the United States of America by Sheridan Books, Inc.

A catalogue record for this publication is available from the British Library.

ISBN 978-1-108-42950-4 Hardback

Contents

Acknowledgments

As with all multiyear projects such as this, we owe a debt to many individuals at a variety of institutions in the United States and abroad. For very thoughtful comments at various stages, we thank Rumi Aoyama, Gregory Chin, Jacques DeLisle, Michael Glosny, Miles Kahler, Evelyn Goh, Avery Goldstein, Andrew Kennedy, Amy King, Wei Liang, Ryan Manuel, Susan Shirk, Michael Tierney, Eric Voeten, Yuhua Wang, and Fengshi Wu. We benefited tremendously from discussions with participants in workshops at the University of Pennsylvania Center for the Study of Contemporary China, University of California, Irvine, School of Law, and the Crawford School of Public Policy at Australian National University. Parts of the manuscript draw from an earlier article published in the journal *Security Studies*.

At Cambridge University Press, we are grateful for the careful guidance of Robert Dreesen and Meera Seth. At various stages, the research benefited substantially from the assistance from Ping-Kuei Chen, Kung-chen Chen, Jiunda Lin, and Liu Wei.

As always, we gratefully appreciate the support of our families. We dedicate this book to Dina, Steve, Benjamin, David, Sarah, Milo, and Aldis.

Abbreviations

6PT	Six Party Talks
AIIB	Asian Infrastructure Investment Bank
AOSIS	Alliance of Small Island States
APEC	Asia-Pacific Economic Cooperation
ASEAN	Association of Southeast Asian Nations
BASIC	Brazil, South Africa, India, and China
BRI	Belt and Road Initiative
BRIC	Brazil, Russia, India, and China
CCP	Chinese Communist Party
CIC	China Investment Corporation
CIS	Commonwealth of Independent States
CMI	Chiang Mai Initiative
COP	Committee of the Parties
CSTO	Collective Security Treaty Organization
DPRK	Democratic People's Republic of Korea
EU	European Union
EurAsEC	Eurasian Economic Community
FDI	Foreign Direct Investment
FTA	Free Trade Agreement
G7	Group of 7
G8	Group of 8
G20	Group of 20

G77	Group of 77
GATT	General Agreement on Tariffs and Trade
GCF	Green Climate Fund
GDP	Gross Domestic Product
GHG	Greenhouse Gases
IAEA	International Atomic Energy Agency
IMF	International Monetary Fund
LCA	Long-term Cooperative Action
MRV	Measuring, Reporting, and Verification
NAMAs	Nationally Appropriate Mitigation Actions
NATO	North Atlantic Treaty Organization
NDB	New Development Bank
NDCs	Nationally Determined Contributions
NDRC	National Development and Reform Commission of the PRC
NGO	Non-Governmental Organization
NPT	Treaty on the Non-Proliferation of Nuclear Weapons
OECD	Organization for Economic Cooperation and Development
PBOC	People's Bank of China
PLA	People's Liberation Army
PRC	People's Republic of China
RATS	Regional Anti-Terrorist Structure
RMB	Renminbi
ROC	Republic of China
SCO	Shanghai Cooperation Organization
SDR	Special Drawing Rights
THAAD	Terminal High Altitude Area Defense
TPP	Trans-Pacific Partnership
UN	United Nations
UNFCCC	United Nations Framework Convention on Climate Change
UNSC	United Nations Security Council
WTO	World Trade Organization

1

Introduction

Explaining China's International Behavior

China's rise as a global power over the last three decades means that, to an increasing extent, Chinese behavior can make or break international cooperation in a given issue area. For example, building and maintaining effective institutions to deal with the North Korean nuclear issue without active Chinese participation is hard to imagine. Likewise, the creation of robust institutions to manage global climate change almost certainly requires active "buy-in" from what is today the world's second largest economy and largest greenhouse gas emitter. Given China's growing importance, an expanding scholarly and popular discourse has considered what type of country China is and what type it is likely to become. Will China emerge as a responsible stakeholder, showing diplomatic leadership to *invest* in reviving and maintaining even those global regimes that it did not play a part in creating because it sees an interest in preserving global stability and prosperity? Will China be a revisionist state, a spoiler, threatening to *hold-up* global multilateralism if it cannot restructure international institutions more to its liking? Or will China simply be a free-rider, content to *accept* the existing rules but to let the United States and other established powers do the heavy lifting needed to maintain international order?

We argue that China has shown, and will continue to show, all three of these patterns of behavior in different issue areas at the same time. In some cases, Chinese actions have helped consolidate and expand international cooperation. To return to the examples used earlier, China's recent increasing willingness to reach international agreements on climate is among the most significant global developments in this issue area in recent years. Similarly, Beijing's efforts to facilitate a resolution to North

Korea's nuclear weapons program, though ultimately unsuccessful, were critical to fostering cooperative interactions on that issue during the 2000s. In these cases, a picture emerges of China as a responsible stakeholder, willing to invest in efforts to preserve and expand international cooperation. At other times, however, Beijing has shown a willingness to play the role of spoiler, to use its bargaining power to push for the restructuring of international institutions to better serve Chinese interests. China's willingness to stand firm in pressing for revisions to the institutional architecture of international financial regulation (most notably by demanding greater representation in International Monetary Fund [IMF] decision-making) serves as a clear example. And in other cases still, China has been content to sit on the sidelines and allow other countries to pay the costs of sustaining and deepening international cooperation. Consider, for instance, China's apparent disinterest in actively working to find a successful resolution in the Doha Round negotiations of the World Trade Organization (WTO), a decision that might come to be seen as an enormous missed opportunity for developing countries in particular.

China's approach to multilateral regimes is part of a more general issue: how rising powers – which in the future may include states beyond China, such as India and Brazil – approach global governance. When, and to what extent, do rising powers passively accept existing rules? When do they actively invest in and help strengthen existing institutional architecture? When do they obstruct or play hold-up with existing institutions? When do they construct new institutions? The way that emerging powers approach global governance issues will have enormous impact on the future of world order. China's decision, for instance, to demand changes to the IMF resulted in greater voice for it and other emerging economies in that body. Likewise, China's more recent decision to establish the Asian Infrastructure Investment Bank (which we discuss at length in this book's concluding chapter) has the potential to dramatically expand development finance in Asia. Understanding why rising powers make the choices they do concerning global governance, in short, will shed important light on the evolution of cooperation in different issue areas and the prospects for future cooperation.

Our thesis is that the strategic setting of a particular issue area will have a strong influence on whether and how a rising power will contribute to global governance. Although we argue that our theory applies in principle to any rising power, our empirical focus in this book is on China's approach to global governance in the post–Cold War world. We show that China's behavior has varied dramatically both over time and across issues, and we use our theory to help make sense of this variation in ways that existing theories cannot. To be clear, we do not argue that other factors – such as Chinese political institutions, ideology, culture, or broader socialization into international institutions – are unimportant. Rather, we make the case that a focus on the strategic setting helps make sense of broad patterns in China's approach to global governance that might otherwise go unaccounted for or underexplored.[1] Our findings have important implications for how we understand not only Chinese behavior in global regimes but, more generally, the way other emerging powers are likely to approach global governance as their influence grows.

1.1 THE PUZZLE

Throughout most of the postwar era, China played a minor role in international governance; not only was the People's Republic of China (PRC) government primarily concerned with domestic issues, but China was also effectively marginalized in most multilateral regimes. Since the end of the Cold War, China's international influence has risen as its relative economic and military potential has grown, yet China remains an *inconsistent* player in multilateral settings. In the language of social science, its behavior varies. Three recent examples help illustrate this variation.

Consider, first, China's behavior within the multilateral trade regime. Beijing went to great efforts to get into the WTO at a time when the PRC was emerging as one of the world's largest exporters. China and the United States engaged in over a decade of on-again, off-again negotiations, culminating in a comprehensive agreement in 1999 that set the stage for the PRC's 2001 entry into the organization. Outside observers viewed China's WTO commitments as more extensive than those made by previous newly admitted members, and Chinese leaders faced substantial domestic criticism for the concessions they made to gain entry into the body.[2] Yet, despite these efforts, since entry China has been more passive within the WTO regarding efforts to revise the international trade

[1] To put it another way, our theoretical expectation is about the behavior of rising powers generally. We explore the practical implications of our theory using a set of observations about China in order to evaluate the theory on its own terms, because the Chinese experience is a good test case for the theory. To the extent that the evidence supports our theory, it should also inform our understanding of China specifically. Our claim is not that China is indistinguishable from every other rising state.

[2] On China's concessions, see, for instance, Nicholas R. Lardy, *Integrating China into the Global Economy* (Washington, DC: Brookings Institution Press, 2002).

regime: although Beijing has largely *accepted* and complied with existing rules, it has not played a constructive role in moving a new round of liberalizing rules forward.[3] During Doha Round negotiations, for instance, China largely sat on the sidelines, even though some observers noted the PRC's unique ability to play a bridging role between developed and developing economies.

Second, China's behavior with regard to global financial governance has been different. As with trade, global financial institutions were created without input from the PRC, which only assumed membership in the IMF in 1980.[4] And, like its behavior in the WTO, China – although compliant with IMF rules – was for many years relatively passive in its approach to governance issues within the IMF. But in recent years, China has been more active in trying to reshape the rules governing global finance. During the global financial crisis, given China's growing economic power, other countries increasingly viewed active PRC participation as critical if efforts to restructure global financial governance were to succeed. But China made its participation conditional on reforms to existing institutions, in particular with regard to voting rules that were stacked against developing countries like China. In other words, China after the financial crisis pursued a strategy of *hold-up* with regard to the international financial regime, conditioning active participation in regime maintenance on a set of concessions favorable to PRC interests.

The third example concerns Chinese behavior with respect to the North Korean nuclear issue. Here, as with the IMF case, Chinese behavior has varied over time. During the first North Korean nuclear crisis in the 1990s, China played a supportive – but mostly secondary and passive – role in managing the issue, largely deferring to Washington and Pyongyang to find a bilateral solution. However, when tensions on the Korean Peninsula spiked again during the second nuclear crisis in 2002–2003, China ended up playing a much more proactive role, ultimately *investing* time and effort in the creation of the Six Party Talks (6PT),

[3] On China's behavior within the WTO in the years after accession, see Margaret M. Pearson, "China in Geneva: Lessons from China's Early Years in the World Trade Organization," in Alastair Iain Johnston and Robert Ross, eds., *New Directions in the Study of China's Foreign Policy* (Stanford University Press, 2006), pp. 587–644.

[4] Although China was an original member of the IMF in 1945, the country was governed by the Republic of China at the time. When the Nationalists lost the Chinese Civil War and retreated to Taiwan in 1949, they retained membership in many international organizations, including the IMF.

a new multilateral dialogue that aimed to resolve the North Korean nuclear issue.

These three cases show that China's behavior in global governance, and in particular with regard to regime creation and maintenance, has exhibited considerable variation across cases and, often, over time within cases.[5] At times, as in the WTO or in the early years of the PRC's entry into the IMF, Beijing behaves passively. In these cases, China was largely in compliance with the rules of the organizations and appeared, by and large, to accept the rules embodied by these organizations. At other times, such as in matters of global financial governance during the global financial crisis, China has played what might be termed a hold-up strategy, in which it tries to leverage its bargaining power to restructure rules so as to better suit its interests. And in other cases, China actively invests in the creation of new institutions or the maintenance of existing institutions, as with the PRC's creation of the 6PT. As we show in the empirical chapters to follow, China's behavior in a large number of settings can be characterized as one of these three types of behavior: accept, invest, or hold-up.

Many existing efforts to explain China's international behavior through the lens of international relations theory focus on the country's innate disposition. Drawing inspiration in particular from the Power Transition Theory literature, China is viewed as either a "status quo" power (likely to acquiesce to and integrate into US-led governance structures) or a "revisionist" state (dissatisfied with existing structures and aiming to change them as able).[6] As we have observed, though, China's behavior since the end of the Cold War has varied greatly across issue areas; China does not approach international regimes with a single, ideologically fixed approach, as predicted by the dispositional theories. What is needed is an understanding of *when* a rising state like China will seek to revise or undermine existing rules, when it will accept them, and when it will actively invest in them.

5 On the point that China has played very different roles in different multilateral regimes, see Hongying Wang and Erik French, "China in Global Economic Governance," *Asian Economic Policy Review*, Vol. 9, no. 2 (2014), pp. 254–71.

6 For an excellent and critical discussion along these lines, see Alastair Iain Johnston, "Is China a Status Quo Power?" *International Security*, Vol. 27, no. 4 (Spring 2003), pp. 5–56. See also: Scott L. Kastner and Phillip C. Saunders, "Is China a Status Quo or Revisionist State? Leadership Travel as an Empirical Indicator of Foreign Policy Priorities," *International Studies Quarterly*, Vol. 56, no. 1 (March 2012), pp. 163–77; and Steve Chan, *China, the U.S., and the Power Transition Theory: A Critique* (New York: Routledge Press, 2008).

A number of prior excellent studies have examined China's behavior within regimes, focusing on the extent to which China behaves in accordance with the rules and norms of multilateral organizations ("compliance").[7] Our question, in contrast, concerns China's willingness to go one level deeper by actively participating in the creation and maintenance of multilateral regimes – what Douglas Heckathorn has termed *second-order cooperation*.[8] We seek to understand the conditions under which China will organize other states to contribute to a common aim and "invest" by compromising on its own objectives for the sake of broader agreement or, conversely, will complicate cooperative efforts, either by attempting to leverage its influence to restructure existing arrangements through "hold-up" or by passively choosing to "accept" existing regimes without contributing to their preservation.

1.2 THE ARGUMENT IN BRIEF

We theorize that the variation in an emerging great power's approach to regime production and maintenance (its second-order cooperation) is strongly influenced by two strategic variables: the balance of outside options the rising power and established powers face, and the degree to which contributions by the rising power are viewed as indispensable to regime success. Outside options are the alternatives – for both rising and established powers – to jointly investing in multilateral regimes. We posit first that a rising power is more likely to invest in new or existing regimes when the rising power's outside options are poor relative to those of established powers. When the rising state's outside options are better, we posit that its approach to multilateralism will depend on the second variable: the degree to which the rising state believes that established powers view contributions from the rising state as indispensable to the overall

7 E.g., Rosemary Foot and Andrew Walter, *China, the United States, and Global Order* (New York: Cambridge University Press, 2011); Elizabeth Economy and Michel Oksenberg (eds.), *China Joins the World: Progress and Prospects* (New York: Council on Foreign Relations, 1999); and Ann Kent, *Beyond Compliance: China, International Organizations, and Global Security* (Stanford, CA: Stanford University Press, 2007). Alastair Iain Johnston's focus on socialization processes applies, we believe, to both compliance and second-order cooperation (which we also define in this paragraph). We discuss socialization arguments at greater length in Chapter 2. See: Alastair Iain Johnston, *Social States: China in International Institutions, 1980–2000* (Princeton, NJ: Princeton University Press, 2008).

8 Douglas D. Heckathorn, "Collective Action and the Second-Order Free-Rider Problem," *Rationality and Society*, Vol. 1, no. 1 (July 1989), pp. 78–100.

success of a regime. When a rising state's outside options are relatively good and when its contributions are generally seen as indispensable, it will possess the leverage to pursue hold-up, where it can extract concessions from established powers as the price of its contributions to regime success. On the other hand, when the rising power's outside options are good but it believes established powers view its cooperation as unnecessary, it will choose to passively accept existing rules, free-riding on the efforts of established powers to construct and maintain regimes.

After developing the theory and deriving testable implications, and following a brief presentation of contextual material concerning China's rise, we explore the utility of the theory in the context of four empirical cases relating to China:

- attempts by great powers to promote security in Central Asia,
- nuclear nonproliferation efforts globally and with respect to North Korea,
- management of the international financial system, and
- cooperation to mitigate climate change.

From the perspective of social science theory, we chose these cases carefully. Not only is there variation across the four cases, but there is also variation within each case. The cases also, of course, are of much contemporary interest. On each issue our analysis brings to light a perspective that is not found in other mainstream treatments of these topics. Our empirical analysis draws from a range of sources, including primary sources from China and original interviews in the United States and China.

Our approach bridges contemporary theories of multilateralism and institutional development with up-to-date research on Chinese foreign policy. Although a number of recent studies have fruitfully examined China's approach to multilateral regimes, these studies typically do not aim to develop generalizable propositions about rising power behavior.[9]

[9] Recent examples include Thomas J. Christensen, *The China Challenge: Shaping the Choices of a Rising Power* (New York: W. W. Norton & Company, 2015); Chien-peng Chung, *China's Multilateral Cooperation in Asia and the Pacific: Institutionalizing Beijing's "Good Neighbor Policy"* (London and New York: Routledge, 2010); Gerald Chan, Pak K. Lee, and Lai-Ha Chan, *China Engages Global Governance: A New Order in the Making?* (Routledge, 2012); David Shambaugh, *China Goes Global: The Partial Power* (New York: Oxford University Press, 2013); and Foot and Walter, *China, the United States, and Global Order* (New York: Cambridge University Press, 2011). Earlier examples include Kent, *Beyond Compliance*; Economy and Oksenberg, *China Joins the World*; Alastair Iain Johnston and Robert Ross, eds., *Engaging China: The*

At the same time, none of the best recent work on the strategic aspects of leadership and institutional development within international organizations[10] is grounded in a detailed and specific empirical examination of decision-making within a rising state. Our hope is that our study makes a unique and important contribution, both to the literature on China's foreign relations and to the broader theoretical literature on international institutions.

1.3 PLAN FOR THE BOOK

We present our theoretical argument in Chapter 2, in which our aim is to provide a general theory of how rising powers approach global governance in a world where most institutions have been set up by established powers. We begin with an extensive discussion of our dependent variable, the strategy a rising power adopts with respect to second-order cooperation within a particular regime. We then develop our core theoretical argument (summarized earlier) in two steps: first by considering the impact of outside options on rising power behavior, and then by considering the impact of perceived indispensability. We show how these factors combine to create incentives for a rising state to pursue strategies of accept, hold-up, or invest. We also consider the possibility of dynamic conditions in which state leaders might try to manipulate their outside options. Finally, we present our research design, used to test the main hypotheses emerging from our theory.

A brief Chapter 3 provides a contextual and background discussion on the economic, security, and diplomatic dimensions of China's rise. We intend this to be useful to readers who are not as familiar with China's recent history. Chapters 4–7 then assess the utility of our theory by examining China's behavior in international regimes.

Management of an Emerging Power (New York: Routledge Press, 1999); and Marc Lanteigne, *China and International Institutions: Alternate Paths to Global Power* (London: Taylor and Francis, 2005). One key exception that does aim to generalize is Johnston, *Social States*.

[10] See, for instance, Allison Carnegie, *Power Plays: How International Institutions Reshape Coercive Diplomacy* (New York: Cambridge University Press, 2015); Tana Johnson, *Organizational Progeny: Why Governments are Losing Control over the Proliferating Structures of Global Governance* (Oxford: Oxford University Press, 2014); Randall Stone, *Controlling Institutions: International Organizations and the Global Economy* (New York: Cambridge University Press, 2011); and Erik Voeten, "Outside Options and the Logic of Security Council Action," *American Political Science Review*, Vol. 95, no. 4 (December 2001), pp. 845–58.

The first two of the four case chapters focus on security issues. In Chapter 4, we consider China's approach to the problem of stability in Central Asia. Following a period in which China largely free-rode on Soviet and then Russian efforts to promote stable regional development, several factors led to an erosion in China's outside options by the mid-1990s. These factors included, most importantly, instability in Xinjiang (and the fear that instability in Central Asia could worsen conditions in Western China) combined with a sharp deterioration in Russian power in the region. After the mid-1990s, in turn, China played an active role in building regional security institutions, culminating in 2001 with the establishment of the Shanghai Cooperation Organization. Chapter 5 examines China's approach to nuclear nonproliferation. After being disengaged from the global nonproliferation regime until the early 1990s, China has since been a regular player, albeit a passive one. Broadly speaking, Beijing has been consistent in its acceptance of the existing regime but provides little affirmative leadership to maintain it. We argue that strong outside options help explain PRC behavior. We then explore in some detail a key exception, involving North Korea's nuclear program, in which China, beginning in 2003, actively invested in institution-building by organizing the 6PT. Discussion of this important exception illustrates and further tests our basic theory.

Chapter 6 shifts the focus to an economic issue, specifically China's approach to global financial governance since the early 2000s. After years of being largely passive, accepting the rules of the international financial regime, China by the late 2000s moved toward a policy of hold-up, whereby it threatened to spoil cooperation as a way to force changes in the IMF to better suit its interests. This shift occurred most notably in the aftermath of the global financial crisis, when there was a widespread perception that Chinese contributions were indispensable to continued effective global financial governance. We explore in detail China's move to hold-up cooperation, as it sought to influence the redistribution of vote shares in the IMF and to secure the inclusion of China's currency, the *renminbi*, in the basket of reserve currencies that constitute the IMF's Special Drawing Rights (SDR).

Chapter 7 considers China's approach to global climate change negotiations. We show that China played a role as spoiler in the 1990s and 2000s climate negotiations in an effort to hold-up cooperation and ensure that future agreements would give it more favorable terms. Though China continued, by and large, to play a hold-up strategy through the 2009 Copenhagen meetings, its approach to climate change negotiations

TABLE 1.1. *Cases and changing PRC behavior*

Case	Chapter	China's behavior	Key institution
Central Asian Stability	4	Accept → Invest	Shanghai Cooperation Organisation
Nuclear Proliferation	5	Accept → Accept	Non-Proliferation Treaty
(North Korea)	5	Accept → Invest → Accept	Six Party Talks
Financial Governance	6	Accept → Hold-up	International Monetary Fund
Climate Change	7	Hold-up → Invest	UN Climate Negotiations

was beginning to change. By the mid-2010s, friction related to worsening environmental conditions within China, combined with the undesirability of an outcome in which the European Union (EU) and United States might proceed with an agreement without China, led to constructive Chinese engagement on climate and an increased willingness to invest in new institutional architecture. Table 1.1 summarizes our key empirical cases and China's changing behavior in each.

Finally, Chapter 8 concludes the book. After summarizing our findings – which underscore the useful leverage that our theory provides in explaining China's approach to global governance – we discuss implications for recent developments as China contemplates its approach to multilateralism with respect to other issues, such as development lending (with the Asian Infrastructure Investment Bank). The chapter ends with a discussion of recent events in the West, including the United Kingdom's vote to exit the EU and the election of Donald Trump as US president. Though events are still unfolding, we speculate briefly on how a shift toward unilateralism in the West might affect China's future approach toward global governance.

2

Theory

When Do Rising Powers Choose to Invest, Hold-Up, or Accept Existing Regime Arrangements?

When do rising powers choose to contribute to the creation and maintenance of multilateral regimes? Our argument begins with the assumption that national leaders choose whether and how to support or revise a regime based, at least in part, on their beliefs about what kinds of benefits they will receive from participation in the regime. National leaders, in other words, try to anticipate their potential payoffs from different options and make choices that leave them in the best position afterward. Their payoffs – the benefits they expect to get from a regime – stem not merely from the presence or absence of gains from cooperation, but from the distribution of those gains, giving states incentives to bargain hard over multilateral governance.[1]

In this chapter, we develop our general theoretical approach; we argue that there are some fundamental structural factors that help condition the strategies China, or any rising state, will adopt when confronted with any given issue. These structural factors are characteristics of the particular

[1] Institutionalized cooperation is as much of a struggle for gain as any other domain of international politics, and distributional conflicts among states ostensibly cooperating with each other within international organizations is a subject of extensive investigation in the study of international relations. See Phillip Y. Lipscy, *Renegotiating the World Order: Institutional Change in International Relations* (New York, NY: Cambridge University Press, 2017), p. 5. A common finding is that the expectations leaders have over distributional conflicts have a major influence on whether and how agreements get negotiated and ratified in the first place. See, for example, Christina J. Schneider and Johannes Urpelainen, "Distributional Conflict between Powerful States and International Treaty Ratification," *International Studies Quarterly*, Vol. 57, no. 1 (2013), pp. 13–27. Concerns over distribution may even prevent states from agreeing to otherwise potentially mutually beneficial agreements in the first place, as in Chad Rector, *Federations: The Political Dynamics of Cooperation* (Ithaca, NY: Cornell University Press, 2009).

issue and can vary across issues or within issues over time; they are not inherent characteristics of countries or features of the international system such as the distribution of power – things that might be expected to be the same across all issues. Our argument focuses more specifically on a state's outside options, which are the expectations leaders have about what will happen if cooperation were to fail, and the beliefs leaders have about whether a rising state's contributions to a regime are indispensable to the success of broader cooperation. We compare different issue areas and argue that a rising state's engagement with multilateral regimes will differ across issues.

This chapter proceeds in several steps. First, we define the dependent variable, the approach rising states take toward second-order cooperation in multilateralism, and explain the scope of our argument. Second, we explain how structural factors – outside options and indispensability – influence the immediate decisions that a rising state like China makes about investments in multilateralism. Third, we expand our analysis to consider a dynamic context and show how a rising state might adopt strategies designed to change the structure of an issue in the longer run. Fourth, we describe some of the observable implications of our argument and place it in the context of other scholarship on our basic question.

2.1 INTERNATIONAL REGIMES AND SECOND-ORDER COOPERATION

A multilateral regime is a system of rules and expectations that countries use to coordinate their actions on a given issue.[2] Regimes are defined by the issue area, rather than by a specific institution. While regimes typically include formal institutions, they also include all of the informal procedures and common understandings connected to that issue. For example, the global multilateral trade regime includes the formal rules of the WTO and of the many other regional and bilateral trade agreements, such as Mercosur and the Asia-Pacific Economic Cooperation (APEC) forum and the European Union, as well as the informal understandings leaders have about the relationships among those institutions, and the norms and customs around how they are negotiated and implemented. Another example is the multilateral nuclear proliferation regime, defined not just by the Treaty on the Non-Proliferation of Nuclear Weapons

[2] Peter J. Katzenstein, Robert O. Keohane, and Stephen D. Krasner, "International Organization and the Study of World Politics," *International Organization*, Vol. 52, no. 4 (1998), pp. 645–85.

(NPT) but by a set of common expectations about how countries will address issues of common concern even when they do not technically fall under the auspices of the NPT. So, negotiations over international supply chains for India's nuclear program, demands for inspections of North Korean sites, economic sanctions on Pakistan, and a *de facto* exemption for Israel are all aspects of the regime even though the countries involved are not formal NPT members.[3]

Regimes are products of negotiations among member states, when those states have at least some common interests in situations of mutual concern. At the simplest level, a regime can be understood as a set of rules about which behaviors are acceptable. Sometimes, of course, the boundaries between actions that are and are not acceptable are subtle. The nuclear nonproliferation regime could be described as "do not build nuclear weapons unless you are China, France, Russia, the United States, or the United Kingdom," although the real rule is probably more complex: "do not make any obvious moves toward building nuclear weapons unless you are China, France, Russia, the United States, or the United Kingdom, or unless you are a client of one of them and have demonstrated that you do not have destabilizing intentions."

At the broadest level, states have two kinds of decisions to make about how to behave in a regime. First, they must choose whether to live up to the letter and spirit of the rules – the formal or informal commitment they made by claiming membership in the regime – by making substantive policies that are in line with commitments; this issue is sometimes referred to as "compliance" or "first-order" cooperation.[4]

Our focus in this book, however, is on a second kind of decision: states must choose which efforts to make on behalf of the regime itself. Following Douglas Heckathorn, we refer to this as "second-order" cooperation.[5] Second-order cooperation involves punishing other members of

[3] On regimes being defined as much by common normative understandings as by formal institutions, see Daniel C. Thomas, "Beyond Identity: Membership Norms and Regional Organization," *European Journal of International Relations*, Vol. 23, no. 1 (2016), pp. 217–40.

[4] This is not to say that issues of compliance are not important; they are obviously substantively critical for whether or not regimes are effective, and there is an increasing recognition that expectations about compliance affect how states negotiate agreements in the first place. Emilie Hafner-Burton, Brad L. LeVeck, and David G. Victor, "No False Promises: How The Prospect of Non-Compliance Affects Elite Preferences for International Cooperation," *International Studies Quarterly*, Vol. 61, no. 1 (2016), pp. 1–13.

[5] Douglas D. Heckathorn, "Collective Action and the Second-Order Free-Rider Problem," *Rationality and Society*, Vol. 1, no. 1 (1989), pp. 78–100.

the regime who fail to follow through on their commitments, enticing new members to join the regime, putting one's own reputation on the line, and sacrificing other goals by accepting that other states will need a voice in regime governance as well, all in order to enhance the operation of the regime generally. Second-order cooperation can also entail investing in the construction of new institutions to help solve problems left un- or under-addressed in extant regimes. And in instances where no regime exists to address a particular problem, second-order cooperation entails investing in the creation of a new regime to manage the issue.

The idea that there are different levels to cooperation is not novel; indeed, it forms the basis for many different versions of the theory of hegemonic stability. Robert Keohane describes the difference between states that *follow* the rules of a regime and states that *enforce* the rules of a regime. He notes, for example, that Britain in the nineteenth century did little to coerce other states (beyond the ones that were subordinate units in its own empire) to open their markets to trade in the same way that Britain itself did. Conversely, by the mid-twentieth century the United States enforced market openness by using leverage stemming from its willingness to selectively open its market to reciprocal cooperators and from its military commitments to Cold War allies, using rewards and punishments to build support for a broader regime.[6] First-order cooperation, in this case, is simply opening up one's own market. Second-order cooperation is coercing other countries to join a regime that commits them to opening their markets.

The relationship between first-order and second-order cooperation has been addressed in a number of other contexts as well. In sociology, for example, Christine Horne distinguishes between norms and "meta-norms." A norm is a rule about behavior, such as, in China prior to the twentieth century, "parents of girls should bind their daughters' feet." A meta-norm is a rule about how rules are to be enforced, such as "people should shun parents who do not practice foot-binding." Norms and meta-norms are analytically and empirically distinct, since actors can comply with the norm without necessarily contributing to enforcement at the meta-level – in the footbinding example, parents may choose to bind their own daughters' feet without necessarily shunning others who choose not to. Meta-norms (or, as we refer to it, "second-order cooperation") guide actions to reward compliance and punish noncompliance.

[6] Robert O. Keohane, *After Hegemony: Cooperation and Discord in the World Political Economy* (Princeton, NJ: Princeton University Press, 1984), p. 37.

An important question in sociology concerns when actors will take action to enforce norms (that is, when they will comply with meta-norms) and when they will not.[7]

The flip side of second-order cooperation is second-order free-riding. Consider an international rule such as the prohibition on nuclear proliferation. A country might violate that rule by building nuclear weapons when it did not previously possess them, perhaps because it concluded that doing so would enhance its own security even at the expense of the security of others; such a country would be a "first-order free-rider" for violating the rule. Other countries might then punish the violator, perhaps by imposing trade sanctions. But imposing trade sanctions is costly, and many countries might ideally prefer not to sanction the violator. Those that *do* sanction are acting as "second-order cooperators" by acting in ways costly to their own interests for the sake of the broader regime. Those countries that *do not* sanction are "second-order free-riders," enjoying the benefits of trade with the violator while relying on others to pay the costs of enforcement.[8]

Experimental and theoretical research in several fields has generally concluded that second-order cooperation is often necessary to sustain first-order cooperation. For example, Ernst Fehr and Simon Gächter found, through a series of experiments, that test subjects who were more willing to withhold cooperation from defectors in a coordination game – even when punishing defectors was costly to those who carried out punishments – were generally able to sustain cooperation longer.[9] Christine Horne also found consistent evidence that cooperation lasted longer when the threat of enforcement from at least some other players was stronger.[10]

For an example that demonstrates the importance of second-order cooperation for sustaining first-order cooperation, consider again the global nonproliferation regime. Leading states, such as the United States, sometimes use economic sanctions to punish states that violate nonproliferation rules, such as Iran. However, economic sanctions are only

7 Christine Horne, *The Rewards of Punishment: A Relational Theory of Norm Enforcement* (Palo Alto, CA: Stanford University Press, 2009), p. 64.

8 For a recent study that explores the issue of second-order free-riding in the case of China, see Andrew B. Kennedy, "China and the Free-Rider Problem: Exploring the Case of Energy Security," *Political Science Quarterly*, Vol. 130, no. 1 (2015), pp. 27–50.

9 Ernst Fehr and Simon Gächter, "Fairness and Retaliation: The Economics of Reciprocity," *The Journal of Economic Perspectives*, Vol. 14, no. 3 (2000), pp. 159–81.

10 Horne, *Rewards of Punishment.*

effective if they are widely observed by all of the target's potential trading partners, and each potential trading partner has an individual interest in violating, or "busting," the sanctions regime to secure economic gains. So, Bryan Early argues that the success of the nonproliferation regime largely rises or falls on securing widespread second-order cooperation on economic sanctions to punish potential violators, but that successful enforcement relies on the ability of leading sanctioners, in turn, to punish countries that threaten to bust sanctions. He concludes that leading states have an especially difficult time punishing sanction busters when those busters are themselves critical allies; for example, the United States was unwilling to punish the United Arab Emirates for violating sanctions placed on Iran because the United States had other issues at stake in the relationship.[11]

Todd Sandler examines the issue using the example of transnational terrorist groups, in which those states that are potential terrorist targets have a *collective* interest in committing to a strategy of not negotiating or paying ransoms, but each state has an *individual* interest in making a side deal to buy off terrorist groups who would then direct their energies elsewhere.[12] International conventions against terrorism, as well as formal alliances and *ad hoc* coalitions, are mechanisms that leading states use to punish states that themselves violate international agreements by paying ransoms.[13]

For a final example of the connection between first-order and second-order cooperation, consider the logic of international environmental agreements. One key difference between, on the one hand, the relatively successful Montreal Protocol to reduce emissions of ozone-depleting chemicals and, on the other hand, the relatively unsuccessful Kyoto Protocol to reduce emissions of carbon dioxide and other GHGs was that although both involved similar first-order commitments to reduce

[11] Bryan R. Early, *Busted Sanctions: Explaining Why Economic Sanctions Fail* (Palo Alto, CA: Stanford University Press, 2015), pp. 110–15. He does not use the phrases "second-order" or "meta-norm" but the logic is the same. See also Bryan R. Early, "Sleeping With Your Friends' Enemies: An Explanation of Sanctions-Busting Trade," *International Studies Quarterly*, Vol. 53, no. 1 (2009), pp. 49–71.

[12] Todd Sandler, *Global Collective Action* (New York, NY: Cambridge University Press, 2004), p. 189. See also Walter Enders and Todd Sandler, *The Political Economy of Terrorism* (New York, NY: Cambridge University Press, 2011).

[13] The case of failed American efforts to stop French and Italian payments to al Qaeda kidnappers underscores the difficulty of maintaining a regime while also highlighting the relationship between weak second-order enforcement and cooperation failure generally. Rukmini Callimachi, "Paying Ransoms, Europe Bankrolls Qaeda Terror," *The New York Times*, July 29, 2014.

emissions, their enforcement structures differed. The Montreal Protocol on ozone depletion included provisions for sanctions on countries that did not adopt cleaner technologies. Moreover, and crucially, the vested interest that the United States had in promoting these alternatives (since a US firm, DuPont, held key patents) gave the United States an interest in enforcement that made sanctioning threats credible. In contrast, not only did the Kyoto Protocol on climate change lack an enforcement mechanism, but the agreement also lacked any state or group of states willing to punish other states that stayed out or that violated their commitments.[14] Separately, the financing provisions of the Montreal Protocol, designed to provide funding for research into alternatives and to help pay for the transition in poor countries, encouraged transparency and allowed for countries to shame and punish free-riders; a general consensus suggests that these provisions helped mitigate the free-rider problem in funding.[15]

In any case, contemporary national policymakers often act as though international regimes with at least some sort of mechanism for sanctioning behavior are the *sine qua non* of international cooperation; a recent survey of policymakers, for example, showed a strong preference for international agreements that had enforcement mechanisms over those that did not.[16] Given the importance of second-order cooperation – actions one state takes to create incentives for other states to engage in first-order cooperation – when will states cooperate at this higher level? In particular, when will rising powers contribute to second-order cooperation in the context of existing or new regimes?

Emerging powers often face a set of international regimes constructed by established, great powers – regimes created with the interests of those

[14] Sandler, *Global Collective Action*; David G. Victor, *The Collapse of the Kyoto Protocol and the Struggle to Slow Global Warming* (Princeton, NJ: Princeton University Press, 2004); Jana von Stein, "The International Law and Politics of Climate Change: Ratification of the United Nations Framework Convention and the Kyoto Protocol," *Journal of Conflict Resolution*, Vol. 52, no. 2 (2008), pp. 243–68.

[15] On the developing of these funding mechanisms and their value in maintaining cooperation, see Scott Barrett, *Why Cooperate? The Incentive to Supply Global Public Goods* (London: Oxford University Press, 2007), p. 123. On second-order cooperation as the basis of human cooperation generally, see Mizuho Shinada, Toshio Yamagishi, and Yu Ohmura, "False Friends are Worse than Bitter Enemies: 'Altruistic' Punishment of In-group Members," *Evolution and Human Behavior*, Vol. 25, no. 6 (2004), pp. 379–93. For chimpanzees as well, cooperation across different domains seems to depend on systems of enforcement. Keith Jensen, Josep Call, and Michael Tomasello, "Chimpanzees are Vengeful but Not Spiteful," *Proceedings of the National Academy of Sciences*, Vol. 104, no. 32 (2007), pp. 13046–50.

[16] Hafner-Burton et al., "No False Promises."

established powers in mind. As emerging countries develop their economic and military potential, however, their approach to multilateral regimes can be increasingly consequential to how those regimes operate. In other words, these rising powers will play a pivotal role in determining whether and how pre-existing regimes continue to function. In some instances, emerging powers may find that existing regimes do not address problems that are important to the emerging powers and, so, if there is to be a regime-based solution to a common problem, the rising power will have to create the regime itself. In other instances, emerging powers may find existing regimes perfectly suitable and enjoy the benefits without making any efforts to sustain the regimes. Alternatively, they may find existing regimes unsuitable to their interests and take steps to undermine them.

For our purposes, the term "rising power" refers to a country that, in the past, has played a minor role in contributing to second-order cooperation on a particular issue, but that is an increasingly consequential actor within that issue area. States are more consequential for international cooperation when their individual choices have a larger impact. A major country increasing its efforts to promote multilateral cooperation will make more of a difference than a minor country that increases its efforts by the same proportion. A rising power is a country whose importance is growing to the point where it is on track to become one of the most consequential countries in a particular issue area.

A state may have a different marginal effect on some issue areas than on others; therefore, what constitutes a rising (or emerging) power in any given case will depend on the context of the particular issue. For instance, India can be thought of as an emerging power in the context of global climate change, since rapid industrialization means that India is an increasingly significant contributor to GHG emissions, though India previously has played a secondary role in the construction and maintenance of international climate change regimes. But India exerts little influence on security issues in Northeast Asia, so it makes little sense to think of India as a rising power in that context. In the global context, with respect to many issues of contemporary concern, China clearly meets our criteria for a rising power. While our focus in the empirical sections is on China's behavior, our theory could also apply to other emerging powers in today's world, or to historical cases such as the United States or Germany at the turn of the twentieth century; we draw on other cases like these as we build our theory. For simplicity, in the theoretical argument that follows, we refer to a single rising state and a single established power, although in practice the relevant established power may be a coalition of states on an issue (such as the United States and the European Union).[17]

The scope of our argument is limited to issues having the potential for joint gains. The empirical chapters that follow, which focus on regional security in Central Asia, nuclear proliferation, global financial stability, and climate change, all concern issues on which cooperation in principle could make all states better off at the same time. This kind of analysis has little to say about situations of pure deadlock – where anything that makes one state better off, by definition, makes its rival worse off. So, for example, competition between the United States and China for regional allies might be an issue for which our argument would not apply.[18]

Throughout our analysis, we seek to explain the approach that a rising state adopts toward a particular issue. Here we are not referring to a *grand strategy* in the conventional sense, although it could be thought of as a *strategy* in the formal sense of a "complete, contingent plan," meaning a description of the actions a state will take for any situation in which it finds itself.[19] For example, a rising state might follow a simple strategy of "never play a leadership role in multilateral settings." It might, on the other hand, follow a more complex strategy in which its actions are contingent on the actions of other states, such as "do not play a leadership role unless it appears no one else will, and then only do it if the costs don't exceed a certain threshold." In the analysis that follows, we argue that a rising state will take different actions based on the strategic

[17] Within the study of international relations, there is increasing mainstream acceptance of the idea that the international system is characterized by hierarchy, rather than an anarchy of equal states, as has been sometimes supposed. Our focus on rising states is warranted, therefore, as a practical recognition that multilateral regimes are at least as much a product of the strategic interaction among states at the apex of the hierarchy as they are of more diffuse interests or norms. David A. Lake, "Rightful Rules: Authority, Order, and the Foundations of Global Governance," *International Studies Quarterly*, Vol. 54, no. 3 (2010), pp. 587–613. Eric Grynaviski and Amy Hsieh, "Hierarchy and Judicial Institutions: Arbitration and Ideology in the Hellenistic World," *International Organization*, Vol. 69, no. 3 (2015), pp. 697–729.

[18] Even here, though, the two sides would have a common interest in avoiding some more extreme possible outcomes, such as a costly bidding war for regional partners (or, of course, an actual war). To be more precise, then, our argument has little to say about issues where great power relations are a zero-sum game along the margins of ordinary day-to-day variations in policy. It is for this reason that, for example, we do not include a case study of territorial disputes in the South China Sea; even though the sides have a common interest in avoiding war, the interaction is mostly zero-sum as long as relations stay short of war.

[19] Vincent P. Crawford, *Thomas Schelling and the Analysis of Strategic Behavior*, (Cambridge, MA: MIT Press, 1991).

setting of the issues it faces. These actions, or tactics, comprise the general approach that a rising state will take on a particular issue. The specific tactics we identify are: exercise leadership to create or sustain a regime, hold-up support to extract concessions on a regime, and passively accept a regime.

When describing regimes as systems of cooperation, our argument applies to long-established regimes as well as to newly created or even hypothetical regimes. When the United States led the creation of the General Agreement on Tariffs and Trade (GATT), it devoted scarce time and political capital to the project, just as Germany invested political capital in maintaining the regime through the 1970s. In each case, a country invested in cooperation by taking steps to induce minor powers to abide by the rules of the regime and ensure that the regime would handle a changing international system appropriately – the United States by creating the regime in the first place and Germany by helping the regime adapt to changing international circumstances following the oil shocks and the end of the Bretton Woods system.[20]

The same applies to hold-up as well. Blocking the creation of a new regime is strategically little different from sabotaging the functioning of an existing one in need of support. In the chapters that follow, as an empirical matter, we show the same logic that led China to play hold-up with proposals to address climate change at the Copenhagen Summit also led China to play hold-up with support for the ongoing functioning of the IMF.[21]

When will rising powers choose to invest – that is, to engage in second-order cooperation – in either existing or new regimes? When will they passively accept existing regimes, essentially free-riding on the second-order cooperative efforts of established powers? And when will they seek instead to change the rules put in place by existing great powers?

In this chapter we try to explain why a rising state adopts the tactics it does, and in the rest of the book we apply our analysis to explain the pattern of Chinese behavior in multilateral settings across a variety of issue

[20] Keohane, *After Hegemony*, describes the roles of the United States and Germany in explicitly parallel terms, as efforts to create and maintain a system of international cooperation.

[21] Similarly, Lipscy, *Renegotiating*, consciously applies his argument about outside options and hold-up both to regimes as they are being created – such as the Internet Corporation for Assigned Names and Numbers (ICANN) and the International Telecommunications and Satellite Organization (ITSO) – and as they are later revised or renegotiated – such as with those same regimes later and with the World Bank and IMF.

areas. We do not, however, try to explain the decisions made by other established powers, including the United States. Consequently, our argument does not seek to explain why multilateral cooperation is sometimes effective and sometimes not – doing so would require a theory about the choices that both rising and established states make at the same time and how their strategies interact, which is beyond our scope.

For example, we will argue that, in some conditions, a rising state will hold-up contributions to a regime and be willing to let the regime collapse if the rising state does not get the concessions it seeks. Whether it gets the concessions depends on the strategies that other established states adopt. So, while we feel we can, for example, characterize China's choices with respect to international financial governance (in which China held-up international cooperation in order to extract greater representation within the IMF and other bodies), we do not seek to fully account, in this book, for the ultimate outcome (eventually the United States and European states relented and acceded to China's demands).

Although we aim to construct a generalizable argument about how rising powers approach second-order cooperation, we do not claim that our theory explains all variation in rising power behavior relating to second-order cooperation. Certainly other factors, such as domestic politics or international socialization, also shape state behavior in important ways. Our more modest claim is that variables relating to bargaining power matter in important ways, independent of these other factors; we argue that, all else equal, outside options and perceptions of indispensability have a significant impact on rising power behavior, even though we of course recognize that not all else is always equal. We return to alternative explanations, and how we handle these in our case studies, at the end of this chapter.

2.2 OUTSIDE OPTIONS AND INDISPENSABILITY

The core of our argument is that a rising state's strategy on how to approach multilateralism for any particular issue is shaped by outside options and indispensability, two factors that we consider in turn in this section. Both of these refer to the expected consequences of the rising state's decision to engage in second-order cooperation – its decision about whether and how to support the creation or maintenance of a regime.

2.2.1 What States Want

When states work together, cooperating for their mutual gain, there are several factors that will influence how valuable their cooperation is to each of them. These include the general effectiveness of their joint efforts, but they also include the way the costs and benefits of the joint project are tuned to the particular preferences that each state has.

First consider the general effectiveness of the joint efforts the states make. How much of a total benefit do these efforts provide? Here, the logic of public goods is instructive. A pure public good is a good that is nonrival and nonexcludable. A classic example is a lighthouse, which is "nonrival" because one ship can "consume" the services that the lighthouse supplies without leaving less for other ships to consume and "nonexcludable" because, if the lighthouse is illuminated, then it provides a service for every ship in the area and cannot be turned off for just one of them without turning it off for all of them. In studies of international cooperation, regimes are often thought of as public goods; if a regime successfully reduces the rate of climate change or nuclear proliferation, then those benefits accrue to all countries and aren't diminished as the benefits are more widely shared.[22] The greater the investment that states make, together, in a regime that supplies them with some sort of public good, the more they will all benefit.

However, just because all states might benefit from a public good doesn't mean that all of them will benefit equally, since both the benefits and the costs of a particular public good can be tuned to states' individual preferences. As examples, a global multilateral trade regime might be liberal or mercantilist, international legal norms might privilege universal human rights or national sovereignty, and security institutions might empower regional powers or subordinate them to a global power. These kinds of choices about how order is provided can themselves be critically important to the players and, by tailoring the regime to suit the preferences of one state more than another, the regime can be negotiated (or renegotiated) in a way that increases its value to one member while reducing its value to another.[23] Phillip Lipscy makes this point when he shows that international development agencies, such as the World Bank,

[22] Public goods contrast with private goods like food, the supply of which decreases as people consume it. On the logic of regimes as public goods, see Randall W. Stone, Branislav L. Slantchev, and Tamar R. London, "Choosing How to Cooperate: A Repeated Public-Goods Model of International Relations," *International Studies Quarterly*, Vol. 52, no. 2 (2008), pp. 335–62.

[23] Within the literature on public goods, this issue is sometimes referred to as the "flavor" of the good produced. See Alberto Alesina, Reza Baqir, and William Easterly, "Public Goods and Ethnic Divisions," *The Quarterly Journal of Economics*, Vol. 114, no. 4 (1999), pp. 1243–84.

make very different kinds of lending decisions depending on which states have more influence in the process.[24]

The costs of creating or maintaining a regime can also be allocated across states differently. In literal terms, many international institutions rely on funding from member state contributions in order to function, and those contributions have to be allocated in some way.[25] Beyond that, creating and maintaining regimes entails diplomatic costs; as we will detail in our discussion of investment as an outcome, this can involve states giving up other prized goals for the sake of maintaining the credibility of a regime. As a practical matter, for our purposes, the extent to which a regime's benefits and costs are more suited to one state or another are two sides of the same coin; distinguishing costs from benefits does not change anything about our analytic argument and, as an empirical matter, policymakers consider them together anyway.

Here we should note that our argument is explicitly rationalist, in the narrow sense that we assume states have a set of preferences that they pursue in a consistent way. We do not need to assume, however, that these preferences are necessarily rooted in economic or material goals – they can just as likely stem from ideological sources or come as a product of long-term international socialization. Indeed, throughout the empirical chapters we try to find instances in which the apparent preferences of Chinese or American leaders change in ways that our argument suggests might lead to a change in their strategies, which we can then observe.

In thinking about the way states make choices about how they value multilateral cooperation, we begin with an examination of things the leaders of those states think they can get in the absence of cooperation; what is their outside option?

2.2.2 Outside Options

The relevant outside option for our analysis is a government's expectation about what would happen if it were to fail to cooperate with other states to promote or maintain a multilateral regime. Outside options are important because they give states leverage in their negotiations over distributions of costs and benefits. Each side's outside option is its "best alternative to a negotiated agreement" against which it compares existing

[24] Lipscy, *Renegotiating*, pp. 4, 125–9.

[25] A. Burcu Bayram and Erin R. Graham, "Financing the United Nations: Explaining Variation in How Donors Provide Funding to the UN," *The Review of International Organizations*, Vol. 12, no. 3 (2017), pp. 421–59.

or proposed deals; as its best alternative improves, the value of any one particular compromise diminishes, putting it in a better position from which to demand more concessions or simply walk away.[26] Since the result if *no one* maintains the regime is that the regime collapses, a rising state can negotiate better terms for itself if it can convince the established power that it is willing to run the risk of a regime collapse. Note that a regime collapse is not a goal in itself, but by claiming that it can tolerate a collapse if one were to come, the rising state can induce the established power to pay a greater share of the costs of regime maintenance or shift the policy outputs of the regime to better suit the rising state's preferences. Here, it is the balance of outside options among states that matters, and not a state's individual outside options in an absolute sense; a state only has more leverage when its outside option is better than that of its partner.

A classic example of how an outside option – the ability to walk away from an agreement – can give a state bargaining leverage within an ostensibly cooperative arrangement is the "empty chair" crisis in the European Commission in 1965–66. The crisis arose when France resisted a series of proposed changes that would merge a number of existing European institutions under a supranational authority. France withdrew its minister from the Commission – leaving the "empty chair" – and demanded a national veto on European policymaking to induce it to return. Even though most other members understood that France benefited from the continuation of the European Economic Community, they nonetheless saw themselves as benefiting even more, and so made substantial concessions to France in order to resolve the crisis.[27]

[26] Roger Fisher and William Ury, *Getting to Yes: Negotiating Agreement without Giving In* (New York, NY: Penguin Books, 1981). Heather Elko McKibben, *State Strategies in International Bargaining: Play by the Rules or Change Them?* (London: Cambridge University Press, 2015). On exit options as a tool for influence, see also Alfred O. Hirschman, *Exit, Voice, and Loyalty: Responses to Decline in Firms, Organizations, and States* (Cambridge: Harvard University Press, 1970).

[27] The crisis was resolved with the Luxembourg Compromise, widely seen as a substantial diplomatic victory for France. For an overview see Andrew Moravcsik, "De Gaulle between Grain and Grandeur: The Political Economy of French EC Policy, 1958–1970 (Part 2)," *Journal of Cold War Studies*, Vol. 2, no. 3 (2000), pp. 4–68; Etienne Davignon, "The Empty Chair Crisis and the Luxembourg Compromise," in Jean Marie Palayret, Helen S. Wallace, and Pascaline Winand, eds., *Visions, Votes and Vetoes. The Empty Chair Crisis and the Luxembourg Compromise Forty Years On* (Brussels: P.I.E.-Peter Lang, 2006), pp. 15–19. Whether or not de Gaulle was ultimately bluffing is beside the point, as his leverage came from his perceived willingness to walk away. On the perception he was bluffing, see N. Piers Ludlow, "Challenging French Leadership in Europe:

Outside options – the opportunity costs of cooperation – are a core feature of most contemporary understandings of how cooperation works in international organizations and in regimes generally.[28] Scholars have shown that this ability to walk away – a state's "go it alone" power[29] – is a resource a state can use to reshape agreements to suit its interests in a variety of contexts. Outside options are being used, for example, by the United States when it threatens unilateral military action in order to win a United Nations Security Council (UNSC) resolution more to its liking,[30] and by North Atlantic Treaty Organization (NATO) members when they use their willingness to accept inaction in a security crisis as a means to shift the military burden to other members.[31]

From the rising state's perspective, the balance of outside options depends on its expectations about what would happen if it were to stop contributing to multilateralism. Again, this is not a question of whether or not the rising state *complies* with a regime (first-order cooperation), but rather it is question of whether or not the rising state *contributes to the production and maintenance* of a regime (second-order cooperation). What would happen next? In particular, how would it expect other established powers to respond? There are three possibilities. First, established powers might do nothing, leaving multilateralism to collapse. Second, one or more established powers might find a way to sustain multilateralism

---

Germany, Italy, the Netherlands and the Outbreak of the Empty Chair Crisis of 1965–1966," *Contemporary European History*, Vol. 8, no. 2 (1999), pp. 231–48.

28 Allison Carnegie, "States Held Hostage: Political Hold-up Problems and the Effects of International Institutions," *American Political Science Review*, Vol. 108, no. 1 (2014), pp. 54–70. Julia Gray and Jonathan B. Slapin, "Exit Options and the Effectiveness of Regional Economic Organizations," *Political Science Research and Methods*, Vol. 1, no. 2 (2013), pp. 281–303. Leslie Johns, "A Servant of Two Masters: Communication and the Selection of International Bureaucrats," *International Organization*, Vol. 61, no. 2 (2007), pp. 245–75. Christina J. Schneider, "Weak States and Institutionalized Bargaining Power in International Organizations," *International Studies Quarterly*, Vol. 55, no. 2 (2011), pp. 331–55. Randall W. Stone, *Controlling Institutions: International Organizations and the Global Economy* (New York, NY: Cambridge University Press, 2011). Phillip Y. Lipscy, "Explaining Institutional Change: Policy Areas, Outside Options, and the Bretton Woods Institutions," *American Journal of Political Science*, Vol. 59, no. 2 (2015), pp. 341–56. Daniel Verdier, "The Dilemma of Informal Governance with Outside Option as Solution," *International Theory*, Vol. 7, no. 1 (2015), pp. 195–229.

29 Lloyd Gruber, *Ruling the World: Power Politics and the Rise of Supranational Institutions* (Princeton, NJ: Princeton University Press, 2000).

30 Erik Voeten, "Outside Options and the Logic of Security Council Action," *American Political Science Review*, Vol. 95, no. 4 (2001), pp. 845–58.

31 Songying Fang and Kristopher W. Ramsay, "Outside Options and Burden Sharing in Nonbinding Alliances," *Political Research Quarterly*, Vol. 63, no. 1 (2010), pp. 188–202.

on their own, through second-order contributions. Third, one or more established powers may take unilateral action to address the problem.

In order to evaluate its outside options, therefore, the rising state first develops a guess about which of those three possibilities is most likely and, second, evaluates how *it* would fare in that outcome as compared with how *the established powers* would fare. These are related, since it will have every reason to expect established powers to choose the option most in line with their own interests. So, we consider the three possibilities in turn.

First, what happens if, in the absence of second-order cooperation from the rising state, established powers are unwilling or unable to sustain meaningful cooperation on their own, and the common problem goes unsolved? Here, the balance of outside options is simply determined by the value that the rising state places on the issue, compared with the value that established powers place on the issue. In other words, what are the stakes? More precisely, the stakes are the prospective cost the rising state and established powers each face in unilaterally adjusting to a world in which no one supports multilateral cooperation. In a world without multilateralism on this particular issue, would the rising state be substantially worse off than before, or would the rising state be just fine? How much worse off would established powers be?

One example of low stakes for a rising state is the role of the United States in European overseas empires in the first half of the twentieth century. Through a series of formal and informal agreements, European states had developed a multilateral regime to resolve territorial disputes among them in their colonial empires and to provide occasional mutual support against anti-colonial uprisings. Although the scramble for Africa in the 1880s and 1890s reflected intense competition among Europeans, they nevertheless acted through an ongoing, albeit mostly informal, regime to advance their collective interests; the Berlin Conference of 1885 was simply one example of this broader cooperation.[32] Despite a common expectation across the continent after World War II that colonial institutions would be revived, leaders in fact discovered that the largest rising state – the United States – had no interest in maintaining colonialism and was almost perfectly indifferent to the system collapsing.[33] American policymakers simply did not value the collective good of coordinating

[32] Michael W. Doyle, *Empires* (Ithaca, NY: Cornell University Press, 1986), p. 287.

[33] David D. Newsom, *The Imperial Mantle: The United States, Decolonization, and the Third World* (Bloomington, IN: Indiana University Press, 2001), pp. 46–53.

colonial enterprises and, if anything, acted to undermine them. Where the Americans did see value in maintaining some aspects of control over peripheral states – as when access to critical resources like uranium or oil was at stake – the United States preferred to act through bilateral relationships entirely outside of any generally agreed colonial framework.[34] At the same time, in contrast, the United States viewed the stakes as being extremely high in the negotiations surrounding the Bretton Woods agreement in 1944, as it understood its own commercial and security interests as being tightly connected to the prospects for postwar recovery and economic integration.

In the absence of a multilateral solution – or any other solution – to the common problem, the rising state might attempt to mitigate the problem on its own, unilaterally. When this is the case, the value of the rising state's outside option is simply the value, to it, of a unilateral solution.[35] Examples here might be efforts by a state to use its own resources to adapt to climate change, neutralize a terrorist threat, or protect against infectious diseases without relying on meaningful international cooperation. To the extent that these solutions are low quality, the rising state's outside option is poor, but where unilateral solutions are cheap and effective, the rising state's outside option is good.

In summary, when the end of multilateralism would substantially raise the rising state's risk of facing an existential crisis like war, revolution, or economic depression, the stakes for the rising state would be high. The stakes would be lower if the rising state gains little from some multilateral endeavor, or if the rising state's leaders believe the gains from multilateral cooperation could readily be replaced by some other arrangement (such as a series of bilateral agreements or unilateral actions). The stakes, by themselves, cannot account for any one particular outcome; we argue that the choices the rising state makes will also depend on what the rising state expects other established powers to do if it doesn't cooperate, since the established powers might end up sustaining an effective regime on their own anyway. If a rising state calculates that it will be able to benefit from global leadership for free, by having others pay the costs of creating

34 Daniel H. Nexon and Thomas Wright, "What's at Stake in the American Empire Debate," *American Political Science Review*, Vol. 101, no. 2 (2007), p. 253.

35 We return to this point later in this chapter, as well as in several of the case study chapters. Our explicit comparisons between multilateral institutionalized cooperation and unilateral action by established states are one of the differences between our analysis and several other leading theories of institutional change, e.g., Lipscy, *Renegotiating*.

and maintaining multilateral institutions, it will find ways to shift those costs to other states even when the stakes are high.

We therefore need to consider a second way that established states might respond to a rising state's non-contribution to regime maintenance: one or more established powers might find a way to sustain multilateralism on their own, through their own second-order contributions. Consider the case of one established power that is willing to pay the costs, itself, of regime maintenance because it has a large enough stake in the outcome that the private benefits it receives from effective multilateralism outweigh the costs of organizing and maintaining a regime. Such an expectation draws directly from the logic of hegemonic stability. To the extent that an established power (or a hegemon) benefits from global public goods directly – as when global economic growth benefits the established power's trade and investment – or indirectly – as when political stability and economic prosperity in the established power's allies deter revisionism – it will have an interest in paying at least some of the costs of supporting institutions that organize the provision of those public goods.

Recent extensions of the logic of hegemonic stability with empirical applications to the period of twentieth century American primacy suggest that this kind of leadership may have structural roots. If the leading state knows that basic security institutions will fail in the absence of a contribution that only it can provide, its outside option will be poor and it will take action to create and support those basic global regimes.[36] This idea reflects a wide consensus in the study of international political economy, which took as its starting off point the persistence of postwar economic institutions and the liberal international order, despite the relative decline of the United States in the 1970s and 1980s. Robert Keohane's classic study made the case that even as the United States and other established powers, including Japan and Germany, found their share of world markets declining, they were still able to sustain multilateral cooperation to stabilize the rules for world trade as well as in financial and energy markets.[37]

This of course is the flip side of the situation in which multilateralism fails. Assuming it is generally understood that rising states are not going

[36] G. John Ikenberry, *After Victory: Institutions, Strategic Restraint, and the Rebuilding of Order after Major Wars* (Princeton, NJ: Princeton University Press, 2009). David A. Lake, *Hierarchy in International Relations* (Ithaca, NY: Cornell University Press, 2009). Randall Stone et al., "Choosing How to Cooperate."

[37] Keohane, *After Hegemony*.

to contribute to multilateralism – that is, that rising states are not going to engage in second-order cooperation – will established powers be willing and able to pay the costs to maintain multilateral order themselves or not?

Finally, the third possibility is that an established power could attempt to solve the problem unilaterally, either without using multilateral regimes at all or with using limited multilateral regimes that exclude the rising power. Provision of some public good by a leading state, or a hegemon, outside of a multilateral agreement may, in some instances, be less desirable for the leading state. One common argument is that liberal hegemons like the United States have a general preference for multilateral institutions for a variety of reasons, including building confidence that they will not use their control in one issue to encroach on the independence of smaller states, allowing smaller states a forum to coordinate their approval or disapproval of the leading state's actions and helping the leading state share the costs of action with other members of the system that benefit from it. Acting through institutions benefits both the leading state and the smaller ones.[38]

So, when the leading state acts unilaterally, both it and weaker and rising states may be worse off than they would be if the leading state acts through regimes. The balance of outside options, however, depends on which one is *even more* worse off. That in turn depends on the manner in which the leading state addresses the problem. Some unilateral solutions to problems that an established or hegemonic power might take would be more to the rising power's liking than others. As we noted previously, apart from the question of *whether* a public good is provided, there is the question of *how* it is provided.

Consider for example potential solutions to the problem of climate change. Even if there is a multilateral regime that attempts to address the problem, there are questions of who shoulders most of the costs – since if states create an enforceable system for regulating carbon emissions below some global limit, they must still decide which states get to pollute more and which are permitted to pollute less within that limit. In a unilateral solution to climate change, one that does not involve institutions, a leading state such as the United States – perhaps in concert with other wealthy democracies – might institute carbon taxes domestically and then impose tariffs (or "border adjustments") on imports deemed to be carbon-intensive; this would be a strategy that pushes adjustment costs

[38] Lake, *Hierarchy*.

onto poor countries.[39] As an alternative, the United States and other established powers might transfer clean energy technology to poor countries under a general license without demanding patent payments, a scheme under which wealthy countries would generally pay more of the adjustment costs.[40] From the perspective of a country like China the latter unilateral course would be much better, and if Chinese leaders calculated that unilateral transfer would be the eventual policy the United States would settle on, then they would see their outside options as relatively favorable.[41]

Another example involves halting the spread of nuclear weapons. In the event that the global nonproliferation regime fails, either systemically or in particular instances, the United States would probably still act unilaterally to halt nuclear proliferation rather than simply accept further proliferation and arms races.[42] These unilateral steps, even if short of war, might still harm the interests of a rising power like China. For instance, boarding ships and quarantining harbors of countries suspected of seeking nuclear technology or materials – actions the United States has threatened under the "Proliferation Security Initiative" but rarely taken as a practical matter – would be contrary to Chinese interests both because of the precedent Beijing might be seen to accept and because their own security ties to North Korea or future Central Asian and African client states might be compromised.[43]

[39] Kateryna Holzer, "Proposals on Carbon-related Border Adjustments: Prospects for WTO Compliance," *Carbon & Climate Law Review*, Vol. 4, no. 1 (2010), p. 51.

[40] Antoine Dechezleprêtre et al., "Invention and Transfer of Climate Change–mitigation Technologies: A Global Analysis," *Review of Environmental Economics and Policy*, Vol. 5, no. 11 (2011), pp. 109–30.

[41] In the climate example there are other unilateral actions the United States could take that would be possibly even worse from China's perspective: the United States could lead a geoengineering effort that might raise risks of local ecological damage or risk a weather modification arms race, or the United States could simply give up on preventing climate change and adapt by diverting resources to desalinization efforts and coastal fortifications that would mitigate the impact on the United States only, while leaving other states on their own. On climate modification technology as a potential minefield, see Sanna Joronen, Markku Oksanen, and Timo Vuorisalo, "Towards Weather Ethics: From Chance to Choice with Weather Modification," *Ethics, Policy and Environment*, Vol. 14, no. 1 (2011), pp. 55–67. On the distributive implications of choosing unilateral adaptation in the face of climate threats, see W. Niel Adger, ed., *Fairness in Adaptation to Climate Change* (Cambridge, MA: MIT Press, 2006).

[42] On the general logic underlying this, with a particular application to the US attack on Iraq in 2003, see Alexandre Debs and Nuno P. Monteiro, "Known Unknowns: Power Shifts, Uncertainty, and War," *International Organization*, Vol. 68, no. 1 (2014), pp. 1–31.

[43] Rosemary Foot, "Selective or Effective Multilateralism? The Bush Administration's Proliferation Security Initiative and China's Response," *Effective Multilateralism* (London: Palgrave Macmillan UK, 2013), pp. 215–31.

How do outside options matter? When the rising power's outside options on an issue are poor – the stakes are high and the established power is unlikely to act unilaterally in a way that suits the rising power's interests – the rising power has a greater incentive to invest in regime maintenance by contributing to the costs of promoting and extending multilateralism. This is because the rising state has the most to lose if cooperation fails, and as such other states can more credibly walk away from cooperation than can the rising state. Even though many of the actions states must take if they are going to create and sustain a multilateral regime are costly, they may be less costly than the alternative of doing nothing, especially when the costs of non-cooperation are lower for other, more established states who can threaten to free-ride or to act unilaterally in ways contrary to the interests of the rising power. In this situation, the rising state will be more willing to sacrifice other diplomatic objectives, and may even be willing to make substantive policy concessions to its partners, in order to achieve broad support for an agreement on joint action. The logic of this strategy is the same whether or not a formal international organization already exists. If the rising power's outside options are bad and an organization exists, then the rising power will help make it function better; if one does not exist, then the rising power will build one.

Germany's role within Europe illustrates the point that leadership in preserving and extending a regime can be costly and may entail sacrificing other policy goals. Germany's interests in European political integration – the stakes – are high, as Germany receives large economic and foreign policy benefits from integration and, as a result, stands to gain more than do most of its partners from political reforms that streamline the efficiency of decision-making in EU institutions.[44] Furthermore, Germany's outside option to effective EU governance is especially poor, since its history makes the unilateral option for European governance a non-starter. Consequently, Germany at times ends up paying the costs of effectively maintaining the regime. When negotiations over what eventually became the Lisbon Treaty stalled in 2005, the impasse was broken when Germany made a number of concessions on voting weights in the Council of the European Union.[45] In the empirical chapters to follow, we

[44] William E. Paterson, "The Reluctant Hegemon? Germany Moves Centre Stage in the European Union," *Journal of Common Market Studies*, Vol. 49, no. 1 (2011), pp. 57–75.

[45] Jonathan Slapin, "Bargaining Power at Europe's Intergovernmental Conferences: Testing Institutional and Intergovernmental Theories," *International Organization*, Vol. 62, no. 1 (2008), pp. 131–62. Robert Thompson, *Resolving Controversy in the European Union:*

argue that China made a similar choice in 2001 with respect to the issue of stability in Central Asia, and again in 2003 with respect to the Korean nuclear crisis.

2.2.3 Indispensability

Conversely, when a rising power's outside options are better, it is in a stronger position at the margins to try to negotiate meaningful international cooperation on its own terms without having to pay, itself, the costs of establishing or maintaining a regime. Where possible, a rising state will try to ensure that the established power or others pay these costs – in effect, arranging for others to play the role that Germany played in the negotiations over the Lisbon Treaty. We expect the rising state's strategy, however, to depend on a further factor in the strategic environment: the rising state's assessment of whether other powers view the rising state's contributions as indispensable to the formation and maintenance of a regime.

With better outside options, there are two different ways that a rising power can try to make its partners pay for producing regimes. First, it can show leadership maintaining a regime but demand compensation for it, either through concessions on other issues or through greater control of the regime itself. That is, it can hold-up contributions in exchange for concessions. Second, it can passively accept regimes produced by other states and free-ride off their second-order investments. We argue that a rising power will be more likely to adopt the first approach – hold-up – when it is widely perceived as having a critical role to play in regime construction and, like a monopolist, demands a high price for its services.

Size alone can make an emerging great power seem indispensable as a contributor to the creation and maintenance of international regimes. For example, if a state's active participation on first-order cooperation is critical to regime success, other states are likely to view that state's active cooperation on second-order issues as crucial. It is inconceivable, for instance, that efforts to revamp the global trading regime would be undertaken without active participation from the United States. As the world's largest economy, the regime depends on some level of US "buy in"; as such, other countries should reasonably demand active US participation in regime construction, so as to have some reassurance that the United States will comply with the new rules.

Legislative Decision-Making before and after Enlargement. (Cambridge: Cambridge University Press, 2011), p. 2.

States may also appear indispensable when their distinct preferences make them necessary, politically, for a multilateral coalition to have credibility. When a hegemonic state (like the United States) tries to entice smaller partners to join it in cooperation – e.g., when it exercises second-order leadership – it can face a credibility problem if smaller states suspect it is likely to abuse its leading position in the regime. Having a second state, one skeptical of the hegemon's broader aims, cooperate on second-order issues can create more confidence in the ultimate aims of the regime. Even relatively weaker secondary powers can therefore be indispensable if the regime works as a "dual key" system in which smaller states are more willing to make investments in cooperation when even states with distinct goals agree on the aims of the regime. For example, some of NATO's political effectiveness has been attributed to the diversity of opinion among member states, so that unanimous actions taken by an organization with a diverse membership have enhanced credibility.[46] For similar reasons, American security officials were highly motivated during the Cold War to ensure that the Soviet Union was seen as an equal partner in efforts to prevent nuclear proliferation, since Soviet acceptance would serve as a strong signal that the regime would not simply be a fig leaf for American aggrandizement.[47]

A rising state that (a) can walk away from cooperation and (b) is perceived by other major players as indispensable to effective regime maintenance will be in a position to threaten to withhold cooperation unless it secures concessions on the structure of the regime itself. Such a state would have a monopoly on a critical component for the regime, to the point where everyone else's contributions alone would be insufficient without the state's cooperation. If the state's outside options were good, it would be able to threaten to withhold cooperation unless it was compensated so that it would be able to cooperate at a profit. The profit it seeks need not be financial – an indispensable state might be able to ensure, for instance, that it had a disproportionate influence in the governance of the regime, or it might demand side-payments through other, linked regimes.[48]

46 Lawrence S. Kaplan, *NATO Divided, NATO United: The Evolution of an Alliance* (New York, NY: Greenwood Publishing Group, 2004).

47 Joseph F. Pilat and Robert E. Pendley, eds., *1995: A New Beginning for the NPT?* (New York, NY: Springer Science and Business Media, 2012).

48 On side-payments through linked issues in bargaining over multilateral regimes, see McKibben, *State Strategies*.

This logic was first developed to describe relations among firms in a supply chain, where one firm with a monopoly on a component critical to a finished product has an incentive to be a bottleneck. The classic example here is the relationship in the 1910s between General Motors (GM) and the Fisher Body Company (Fisher), which made high-quality auto bodies for GM and other car manufacturers; GM designed both its cars and its marketing around Fisher's brands and production. At the time, Fisher was indispensable to the joint project of producing cars, and GM understood that. Throughout the 1910s there were a series of episodes in which the contracts between Fisher and GM were renegotiated to the benefit of Fisher. This is commonly described as "opportunistic" behavior by Fisher, although it should be understood that this does not necessarily imply malevolence or dishonesty on Fisher's part. For example, Fisher's production slowed down at one point because of a shortage of the raw materials that it used, and Fisher went to GM for financial help in resolving the problem. The shortage was not Fisher's fault; however, if Fisher had not been in an indispensable position – if it had had competitors who also could have made auto bodies for GM – then Fisher would have had to resolve the shortage itself, without getting help from GM, or lose its contract.[49]

The lesson of this story from the early industrial era is that when firms cooperate, the firm that is indispensable to cooperation can often find ways to make its partners (rather than itself) bear the costs of managing their joint enterprise. Note that, in the story, Fisher did not have to explicitly threaten to stop cooperating and walk away entirely in order to induce GM to increase its payments to Fisher. Rather, because a delay in production hurt GM more than it hurt Fisher, each labor dispute, materials shortage, supply problem, and so on was a bigger problem for GM than for Fisher.[50]

The evolution of the Lisbon Treaty in Europe illustrates a way in which partners that are perceived as indispensable, even if they are smaller, have

[49] The foundational study on Fisher, GM, and indispensability is Benjamin Klein, Robert G. Crawford, and Armen A. Alchian, "Vertical Integration, Appropriable Rents, and the Competitive Contracting Process," *The Journal of Law and Economics*, Vol. 21, no. 2 (1978), pp. 297–326. Note that the particular historical example is in dispute; see Ramon Casadesus-Masanell and Daniel F. Spulber, "The Fable of Fisher Body," *The Journal of Law and Economics*, Vol. 43, no. 1 (2000), pp. 67–104. Much of the dispute, however, is about the extent to which Fisher was actually indispensable to the production process, rather than whether or not a firm that is indispensable can arrange for other firms to pay the costs of adjustment.

[50] In the end, GM bought and integrated Fisher, solving the problem.

used their leverage to restructure regimes to serve their interests. During the final round of treaty negotiations in 2007, Polish leaders adopted a high public profile, blocking agreement on the new voting system. Poland's size, combined with its preferences (which were distinct from Germany's but resonated with other smaller Central European states) made it indispensable in the negotiations that followed, in which Poland won a voting system better suited to its interests.[51] In a similar vein, we note in the case study on international finance that China is seen as increasingly indispensable in global financial governance; this has given it the leverage to revise aspects of IMF governance.

What about situations in which the rising state is not perceived as indispensable? Here, the rising state has little independent incentive to devote resources to supporting the regime – second-order cooperation – even though it may engage in first-order cooperation.[52] In such cases, rising states will passively accept existing institutional rules, while relying on larger established states to make efforts to build and maintain the regime themselves. This follows the simple logic of free-riding, in which each state has an incentive to play along with an existing regime but has no incentive to expend effort to maintain it (by punishing cheaters or working to build a consensus around extensions to the regime, or by attempts to modify it to better suit changing circumstances).

To be sure, a rising state that has a good outside option and that is not perceived as indispensable will have no particular reason to actively undermine multilateralism – although it may be inclined to stretch the rules when its own interests are at stake, even if that makes it harder for established leaders to maintain the regime. As the United States was a rising power in the late nineteenth century, it mostly complied with the British-led regime of economic openness but gradually moved to being a spoiler, driven by the domestic political logic of appeasing particular protectionist interests. From the American perspective, any indirect

51 Paterson, "The Reluctant Hegemon?" Small European states have used bargaining leverage that comes from their distinctive assets and niches in sometimes surprising ways to win concessions, especially when they are seen as being critical to reaching a broader agreement. Stefanie Bailer, "Bargaining Success in the European Union: The Impact of Exogenous and Endogenous Power Resources," *European Union Politics*, Vol. 5, no. 1 (2004), pp. 99–123.

52 Neal G. Jesse, Steven E. Lobell, Galia Press-Barnathan, and Kristen P. Williams, "The Leader Can't Lead when the Followers Won't Follow: The Limitations of Hegemony," in Neal G. Jesse, Steven E. Lobell, Galia Press-Barnathan, and Kristen P. Williams, eds., *Beyond Great Powers and Hegemons: Why Secondary States Support, Follow, or Challenge* (Palo Alto, CA: Stanford University Press, 2012).

consequence from its actions that did have the effect of undermining the regime was entirely unintended.[53]

As a long as the rising state knows that others will make sure the regime is well tended, it will not, itself, have an incentive to work on it. In other words, a state might still comply with a regime (first-order cooperation) without contributing to uphold it (second-order cooperation). Here the example of nonproliferation is again instructive, as many countries in the post–Cold War era were second-order free-riders, trading with Iraq, Iran, or North Korea in violation of economic sanctions meant to punish or deter the development of nuclear weapons. Bryan Early describes how Turkey and the United Arab Emirates traded surreptitiously with Iran in violation of US-led economic sanctions, undermining the enforcement of the nonproliferation regime. At the same time, though, these countries themselves scrupulously complied with international rules concerning the development and inspection of nuclear sites within their own territories.[54]

Second-order free-riding may be accompanied by first-order free-riding (or noncompliance) as well. Returning to the example of the United States during the period in which British global domination was winding down, although the United States was a minor power through most of the end of the nineteenth century, by the early 1900s American free-riding was more consequential. Britain, the established leading state, invested heavily in a regime, but most middle and rising powers (such as the United States) refrained from acting to support the regime even as they accepted its rules and benefited from the growth and stability it fostered. Prior to the collapse of world trade in the 1930s, leaders from the United States (a classic rising state) understood that they benefited from the openness Britain maintained among its colonies and allies, even as Americans did little to reproduce norms of economic openness. The British example demonstrates the central importance of perceptions as well, since the key factor affecting outcomes was the common view that

[53] David A. Lake, *Power, Protection, and Free Trade: International Sources of US Commercial Strategy, 1887–1939* (Ithaca, NY: Cornell University Press, 1988).

[54] Early, *Busted Sanctions*, pp. 1–3. The United Arab Emirates is a clear case here, as it is an American ally with a clear interest in maintaining the international nonproliferation regime that nonetheless busted sanctions on Iran knowing that its individual contributions to the maintenance of the nonproliferation regime would be a drop in the bucket, whereas the individual costs of regime maintenance (in the form of sanctioning Iran) would have been extremely costly. The UAE busted sanctions on Iran even as it, itself, complied with the regime. See also Bryan R. Early, "Acquiring Foreign Nuclear Assistance in the Middle East: Strategic Lessons from the United Arab Emirates," *Nonproliferation Review*, Vol. 17, no. 2 (2010), pp. 259–80.

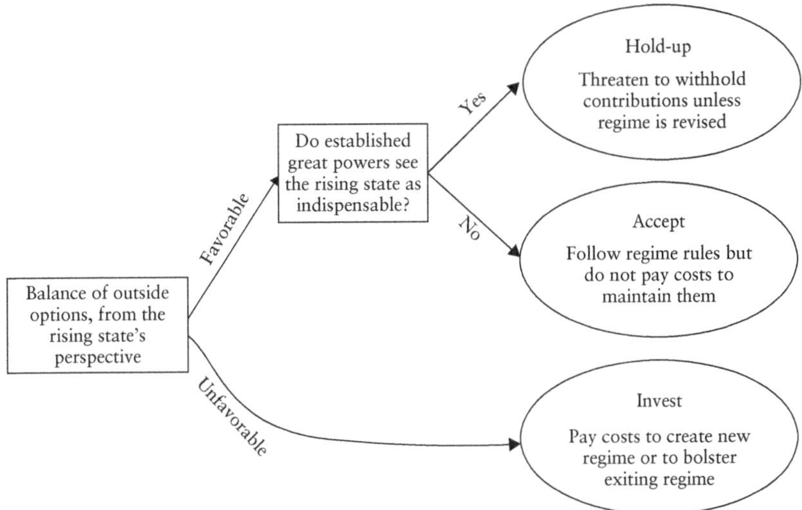

FIGURE 2.1. *Three stable outcomes: hold-up, accept, and invest*

none of the rising middle powers were themselves indispensable to the maintenance of the regime. In reality (and in retrospect) they probably were, and their attempts to have it both ways eventually resulted in the collapse of the regime.[55]

2.2.4 Summary

In summary, our theory entails two steps, detailed in Figure 2.1. The rising state has either a favorable or an unfavorable outside option, relative to the outside option of the established state. If the rising state's outside option is poor, we expect it to show leadership, devoting time and energy to building and maintaining an international regime. If the rising state's outside option is good, then its strategy will depend on the extent to which the emerging state believes the established power views the rising state's contributions as indispensable to a regime. When there is a perception of rising state indispensability, the rising state will play a strategy of restructuring through hold-up, only lending support to a regime in

[55] On turn-of-the-century trade policy, focusing on British attempts to build institutions despite rampant free-riding, see Steven E. Lobell, *The Challenge of Hegemony: Grand Strategy, Trade, and Domestic Politics* (Ann Arbor, MI: University of Michigan Press, 2003).

exchange for concessions from the established power. Where the rising state is not seen as indispensable, it will accept an established state-led regime but will not invest heavily in building or maintaining it.

2.3 DYNAMIC CONDITIONS

Our discussion until now has assumed that outside options and perceptions of indispensability are, for each issue, fixed. Or, equivalently, that any changes in those parameters happen unpredictably and for reasons that are outside of any one state's control, so that national leaders have no ability to influence them at the margins. What if, however, national leaders had the ability to try to influence changes in our key parameters? Having this ability would have important implications for the way states might behave. This is particularly true if international regimes have inertia, or "stickiness," so that decisions getting made about regimes in the present will influence how those regimes operate for years to come.

Suppose that international institutions are sticky, and that overturning an existing precedent can be more difficult than establishing a new one where none had previously existed.[56] At a minimum, a long time horizon combined with institutional stickiness suggests that when countries negotiate the setup of multilateral regimes, the stakes will be high. Under such conditions, even seemingly minor changes in the present can have large implications for the accumulated future divisions of gains, in the same way that a small financial investment can lead to a large fortune through compound interest.[57] The corollary to this assumption of institutional

[56] This assumption is common to several rival schools of thought in the study of multilateralism, including the historical institutionalist and rational design approaches. On historical institutionalism in studies of multilateral institutions, see Orfeo Fioretos, "Historical Institutionalism in International Relations," *International Organization*, Vol. 65, no. 2 (2011), pp. 367–99. On the rational design of institutions where the cost of creating or changing a regime is a factor, see Barbara Koremenos, Charles Lipson, and Duncan Snidal, "The Rational Design of International Institutions," *International Organization*, Vol. 55, no. 4 (2001), pp. 761–99. The costs of creating or changing institutions is also a common assumption underlying some other recent strands of analysis about China's approach to multilateralism, even among scholars from the "realist" school, who traditionally downplay the constraining role of international institutions. Randall Schweller and Xiaoyu Pu, for example, argue that China must take costly diplomatic actions to delegitimize US-led institutions before it can replace them with its preferred alternatives. Randall L. Schweller and Xiaoyu Pu, "After Unipolarity: China's Visions of International Order in an Era of US Decline," *International Security*, Vol. 36, no. 1 (2011), pp. 41–72.

[57] James D. Fearon, "Bargaining, Enforcement, and International Cooperation," *International Organization*, Vol. 52, no. 2 (1998), pp. 269–305.

inertia is that building a new institution takes time. New institutions are created gradually, as they adapt to manage unintended consequences and learn how to most effectively carry out specialized tasks; the incremental development and expansion of the European Union through trial-and-error is an example.[58] It can take time for international agencies to develop expertise, and it can be even longer before they develop the credibility or authority to carry out their core functions.[59]

From these assumptions we derive two conclusions, which we explain in this section. First, rising states are always motivated to enhance their outside options, but they are especially motivated to enhance their outside options when they are seen as being indispensable. Second, because regimes are costly to build and slow to change, the more a rising state is investing in outside options in the present, the more it will be able to delay committing to second-order cooperation in the future.

Consider, first, the question of designing shifts. Our argument addresses the question of why a rising state like China sometimes plays a leadership role in global multilateralism and sometimes acts passively or as a spoiler. Our analysis, however, also suggests that there may be a systematic pattern to the kinds of investments that a rising state will tend to make in its outside options over time. Investments in outside options are therefore an independent implication of the argument and give us an opportunity to test, separately, the basic logic of the argument. To shift the balance of outside options to be more in its favor, a rising state can adapt so as to minimize the costs it faces if the common challenge goes unsolved, develop an ability to solve the problem independently of other established states, or sabotage the outside options of other established states.

Adaptation simply means preparing for, or self-insuring against, a global coordination failure. A state that builds coastal defenses in anticipation of a global failure to reduce carbon emissions, or that amasses currency reserves in anticipation of a financial crisis that is not resolved

58 Nikitas Konstantinidis, "Gradualism and Uncertainty in International Union Formation: The European Community's First Enlargement," *The Review of International Organizations*, Vol. 3, no. 4 (2008), pp. 399–433.

59 On the gradual development of credibility and authority generally, see Deborah D. Avant, Martha Finnemore, and Susan K. Sell, eds., *Who Governs the Globe?* (London: Cambridge University Press, 2010). For a specific example, the International Atomic Energy Agency only gradually developed a set of institutions that gave it the ability to command authority. Robert L. Brown, *Nuclear Authority: The IAEA and the Absolute Weapon* (Washington, DC: Georgetown University Press, 2015).

by international lending, is adapting. In the terms of the analytic model we present in this chapter, adaptation lowers the stakes.[60]

A state that lowers the stakes it faces on an issue will naturally enhance its own outside option, because it will be more insulated against the consequences of a regime failure. Enhancing its own outside option can allow a state to avoid having to invest in a new or existing regime. Ultimately, whether a state uses its new, improved position to play hold-up to demand a better position within existing regimes or to simply free-ride on the contributions of established states will depend on how indispensable it is to regime maintenance. So, the logic of our argument suggests that building an outside option (or even an entire alternate regime, waiting in the wings, such as the New Development Bank [NDB] or the AIIB) is not necessarily or inevitably a move to act as a spoiler – it depends on the larger strategic setting.[61]

Finally, sabotaging the outside options of established states can also shift the balance. Since the relevant aspect of the rising state's calculation is the balance of outside options between the rising state and the established state (rather than the quality of the rising state's outside options on any sort of absolute scale), undermining the established state's options has the same effect as enhancing the rising state's own. So, actions to delegitimize a set of global regimes, or to link cooperation in one regime to the survival of another regime, can raise the costs of a regime collapse to other established states. Lloyd Gruber provides several examples of this, such as when the United States threatened to withdraw from several other bilateral treaties with Mexico if Mexico did not agree to particular provisions of the North American Free Trade Agreement.[62]

Our argument suggests that states would always prefer to have better outside options, and would always have an incentive to do things to enhance their outside options.[63] However, one implication of our argument

[60] Adaptation can be purely unilateral, or it can be cooperative with an alternate group of states from the main multilateral regime. For example, a state wary of depending on the IMF in a crisis can build up its own currency reserves, and might also enter into swap agreements with other states as a way to further insure itself.

[61] Johannes Urpelainen and Thijs Van de Graaf, "Your Place or Mine? Institutional Capture and the Creation of Overlapping International Institutions," *British Journal of Political Science*, Vol. 45, no. 4 (2015), pp. 799–827. On competition between regimes, see also Erik Voeten, "Competition and Complementarity between Global and Regional Human Rights Institutions," *Global Policy*, Vol. 8, no. 1 (2017), pp. 119–23.

[62] Gruber, *Ruling the World*.

[63] An exception to this is when a state might seek to prevent its own outside options from improving in the future, as a way to reassure potential partners that it will refrain from exploiting their dependence later. This can happen when there are relationship-specific

is that the value of having a strong outside option also depends on a state's indispensability, and *vice versa*. If a state is indispensable, then moving from poor outside options to good outside options will create a situation in which it can play hold-up – that is, it can have a chance to win a multilateral regime structured on its terms and still be in a position to push some of the costs of the regime on to other states. In contrast, if the state is not indispensable, it moves to a position in which it will simply accept existing regimes and free-ride on their provision. In this case, it also does not have to pay the costs of upholding a regime, but neither does it get a regime structured along its preferred terms. So, when a rising state expects that it may be indispensable in the future, it has an additional incentive to invest in a better balance of outside options for itself. We discuss this dynamic later in the book with reference to international finance, where China both saw itself as increasingly indispensable and was especially active in creating mechanisms to adapt after the Asian financial crisis, as well as organizing alternative coalitions to address international financial issues without relying on established great powers.

To the extent that regimes are costly to build and costly to change, a rising state's investment in outside options gives it an additional reason to hold back from second-order cooperation in the present. Costly actions to build or maintain a regime in the present are just that – costly. Enforcing nonproliferation sanctions can alienate allies and can entail passing up commercial gains; rewarding states that maintain open financial systems and backstopping international lending institutions diverts from other foreign policy priorities. Once allies are alienated, commercial opportunities are forgone and other goals are sacrificed, those costs become sunk, and the rising state may find itself in a position of being trapped into maintaining a regime that is different from the one that it would otherwise have ideally preferred. As a result, a state investing in enhancing its outside options will be less likely to contribute to regime-building in the present. That is, it may still comply with regimes (first-order cooperation) without contributing to them (second-order cooperation).

In the empirical chapters that follow, we find several situations in which China's behavior might best be understood as building itself enhanced outside options. The Belt and Road Initiative is both an investment in Chinese capabilities as well as a tool that China could use, in principle,

investments at stake; these are more prevalent in instances of deep economic or military cooperation, and are generally less of a factor in the kinds of global multilateral issues we examine in this project; see Rector, *Federations*.

to try to accomplish the same objectives as the Shanghai Cooperation Organization, on a unilateral basis. Similarly, the Chiang Mai Initiative could be seen as giving China a stronger exit option and, therefore, a better position from which to approach the global financial system generally.

2.4 OBSERVATION

In the following empirical chapters, we explore the explanatory power of our argument in the context of a series of in-depth case studies relating to China's approach to particular issues. Our empirical focus on China is, obviously, not happenstance. The question of whether and how China engages with multilateral regimes to address issues of global concern is critically important to whether or not the world finds productive ways to manage those issues. China is therefore the primary motivating case for our theory and, although the theory is applicable to any state rising in a world populated by multilateral regimes, as a practical matter, the most meaningful tests of the theory will involve China. So, while we recognize that there is the potential for some circularity, with the theory being tested on the case that inspired it, we feel that the empirical analysis that follows is still a meaningful test of the theory for two reasons.

First, the theory itself is deductive; we begin with some basic premises that are generally uncontroversial in the study of international organizations and arrive at a set of conclusions that follow from those. Because the theory was not built in reverse inductively from the Chinese cases, whether or not the Chinese experience is consistent with our argument is an empirical question rather than something we assume.

Second, the units of analysis are issue areas rather than China as a whole. We chose a series of cases in order to maximize the variation we could obtain on the independent variables of interest – outside options and indispensability – which exhibit variation across the four cases. Critically, they also show exogenous variation within each case. That is, within each case a series of political changes that were not themselves connected to China's foreign policy stance led to observable changes in the balance of outside options and perceptions of indispensability, creating a kind of natural experiment to test the theory. Likewise, the cases show variation on our dependent variable – a rising power's (in our cases, China's) investments in second-order cooperation. Several of the cases also allow us to observe, directly, actions by Chinese leaders to enhance their outside options in ways consistent with our argument.

Because our cases are good ones from the perspective of hypothesis testing, to the degree we can show that our theory adds explanatory leverage in these cases, our confidence in our argument's broader utility is increased.[64] Nevertheless, we are cognizant that any small-n qualitative design will face questions about generalizability, and we are appropriately cautious in this regard. Future research should further probe the argument's generalizability. Such research should apply our theory to China's behavior in other settings, and should assess the extent to which our theory can help explain the behavior of other rising powers (both historical and contemporary) with regard to second-order cooperation.

We also wish to emphasize that our theory, like all theories of political behavior, greatly simplifies complex realities. In practice, for instance, both outside options and perceptions of indispensability vary continuously rather than dichotomously; our dependent variable – the rising power's strategy – can likewise vary by degrees. In the case studies that follow, we therefore describe both changes in China's outside options and changes in China's perceptions of its indispensability as gradations, as well as how these changes are linked to changes in its foreign policy strategy at the margins.

More broadly, Chinese decision-making in the cases we have selected has undoubtedly been shaped by factors that lie outside of our theoretical framework. Our theory, for instance, abstracts away from domestic political dynamics within China, even though it is certain that factors such as public and elite opinion and bureaucratic interests have, at times, influenced Beijing's approach to international regimes.[65]

64 In the ecosystem of political science research, our argument and empirical project likely falls in the "analyticist" category, in that we have a model (of a rising state's approach toward multilateralism) that we then evaluate by examining the relationship between different observable implications of the argument and the dynamics of a single set of related observations (China's tactics on a variety of issues). For an explanation of this approach in considerable depth, see Patrick Thaddeus Jackson, *The Conduct of Inquiry in International Relations: Philosophy of Science and its Implications for the Study of World Politics* (New York, NY: Routledge, 2010).

65 For examples from a variety of policy areas of domestic politics influencing Chinese foreign policy behavior, see the chapters in David M. Lampton, ed., *The Making of Chinese Foreign and Security Policy in the Era of Reform, 1978–2000* (Palo Alto, CA: Stanford University Press, 2001); and also Miles Kahler, "Rising Powers and Global Governance: Negotiating Change in a Resilient Status Quo," *International Affairs*, Vol. 89, no. 3 (2013), pp. 711–29. For a more recent study of the interaction between China's domestic politics and its foreign policies, see Jessica Chen Weiss, *Powerful Patriots: Nationalist Protest in China's Foreign Relations* (New York, NY: Oxford University Press, 2014). For an argument that investments in multilateral regimes may sometimes be simply a smokescreen to facilitate networks of corruption or disguises for

Likewise, some scholars have pointed to the role of ideology and strategic culture in shaping China's approach to multilateralism. For instance, Rosemary Foot,[66] drawing in part from Alastair Iain Johnston,[67] argued that a realpolitik strategic culture may have served as a constraint on China's willingness to engage in "multilateralist behavior" during the 1990s. Our analytic assumptions are entirely consistent with ideology being an important intervening factor in Chinese decisions. Ideology can, in principle, influence both the ends that leaders seek to pursue as well as their beliefs about cause and effect. So, for example, perhaps Chinese leaders have expectations about future American actions that are partly conditioned by their own ideological dispositions. We are more interested in the consequences of the beliefs that Chinese leaders hold than the process by which they arrived at them, so in the cases that follow we simply attempt to observe those beliefs, in order to test empirically whether they seem to have the effects we hypothesize.

Phillip Lipscy presents a theory, related to ours in its focus on outside options, that operates at the systemic level. His interest is in the flexibility of multilateral regimes, and he seeks to explain why some regimes change in order to give more voice to rising states as they rise but other regimes are less flexible. His thesis is that when network effects (the value of adding more states to an existing regime) and barriers to entry (the fixed costs of starting a new regime) are low, it is easier to start an alternative regime to compete with existing regimes, and so existing regimes will be more flexible and quicker to accommodate rising powers in order to stave off regime competition. When network effects and barriers to entry are high, it is much harder to start an alternative regime, so existing regimes are not compelled by competitive pressures to adapt; they will survive regardless and so can continue to privilege the interests of whichever legacy states happen to be overrepresented (relative to their real, current power).[68]

Lipscy's argument is an important advance in the study of multilateral institutional change. One advantage of his parsimonious approach to the

covert military or intelligence activities, see Evgeny Vinokurov and Alexander Libman, *Re-Evaluating Regional Organizations: Behind the Smokescreen of Official Mandates* (London: Springer, 2017).

[66] Rosemary Foot, "China in the ASEAN Regional Forum: Organizational Processes and Domestic Modes of Thought," *Asian Survey*, Vol. 38, no. 5 (1998), pp. 425–40.

[67] Alastair Iain Johnston, *Cultural Realism: Strategic Culture and Grand Strategy in Chinese History* (Princeton, NJ: Princeton University Press, 1995).

[68] Lipscy, *Renegotiating*.

theory is that it is systemic; the flexibility of a regime in his argument is determined solely by the characteristics of the issue and not by the situational preferences of individual states. Our approach, in contrast, permits state preferences to vary based on contextual factors. This allows us to consider situations where the stakes of an issue might be higher for one state than another, as well as situations in which the balance of outside options between states might change. An example of this might be climate change, where changes in the domestic salience of pollution in China raised the stakes for Chinese policymakers through the 2010s, even as partisan shifts in the United States led the American government to treat climate change as a lower priority with the election of President Trump. Our expectation, borne out by the case studies in the empirical chapters that follow, is that although these variations and shifts are unexplainable at the systemic level, they nevertheless seem to be triggering meaningful changes in China's willingness to invest, hold-up, or accept global multilateralism.[69]

Other studies have traced changes in Chinese behavior to changes in the way that Chinese policy-makers think about international regimes. Evan Medeiros and Taylor Fravel, for instance, argue that broad shifts in the post-Mao Chinese leadership's approach to international affairs ("China's new diplomacy") contributed to an increased willingness to engage with international institutions after the late 1990s.[70] More recently, some scholars have argued that China's leaders have deliberately undertaken more cooperative stands in order to increase the nation's international status.[71]

[69] Another important implication of Lipscy's systemic approach is that, for him, outside options all take the same form: building a rival multilateral institution. We argued in this chapter, and show in several of the empirical chapters, that both the United States and China had other more relevant alternatives as well. The threat of unilateral American military action against North Korea might have been entirely outside of any formal multilateral institution governing nuclear proliferation, but it still "competed" with the Six Party Talks as a potential solution to North Korea's nuclear program. Similarly, hypothetical US or European "green tariffs" on carbon-intensive imports might be implemented without Chinese assent, but would still compete with multilateralism. The availability of these kinds of uncoordinated unilateral actions suggests that we should be careful to clearly specify the outside options that established states have at their disposal.

[70] Evan S. Medeiros and M. Taylor Fravel, "China's New Diplomacy," *Foreign Affairs*, Vol. 82 (2003), p. 22.

[71] On status-seeking as a driver of behavior, see Xiaoyu Pu, "Ambivalent Accommodation: Status Signaling of a Rising India and China's Response," *International Affairs*, Vol. 93, no. 1 (2017), pp. 147–63. On China renegotiating the international public health regime out of a desire for enhanced international status, see Lai-Ha Chan, *China Engages Global Health Governance: Responsible Stakeholder or System-Transformer?* (London: Springer, 2011), p. 14.

Other scholars have considered how regimes may socialize leaders of states or the very states themselves.[72] In the case of China, Johnston shows that socialization has, at times, played an important role in shaping PRC behavior in international security institutions. Though much of Johnston's book is focused on first-order issues (such as China's decision to sign the Comprehensive Test Ban Treaty), he also addresses second-order issues (such as China's increased interest in contributing to multilateral security discourse in the context of the Association of Southeast Asian Nations [ASEAN] Regional Forum). Johnston traces shifts in China's approach to security institutions to socialization processes such as – in the ASEAN Regional Forum case – persuasion.[73] Allen Carlson, meanwhile, attributes subtle shifts in the PRC's approach to sovereignty and intervention over the course of the 1990s, in part, to the influence of changing international norms regarding humanitarian intervention, and the impact of these changing norms on the thinking of Chinese scholars and – eventually – China's broader foreign policy community.[74] These broader effects of multilateral regimes are not inconsistent with our thesis, as we argue that the structural factors we identify have an effect on a rising state's approaches to regimes as well. And, in some cases, our theory may offer insight into shifts in Chinese behavior that may be hard for socialization theories to account for: for instance, in Chapter 5 we characterize China's approach to the North Korean nuclear issue as moving from "accept" to "invest," but then back to "accept" more recently. Socialization processes may have a hard time accounting for this sort of retrogression (or, indeed, other types of behavior that we describe, especially our concept of "hold-up").

Before considering, in turn, each of our four cases of China's international behavior, we offer a brief introduction to the context of China's rise. Chapter 3 considers some of the most important parameters of that ascent – most notably economic, security, and diplomatic dimensions of China's post-Mao trajectory.

[72] David. H. Bearce and Stacy Bondanella, "Intergovernmental Organizations, Socialization, and Member-state Interest Convergence," *International Organization*, Vol. 61, no. 4 (2007), pp. 703–33. Judith Kelley, "International Actors on the Domestic Scene: Membership Conditionality and Socialization by International Institutions," *International Organization*, Vol. 58, no. 3 (2004), pp. 425–57.

[73] Alastair Iain Johnston, *Social States: China in International Institutions*, 1980–2000 (Princeton, NJ: Princeton University Press, 2008).

[74] Allen Carlson, "More than Just Saying No: China's Evolving Approach to Sovereignty and Intervention since Tiananmen," in Alastair Iain Johnston and Robert S. Ross, eds., *New Directions in the Study of China's Foreign Policy* (Palo Alto, CA: Stanford University Press, 2006), pp. 217–41.

3

The Context and Content of China's Rise

From the first century through the eighteenth century, China's economy was one of the largest in the world, along with that of India. As late as 1800, China's market-based system produced one-third of global gross domestic product (GDP) and dominated global trade in manufactures such as ceramics and silk.[1] Through much of this time, Chinese dynastic rulers also considered their peoples to be the world's most civilized, as well as – pointing to numerous important inventions – the most innovative. Dynastic rulers, committed to protecting the "heartland," engaged in the frequent, albeit geographically limited, use of force against surrounding enemies when they encroached on China's periphery.[2] During the late 1700s and early 1800s, proximate with the Industrial Revolution in the West, China's position in the world declined. The decline was not just relative to the West, but was absolute, as measured in terms of rates of economic output and the country's ability to protect itself from external military, economic, and political encroachment. The fall of the dynastic system, with the end of the Qing dynasty in 1911, is commonly viewed as the result of a combination of demographic pressure, domestic political reluctance by the Qing court to modernize under threat by imperialist powers, exploitation by those same powers as well as by a parasitic gentry class, and upheaval in the form of popular rebellion and – eventually – civil war.

[1] Angus Maddison, *The World Economy* (Paris: OECD, 2007).

[2] On defense strategy, see Michael D. Swaine and Ashley J. Tellis, *Interpreting China's Grant Strategy: Past, Present and Future* (Santa Monica, CA and Washington, DC: RAND, 2000).

The emergence in 1912 of the successor regime, the Republic of China (ROC), did not end the country's problems. While economists and historians debate the degree to which the economy was moribund before the 1949 Revolution,[3] this period saw a gradual but unambiguous shift, domestically, from the view of China as a "great civilization" to a more contemporary, if not yet modern, "nation-state." The ROC's inclusion in the great World War II alliance structure and its permanent seat on the UNSC conferred a symbol of China as a major nation, even though its economic and military strength fell short of conventional great-power status. Nevertheless, the country continued to be plagued by interference from foreign powers during the Republican era, particularly the Japanese invasion, and after the defeat of Japan, the civil war (1945–1949) between the Nationalist Party (which controlled the ROC government) and the Communist Party.

When the communist government took over in the autumn of 1949, Mao Zedong spoke of the Chinese people as having "stood up." This "rise" focused in part on China taking its place as a sovereign independent nation with a political regime that could protect its borders. As important was the development of a socialist economy that would move its citizens out of widespread poverty. The Maoist regime faced major challenges from both home and abroad. Domestic interruptions came in the form of the political movements of the Great Leap Forward (1958–1961) and the Cultural Revolution (1966–1976). On the international front, China quickly became enmeshed in the Korean War. The country faced a sustained threat from the United States, including (in addition to the Korean War) a trade embargo, the Vietnam War, and ongoing US support of the ROC government on Taiwan. Beijing faced yet an additional major threat, from the Soviet Union, after the Sino-Soviet split in 1960. The People's Republic was excluded from many international organizations, most notably the United Nations (UN), but also the GATT, the IMF, and the World Bank. In all of these, the "China" seat was held by the ROC. All told, external challenges kept the PRC government

[3] Historians tend to see the economy as a shambles, whereas economists are more likely to view traditional Chinese society as supportive of development, providing a solid basis for the growth in the Mao and post-Mao eras. On this latter view, see Loren Brandt, Debin Ma, and Thomas G. Rawski, "Industrialization in China," in Kevin O'Rourke and Jeffrey Williamson, eds., *The Spread of Modern Industry to the Global Periphery Since 1871* (Oxford: Oxford University Press, 2017), pp. 197–228. The debate is summarized in Philip Richardson, *Economic Change in China, c. 1800–1950* (Cambridge: Cambridge University Press, 1999).

in a defensive posture globally and, to some degree, regionally, although improving relations with Washington in the early 1970s helped to stabilize this environment. Economically, the end of the Japanese invasion and the civil war permitted the new government's policies to organize for growth, such as by promoting modest mechanization of agriculture and massive investment in extensive development. Still, China remained overwhelmingly rural and at a very low level of development. Consistent with the party's security strategy, to secure the heartland and periphery, the economic development strategy was largely autarkic and gradually minimized the role of markets in favor of planning. From 1949 until a modest re-engagement as Mao turned toward the West in the early 1970s, foreign trade – never at more than 10 percent of GDP[4] – was minimal and geographically limited (mainly to the Soviet bloc in the 1950s). Both inward and outward foreign direct investment (FDI) were non-existent. Despite historic links to the financial center of colonial Hong Kong, Chinese participation in international financial and capital markets also was absent. China was not a significant economic player in the Asian region, in terms of flows of goods and services, or in regional economic organizations.

Thus, by the time of Mao's death in 1976, although China had achieved a greater degree of external security and some economic progress, the country remained underdeveloped and largely outside of global markets, and had suffered from considerable domestic upheaval during the final two decades of Mao's life. Since then, however, the country has experienced a dramatic resurgence and has regained much of its lost economic, military, and cultural status. The case studies of China's strategic multilateralism in the following chapters occur in the broader context of what is generally considered the "rise" of China following the death of Mao. This largely descriptive chapter provides a general background of the economic, security, and diplomatic aspects of China's rise.

3.1 CHINA'S ECONOMIC RISE

Prior to Deng Xiaoping's 1978 ascendance as paramount leader, China's legacy, very broadly speaking, was one of past greatness and, more recently, extreme upheaval and poverty. The post-Mao regime, however, was able to achieve relative stability and, on this basis, begin China's economic rise.

4 Barry Naughton, *The Chinese Economy: Transitions and Growth* (Cambridge, MA: MIT Press, 2007), pp. 377–8.

FIGURE 3.1. *China GDP growth rate*
Source: The World Bank (https://data.worldbank.org)

By 2015, the picture of an underdeveloped and autarkic China had completely changed. Indeed, perceptions of China's rise are based, first and foremost, on the country's economic growth trajectory. Between 1978 and 2012, China's annual GDP growth averaged 9.8 percent, a rate the World Bank called "the fastest sustained expansion by a major economy in history."[5] Although Chinese official data has been called into question for overstating economic performance, and growth rates clearly have slowed since 2012, no one disputes that the sustained growth rates are historically notable (see Figure 3.1). In 2010, China surpassed Japan to become the second largest economy in the world, after the United States (excluding the European Union as a single economic bloc).

Deng Xiaoping's "reform and opening" program (*kaifang gaige*) radically altered the ways in which China's economy operated. China's extensive planning system gradually became subordinate to market mechanisms, so that today even state enterprises operate largely subject to market forces.[6] Over this period, China's economy became dominated (in terms of output and employment) by privately-owned enterprises,

[5] See World Bank figures and assessment at www.worldbank.org/en/country/china/overview, and Arthur R. Kroeber, *China's Economy: What Everyone Needs to Know* (New York, NY: Oxford University Press, 2016), pp. 263–6.

[6] Naughton has aptly termed this process "growing out of the plan." See Barry Naughton, *Growing Out of the Plan: Chinese Economic Reform, 1978–1993* (New York, NY: Cambridge University Press, 1995).

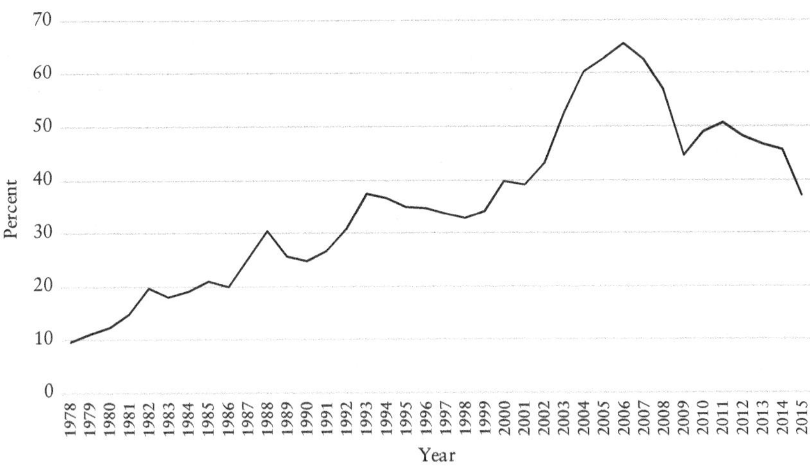

FIGURE 3.2. *China trade/GDP*
Source: The World Bank (https://data.worldbank.org)

although the largest, most strategic, and capital-intensive companies in China remain state owned.[7] The PRC also emerged as the world's largest trading nation in 2013, demonstrating the centrality of economic globalization to the regime's economic modernization strategy. The ratio of trade to GDP skyrocketed to 65.6 percent in 2006, before dropping off to a still substantial (by continental economy standards) 40 percent by 2015.[8] (See Figure 3.2.)

Along with the increase in trade came China's integration into cross-border production networks involving especially Asia's newly industrialized areas such as Hong Kong, Taiwan, and South Korea. Until the turn of the century, the direction of China's growing international economic integration was primarily outside-in. But, particularly as export earnings led to the growth of tremendous state-held foreign exchange reserves, and as many large Chinese state-owned enterprises amassed great wealth, the resources available for China to turn outward exploded. A sovereign debt fund, the China Investment Corporation (CIC, formed in 2007), became a major conduit through which the Chinese government has converted

7 See the discussion of the relationship between China's private and state-owned economies in Kroeber, *China's Economy*, chapter 5.

8 Data from the World Bank: http://data.worldbank.org/indicator/NE.TRD.GNFS.ZS.

its foreign exchange holdings to purchases, most notoriously of US government debt. This has led China to rival Japan as the largest foreign purchaser of US government debt (though their holdings remain far less than the amount of US debt held by US government and private sources). A related aspect of China's "going out" policy has been its outward FDI, as Chinese firms have purchased assets in both developed and developing countries. Chinese firms, quite naturally, are interested in uncovering new sources of growth and reaping a share of the profits historically realized by multinational corporations investing abroad. In some circumstances, these efforts may also serve the state's strategic interests.

Even in just the short previous discussion of China's new economic strength, we can observe the impact of three interrelated factors: government policies, domestic factors of production, and global context.[9] First, reform leaders substantially reoriented China's economic policy. Their basic push was away from the focus on "politics-in-command" of Mao's later years toward economic growth and development. Such a shift in focus required accepting, ideologically, market-supporting economic concepts (such as comparative advantage) that had been declared "bourgeois" under Mao. While this reorientation was politically volatile for the first years of the reform, Deng's "Southern Tour" of 1992 made it clear that the reform outlook was now "in command" and offered a combination of explicit and tacit government permission for new markets and private enterprises to grow alongside the state-led planned economy. Firms and local governments in particular experimented with new forms of economic activity before these experiments were formally sanctioned with laws and regulations.[10] For example, firms began making direct links with foreign purchasers and suppliers, and integrating into Asian and international supply chains. These domestic reforms were accompanied by a foreign economic policy designed to promote overall economic growth but also foster technological upgrading of the economy.[11] New policies permitted firms in China's coastal areas to engage

[9] Excellent discussions of the economic and political conditions enabling China's post-Mao growth are: Barry Naughton and Kellee Tsai (eds.), *State Capitalism, Institutional Adaptation, and the Chinese Miracle* (Cambridge: Cambridge University Press, 2015); Kroeber, *China's Economy*; and Naughton, *The Chinese Economy*.

[10] On the role of local experimentation in China's policy process, see Sebastian Heilmann, "Maximum Tinkering under Uncertainty: Unorthodox Lessons from China," *Modern China*, Vol. 35, no. 4 (2009), pp. 450–62.

[11] On policies to integrate into the global economy, see Nicholas Lardy, *Foreign Trade and Economic Reform in China, 1978–1991* (New York, NY: Cambridge University Press, 1993).

in increasingly independent contracting to produce high-quality, low-priced, manufactured goods to be sold in the West. Over time, the nature of goods produced in these areas – and increasingly throughout the country – became more sophisticated, moving up the value chain from toys and textiles to machinery and equipment, such as electronics and automobile parts. Using foreign currency earned through exports, as well as being encouraged by new policies to accept FDI in the form of joint ventures and wholly foreign-owned enterprises, Chinese firms obtained crucial new sources of technology that further promoted upgrading. Not content to remain at the low end of the value chain, the government made strong efforts to ensure that foreigners participating in the China market brought foreign "advanced" technology.

While the extent and rapidity of China's economic growth was remarkable, and historically unprecedented, the PRC government did not lay out *ex ante* a vision for its rise or a cohesive plan. Rather, as described in the phrase "crossing the river by feeling the stones," party leaders took incremental steps to promote growth guided by a sense of what would (or had been shown in experiments to) work and would not be too politically unpalatable to potential opposition interests. Through this process, the leadership was able to demonstrate payoffs from "easy wins"; dismantling the communes in the countryside, for example, not only increased wealth and contentedness for many rural dwellers, but also stimulated the production of more consumer goods – especially food – that were popular in cities. The regime waited until the reforms were more politically secure to tackle more sensitive issues, such as permitting bankruptcies of moribund firms. The patchwork of policies led to a patchwork economic system, comprising a mix of state-owned and private firms, as well as a mixture of dirigiste controls and laissez-faire markets.[12]

The gradualist policy measures complemented a second aspect of the regime's approach: the seeming willingness of the Chinese party-state to pull back its reach in favor of market forces. In the early reform years, China's main comparative strength – an abundance of underused, low-cost, and relatively skilled labor – could be mobilized together with capital and technology, much of it from overseas, to remarkable advantage. Although China continued to serve largely as an assembly location, in

[12] On the tensions between these statist and market-led forces in China's economic globalization, see Margaret M. Pearson, "China's Foreign Economic Relations and Policies," in Saadia Pekkanen, John Ravenhill, and Rosemary Foot, eds., *The Oxford Handbook of the International Relations of Asia*, (New York, NY: Oxford University Press, 2015), pp. 160–78.

which labor remained an important advantage, this, too, began to change at the turn of the century, as Chinese production for export moved up the value chain. The government also has been willing to cede former areas of control to market forces. For example, under the 1997 slogan "grasp the large and release the small" (*zhuada fangxiao*), the government sanctioned the ongoing massive privatization of small and medium enterprises in non-strategic sectors, while retaining a commitment for state management of large and strategic sectors of the economy. As another example, the government loosened its longstanding view of the necessity to control and guarantee domestic food production and, in the context of its WTO accession agreements lowering tariffs on grain imports, effectively recognized that grain production is not in China's comparative advantage.

The global economic context was a third important factor driving China's economic takeoff. The mobilization of China's comparative advantage in low-cost and skilled labor occurred at a time when China could realize payoffs in international markets; it faced seemingly insatiable demand for the goods it produced at a lower cost than those with whom it would compete – such as Mexico and Taiwan. Loose credit in the Organization for Economic Cooperation and Development (OECD) countries, and declining costs of transportation and logistics, further supported demand for Chinese goods. As noted earlier, the attractiveness of the Chinese labor market for low-cost production brought in foreign capital, first from Hong Kong and later from the West, Taiwan, and elsewhere in Asia. By the mid-1990s, the PRC was the top recipient of FDI in the developing world, monopolizing the flow of foreign capital, which otherwise might have gone to other developing countries. Major multinationals competed not to be left out of China.

There is a pronounced regional dimension to China's international economic integration. PRC firms – both state-owned and non-state-owned – have been vertically integrated into cross-border networks built by regional and multinational firms. By 2012, China had become the center of Asia's supply chain. As noted, this integration has been especially, but not exclusively, important for China's export industries. But it also has linked China deeply to other Asian economies, on which China relies for intermediate goods to process for re-export.[13] Overall, then, China's economic performance is central to the Asian region. Regionalization has

[13] Lee Branstetter and Nicholas Lardy, "China's Embrace of Globalization," in Loren Brandt and Thomas G. Rawski, eds., *China's Great Economic Transformation* (New York, NY: Cambridge University Press, 2008), pp. 633–82.

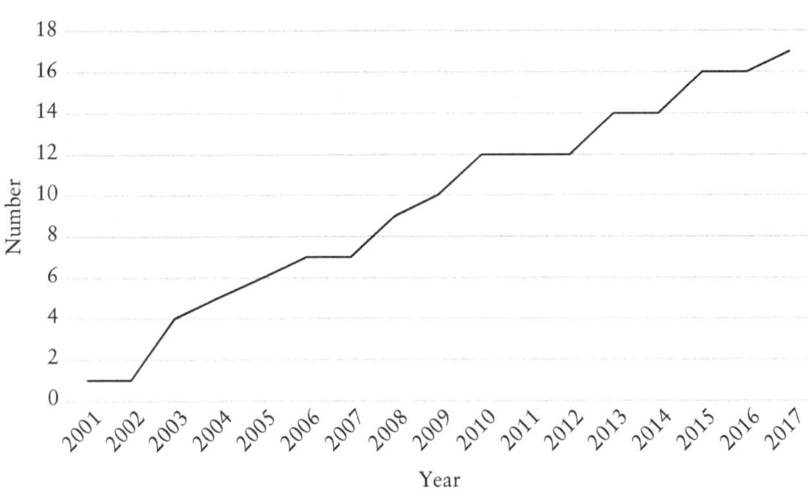

FIGURE 3.3. *China signed FTAs (cumulative)*
Source: Asian Development Bank, Asia Regional Integration Center (https://aric.adb.org/fta-country). This count includes signed agreements, but not those under negotiation.

been supported by the PRC government's eagerness to conclude bilateral free trade agreements (FTAs); more recently, Chinese proposals for a broader regional trade agreement took up steam in competition with the US-proposed Trans-Pacific Partnership (TPP), especially after the Trump administration withdrew from the TPP. More generally, China's leaders have invested heavily in FTAs. As of the end of 2017, Beijing had signed seventeen FTAs with a wide variety of countries and regions, within and outside of Asia, and was negotiating to form several new ones (Figure 3.3).

China's integration has also proceeded at the level of international and regional organizations. From its starting position as a non-participant, Beijing is now an active presence in numerous economic institutions. These institutions include those situated in Asia – APEC, ASEAN Plus Three, Asian Development Bank, and the newly established AIIB, for example. As we shall discuss in Chapter 6, moreover, China has become a major figure in the major international economic institutions, including the World Bank, the IMF, the WTO, and the Group of Twenty (G20).

3.2 INCREASES IN CHINA'S STRATEGIC CAPABILITIES

Along with the increase in China's economic capabilities has come an increase in China's security capabilities, both defensive and offensive.

During the Chinese civil war and the Mao era, the People's Liberation Army (PLA) relied heavily on mobilization of its large standing army for security, and it continued to rely on relatively underequipped ground troops during the early reform era. The desire for professionalization and sophisticated hardware was always present, as exemplified by China's successful push to become a nuclear power in 1964. The effort to modernize the PLA – to develop not just ground forces, but also air power and, eventually, naval power – gained steam in the early 1990s, and relied significantly on funds and technology obtained through economic modernization. Several events around this time period caused Chinese leaders to become more wary about external threats to regime stability. Leaders framed the civilian uprising at Tiananmen Square in 1989 as a result of external forces that were bent on "peaceful evolution" of the regime away from communism. The demise of ruling communist parties in Eastern Europe in the late 1980s, and the collapse of the Soviet Union in 1991 raised further concerns about how to ensure the durability of the regime.[14] The demonstration of US superior technology during the 1991 Gulf War and, later, the 1996 Taiwan Strait crisis, called into question the reliability of China's military readiness.

As a result, subsequent years saw sharp increases in military expenditures. Between 1997 and 2012, Chinese military spending increased in real terms by over 600 percent, moving the PRC to second place (behind the United States) among all countries, although at absolute levels that remained much smaller than expenditures by the US government.[15] As Figure 3.4 illustrates, PRC military spending has continued to increase in recent years. Indeed, between 2007 and 2016, China saw the biggest growth in military spending of all countries, with an increase of 118 percent.[16] Key goals for modernization have been the mechanization of systems (with concomitant reductions in personnel), the upgrading of

[14] We discuss in detail the perceptions of threats to PRC stability from the Tiananmen events and the collapse of the Soviet Union in our chapter on stability in Central Asia.

[15] A succinct description of expenditure increases is in Richard Bitzinger, "Modernizing China's Military, 1997–2012," *China Perspectives*, Vol. 2011, no. 4 (2011), pp. 7–15. According to the Stockholm International Peace Research Institute (SIPRI), the United States alone counted for 36 percent of the total $1.6 trillion worldwide military spending, and roughly the size of the next seven military budgets combined, including China in the number two position, with 13 percent (www.sipri.org/databases/milex). Military spending is notoriously difficult to calculate.

[16] See Aude Fleurant, Pieter D. Wezeman, Siemon T. Wezeman, and Nan Tian, Trends in World Military Expenditure, 2016 (Stockholm: SIPRI, 2017): www.sipri.org/sites/default/files/Trends-world-military-expenditure-2016.pdf.

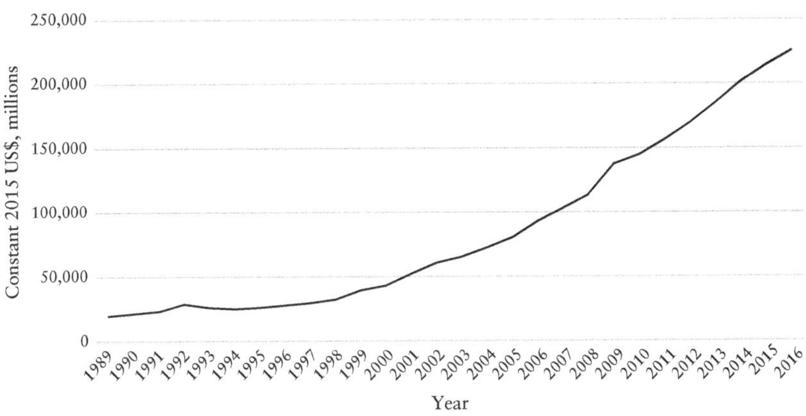

FIGURE 3.4. *PRC military spending*
Source: Stockholm International Peace Research Institute Military Expenditure Database (www.sipri.org/databases/milex)

remaining personnel, the development of command and control software systems, and overall informatization.[17] China also has been more willing to engage in joint maneuvers (as in Central Asia through the Shanghai Cooperation Organization [SCO]) and in more limited military-to-military cooperative exchanges with major powers including the United States.

While PRC military capabilities obviously and understandably have improved, and the government was willing to deploy its military at key strategic moments – most notably over Taiwan – China has remained relatively isolated from direct participation in regional and global conflict. Other than participating in UN peacekeeping missions, China has limited its military deployments to its own sovereign territory, to its new base in Djibouti, and to some activities in disputed (especially maritime) regions in Asia, especially in the South China Sea. We can understand this relative peace during the first forty years of the post-Mao era, at least in part, as a result of the broader strategy of "peace and development" espoused by Deng Xiaoping. After the fall of the Soviet Union, in particular, China sought to build a non-threatening strategic environment on its periphery, with the explicit goal of allowing focus on economic development. "Peace and development," then, referred to the idea that China needed peace, specifically cooperation with the United States, and especially in

[17] See Dennis J. Blasko, *The Chinese Army Today: Tradition and Transformation for the Twenty-First Century* (London: Routledge, 2012).

the Asian region, if it were to achieve economic development. So while some instances of military tension occurred (e.g., over Taiwan), and the continued US naval presence in Asia rankled nationalist sensibilities, Deng nevertheless viewed the benefits to China from residing in a peaceful region and avoiding entanglement overseas as crucial. An extension of the "peace and development" line, indicating that peace today would bode well for China's future military capabilities, was his "*tao guang yang hui you suo zuo wei*" often translated as "hide our capacities and bide our time, but also get some things done."

Internal debates have occurred over how long the PRC should abide by the "peace and development" line, as we will discuss. These debates became more prominent following the financial crisis of 2008 and the Obama administration's so-called "rebalance to Asia," consisting of negotiations for a TPP that (initially, anyway) excluded China, and a renewal of US defense partnerships in the Asian region (particularly with the Philippines and Japan). The US reorientation of attention to Asia reignited in Beijing a never truly dormant suspicion of US efforts to "contain" China. These occurred in concert with threats to stability that did emerge, notably on the Korean peninsula and in Central Asia, as our chapters on these topics show.

3.3 CHINA'S DIPLOMATIC "GOING OUT"

China was less isolated internationally during the Mao era than is often assumed. It allied, albeit uneasily, with the Soviet Union, and had substantial ties to the international communist countries and movements. It also developed strong ties to the non-aligned movement, beginning with the Bandung conference in 1955. Yet China was, in fact, isolated from the West and the developed world. Beijing resisted – or was barred from, due to lack of formal diplomatic recognition – membership in organizations controlled by the post–World War II established powers; it generally eschewed alliances and costly entanglements, and sought to maintain maximum flexibility in foreign relations.[18]

[18] For analyses citing Beijing as a free-rider in international cooperation during the Mao era, see Samuel Kim, "China and the United Nations," in Michel Oksenberg and Elizabeth Economy, eds., *China Joins the World: Progress and Prospects* (New York, NY: Council on Foreign Relations Press, 1999), pp. 42–89; and for the post-Mao era, see Stephanie Klein-Ahlbrandt, "China: Global Free-Rider," *Foreign Policy* (November 12, 2009): http://foreignpolicy.com/2009/11/12/beijing-global-free-rider.

In the late Mao era, with diplomatic recognition from the West won, China increasingly became involved in the UN system.[19] The new economic policy of "reform and opening to the outside world" was perhaps the most direct driver of international integration, but integration occurred on nearly all fronts. Formal diplomatic relations were opened with many countries – as of 2017, numbering 175. Many resources have been spent training the diplomatic and foreign affairs corps, opening missions, and supporting constant travel by leaders and diplomats.[20] As part of this "new diplomacy," soft power tools – such as the establishment of Confucius Institutes and funding for international educational exchanges – were deployed as a state-directed strategy to improve perceptions of China in the Asian region and around the world.[21] In addition, the PRC joined many international organizations over a relatively short period of time. As Johnston notes, "From the mid-1960s to the mid-1990s, China moved from virtual isolation from international organizations to membership numbers approaching about 80 percent of the comparison states."[22] Much Chinese diplomacy was in the service of the leaders' economic development goals, notably signing bilateral FTAs, regional economic arrangements (such as APEC) and international finance organizations (joining the IMF and World Bank, and acceding to the WTO). It also engaged in security agreements, such as the NPT (as discussed in our chapter on non-proliferation), and notably becoming the largest contributor to UN peacekeeping missions. After focusing on building relations with Western and developed countries (and with international organizations closely tied to them) during much of the post-Mao era, more recent years have seen a return to an emphasis on developing relations with other emerging and developing economy nations. Support of the BRICS organization (encompassing Brazil, Russia, India, China, and South Africa) is evidence of this push toward like-economies, as is Beijing's effort to foster the activity of the G20 as a successor to the OECD-dominated Group of Seven (G7). At the same time, as our cases show, this greater engagement has not led to uniform

[19] See Samuel Kim, *China, The United Nations and World Order* (Princeton, NJ: Princeton University Press, 1979).

[20] Evan S. Medeiros and M. Taylor Fravel, "China's New Diplomacy," *Foreign Affairs*, Vol. 82 (2003), p. 22.

[21] Among many excellent studies of China's new soft power initiatives, one of the most comprehensive is Joshua Kurlantzick, *Charm Offensive: How China's Soft Power Is Transforming the World* (New Haven, CT: Yale University Press, 2007).

[22] Quoted in Johnston, "Is China a Status Quo Power?" p. 12.

behavior in these organizations; quite different behaviors – relatively passive acceptance, hold-up to gain concessions, and investment in cooperation – are evident.

3.4 TURNING POINTS: THE GLOBAL FINANCIAL CRISIS AND US "REBALANCE"

Two recent events have led China's leaders to reconsider the country's place in the global order. The first was the global financial crisis that began in 2008. As discussed more extensively in our chapter on global financial governance, this crisis was viewed widely in China as being caused by US financial firms' ill-advised practices, by poor regulation by the US government, and by poor surveillance mechanisms of the IMF. The PRC escaped the worst effects of the crisis due to its capital controls and abundant foreign reserves. Yet the crisis was widely discussed in China as a marker of the decline of US power, of US responsibility, and of US moral leadership in the financial – and, by extension, other – realms of global governance.[23] It was seen as a harbinger of the decline of the "Washington Consensus" and the rise of a new "Beijing Consensus." While Beijing publicly rejected these notions, perhaps reluctant to take on the mantle of leadership, the issue of China's appropriate response became a popular theme.[24]

The second turning point, on the heels of the global financial crisis, was the move by the US government, under the Obama administration, to "rebalance" or "pivot" to Asia, implicitly away from an over-emphasis in US policy on the Middle East.[25] As noted previously, Chinese officials had long been uncomfortable with US alliances and naval power in the region, even as they recognized benefits to China's development that were possible in the context of regional peace. The rebalance, on the heels of questions about US leadership in global finance, raised to

[23] Wang Yong and Louis Pauly, "Chinese IPE Debates on (American) Hegemony," *Review of International Political Economy*, Vol. 20, no. 6 (2013), pp. 1165–88.

[24] See Scott Kennedy, "The Myth of the Beijing Consensus," *Journal of Contemporary China*, Vol. 19, no. 65 (2010), pp. 41–62.

[25] An excellent summary of the idea that a pivot occurred is Robert G. Sutter, Michael E. Brown, and Timothy J. A. Adamson, "Balancing Acts: The U.S. Rebalance and Asia-Pacific Stability" (Elliot School of International Affairs, George Washington University, August 2013): www2.gwu.edu/~sigur/assets/docs/BalancingActs_Compiled1.pdf. Others, such as Christensen (*The China Challenge*), argue that no sharp pivot occurred, as policy from the Bush to the Obama administrations demonstrated consistency in their attention to the Asia-Pacific region.

new heights suspicions about underlying and inevitable US efforts to "contain" China and keep the country from its "rightful place." Many in the West have interpreted Chinese policy as marked by a "new assertiveness,"[26] an impression deepened by President Xi Jinping who, upon ascension to the apex of power, made his hallmark policy the "China Dream of National Rejuvenation" (*Zhongguo guojia fuxing zhi meng*).[27] China's actions in the South China Sea were seen as the clearest mark of a new posture.

But despite increased dissatisfaction with the US role, there remain in China diverse views among officials and scholars as to whether the era of "hiding our capabilities and biding our time" should truly be over. Critical voices have not been clear about what Beijing should do about China's place in the world. Indeed, internal debate about whether China's rise should cause it to alter its policy reveals a split between those who feel China should more aggressively assert its interests on the world stage, and those who wonder whether to do so would put undue pressure on China and divert attention away from the continued need to focus on domestic problems.[28] Even with the election of Donald Trump as US President and his withdrawal from (or minimized participation in) many international fora, there is not a clear consensus in China for how to proceed in terms of global cooperation. We return to this issue in our final chapter.

[26] Susan Shirk discusses a general trend toward "new assertiveness" beginning in around 2009, particularly in the Asian region, although her analysis – consistent with the theme of variance in this book – shows that Chinese behavior bore marks of assertiveness before this time. Susan Shirk, "The Domestic Context of Chinese Foreign Security Policies," in Saadia Pekkanen, John Ravenhill, and Rosemary Foot, eds., *The Oxford Handbook of the International Relations of Asia* (New York, NY: Oxford University Press, 2015), pp. 390–410.

[27] An aspect of "national rejuvenation" was seen to be the search in China's Confucian roots for a revived traditional posture in foreign affairs. See Qin Yaqing, "Development of International Relations Theory in China," *International Studies*, Vol. 46, issue 1–2, pp. 185–201.

[28] A lively debate about whether China is "newly assertive" and its implications for global order is: Alastair Iain Johnston, "How Assertive is China's New Assertiveness?" *International Security*, Vol. 37, no. 4 (2012), pp. 7–48; and Dingding Chen, Xiaoyu Pu, and Alastair Iain Johnston, "Debating China's Assertiveness," *International Security*, Vol. 38, no. 3 (2013/2014), pp. 176–183.On differences between more cautious official statements by Beijing, compared to less authoritative but more bellicose statements, see Michael Swaine, "Chinese Leadership and Elite Responses to the US Pivot," *China Leadership Monitor*, no. 38 (2012), http://media.hoover.org/sites/default/files/documents/CLM38MS.pdf.

3.5 CONCLUSION

China's dramatic rise, along economic, military, and diplomatic dimensions, suggests that our theory is likely to apply to the PRC across a range of issue areas. In the theory chapter, we defined a "rising power" as a country that, in the past, has played a minor role in contributing to second-order cooperation on a particular issue, but that is an increasingly consequential actor within that issue area. China's emergence as the world's second largest economy and largest trading state suggests, for instance, that actions taken in Beijing on a broad array of economic issues will have large global consequences. Decisions on the value of China's currency will have significant economic consequences in countries across the world. Likewise, as the world's leading emitter of GHGs, China's approach to the climate change issue will have large implications for international efforts to curb global warming. And China's growing military clout means that Beijing is an increasingly consequential actor on regional and, to some degree, global security issues. In the empirical chapters that follow, we explore how China – as a rising power – has approached second-order cooperation across a range of issue areas, some regional in scope, some global. We begin in the next chapter with a case study of China's evolving approach to stability and order-provision in Central Asia.

4

Order in Central Asia

From Accept to Invest

4.1 INTRODUCTION

On June 15, 2001, six countries – China, Russia, Kazakhstan, Kyrgyzstan, Tajikistan, and Uzbekistan – established the Shanghai Cooperation Organization (SCO) in Shanghai. The principal focus of the new organization, as emphasized by Chinese President Jiang Zemin in his speech at the inaugural meeting of the SCO, was "maintaining the regional security."[1] As Russian President Vladimir Putin noted at the same meeting, the SCO "will manage to reinforce stability in the region, something which clearly will have a beneficial impact on all of Asia."[2] In addition to establishing the SCO, the six countries at this meeting signed an agreement to crack down on terrorism, separatism, and extremism, underscoring the centrality of stability in the SCO mandate. The SCO emerged primarily as a consequence of proactive PRC efforts to create a new regional security architecture, and China in subsequent years continued to be the key driver for further institutionalization of the organization, including the opening of the Regional Anti-Terrorist Structure (RATS) in 2003 and the creation of a permanent secretariat in 2004.

In this chapter, we explore China's motivations for investing in the SCO and the way those motivations have changed over time. To preview, we argue that our theory offers substantial leverage in this regard. We emphasize that, during the 1990s, Beijing had an increasing stake in

[1] "Jiang Zemin's Speech at Inaugural Meeting of 'Shanghai Cooperation Organization,'" *Xinhua Domestic Service*, June 15, 2001, in *World News Connection*, June 18, 2001.

[2] "Putin Says New Shanghai Organization to Promote Security across Asia," *ITAR-TASS*, June 15, 2001, in *World News Connection*, June 18, 2001.

cooperation on the issue of Central Asian stability, just as Russia – the other key regional actor at the time – had declining capacity to impose order in the region.[3] Instability in Central Asia was of growing concern to Beijing at the time because of increasing ethnic unrest in the Xinjiang Uyghur Autonomous Region. Beijing worried that instability in Central Asia could contribute to further unrest in Xinjiang. Meanwhile, Russian hegemony in Central Asia faded sharply following the collapse of the Soviet Union in 1991, and Russia's subsequent economic struggles persisted during the 1990s, which undermined Moscow's ability to provide stability in the region. In combination, a growing PRC stake and declining Russian capacity implied that China's outside options, relative to those of the established power (Russia) were worsening on the issue of order-provision in Central Asia. Consistent with our theory, Beijing in turn invested in building new regional security architecture that could contribute to stability in the region, beginning with the Shanghai Five in the late 1990s and culminating with the SCO in 2001.[4]

In the years after the SCO was established, China faced an ambiguous array of constraints in Central Asia. On the one hand, Russian resurgence under Vladimir Putin meant that Moscow was increasingly willing and able to reassert Russian dominance in the region. This resurgence, in turn, opened the possibility of some PRC free-riding on Russian provision of order in Central Asia. On the other hand, however, Beijing had reason

[3] It is worth noting here that this case differs from our other empirical studies, in that the principal established power interacting with China in this case is Russia, rather than the United States.

[4] We note at the outset that our focus on outside options may seem counterintuitive in this case, particularly prior to the emergence of regional institutions in the late 1990s. Typically, when scholars write about outside options in the context of international institutions, they have in mind the creation of new institutions outside of existing institutions (Phillip Y. Lipscy, *Renegotiating the World Order: Institutional Change in International Relations* (New York, NY: Cambridge University Press, 2017)) or, perhaps, unilateral actions outside of existing institutions. In Chapter 2, we defined outside options more broadly, as "a government's expectation about what would happen if it were to stop cooperating with other states to promote or maintain a multilateral regime." But here, prior to the emergence of regional institutions, we conceptualize outside options more abstractly, as Beijing's alternatives to promoting cooperation that could address the worsening problem of Central Asian stability. Outside options, in other words, are conceptualized here as the opportunity costs of organizing multilateral cooperation to address the problem. In our analysis, we focus much of our attention on the concept of "stake," which we identified in Chapter 2 as being a core determinant of an actor's outside options. As China's stake in a cooperative solution to the problem of Central Asian stability increased, China's outside options were worsening, given the unattractiveness (and, indeed, the increasing infeasibility) of a Russian unilateral option in the 1990s.

to be wary of Russia's unilateral option: perhaps most importantly, the reestablishment of Russian hegemony in the region could undercut access to Central Asian oil and gas resources for a China that was increasingly dependent on imported energy. Finally, the stakes remained high for China throughout. In the early 2000s, the US-led intervention in Afghanistan generated fears in Beijing of possible US encirclement, as Washington burst onto the scene as a leading actor in Central Asia. Later, as the Color Revolutions swept through the region and the war in Afghanistan dragged on, China had reason to fear continued regional instability, especially after violence in Xinjiang spiked in 2009. Thus, although (from Beijing's perspective) the balance of outside options relating to Central Asian order-provision improved somewhat beginning in the early 2000s, those outside options remained relatively poor. Our theory predicts continued PRC investment in institution-building in the region. We show that PRC policy and behavior have been moderately consistent with this expectation, though conflicting interests among SCO member-states has limited the institutionalization and efficacy of the organization. We conclude by considering implications of more recent PRC economic initiatives in the region – including, most notably, the Belt and Road Initiative (BRI).

4.2 BACKGROUND: CHINA, CENTRAL ASIA, AND THE PROBLEM OF STABILITY IN XINJIANG BEFORE THE END OF THE COLD WAR

China's current interest in Central Asian stability is not new. Rather, Chinese leaders have been concerned about the influx of destabilizing forces from the northwest frontier for millennia. Successive imperial dynasties struggled with the question of how best to manage relations with, and avoid violent incursions from, the nomadic populations of Inner Asia, which could put regime stability at risk. Thomas J. Barfield writes, for instance, that "intentionally destructive" Xiongnu (a confederation of nomadic Turkic tribes) raids during the Han dynasty generated instabilities that the Han court feared could "lead to an unraveling of empire."[5] The Tang dynasty at its height established protectorates deep into Central Asia, though the costs of overexpansion would help undo the dynasty. As Fairbank notes, by the end of the Tang in the early tenth century, "Turkic and other non-Chinese peoples occupied much of North

[5] Thomas J. Barfield, "The Hsiung-nu Imperial Confederacy: Organization and Foreign Policy," *Journal of Asian Studies*, Vol. 41, no. 1 (1981), p. 54.

China."[6] Later, even before the Mongols established the Yuan dynasty in 1271 and defeated the Southern Song in 1279, northern China had been under the control of non-Chinese rulers for more than a century.[7] For centuries after defeating the Yuan, the Ming continued to view the Mongol tribes along their northern and northwestern borders as representing their "primary security problem."[8] And Western Mongol tribes later posed a threat to the Qing – themselves Inner Asians – who ultimately conquered the Western Mongols and expanded their empire deep into Central Asia.[9] Today, of course, the Chinese state does not fear armed incursions originating in Central Asia, but the fear of destabilizing ideologies and support networks in some sense parallels this historical challenge to Chinese rule.[10]

After expanding the empire to include what is now Xinjiang, the Qing continued to face significant challenges along its northwest frontier – both external, including pressures from the Russian and British empires, and internal, including large-scale Muslim revolts during which the Qing lost control of the region.[11] These challenges – combined with growing threats from the European colonial powers and Japan in the east, and the reality that Xinjiang was a persistent drain on resources – led some high-ranking officials to advocate for the abandonment of Xinjiang altogether.[12] Although the Qing court ultimately decided against abandonment

[6] John King Fairbank, *China: A New History* (Cambridge, MA: Harvard University Press, 1992), pp. 86–7.

[7] Ibid., chapter 4.

[8] Alastair Iain Johnston, *Cultural Realism: Strategic Culture and Grand Strategy in Chinese History* (Princeton, NJ: Princeton University Press), p. 183.

[9] John King Fairbank, *China: A New History* (Cambridge, MA: Harvard University Press, 1992), pp. 152–3.

[10] For a discussion of the calculations facing nomadic tribes concerning whether or not to engage in violent raids, see Sechin Jagchid and Van Jay Symons, *Peace, War, and Trade along the Great Wall: Nomadic-Chinese Interaction through Two Millennia* (Bloomington, IN: Indiana University Press, 1989). The authors show that raiding behavior was least likely to prevail when institutions (trade, tributary, and intermarriage) were in place that enabled nomads to obtain needed goods (such as grain) peacefully. See also Thomas J. Barfield, *The Perilous Frontier: Nomadic Empires and China* (Cambridge, MA: Blackwell, 1989). For a discussion of different Chinese grand strategies for dealing with the security threat posed by nomadic tribes – with a focus on the Ming – see Johnston, *Cultural Realism*. Johnston describes three broad Chinese strategies, including offense, static defense (such as wall-building), and accommodation.

[11] See, e.g., Fairbank, *China*; Nadine Godehardt, *The Chinese Constitution of Central Asia: Regions and Intertwined Actors in International Relations* (New York, NY: Palgrave MacMillan, 2014), p. 117.

[12] Gardner Bovingdon, *Uyghurs: Strangers in Their Own Land* (New York, NY: Columbia University Press, 2010), pp. 32–3; James A. Millward, *Eurasian Crossroads: A History of Xinjiang* (New York, NY: Columbia University Press, 2007), p. 126.

and Qing forces were able to reestablish control in Xinjiang, it was only in 1884 that Xinjiang was transformed into a province of China. After the Qing collapse, Xinjiang was largely self-ruled by local (ethnic Chinese) warlords during the Republican era. Even after Chiang Kai-shek's Northern Expedition in the 1920s, these warlords remained autonomous from the reconstituted central government in Nanjing.[13] The period was characterized by frequent rebellions, triggered in part by harsh repression of local (non-Han) populations; in 1933, one of these rebellions resulted in the establishment within Xinjiang of the short-lived Eastern Turkestan Republic.[14] The Soviet Union provided assistance in putting down these rebellions and, in turn, Soviet influence in Xinjiang grew sharply in the 1930s and early 1940s.[15] Fravel observes that the ethnic Han Chinese warlords in Xinjiang at the time "usually maintained far closer administrative and economic ties with the Soviet Union than with China proper."[16] These ties to the Soviet Union lingered after World War II: even as the Nationalist government tried to reassert Chinese authority in the region, Moscow supported the establishment of a second Eastern Turkestan Republic in areas along the border.[17] And, although the People's Liberation Army (PLA) moved into Xinjiang shortly after the establishment of the PRC in 1949 and Chinese authorities gradually constructed a new administrative apparatus that brought Xinjiang under greater institutional control of the central government,[18] central government authority in the region remained relatively weak nevertheless.[19]

PRC efforts to consolidate control over Xinjiang in the 1950s helped lay the groundwork for further unrest in the early 1960s. Leaders in Beijing worried about continued Soviet influence in the region – Mao at one point referred to Xinjiang as a Soviet "semi-colony" – and by the late 1950s, as the relationship with Moscow began to deteriorate, non-Han

[13] Bovingdon, *Uyghurs*, p. 35.

[14] Ibid., pp. 36–7; Millward, *Eurasian Crossroads*, chapter 5.

[15] Godehardt, *Chinese Constitution of Central Asia*, p. 119.

[16] M. Taylor Fravel, *Strong Borders Secure Nation: Cooperation and Conflict in China's Territorial Disputes* (Princeton, NJ: Princeton University Press, 2008), p. 102.

[17] Ibid., pp. 101–2.

[18] Millward, *Eurasian Crossroads*, chapter 6.

[19] Fravel, *Strong Borders*, p. 102. In 1955, Xinjiang was designated an autonomous zone (the Xinjiang Uyghur Autonomous Region), but as Millward (*Eurasian Crossroads*, p. 246) notes, this was mostly a superficial designation: "The system of local and regional autonomous areas, ... although it placed members of the various recognized ethnic groups at each level of government in Xinjiang, does not provide what most people would understand to be 'autonomy.'"

cadres in Xinjiang were increasingly attacked for being pro-Soviet "local nationalists."[20] Meanwhile, despite a formal veneer of regional autonomy, Beijing adopted a more assimilationist policy in Xinjiang beginning in 1958;[21] the late 1950s and early 1960s also saw a surge in Han migration to the region.[22] The growing repression of the non-Han population, combined with the economic dislocations triggered by the Great Leap Forward, helped spark a massive exodus of non-Han (mostly Kazak) residents in the spring of 1962. Approximately 60,000 refugees fled to the Soviet Union, and Chinese officials blamed Moscow for encouraging the migration, believing that the Soviet Union was deliberately seeking to destabilize the region.[23] As Beijing moved to stop the exodus by sealing the border, a large riot erupted in the town of Yining near the Soviet border. The sudden migration also caused significant economic dislocations in northwest Xinjiang as the size of the local labor force dropped sharply, leading PRC officials to fear further instability in the region.[24] As Fravel emphasizes, the out-migration and subsequent unrest and economic disruptions "brought into stark relief China's own weaknesses in Xinjiang as well as the latent challenge of Soviet influence."[25] After 1962, the PRC dramatically increased troop deployments along Xinjiang's borders, while ending border trade with the USSR and closing Soviet consulates in Xinjiang.

Xinjiang, like the rest of China, slipped into political chaos during the Cultural Revolution. James Millward writes that the Soviet border became tense during this time, and "the historical connections of Xinjiang's non-Han political elites with the Eastern Turkestan Republic and the Soviet Union were invoked against them"; most non-Han cadres

[20] See Millward, *Eurasian Crossroads*, pp. 255–6; and Sergei N. Goncharov, John W. Lewis, and Xue Litai, *Uncertain Partners: Stalin, Mao, and the Korean War* (Stanford, CA: Stanford University Press, 1993), pp. 121–6. Goncharov et al. note that the secret Additional Agreement to the 1950 Sino-Soviet alliance treaty, along with other secret protocols signed by the two countries, aimed to protect Soviet influence in Xinjiang. For instance, the Additional Agreement barred citizens from third countries from settling in Xinjiang (a restriction meant to help reinforce Soviet influence and protect it from foreign competition), and another secret protocol guaranteed the USSR preferential access to Xinjiang's natural resources (see Goncharov et al., *Uncertain Partners*, pp. 122, 125).

[21] Millward (*Eurasian Crossroads*, p. 261) notes that the Chinese Communist Party (CCP) "launched a series of anti-Islamic measures" in the late 1950s, including the end of press acknowledgment of Islamic holidays and refusing permission for Muslims to go on hajj.

[22] Ibid., p. 263.

[23] Fravel, *Strong Borders*, p. 104.

[24] Ibid., pp. 101–4; Millward, *Eurasian Crossroads*, pp. 264–5.

[25] Fravel, *Strong Borders*, p. 104.

were purged from power.[26] The end of the Cultural Revolution and the rise of Deng Xiaoping led to greater political stability in Xinjiang during the late 1970s and 1980s. This is not to say there were no ethnic tensions at the time; episodic demonstrations and riots, in fact, occurred throughout the 1980s.[27] But, in comparison with the instability of the past and the growing unrest that would characterize the 1990s (as we will discuss), the 1980s appeared quite calm. Indeed, even the perceived subversive danger posed by the Soviet Union – and its historical linkages with Xinjiang – was becoming obsolete as Moscow, under Mikhail Gorbachev, sought to improve relations with Beijing.

To summarize, Chinese leaders have long worried about the influx of destabilizing forces along China's northwestern frontier. Prior to the Qing, successive Chinese dynasties struggled with the challenge posed by incursions of nomadic tribes from Inner Asia. After the Qing incorporated Xinjiang into the empire, stability within Xinjiang became a persistent problem for successive Chinese governments, a problem at times magnified by external influences such as Soviet intervention. After a brief respite in the 1980s, these historical problems would reemerge in the 1990s, when Beijing faced growing resistance to CCP rule in Xinjiang combined with a new set of challenges in Central Asia in the aftermath of the Soviet Union's collapse.

4.3 CHINA AND CENTRAL ASIA IN THE 1990S: WORSENING OUTSIDE OPTIONS

The balance of outside options relating to Central Asia was clearly quite favorable to China during the later stages of the Cold War. Relative stability in Xinjiang during the 1980s meant that the stakes were relatively low for China at the time, and it almost goes without saying that order-provision in the region was viewed in Moscow as an internal Soviet matter (meaning that China was certainly not seen as indispensable in this regard). In turn, China had little reason to be engaged in the region; that is, consistent with our theory, China's behavior at the time was relatively passive.

Over the course of the 1990s, however, China faced a worsening balance of outside options with regard to the provision of order in Central

[26] Millward, *Eurasian Crossroads*, p. 272.

[27] For key instances, see Michael Dillon, *Xinjiang: China's Muslim Far Northwest* (London and New York, NY: Routledge Press, 2004), pp. 59–62.

Asia. During this time, the PRC's stake in regional stability increased sharply as a consequence of several factors, including (most importantly) increased unrest in Xinjiang. At the same time, however, the attractiveness of the Russian unilateral option in providing that stability was declining, from Beijing's perspective. While a Moscow-centered regional order could, in principle, help provide stability in the region, it would likely do so in a way that neglected growing Chinese economic interests in Central Asia. And declining Russian power called into question the capacity of post-Soviet Russia to provide effective regional order in any event. China's worsening outside options relative to Russia, in turn, gave Beijing strong incentives to make investments of its own in Central Asia.

4.3.1 China's Growing Stake in Central Asian Stability

Several factors combined to dramatically increase China's stake in the problem of Central Asian stability during the 1990s. First, and most important, was the reemergence of serious ethnic unrest in Xinjiang. Renewed unrest in Xinjiang was especially alarming to PRC leaders, since it came on the heels of the large-scale Tiananmen Square protests and the demise of Communist regimes in Eastern Europe and the Soviet Union. These events heightened PRC sensitivities to unrest, especially since they viewed mismanagement of relations with ethnic minorities in the Soviet periphery as a key factor driving the USSR collapse. While PRC leaders focused primarily on internal solutions to the unrest, they also viewed diplomacy with Central Asian countries as an important component of their strategy to reduce instability in Xinjiang. Second, the collapse of the Soviet Union led to an increasing risk of instability in Central Asia, which could potentially spread to China's Western regions. Finally, China's outward-oriented economic reforms and rapid economic development meant that China had an increasing (though admittedly still relatively small) economic stake in Central Asia.

4.3.1.1 Xinjiang Unrest in the 1990s

Although – as discussed in the previous section – Xinjiang experienced periodic unrest after the establishment of the PRC in 1949, the area had been relatively stable during the 1980s. By 1989, however, this stability appeared increasingly tenuous: in March, violent protests in Lhasa led the PRC to impose martial law in Tibet and, in May, thousands of students took to the streets in Urumqi to support the Tiananmen Square demonstrations and to protest the publication of a book in Shanghai that was seen as disparaging to Islamic customs.[28] Unrest became more pronounced in 1990. The key event occurred in April of that year, when approximately 200 armed men initiated a violent uprising in the town of Baren in southwestern Xinjiang. The uprising was motivated by grievances against CCP rule in Xinjiang (which ranged from dissatisfaction with the PRC's treatment of religious minorities to nuclear weapons testing in the region). Participants, who soon numbered in the thousands, kidnapped local officials and surrounded the town hall compound in Baren, with some calling for the establishment of an East Turkmenistan state in Xinjiang. The insurrection was ultimately suppressed when People's Armed Police reinforcements – and possibly regular PLA troops – arrived; some reports suggested that as many as sixty people died during the episode.[29] Several other Xinjiang towns and regions saw uprisings in 1990.[30]

As Fravel writes, the Baren insurrection "sparked a decade of ethnic unrest and instability in Xinjiang that challenged the regime's authority in this vast frontier."[31] Over the next several years, this unrest spread across Xinjiang and included several violent incidents, such as bomb attacks that occurred in Urumqi in 1992 and in Kashgar in 1993, reported armed insurrections that occurred in northwest Xinjiang in 1991, large-scale rioting and strikes which occurred in several towns in 1995,[32] and the assassination of several policemen and a pro-Beijing cleric in 1996.[33] In 1996, the PRC launched its "strike hard" campaign, which Michael Dillon emphasizes was directed not just at criminal activities, but also at separatist activities in Tibet and Xinjiang.[34] During the campaign, authorities arrested large numbers of suspected separatist sympathizers across Xinjiang,[35] and unrest was sufficiently pronounced in 1996 to require the deployment of PLA units in some instances.[36] In 1997, the arrest of a large number of Uyghurs in early February helped trigger large-scale protests and riots in Yining; Dillon writes that the Uyghur protestors

[28] Dillon (*Xinjiang*, p. 60) writes that these protests were originally reported as being orderly, but later (after the crushing of the Tiananmen Square protests) were reported to have been violent. See also Fravel, *Strong Borders* (pp. 151–2); and Felix K. Chang, "China's Central Asian Power and Problems," *Orbis*, Vol. 41, no. 3 (1997), pp. 408–9.

[29] See Dillon (*Xinjiang*, pp. 62–5) for a detailed discussion of the Baren uprising. See also Fravel, *Strong Borders*, pp. 152–3.

[30] Ibid; Chang, "China's Central Asian Power," p. 409.

[31] Fravel, *Strong Borders*, p. 153.

[32] Dillon, *Xinjiang*, pp. 66–8.

[33] Chang, "China's Central Asian Power," p. 410.

[34] Dillon, *Xinjiang*, p. 84.

[35] Ibid., chapter 9.

[36] Chang, "China's Central Asian Power," p. 410.

targeted Han residents, killing at least ten and setting their bodies on fire.[37] Dillon further reports that, according to one eyewitness account, hundreds of protestors were killed during the subsequent crackdown and numerous participants were executed shortly thereafter.[38] The violence spread to other towns and, later in the month, three bombs were detonated on buses in Urumqi on the day of Deng Xiaoping's funeral. Nine people were reportedly killed in those bombings.[39] Xinjiang, in short, was characterized by considerable ethnic unrest during the 1990s.[40]

Moreover, PRC leaders were especially sensitive to instability in Xinjiang, given recent events in China and in the previous Communist bloc countries. Within China, the regime had been shaken by the massive Tiananmen Square protests in the spring of 1989. The protests – which, at their peak, included hundreds of thousands of participants and spread to more than one hundred cities across China (including, as noted earlier, Urumqi) – suggested that the legitimacy of CCP rule was faltering among China's urban population. The protestors, frustrated with endemic corruption and rising inflation, demanded political reform and greater government accountability. Although high-level PRC officials were initially divided in how to respond, hardliners ultimately won out: viewing the massive protests as a threat to continued CCP rule, the leadership used the military to crush the movement. The episode underscored to top officials the tenuousness of Communist Party rule in China and highlighted the degree to which unrest could quickly escalate to a point that threatened that rule. Indeed, Joseph Fewsmith writes that Tiananmen had the effect of fundamentally restructuring debates in China about political reform: "whereas reform and maintaining the new system had seemed the only alternatives in the 1980s, after Tiananmen the alternative of social and political collapse had to be considered as well."[41] Tiananmen crystalized the potential dangers of social unrest in the minds of top Chinese leaders,

[37] Dillon, *Xinjiang*, p. 94.

[38] Ibid., pp. 94–5. Though Chang, "China's Central Asian Power," p. 410 reports much lower casualties on the basis of media reports at the time.

[39] Chang, "China's Central Asian Power," p. 411.

[40] Although concurring with the view that there was considerable unrest in Xinjiang in the 1990s, James Millward observes that making definitive comparisons with earlier periods is hard, because there was increased media attention to Xinjiang – particularly among Western journalists – starting in the late 1980s. See James Millward, *Violent Separatism in Xinjiang: A Critical Assessment* (Washington, DC: East-West Center, 2004).

[41] Joseph Fewsmith, *China since Tiananmen: The Politics of Transition* (New York, NY: Cambridge University Press, 2001), p. 106.

who took away a key lesson from the episode: the need to prevent similar unrest by nipping nascent protest movements in the bud.[42]

Further reinforcing leadership fears were the collapse of Communist regimes across Eastern Europe in the fall of 1989 and the disintegration of the Soviet Union itself in 1991. As Shirk emphasizes, having experienced their own brush with mass upheaval in 1989, Chinese leaders since then "have worried obsessively that they might meet the same fate as their Soviet and Eastern European comrades."[43] Chinese officials and analysts have grappled with the determinants of the Soviet demise, hoping to learn lessons that might enable the PRC to avoid a similar destiny. Although different Chinese analysts have emphasized different variables as central to the Soviet collapse,[44] there is a widely held view in China that mismanagement of the USSR periphery – and an ineffective approach toward ethnic minorities – was an important contributing factor. In particular, Chinese officials believed that excessive decentralization and nativization (allowing local minority officials to dominate local governments), along with economic stagnation in the periphery and political liberalization (*glasnost*) that legitimized dissent, combined to produce a highly unstable environment that ultimately contributed to the Soviet Union's collapse.[45] In turn, given that they viewed mismanagement of ethnic minority regions as a key factor driving the Soviet Union's collapse, growing unrest in Xinjiang must have been especially alarming to Beijing.

Thus, the PRC leadership had reason to be worried about growing unrest in Xinjiang during the 1990s. CCP control in the region, which had always been more tenuous than in China proper to begin with,

42 For a detailed discussion concerning some of the lessons top Chinese leaders took away from Tiananmen, see Susan L. Shirk, *China, Fragile Superpower: How China's Internal Politics Could Derail its Peaceful Rise* (New York, NY: Oxford University Press, 2008), chapter 3.

43 Ibid., p. 38.

44 Meisels reviews the vast Chinese literature on the Soviet collapse and finds three broad classes of explanation: those that blame Gorbachev and his liberalizing policies; those that blame the sclerotic Soviet system; and those that blame external influences (particularly efforts by the West to undermine the USSR). See Greer A. Meisels, "Lessons Learned in China from the Collapse of the Soviet Union," The University of Sydney China Studies Centre, Policy Paper Series, Paper no. 3 (January 2013). On the CCP's extensive efforts to take lessons from the Soviet collapse for its own regime stability, see David M. Shambaugh, *China's Communist Party: Atrophy and Adaptation* (Berkeley, CA: University of California Press, 2009).

45 Greer A. Meisels, "Lessons Learned in China from the Collapse of the Soviet Union," The University of Sydney China Studies Centre, Policy Paper Series, Paper No. 3 (2013), p. 15.

appeared to be unraveling. As Fravel emphasizes, moreover, central leaders viewed instability in Xinjiang as driven in part by external factors. Leaders, of course, saw the United States as partially to blame, as was the case with Tiananmen. But they also worried about the influx of destabilizing forces coming from Central Asia, including more radical ideologies and material support for separatist groups.[46] Consider, for instance, the contents of a leaked document that appears to be the recorded minutes of a March 1996 meeting – held to address instability in Xinjiang – of the Standing Committee of the Politburo.[47] Although the record of the meeting shows that leaders focused mostly on domestic policy changes – such as governance reforms, heightened religious restrictions, more effective propaganda, and increased military presence – to address instability in Xinjiang, leaders also directed some attention to linkages between Xinjiang and Central Asia.[48] Records from the meeting emphasize the need to "tighten measures controlling the border and border defense posts," to "prevent the entry of outside ethnic separatists, weapons, and propaganda materials," and to "prevent internal and external ethnic separatists from coming together and joining hands." Leaders also emphasized the need to "use diplomacy" to encourage countries such as Kazakhstan and Kyrgyzstan to "limit and weaken the activities of separatist forces inside their countries."[49] Fravel shows that instability

[46] Fravel, *Strong Borders*, pp. 155–6. On the dangers of groups supporting the creation of an East Turkistan in Central Asia "penetrating" and undertaking "separatist activities" in Xinjiang, see Liu Fenghua, "Zhongguo zai Zhongya: Zhengce de Yanbian" [China in Central Asia: Policy Evolution], *Eluosi Zhongya Dongou Yanjiu*, 2007, no. 6, p. 66. See also Wang Jiayin, "Sulian Jietihou de Zhongya yu Zhongguo" [Central Asia and China after the Disintegration of the Soviet Union], *Guoji Zhengzhi Yanjiu*, 1995, no. 4, p. 24. Fravel (*Strong Borders*, p. 156) writes that "China's leaders believed that neighboring states were providing crucial material support for separatist groups within China." He notes in particular that Uyghur political parties were active in neighboring states, and that these organizations helped foster increased Uyghur nationalism in China by, among other things, funding religious schools in China in the 1980s.

[47] See "Chinese Communist Party Central Committee Document No. 7 (1996): Record of the Meeting of the Standing Committee of the Politburo of the Chinese Communist Party Concerning the Maintenance of Stability in Xinjiang;" translated in full in *China: State Control of Religion, Update Number 1*, Human Rights Watch, Vol. 10, no. 01(C) (March 1998), pp. 10–14. Karrar writes that because "the authenticity of the document is impossible to verify ... it needs to be treated with caution." See Hasan H. Karrar, *The New Silk Road Diplomacy: China's Central Asian Foreign Policy since the Cold War* (Vancouver: University of British Columbia Press, 2009). Still, the document is widely cited, and Fravel (*Strong Borders*, chapter 3) uses it extensively.

[48] "Central Committee Document No. 7."

[49] Ibid.; Fravel (*Strong Borders*, p. 158) also highlights these passages to show PRC leadership concerns about external sources of instability in Xinjiang and the consequent need for cooperative relations with neighboring countries.

in Xinjiang helped compel PRC leaders to pursue compromising strategies with regard to territorial disputes along China's northwest frontier.[50] More broadly, growing worries about instability in China's northwest, combined with a perception that external linkages helped fuel this unrest, had the effect of increasing China's stake in stability in Central Asia and in good diplomatic relationships with Central Asia's newly independent republics.

4.3.1.2 *The Soviet Collapse and Growing Instability in Central Asia*

In addition to increasing Beijing's sensitivity to ethnic unrest in China's frontier regions, the collapse of the Soviet Union also directly raised the stakes in Central Asia from Beijing's perspective. Before the 1990s, of course, Moscow exercised hegemonic control over the region. While poor relations with Moscow could potentially magnify Beijing's difficulties in managing ethnic unrest,[51] China could nevertheless free-ride on Soviet-imposed order in Central Asia. Soviet control in the region, for instance, could help prevent revolutionary ideologies, or insurgency movements, from gaining a foothold in Central Asia and spreading to Xinjiang (and would limit the ability of insurgency groups in Xinjiang from using Central Asia as a safe haven). The Soviet collapse, however, signaled a growing risk of instability in the region.

To be clear, Russia continued to exert considerable influence in Central Asia in the years following the Soviet dissolution. The countries in the region remained heavily dependent on the Russian economy, and Moscow continued to station troops in the region and to provide border security for Kazakhstan, Kyrgyzstan, and Turkmenistan.[52] Yet, as we will describe when discussing the declining attractiveness of the Russian unilateral option from Beijing's perspective, Moscow faced daunting challenges in the 1990s that undercut its ability to provide effective order in Central Asia. The decline of Russian power in the region, in turn, had the potential to generate greatly increased instability in the region, which Beijing feared could spill over to Xinjiang.

Indeed, instability was already increasing in Central Asia during the 1990s, highlighting the dangers that Beijing potentially faced in a post-Soviet Central Asia. The most obvious manifestation of increased instability in the region was the violent civil war that erupted in Tajikistan – which

[50] Fravel, *Strong Borders*.

[51] Ibid.

[52] Karrar, *New Silk Road Diplomacy*.

borders Xinjiang to the southwest – shortly after independence. Despite Russian (and Uzbek) intervention, the conflict lasted until 1997 and had a devastating impact on the country: over 60,000 dead, over 700,000 displaced, and an economy that was left in ruins.[53] The ongoing civil war in Afghanistan, meanwhile, had the potential to spread instability across the region. As Lena Jonson writes, "turmoil, war and religious extremism exploded during the 1990s and Afghanistan became a 'black hole,' which threatened to swallow neighboring Central Asian societies."[54] Jonson notes, for instance, that opposition leaders in the Tajikistani civil war were able to establish bases in Afghanistan.[55] The rise of the Taliban in Afghanistan was especially alarming to the government of Uzbekistan, which borders Afghanistan to the north. The country's strongman leader, Islam Karimov, presided over a secular government that harshly and systematically repressed any groups that sought to politicize Islam in the country.[56] By the late 1990s, the Taliban was giving refuge to an organization (the Islamic Movement of Uzbekistan) that aimed to overthrow the Uzbek government and establish an Islamic state.[57] Uzbek insurgents, moreover, were gaining combat experience by participating in the Taliban's war against the Northern Alliance in Afghanistan.[58] And in 1999, several bombs exploded in Tashkent in a coordinated terrorist attack that killed sixteen and, as Dilip Hiro writes, "shattered the image of Uzbekistan as a haven of stability."[59]

Beyond an increased propensity for armed conflict and insurgency, Hasan Haider Karrar writes that the Soviet withdrawal from Central Asia led as well to an expanding "war economy that spilled over the borders from Afghanistan."[60] Most notably, narcotics production in Afghanistan increased sharply in the early 1990s, and the vast majority of these illicit drugs were smuggled through Central Asia on their way to

[53] Johnson puts the death toll at 60,000, with over a million refugees. See Rob Johnson, *Oil, Islam, and Conflict: Central Asia since 1945* (London: Reaktion Press, 2007). Hiro writes that death toll estimates range from 60,000 to 100,000 and puts the number displaced at 730,000. See Dilip Hiro, *Inside Central Asia: A Political and Cultural History of Uzbekistan, Turkmenistan, Kazakhstan, Kyrgyzstan, Tajikistan, Turkey, and Iran* (New York, NY and London: Overlook Duckworth, 2009).

[54] Lena Jonson, *Vladimir Putin and Central Asia: The Shaping of Russian Foreign Policy* (London and New York, NY: I.B. Tauris, 2004), p. 49.

[55] Ibid., p. 50.

[56] Hiro, *Inside Central Asia*, p. 150.

[57] Ibid., p. 165.

[58] Karrar, *New Silk Road Diplomacy*, p. 68.

[59] Hiro, *Inside Central Asia*, p. 169.

[60] Karrar, *New Silk Road Diplomacy*, p. 49.

markets in Europe. In turn, drug smuggling provided a convenient way for opposition groups in Tajikistan and Uzbekistan to raise money that they could use to purchase arms.[61]

This is not to say that Central Asia was on the verge of slipping into a cauldron of insurgency and armed conflict; to the contrary, in countries like Kazakhstan, Turkmenistan, and (to some degree) even Uzbekistan, strongman leaders were able to repress dissent quite effectively. But a violent civil war in Tajikistan, a persistent Islamist opposition in Uzbekistan, and the negative spillover effects of a prolonged civil war in Afghanistan underscored future downside risks. This all served to increase China's stakes in the region, particularly given growing instability in Xinjiang in the 1990s and the PRC's fear that opposition groups in Xinjiang might link up with insurgent groups elsewhere in the region.[62]

4.3.1.3 China's Economic Reforms and Growing Demand for Imported Energy

Finally, it is worth emphasizing that stability in Central Asia (and cooperative relationships between China and the Central Asian republics) increasingly dovetailed with China's economic interests over the course of the 1990s. Although growth slowed sharply during the post-Tiananmen retrenchment, economic reforms picked up steam again following Deng Xiaoping's 1992 "southern tour." Over the next several years, the economy grew at breakneck speed (see Figure 3.1) as leaders embraced an outward-oriented development strategy.[63] In turn, China's stake in Central Asian stability increased for two reasons.

First, the PRC was increasingly needing to import energy to fuel its booming economy. China became a net oil importing country in the early

[61] Ibid., pp. 66–7.

[62] Karrar writes, for example, that "as the 1990s progressed, Beijing grew increasingly apprehensive at the prospect of Uyghurs from Xinjiang travelling to Afghanistan to participate in" new transnational anti-state movements. See Ibid., p. 68. For another analysis highlighting the pernicious impact that instability in Central Asia could have on Xinjiang in the 1990s, see, for instance, Liu, "Zhongguo zai Zhongya," p. 64. See also Yang Xiqian, who, writing in 1992, emphasized the risk of an influx of pan-Turkism and Islamic fundamentalism into Central Asia in the aftermath of the Soviet collapse, which in turn could potentially threaten Xinjiang: Yang Xiqian, "Sulian Jietihou de Zhongya Xingshi" [The Situation in Central Asia after the Soviet Disintegration], *Sulian Yanjiu*, September 1992, p. 5.

[63] See, for instance, Susan L. Shirk, *How China Opened its Door: The Political Success of the PRC's Foreign Trade and Investment Reforms* (Washington, DC: Brookings Institution Press, 1994); Nicholas R. Lardy, *Integrating China into the Global Economy* (Washington, DC: Brookings Institution Press, 2002).

1990s, and oil imports constituted a rapidly growing share of China's total petroleum consumption over the course of the 1990s. As China became more dependent on imported energy, Chinese leaders began to view the growing gap between oil production and consumption as "a long-term strategic issue."[64] In 1997, top leaders endorsed a "walking on two legs" strategy, whereby emphasis would be given both to intensified domestic production and to efforts to enter the international petroleum market more aggressively.[65] And Central Asia represented an important potential opportunity, given rich energy reserves in the region. Kazakhstan, the key country in this regard, has Eurasia's second largest endowment of proved oil reserves, behind only Russia and roughly comparable to US reserves. Turkmenistan also has significant – though considerably smaller – oil reserve endowments. Turkmenistan, and to a lesser degree Kazakhstan and Uzbekistan, also has large deposits of natural gas.[66] China's growing dependence on foreign energy (and its recognition that this would require its energy companies to be more engaged internationally), combined with Central Asia's rich energy reserves and proximity to China, served to increase Beijing's stake in stability in the region. This was especially the case after 1997, when China reached an agreement with Kazakhstan on the construction of an oil pipeline to China.[67]

[64] Bo Kong, *China's International Petroleum Policy* (Santa Barbara, CA: Praeger Press, 2010), p. 44.

[65] See Ibid., pp. 44–6. Kong quotes Jiang Zemin, then General Secretary of the Communist Party, as noting: "China's petroleum industry should walk on two legs, namely base its development on domestic resources and also utilize international petroleum resources." Then-Premier Li Peng also, as Kong writes, endorsed a "two legs" approach in a 1997 article on energy policy published in the Central Party School's journal *Qiu Shi*, though it is worth noting that the article focuses more attention on domestic production. See Li Peng, "Zhongguo de Nengyuan Zhengce" [China's Energy Policy], *Qiu Shi*, 1997, no. 11, pp. 524–532. See also Ma Hong, "Jiakuai Zhongguo Shiyou Gongye Fazhan de Guanjian shi Shenru Gaige Kuada Kaifa" [The Key to Speeding up the Development of China's Petroleum Industry is to Deepen Reform and Expand Openness], *Shiyou Qiye Guanli*, 1995, no. 5, pp. 3–7. For an analysis that emphasizes the need for China to develop a foreign energy policy with Chinese characteristics, including the need to maintain good diplomatic relations with other countries, see Wang Weimin, "Qianxi Shijiezhijiao de Shiyou Zhengduozhan" [An Analysis of the Battle for Oil at the Turn of the Century], *Xiandai Guoji Guanxi*, 1998, no. 3, pp. 19–23.

[66] On Kazakhstan's oil and gas reserves, see US Energy Information Administration, "Kazakhstan," last updated January 14, 2015: www.eia.gov/beta/international. Data on other Central Asian countries is available from the US Energy Information Administration at: www.eia.gov/beta/international.

[67] Wang, "Qianxi Shijieshijiao de Shiyou Zhengduozhan," p. 23. Interestingly, in making the point that good diplomatic relations can facilitate energy cooperation, Wang also writes that the Kazakhstan pipeline agreement was "not unrelated" to the border

Second, China's outward-oriented growth strategy meant that stability in Central Asia would potentially facilitate increased economic linkages between China's western provinces and Central Asia, which would help spur growth in those provinces. As noted earlier, top leaders wanted to "speed up economic development and improve the life of the people" in Xinjiang, viewing development as an important part of efforts to increase stability in the region.[68] And leaders clearly believed that increasing Xinjiang's linkages to the global economy – "broadening the scope of the open-door policy" in Xinjiang – would facilitate development there.[69] Though there were clear limits to the degree to which increased economic integration with Central Asia could enhance development in Xinjiang (most obviously, the Central Asian economies had contracted sharply in the years after the Soviet dissolution), on the margins at least instability in the region would work against PRC development goals in Xinjiang.[70]

In sum, China's interest in the provision of order in Central Asia was increasing during the 1990s. Growing unrest in Xinjiang was occurring at a time that the Moscow-led order in Central Asia was unraveling. Against this backdrop, Beijing worried that growing instability in Central Asia could potentially spread to China's restive northwest. Further increasing China's interest in the region at the time (at least marginally) was the PRC's growing demand for imported energy and the leadership's desire to see economic development in Xinjiang.[71] By the late 1990s, in short,

demarcation agreement reached between Russia, China, Kazakhstan, Kyrgyzstan, and Tajikistan.

68 "Central Committee Document No. 7."

69 Ibid. See also Fravel, *Strong Borders*, p. 157.

70 Even in the mid-1990s, China's leaders viewed increased economic ties with Central Asia as potentially beneficial to development in Western China. Li Peng, for instance, argued in 1994 that a new Silk Road should be constructed through Central Asia. See Chien-peng Chung, "The Shanghai Co-operation Organization: China's Changing Influence in Central Asia," *The China Quarterly*, Vol. 180 (December 2004), p. 1002. See also Liu, "Zhongguo zai Zhongya," p. 64, who lists among China's important national interests in Central Asia in the 1990s "opening and expanding economic cooperation" with the region so as to "push forward economic development in Western China." On the limits of "open door" policies in facilitating development in Xinjiang, see for instance Nicolas Becquelin, "Staged Development in Xinjiang," in David S. Goodman, ed., *China's Campaign to "Open up the West": National, Provincial, and Local Perspectives* (Cambridge: Cambridge University Press, 2004), p. 57.

71 To be clear, China's economic stake in Central Asia remained quite limited in the 1990s. Trade was paltry and, though Central Asian energy reserves were beginning to pique China's interest, Chinese companies had not yet begun to initiate significant investments in Central Asian energy. As we describe at greater length later, this all changed after the early 2000s, as Chinese trade with the region grew rapidly and Chinese companies entered regional energy markets in force. Thus, growing economic stakes in the region

China simply had more to lose from a breakdown of order in Central Asia. From the perspective of our theory, these trends implied that the potential benefits to China of cooperative efforts to stabilize Central Asia (or, alternatively, the opportunity costs of such efforts not materializing) were increasing during the 1990s. In other words, China had a growing stake in a (as yet unrealized) cooperative solution to the problem of order in Central Asia.

4.3.2 The Declining Attractiveness of Russia's Unilateral Option

Just as China's stake in Central Asia was increasing during the 1990s, the possibility of free-riding on others – in particular Russia – to provide order was becoming untenable. Simply put, the capacity of post-Soviet Russia to impose order in Central Asia was declining dramatically over the course of the 1990s. Karrar describes the leaders of the Central Asian republics as shocked and angry after the dissolution of the Soviet Union was announced in December, 1991: the decision to dissolve had been made by the leaders of the major Slavic republics, and the Central Asian leaders were out of the loop.[72] Despite this slap in the face, however, the Central Asian republics decided to enter into the Soviet successor organization, the Commonwealth of Independent States (CIS). In fact, they had little choice: as Karrar notes, their economies were "thoroughly integrated into the Soviet Union," meaning that close cooperation with Moscow would continue to be important.[73] Moreover, not only were the newly independent Central Asian republics highly dependent on Russia economically, they continued to depend on Russia for security needs. In the aftermath of the Soviet collapse, Russia continued to deploy large numbers of security forces to Central Asia, and continued to protect the borders of Kazakhstan, Kyrgyzstan, and Turkmenistan.[74] In short, Russia maintained considerable hegemony over Central Asia in the years immediately after the collapse of the Soviet Union.

Karrar argues that China accepted, and indeed welcomed, continued Russian influence in Central Asia in the early 1990s. Relations between Moscow and Beijing had improved dramatically, beginning in the late

helped shape Beijing's approach to second-order cooperation in Central Asia during the 2000s, but economic factors were largely peripheral to the investments China made in regional stability up until the establishment of the SCO in 2001.

72 Karrar, *New Silk Road Diplomacy*, pp. 50–1.

73 Ibid., p. 51.

74 Ibid.

1980s, helping alleviate PRC worries about continued Russian power in the region. More fundamentally, as discussed, Beijing feared that the collapse of Soviet power could trigger instability in Central Asia – which might in turn spread to Xinjiang. As Karrar puts it: "The continuation of Russian influence in Central Asia – both directly and through the Russian-instituted secular oligarchy – was Beijing's surest bet for stability in westernmost China."[75]

Yet Russia faced a number of daunting challenges in the 1990s. Russia's most significant immediate challenge was a sputtering national economy, as leaders implemented market-oriented reforms to try to jump-start an economy that had collapsed in the USSR's final years. The Soviet economy, by 1990, was characterized by declining output, exploding budget deficits, and skyrocketing inflation.[76] Russian economic malaise continued during the 1990s: according to World Bank statistics, per capita income declined in the years after 1991, and the country experienced negative economic growth for much of the decade.[77] Unemployment rates were high (especially if those who had given up looking for work are factored in), the population declined over the course of the decade (reflecting low fertility rates and an uptick in mortality rates), and the country's economic malaise was punctuated by a severe financial crisis in 1998.[78] Although Andrei Shleifer suggests that official statistics and conventional wisdom overstate the degree to which the Russian economy collapsed in the 1990s,[79] there is no doubt that the country faced extensive economic hardships in the years after the dissolution of the Soviet Union. Beyond economic malaise, other problems facing Russia in the 1990s included a devastating war in Chechnya, pervasive corruption and the rise of a robber baron oligarchy, and weak political leadership.

The imposing challenges faced by post-Soviet Russia in the 1990s, in turn, undercut the ability of Russia to provide effective order in Central Asia as the decade wore on. As Alexander Cooley writes, Russia under Boris Yeltsin "remained relatively weak and focused on muddling through its domestic reforms and economic troubles." Although "Russia remained

75 Ibid., pp. 54–5.

76 See Anders Aslund, *Russia's Capitalist Revolution: Why Market Reform Succeeded and Democracy Failed* (Washington, DC: Peterson Institute for International Economics, 2007), pp. 67–73.

77 The World Bank: https://data.worldbank.org.

78 See Steven Rosefielde, *The Russian Economy: From Lenin to Putin* (Malden, MA: Blackwell Publishing, 2007), pp. 179–82.

79 Andrei Shleifer, *A Normal Country: Russia after Communism* (Cambridge, MA: Harvard University Press, 2005), chapter 10.

the most powerful actor" in Central Asia, it was "more by default rather than by choice." And, indeed, to the degree Russia was engaged in the region, it was mostly focused on dealing with "problematic Soviet-era legacies," such as how to manage external borders and what to do with defense assets left over from the USSR.[80] David Kerr and Laura C. Swinton write along similar lines that "in the years before [1999], Russian policy [in the space occupied by the former Soviet Union] could be characterized by complacency and romanticism."[81] Thus, although China had reason to welcome Russian efforts to provide order in Central Asia, Russia's capacity to do so was increasingly in doubt during the 1990s.[82] It is worth noting as well that, even as Russian power was declining, China in the 1990s was effectively excluded from the security architecture of Central Asia, as Russia attempted to maintain a near-monopoly on military and diplomatic coordination through its preferred mechanism, the CIS. Over time, this exclusion from existing institutional architecture further undercut the attractiveness of a Russia unilateral option, as it implied that China would be left outside of any regional economic integration initiatives.

4.3.3 Summary

In sum, China faced a worsening balance of outside options with regard to the problem of order in Central Asia over the course of the 1990s. First, Beijing had a growing stake in (as yet unrealized) regional cooperation on the issue of Central Asian stability. As unrest grew in Xinjiang during the decade, Chinese leaders feared that instability in Central Asia could make things worse. Beijing especially worried about the possibility

[80] Alexander Cooley, *Great Games, Local Rules: The New Great Power Contest in Central Asia* (Oxford: Oxford University Press, 2012), p. 20.

[81] David Kerr and Laura C. Swinton, "China, Xinjiang, and the Transnational Security of Central Asia," *Critical Asian Studies*, Vol. 40, no. 1 (2008), p. 132.

[82] Interestingly, some PRC analysis suggests that Russia became more willing to work with China on providing security in Central Asia in part because Moscow recognized the limits in its ability to do so unilaterally. A Chinese Academy of Social Sciences analysis of post-Soviet Central Asia notes (in discussing the 1990s), for instance, that "although Russian attention to and worries over growing Chinese influence in Central Asia cannot be completely denied, the smooth development in Sino-Russian relations, similar understandings and interests for the two countries concerning Central Asian security, and the experience of the inability of the CSTO to get the civil war in Tajikistan under control all nevertheless combined to make Russia more willing to work with China to jointly preserve stability in the region." See Zheng Yu, ed., *Dulianti Shinian: Xianzhuang, Wenti, Qianjing* [Ten Years of the Commonwealth of Independent States: Current Situation, Problems, and Prospects] (Beijing: Zhongguo Shehui Kexue Chubanshe, 2007), p. 531.

that extremist groups in Xinjiang might link up with organizations in Central Asia, which implied an increased stake in regional cooperation to limit the activities of such organizations. Further increasing the stakes for Beijing was the uptick in instability in Central Asia following the collapse of the Soviet Union: the civil wars in Afghanistan and Tajikistan, for instance, highlighted to Beijing the increased downside risks of instability in the shadow of waning Russian power – instability which Beijing feared could spread to Xinjiang. China's growing demand for imported energy and a PRC belief that economic cooperation with Central Asia could facilitate development in China's west also served to increase Beijing's stake in stability in Central Asia.

Meanwhile, as China's interests in Central Asian stability were increasing, there were also limits to relying on Russia, the key power in the region in recent decades, to provide order. Most importantly, Russian power in the 1990s was declining, and there were clear constraints on its capacity to provide stability in Central Asia. Furthermore, Russia-led institutions in the region generally excluded the PRC, so relying solely on Russia to organize cooperation in Central Asia risked the creation of institutions that would ignore Chinese interests, particularly with regard to energy and economic integration.

Thus, with a growing stake in regional stability and a Russian unilateral option that was not particularly attractive, Beijing's outside options on the issue of order-provision in Central Asia looked to be getting worse. Our theoretical framework predicts that worsening outside options, in turn, should have been pushing China to invest in regional order – that is, to try to organize and sustain cooperation that would help bring stability to Central Asia. In the next section, we argue that the Shanghai Five and the SCO can be seen (at least partially) in this light, as investments in cooperation on the issue of Central Asian stability.

4.4 INVESTING IN STABILITY

Broadly speaking, China's behavior since the mid-1990s has been consistent with our expectations. In particular, China has invested in new institutions in Central Asia that – at least to some extent – helped contribute to stability in the region. In 1996, China was the main force behind the establishment of the "Shanghai Five," a grouping that included China, Russia, Kazakhstan, Kyrgyzstan, and Tajikistan. Later, in 2001, China organized the SCO, a more institutionalized organization that also included Uzbekistan. In this section, we describe these organizations and China's role in constructing them, and we connect China's efforts in this regard to Beijing's worsening outside options (relative to Russia) at the time.

4.4.1 The Shanghai Five

The Shanghai Five forum grew out of border demilitarization talks between China and four Soviet successor states: Russia, Kazakhstan, Kyrgyzstan, and Tajikistan. Sino-Soviet relations had improved dramatically in the years before the Soviet collapse, and the two countries had embarked on negotiations to demarcate and reduce the large military presence along their disputed borders.[83] These negotiations continued after the dissolution of the USSR, and in 1996 the presidents of the five countries met in Shanghai to discuss confidence-building in border areas. The Shanghai meeting culminated in the Agreement between the Russian Federation, the Republic of Kazakhstan, the Kyrgyz Republic, the Republic of Tajikistan, and the People's Republic of China on Confidence-Building in the Military Field in the Border Area (hereafter, the "1996 Shanghai Declaration"), which outlined military confidence-building steps to be taken by the five states, including increasing information exchanges, refraining from exercises directed against the other parties, and notifying the others of military activities undertaken near the previous Sino-Soviet border.[84] The preamble to the agreement emphasized more broadly the importance of maintaining and developing "long-term good-neighbor relations and friendship" among the five signatories, and highlighted the importance of "maintaining peace and stability in the border area."[85]

After signing the Shanghai Declaration, the leaders of the five countries continued to meet with each other on an annual basis. The second summit, held in Moscow in 1997, again focused on military confidence-building in border areas and resulted in an agreement to reduce military forces along the former Sino-Soviet border.[86] As Karrar notes, by the

[83] See Fravel, *Strong Borders*, chapter 3 for a description of these talks.

[84] The agreement is technically between the PRC and a joint party composed of the four former Soviet republics. For the full text, see Andrei Melville and Tatiana Shakleina, eds., *Russian Foreign Policy in Transition: Concepts and Realities* (Budapest and New York, NY: Central European University Press, 2005), pp. 65–74.

[85] Ibid., p. 65.

[86] Jyotsna Bakshi, "Shanghai Cooperation Organization (SCO) before and after September 11," *Strategic Analysis*, Vol. 26, no. 2 (2002), p. 266.

conclusion of the 1997 summit, the key issue giving rise to the Shanghai Five forum – security and confidence-building in border areas – had largely been accomplished, leaving member states with two options: "the forum could be disbanded or a new agenda could be developed."[87] The member countries, of course, chose the latter, and the Shanghai Five mechanism became a platform for discussing broader regional economic and security issues. At the 1998 meeting, held in Kazakhstan, the five countries reached agreement to oppose "evils" like "national splittism" and religious extremism while promising to work together to fight terrorism, organized crime, and drug smuggling. The countries also agreed that "they would not permit the use of their own territory to engage in the activities that damage the state sovereignty, security, and social order of any of the five nations." And the countries pledged to increase economic cooperation.[88] The following year, meeting in Bishkek, the members agreed in principle to the creation of an anti-terrorism center.[89]

The Shanghai Five member countries committed to further institutionalization of the forum during the 2000 summit in Dushanbe. In the agreement emerging from the summit (the Dushanbe Declaration), the parties agreed to regular meetings of defense ministers and law enforcement officials from the member countries, and agreed that it would be "expedient to practice holding annual meetings of the Ministers of Foreign Affairs." The declaration called for the creation of a new Council of National Coordinators, to be composed of officials appointed by each member country. Furthermore, the member countries reiterated "their determination to wage a joint struggle against international terrorism, religious extremism, and national separation, which together represent the main threat to regional security, stability and progress." In pursuing this goal, the declaration committed the member countries to "draw up an appropriate multilateral Program and sign the necessary multilateral treaties and agreements on cooperation" and they agreed to begin holding exercises "to counter terrorist activities and violence" as warranted by developments. Like statements issued at earlier summits, the Dushanbe Declaration again highlights the desirability of increased economic cooperation and notes in particular that "the Parties support the interest of the People's Republic of China in the active participation of Russia and

[87] Karrar, *New Silk Road Diplomacy*, p. 84.

[88] "China: Xinhua Roundup on Jiang's Visit to Kazakhstan," *Xinhua Domestic Service*, July 6, 1998, in *World News Connection*, July 7, 1998.

[89] Jing-Dong Yuan, "China's Role in Establishing and Building the Shanghai Cooperation Organization (SCO)," *Journal of Contemporary China*, Vol. 19, no. 67 (2010), p. 861.

the Central Asian countries in developing the western regions of China."[90] In sum, the Dushanbe Declaration was, as Bates Gill and Matthew Oresman write, "a far-reaching and ambitious statement" that put the Shanghai Five forum on a path to deeper institutionalization that would culminate in the creation of the SCO the following year.[91]

China is generally seen as the "driving force" behind the creation and strengthening of the Shanghai Five forum; as Chien-peng Chung emphasizes, "the SCO, and its predecessor, the Shanghai Five, is the first multilateral security organization largely initiated and promoted by China."[92] China's key role in the group is clearly evident in the text of the Dushanbe Declaration. In addition to the statement noted earlier relating to developing the western regions of China, several other clauses touch directly on China's national interests, including interests with little direct relevance to Central Asia. Most obviously, Article 8 supports the "strict observance" of the 1972 Anti-Ballistic Missile Treaty and includes a statement opposing Taiwan's inclusion in theater missile defense systems (an issue that worried Beijing at the time). Parts of the declaration also give a nod to China's "New Security Concept," unveiled in 1996 and billed as a model for security that moves beyond a "Cold War mentality" by seeking to create trust via dialogue and improve security via cooperation. Article 3 of the Dushanbe Declaration, for instance, hails the border settlement and military confidence-building agreements reached by the five countries as embodying "a new concept of security, based on mutual confidence, equality, and cooperation" and as assisting "in strengthening mutual understanding and good-neighborliness."[93] As Gill and Oresman note, these features of the Dushanbe Declaration "reflected

[90] The full name of the declaration is the "Dushanbe Declaration by the Heads of State of the Republic of Kazakhstan, the People's Republic of China, the Kyrgyz Republic, the Russian Federation, and the Republic of Tajikistan." Full text is available in Melville and Shakleina, eds., *Russian Foreign Policy*, pp. 147–152.

[91] Bates Gill and Matthew Oresman, *China's New Journey to the West: China's Emergence in Central Asia and Implications for U.S. Interests*, Center for Strategic and International Studies, CSIS Report, 2003, p. 7.

[92] Chien-peng Chung, *China's Multilateral Cooperation in Asia and the Pacific* (London and New York, NY: Routledge, 2010), p. 61.

[93] See Melville and Shakleina, eds., *Russian Foreign Policy*, p. 148. Chinese government descriptions of the New Security Concept emphasize a conceptualization of security that moves beyond military concerns to include economics, the environment, culture, and other areas, and highlight concepts like mutual trust (or confidence), mutual benefit, equality, coordination, and cooperation. See, for instance, Foreign Ministry of the People's Republic of China, "China's Position Paper on the New Security Concept," online at: www.fmprc.gov.cn/ce/ceun/eng/xw/t27742.htm.

China's dominant role" and "its ability to shape the organization's agenda consistent with Beijing's foreign policy."[94]

4.4.2 The Establishment of the SCO

At the 2001 leaders' summit in Shanghai, the member countries of the Shanghai Five built on the Dushanbe Declaration by further institutionalizing their grouping – renaming it the Shanghai Cooperation Organization and adding Uzbekistan as a sixth member state. The Declaration on the Creation of the Shanghai Cooperation Organization, released during the summit on June 15, outlined the goals and principles of the new international organization. Key objectives of the SCO highlighted by the 2001 declaration include "strengthening mutual trust ... between member countries; promoting effective cooperation between member countries in political, economic ... and other areas; working together to preserve and safeguard regional peace, security, and stability; and building a democratic, just, and rational international political and economic new order." The Declaration called for continued annual leadership summits, as well as the creation of new "meeting mechanisms" and "provisional working groups," and instructed the council of national coordinators to draft a charter for the organization. And the declaration emphasized that the SCO "attaches special importance to safeguarding regional security and will make all necessary efforts to do so."[95] The member countries also released a separate document during the 2001 summit – the Shanghai Convention on Combating Terrorism, Separatism, and Extremism – that defines what is meant by these three terms and commits the SCO member countries to cooperate and exchange information relating to counterterrorism and to separatist groups. It also commits the parties to conclude a separate agreement to establish a regional counter-terrorism center in Bishkek.[96]

As with the Shanghai Five, China played a leading role in the creation of the SCO. The naming of the organization for a Chinese city in itself underscores this point, something not lost on Chinese commentators at

[94] Gill and Oresman, *China's New Journey to the West*, p. 7.

[95] For the full text of the declaration, see "'Text' of Shanghai Cooperation Organization Declaration Issued in Shanghai," *Xinhua Domestic Service*, June 15, 2001, in *World News Connection*, June 18, 2001.

[96] The full text of the convention is available from the Council on Foreign Relations at: www.cfr.org/counterterrorism/shanghai-convention-combating-terrorism-separatism-extremism/p25184.

the time.[97] In the years preceding the establishment of the SCO, Chinese leaders were outspoken in calling for expanding cooperation and increasing institutionalization in the Shanghai Five mechanism, a process culminating in the creation of the SCO.[98] China's leading role in establishing the SCO can also be seen in the documents and statements issued during the 2001 summit, which are clearly reflective of broader PRC foreign policy principles. The Declaration on the Creation of the SCO, for instance, references the Five Principles of Peaceful Coexistence in stating that SCO member countries will "respect each other's independence, sovereignty, and territorial integrity"; "will not interfere in each other's internal affairs"; "will not use threat or force against each other"; will deal with each other "on an equal footing"; and will "resolve all issues through consultations."[99] The Chinese domestic goal of combating the "three evils" of "separatism, extremism, and terrorism" was likewise highlighted by the declaration and was obviously the focal point of the Shanghai convention. The declaration hails the "Shanghai spirit," a concept that Jiang Zemin – in his speech to the summit – described using language that draws from China's "New Security Concept." The Shanghai spirit, Jiang suggests, is characterized by "mutual trust and benefit, equality, consultation, mutual respect to different civilizations, and common prosperity." Elsewhere in the same speech, he explicitly describes the Shanghai Five mechanism as initiating a "new type of security concept featuring mutual trust, disarmament, and cooperation security," and emphasizes

[97] One *Jiefangjun Bao* op-ed, for instance, notes that "the naming of the 'Shanghai Five' after Shanghai itself entrusts credit and a lofty mission to the Chinese people. At the same time, it also serves as a successful example of China's independent and peaceful diplomatic policy." See Wang Guifang, "'Shanghai Five' Mechanism: Testimony of the Elevation of China's International Status," *Jiefangjun Bao*, June 15, 2001, in *World News Connection* ("JFJB Article Views on China's Unique Role in Developing 'Shanghai Five' Mechanism"), June 19, 2001. One scholar writes that the SCO is the "first regional cooperation organization in history to be initiated by China, to be created in China, and to use the name of a Chinese city." See Xia Yishan, "'Shanghai Hezuo Zuzhi' de Tedian ji qi Fazhan Qianjing" [The Characteristics and Development Prospects for the "Shanghai Cooperation Organization"], *Heping yu Fanzhan*, 2001, no. 3, p. 22.

[98] For instance, Jiang Zemin – at the 1999 leadership summit – called for "strengthening cooperation on regional security issues" and expanding economic cooperation, among other points. See Xing Guangcheng and Sun Zhuangzhi, *Shanghai Hezuo Zuzhi Yanjiu* [A Study of the Shanghai Cooperation Organization] (Changchun: Changchun Chuban She, 2007), p. 142.

[99] "'Text' of Shanghai Cooperation Organization Declaration Issued in Shanghai."

that the organization represents a "partnership but not alignment."[100] In an important sense, then, China had a very strong influence on the organization's basic principles as laid out in the SCO's founding documents.[101]

4.4.3 Why Invest?

Why did China choose to play a leading role in creating and then expanding the scope of the Shanghai Five forum, culminating in the creation of the SCO in 2001? Certainly many factors, including some beyond the scope of our theory, were at play. For instance, China seemed motivated in part by a desire to showcase its "New Security Concept," and the Shanghai Five, and later the SCO, were part of a broader "new diplomacy" that sought to improve China's image in the region.[102] But our theory's focus on the balance of outside options also provides insight into Beijing's behavior. Recall that China's outside options relating to Central Asia were worsening during the 1990s, a consequence of growing unrest in Xinjiang, increasing instability in Central Asia (which Beijing saw as linked to the unrest in Xinjiang), China's increasing reliance on imported energy, and a diminished Russia with declining capacity to provide order

100 Ibid. For the full text of Jiang's speech, see "Jiang Zemin's Speech at Inaugural Meeting of 'Shanghai Cooperation Organization.'" See also Robert G. Sutter, *Chinese Foreign Relations: Power and Policy since the Cold War* (Lanham, MD: Rowman and Littlefield, 2008), p. 316.

101 It is worth noting, moreover, that China invested significant resources to establish the SCO. While, as we note later, the budget of the SCO was rather small, China (along with Russia) paid the largest share. China also provided logistics, such as office space for the Secretariat. See Jianwei Wang, "China and the SCO: Towards a New Type of Interstate Relations," in Guoguang Wu and Helen Lansdowne, eds., *China Turns to Multilateralism: Foreign Policy and Regional Security* (London and New York, NY: Routledge Press, 2008), p. 112. But beyond these immediate financial costs, China invested diplomatic resources to get the organization off the ground and, to some degree, put its reputation on the line with it. And it was clearly an important priority for top leaders, who were involved in its creation and who have participated in activities such as summits. As Phillip Saunders has argued, high-level attention represents the single scarcest resource in government; that top Chinese leaders directed so much attention to this initiative implies significant opportunity costs in terms of the myriad other priorities that could have occupied their attention. On the "Phillip Saunders axiom," see Scott L. Kastner and Phillip C. Saunders, "Is China a Status Quo or Revisionist State? Leadership Travel as an Empirical Indicator of Foreign Policy Priorities," *International Studies Quarterly*, Vol. 56, no. 1 (March 2012), pp. 163–77.

102 Evan S. Medeiros and M. Taylor Fravel, "China's New Diplomacy," *Foreign Affairs*, Vol. 82 (2003), pp. 22–35; Shirk, *China, Fragile Superpower*.

in Central Asia unilaterally. In turn, our theory suggests that the costs of pursuing an "accept" strategy (that is, accepting existing Russian-dominated institutional arrangements in Central Asia) were increasing for China, especially since Beijing viewed unrest in Xinjiang as linked to instability in Central Asia. In other words, all else equal, the factors that were making China's outside options in Central Asia less attractive should have been "pushing" China to pay the costs of constructing institutions in Central Asia that would help provide greater stability in the region.

And, in fact, these factors did appear to be central to Beijing's investment in the Shanghai Five forum and, later, the SCO.[103] Many PRC analysts highlight, in particular, the link between China's growing concerns over stability in Xinjiang and its interest in building institutions that would contribute to stability in Central Asia and facilitate cooperation with Central Asian countries on fighting separatist groups. For instance, Zhao Huasheng, a leading PRC expert on the SCO and Central Asia, emphasizes that China's primary interest in the SCO was security and, in particular, China was interested in using the organization to address the "East Turkistan problem" and to serve as a mechanism for multilateral cooperation in dealing with that problem.[104] In their study of the SCO, Xing Guangcheng and Sun Zhuangzhi likewise view stabilizing China's Northwest as the foremost PRC interest in the organization.[105] And most

[103] To be clear, at its outset, the Shanghai Five forum was quite narrowly focused on the issue of military confidence-building mechanisms in border areas. But after 1998, as we showed, the Shanghai Five (and, subsequently, the SCO) became more broadly focused on stability in Central Asia and on serving as a locus of cooperation among member countries for fighting terrorism, extremism, and separatism movements. Other studies likewise highlight this evolution. See, for instance, Karrar, "New Silk Road Diplomacy."

[104] Zhao Huasheng, *Zhongguo de Zhongya Waijiao* [China's Central Asian Diplomacy] (Beijing: Shishi Chubanshi, 2008), pp. 406–7. See also Zhao Huasheng, "Central Asia in Chinese Strategic Thinking," in Thomas Fingar, ed., *The New Great Game: China and South and Central Asia in the Era of Reform* (Stanford, CA: Stanford University Press, 2016), especially pp. 176–7. Note that use of the term "East Turkistan problem" only became common in Chinese writings after the September 11 terrorist attacks; before that, Chinese writings tended to use terms like "national separatist groups"; see Millward, *Eurasian Crossroads*, pp. 339–40.

[105] Xing and Sun, *Shanghai Hezuo Zuzhi Yanjiu*, p. 149. Elsewhere Xing and Sun emphasize that absent external support, separatist groups in Xinjiang would have little capacity to cause unrest, but if given the opportunity to link up with external forces, such groups would pose a more serious threat (see p. 171). Some analysts, in describing the meaning of the SCO's founding for China, highlight the symbolic importance of China's role in creating the organization and that the SCO showcases the New Security Concept. Li Minlun, for instance, writes that the SCO's establishment "indicates that Chinese foreign policy had entered a phase of actively entering into global society" and

accounts of the SCO by non-PRC-based analysts likewise highlight the importance of concerns over instability in Xinjiang – and fears that separatist groups there might link up with external groups in Central Asia – as central to China's push for the institutionalization of the Shanghai Five and, later, the SCO.[106]

Moreover, the two documents released during the SCO's inaugural meeting clearly suggest that the SCO member states – including China – viewed cooperation on preserving regional stability as the principal purpose of the new organization.[107] Statements made by leaders attending the 2001 summit further underscore this point. For instance, in his speech at the meeting, PRC President Jiang Zemin explicitly emphasized that "maintaining the regional security is the focus of our cooperation." Although Jiang also touched on other areas of cooperation, such as in economic areas, he clearly prioritized security in his speech.[108] Russian President Vladimir Putin likewise stressed security cooperation as the core purpose of the new organization in his remarks delivered at the summit. Putin suggested that "our organization may be viewed as the visible embodiment of the concept of security through cooperation," and he expressed hope that SCO-induced cooperation would enable member countries to "reinforce stability in the region."[109]

To be clear, we are not suggesting that China lacked other options for dealing with unrest in Xinjiang; to the contrary, Beijing's primary way of dealing with this unrest was to increase internal controls.[110] Rather,

---

suggests that the SCO's development will influence the "vitality" of the New Security Concept. But Li also emphasizes the security benefits of the SCO, writing that the "smooth development of the SCO clearly will ease security pressures in Western China." Li Minlun, *Zhongguo "Xin Anquanguan" yu Shanghai Hezuo Zuzhi Yanjiu* [Research on China's "New Security Concept" and the Shanghai Cooperation Organization] (Beijing: Renmin Chubanshe, 2007), pp. 158–61. See also Xu Tongkai, who writes that the founding of the SCO represented a breakthrough for Chinese diplomacy, but also highlights its importance in improving China's security along its periphery. Xu Tongkai, *Shanghai Hezuo Zuzhi Quyu Jingji Hezuo* [The Shanghai Cooperation Organization's Regional Economic Cooperation] (Beijing: Renmin Chubanshi, 2009), pp. 22–4.

106 See, for instance: Shirk, *China, Fragile Superpower*; Gill and Oresman, *China's New Journey*; Fravel, *Secure Borders*; Sutter, *Chinese Foreign Relations*; Karrar, *New Silk Road Diplomacy*; and Millward, *Eurasian Crossroads*, pp. 336–7.

107 On this point, see Chien-peng Chung, "China and the Institutionalization of the Shanghai Cooperation Organization," *Problems of Post-Communism*, Vol. 53, no. 5 (September/October 2006), p. 5. See also Gill and Oresman, *China's New Journey*, p. 8.

108 "Jiang Zemin's Speech at Inaugural Meeting of 'Shanghai Cooperation Organization.'"

109 "Putin Says New Shanghai Organization to Promote Security across Asia."

110 For a detailed discussion of the different internal mechanisms used by Beijing to maintain control in Xinjiang, see Bovingdon, *Uyghurs*, chapter 2.

our argument here is that China, by the late 1990s, had a growing stake in regional cooperation to deal with stability in Central Asia as a consequence of unrest in Xinjiang and Chinese fears about the potential for Uyghur separatist groups to link up with external forces in the region. Indeed, the fact that China was pursuing multiple costly approaches to deal with instability in Xinjiang underscored the importance Beijing placed on this issue. China's outside options, in other words, were worsening, and our argument suggests that this should have been pushing China – ceteris paribus – to be more proactive in building institutions in the region that might provide some order and, as such, help address PRC fears about Central Asian instability. China's efforts to create the SCO – particularly given apparent Chinese motivations in decreasing regional instability, combined with the organization's clear security focus – were thus consistent with our theory.

4.5 THE EVOLUTION OF THE SCO AFTER 2001

In the years after the SCO was established, China continued to invest in the organization and promote its institutionalization. Beijing's efforts on this front met some success. By the mid-2000s, for instance, the SCO possessed a permanent secretariat (located in Beijing) and an organization (located in Tashkent) that focused on anti-terrorism. The SCO also conducted regular military exercises and facilitated frequent high-level leadership meetings among SCO members. On the other hand, however, the organization remained relatively weak, possessing a small operating budget and few tangible accomplishments outside the security realm. In this section, we explore whether our theory offers useful guidance to China's approach to the SCO after 2001. We begin with an overview of the balance of outside options relating to Central Asia (in particular, relating to stability in the region) and how those options evolved after 2001. We here suggest that this balance – though subject to (at times) competing influences – generally remained relatively unfavorable for China in the years after the SCO's establishment. We then show that Beijing continued to be the principal driver behind SCO institutionalization after 2001, and we attribute this behavior to China's poor outside options. But we also suggest that China has only been moderately successful at constructing institutions that facilitate cooperation on order-provision in Central Asia, which we (following other analysts) attribute to the (at times) conflicting interests of the SCO member countries. Broadly, the evolution of the SCO since 2001, and China's role in that evolution, is moderately consistent with our theory.

4.5.1 Chinese Outside Options Relating to Central Asia after 2001

In the years following the establishment of the SCO in 2001, China's outside options relating to Central Asia were subject to confounding influences. Some factors had the effect of improving China's outside options (relative to Russia). Most obviously, Russian resurgence under Putin suggested that Chinese inattentiveness to Central Asia would not necessarily lead to spiraling instability; rather, free-riding on Russian order-provision again became – in theory at least – a plausible course of action. Meanwhile, though instability in Xinjiang remained a serious concern, violence in the region subsided during much of the 2000s – before flaring again in 2009. Increased stability in Xinjiang, prior to 2009, should have had the ceteris paribus effect of reducing the PRC stake in Central Asian stability, for reasons outlined earlier. Yet other factors were hurting China's outside options in the years after 2001. Some events had the effect of increasing PRC stakes in the region. For instance, the September 11, 2001, terrorist attacks underscored the dangers posed by transnational terrorism and the importance of rooting out terror groups in Central Asia. Likewise, the Color Revolutions of the mid-2000s, including the Tulip Revolution in Kyrgyzstan, again raised the specter of internal instability and challenges to authoritarian rule spreading through the region. Meanwhile, the US intervention in Afghanistan – particularly as it dragged on over the course of the decade – sparked fears in China of US encirclement. Finally, China's growing stake in Central Asian energy meant that there were reasons for Beijing to worry about the consequences of being excluded from institution-building initiatives in the region. From Beijing's standpoint, in short, the outside option of addressing issues like instability in Xinjiang via unilateral measures remained relatively unattractive: China's large stakes in the region gave it a strong incentive to be involved, and there were reasons for it to be skeptical of the degree to which a Russian unilateral option would accommodate key PRC concerns.

4.5.1.1 A Resurgent Russia

After a decade of economic malaise and declining influence in Central Asia, Moscow's approach to Central Asia became much more assertive in the years after Vladimir Putin was elected Russian president in 1999. Putin aimed to reestablish Russia's role as a global great power and to reinforce Russian primacy in the country's immediate periphery – particularly in Central Asia. Putin was abetted in this regard by an economy that grew rapidly in the years after his election, aided in large part by rising energy prices. While Russia continued to cooperate with Beijing in the context of the SCO, Moscow under Putin also pursued unilateral options in Central Asia – constructing new Russo-centric security and economic institutions in the region that excluded China.

On the security front, Russia established the Collective Security Treaty Organization (CSTO) in 2002, an organization that included Russia, Armenia, Belarus, Kazakhstan, Kyrgyzstan, and Tajikistan. Uzbekistan later joined, in 2006. The CSTO has been entirely bankrolled by Moscow and aims to enhance Russian-led security cooperation in the region; Russia has aimed (unsuccessfully) to use the organization as the key point of engagement with NATO on issues – such as the war in Afghanistan – pertaining to Central Asia. The CSTO increases military coordination between member countries, including via the development of a rapid reaction force (comprising mostly Russian and Kazakhstani troops, and focused mainly on countering terrorism and narcotics trafficking). Russia has also increased its military base presence in the region under the aegis of the organization.[111]

The 2000s also saw increasing economic ties between Russia and the Central Asian states. Trade grew rapidly, and Moscow constructed new economic institutions that sought to tie the countries in the region more closely to the Russian economy. The Eurasian Economic Community (EurAsEC), which included Russia, Belarus, Kazakhstan, Tajikistan, and Kyrgyzstan, was established in 2000 to enhance regional trade and to begin moving members toward a harmonized set of external trade policies.[112] But Russian economic influence in the region suffered at least a temporary setback after the onset of the 2008 global financial crisis, when Russian trade and investment in Central Asia declined sharply (even as economic ties between China and the region continued to grow).[113]

Russian resurgence in Central Asia, in turn, changed the nature of the Russian unilateral option in the region. Whereas, in the 1990s, Beijing had to worry about Russian weakness in Central Asia, and inability to provide effective order unilaterally, by the 2000s Russia appeared more capable to organize effective and stabilizing institutions in the region. But, as we will emphasize when discussing China's growing economic stakes in Central Asia, Beijing still had reason to worry about the Russian

[111] This discussion of the CSTO draws heavily from Cooley, *Great Games, Local Rules*, pp. 56–9.

[112] In 2010, Russia, Belarus, and Kazakhstan entered into a full customs union with common external policies. See Cooley, *Great Games, Local Rules*, pp. 59–62.

[113] See Cooley, *Great Games, Local Rules*, pp. 66–7.

unilateral option. In particular, since Russia (as Cooley writes) appeared motivated in large part by a desire for prestige – a privileged role – in the region, the Russian unilateral option also implied costs for China, including the possibility of being excluded from regional institutional initiatives.[114]

4.5.1.2 *Instability in Xinjiang*

Recall that Xinjiang was wracked by frequent bouts of violence from 1990–1998. However, after 1998, violent unrest in Xinjiang appeared to subside. As Millward wrote in 2004, "Acts of violent anti-Chinese resistance in Xinjiang have declined in frequency and severity since the late 1990s."[115] To be clear, Millward also emphasized at the time that tensions remained high, and that relations between Han Chinese and Uyghurs in Xinjiang, if anything, were worse in the early 2000s than was the case in the 1990s.[116] Moreover, violent unrest would again erupt in Xinjiang in the late 2000s, particularly during 2009.[117] So, increased stability in Xinjiang in the early to mid-2000s likely had the ceteris paribus effect of improving China's outside options, by reducing its direct stake in Central Asian stability to some degree. However, this improvement was temporary (ending when violence resumed in the late 2000s) and limited, given continued tense inter-ethnic relations in Xinjiang.

4.5.1.3 *Color Revolutions*

While Russian resurgence and declining violence in Xinjiang may have improved – at least to some degree – China's relative outside options relating to Central Asian stability during the early to mid-2000s, other factors were hurting those options. For instance, the Color Revolutions that affected former Soviet republics during the mid-2000s – including the 2005 Tulip Revolution in Kyrgyzstan – generated renewed concern in China about possible diffusion of instability in Central Asia.[118] The

[114] Cooley, *Great Games, Local Rules*.

[115] Millward, *Violent Separatism in Xinjiang*, p. 32.

[116] Ibid.

[117] Violent riots erupted in Urumqi in July, 2009. Official Chinese sources reported that nearly 200 were killed and over 1,700 injured during the riots; Uyghur sources suggested that these numbers, which reflected mostly Han casualties, underestimated Uyghur casualties at the hands of Han vigilantes. See "Chinese President Visits Volatile Xinjiang," *The New York Times*, 25 August 2009: www.nytimes.com/2009/08/26/world/asia/26china.html.

[118] Cooley, *Great Games, Local Rules*, p. 82 writes – based on interviews conducted in China in 2009 – that "China was concerned that such democratizing forces might spill

Color Revolutions received a considerable amount of official and scholarly attention in China, as the CCP tried to determine the causes of the revolutions and the possible implications for China. Much of this analysis blamed a combination of domestic (such as legitimate popular grievances over corruption and inequality) and international (especially Western support, including the role of nongovernmental organizations – NGOs – in affected countries) factors as driving the revolutions, while emphasizing the need for Beijing to place stricter limits on NGOs operating in China.[119]

4.5.1.4 9/11 and Increased US Presence in Central Asia

The September 11, 2001, terrorist attacks affected China's outside options relating to Central Asian stability in several ways. Perhaps most directly and obviously, the attacks demonstrated the risks posed by transnational terrorist networks and underscored the continued stake Beijing had, both in regional stability and in continued interstate cooperation, to root out terrorist networks.[120] As Central Asia expert Pan Guang writes, moreover, the subsequent launching of the US-led War on Terror underscored to the SCO member states that they still lacked an effective institutional structure to combat terrorism; in turn, Pan argues that there was an increased urgency to act quickly to build such a structure.[121] On the other hand, the sudden defeat of the Taliban government was seen – by at least some PRC experts on Central Asia – as temporarily having a stabilizing

over and destabilize its Western province of Xinjiang, as well as potentially empowering political dissidents and subversive groups in the rest of China." See also Li Baozhen, *Shanghai Hezuo Zuzhi yu Zhongguo de Heping Fazhan* [The Shanghai Cooperation Organization and China's Peaceful Development] (Beijing: Xinhua Chubanshe, 2011), p. 160; and He Zhilong and Zhao Xinggang, "Zhongya 'Yanse Geming' de Genyuan ji qi dui Zhongguo de Yingxiang" [The Root Causes of Central Asia's 'Color Revolutions' and their Impact on China], *Gansu Qingnian Guanli Ganbu Xueyuan Xuebao*, Vol. 18, no. 2 (2005), p. 48. He and Zhao also write that the spread of Color Revolutions in Central Asia could increase US power in the region and thereby undercut China's security and access to energy in the region.

119 Ibid. For a detailed overview of Chinese scholarship relating to the Color Revolutions, see Titus C. Chen, "China's Reaction to the Color Revolutions: Adaptive Authoritarianism in Full Swing," *Asian Perspective*, Vol. 34, no. 2 (2010), pp. 5–51.

120 Note that Beijing also used the 2001 attacks as an opportunity to reframe instability in Xinjiang "from a local sovereign affair within China to a frontline in the new global war on terror." Cooley, *Great Games, Local Rules*, p. 81. See also Millward, *Eurasian Crossroads*, pp. 338–9.

121 Pan Guang, "Cong 'Shanghai Wuguo' Dao Shanghai Hezuo Zuzhi" [From the 'Shanghai Five' to the Shanghai Cooperation Organization], *Eluosi Yanjiu*, no. 124, 2002, issue 2, p. 34.

impact on the region. Zhao Huasheng writes, for instance, that the collapse of the Taliban meant "the most serious threat to Central Asia was eliminated," thereby "greatly improving the security environment" in the region.[122] Still, as other analysts pointed out, the gains in this regard were to some degree temporary, particularly as the war in Afghanistan dragged on. One study emphasizes, for instance, that terrorist forces and other illicit groups in the region were, after 2001, "dispersed but not defeated," and soon were again causing trouble.[123]

Meanwhile, the US-led war in Afghanistan also led to a dramatic increase in the United States military presence in Central Asia – which included operating military bases in SCO member states Uzbekistan and Kyrgyzstan to help conduct the war. As Zhao Huasheng writes, this increased presence led to a sharp shift in the Central Asian balance of power, with the United States suddenly emerging as the most influential country in the region.[124] Cooley observes that the post–9/11 United States entry into Central Asia "raised alarm throughout Chinese foreign and defense policy circles," as Beijing increasingly felt encircled by US bases and worried that the United States might establish a long-term presence in the region.[125] Cooley's interviews with Chinese analysts reveal a range of PRC concerns at the time, including the possibility that these bases "could be used to choke off Chinese energy supplies, conduct surveillance operations in Western China, or even provide a springboard for the US government or its allies to destabilize Xinjiang."[126]

122 Zhao Huasheng, "Zhongya Xingshi Bianhua yu 'Shanghai Hezuo Zuzhi'" [The Changing Situation in Central Asia and the 'Shanghai Cooperation Organization'], *Dongou Zhongya Yanjiu*, 2002, no. 6, p. 55. Note that Hua later emphasized in the same article (p. 57) that the SCO's anti-terrorism function remained important even after the defeat of the Taliban, as terrorism, separatism, and religious extremism remained serious problems in the region.

123 Yu Jianhua, *Shanghai Hezuo Zuzhi Feichuantong Anquan Yanjiu* [Shanghai Cooperation Organization Nontraditional Security Research] (Shanghai: Shanghai Shehui Kexueyuan Chubanshe, 2009), p. 308.

124 Zhao, "Zhongya Xingshi Bianhua," p. 55.

125 Cooley, *Great Games, Local Rules*, p. 81. Li, *Zhongguo 'Xin Anquanguan,'* p. 161 writes that the increased US military presence near China's western borders represented a "sword of Damocles" hanging over China's head.

126 Cooley, *Great Games, Local Rules*, p. 81. For an analysis along these lines, see Zhao Longgeng, "Shixi Meiguo Zhujun Zhongya Hou de Zhanlue Taishi ji qi dui Woguo Anquan Liyi de Yingxiang" [An Analysis of the Situation after the US Deployment of Troops in Central Asia and its Implications for China's Security Interests], *Eluosi Zhongya Dongou Yanjiu*, 2004, no. 2, especially pp. 70–2. Zhao argues that US troops in Central Asia have several negative implications for China, including: creating a situation of strategic encirclement; making China more vulnerable to US reconnaissance

4.5.1.5 *Growing Economic and Energy Stakes in Central Asia*

In the years after 2000, China's economic ties with Central Asia grew rapidly. PRC trade with the region stood at less than US$2 billion in 2001, but by 2010 exceeded US$30 billion. Moreover, in the aftermath of the 2008 global financial crisis, Chinese trade with the region, for the first time, surpassed Russian trade with Central Asia. PRC investment in the region also skyrocketed, and by the late 2000s China was the largest foreign investor in several Central Asian states.[127] Even more importantly, China's stake in Central Asian energy rose sharply during the 2000s. As we discussed earlier, Chinese leaders recognized in the 1990s that the PRC was going to need to rely increasingly on imported energy as the economy boomed and domestic oil production stagnated. Central Asia was especially attractive in this regard, because of its proximity and its potential to diversify imports away from sources requiring passage through the Strait of Malacca.[128] After some initial forays into Central Asian energy development projects during the 1990s, PRC energy interests in the region increased markedly during the 2000s. The China-Kazakhstan oil pipeline project, originally agreed to in 1997 but then placed on the backburner, was relaunched in 2003.[129] A gas pipeline extending from Turkmenistan to China was completed in 2009, and in 2012 Uzbekistan also started to export natural gas to China.[130] Meanwhile, Chinese oil companies poured investments into Kazakhstan's oil industry during the 2000s.[131]

China's increasing economic and energy ties to Central Asia, in turn, implied a ceteris paribus growing stake in Central Asian stability, as instability could put those ties at risk. And here, it is worth noting as well that although China's trade with Central Asia has remained a small percentage of the PRC's total foreign trade, it represents a large percentage

and possible use of force (though the latter is seen as unlikely); making it easier for the United States to interfere in Xinjiang by supporting separatists; undercutting the cohesiveness of the SCO by driving a wedge among its members, and complicating Chinese energy strategy in the region. For a less alarmist perspective on the implications of US military presence in Central Asia, see for instance Zhao, "Central Asia in Chinese Strategic Thinking," p. 182, who writes that while "the US military presence in China is not welcomed by China," it also "is not regarded as a pressing security threat."

[127] See Cooley, *Great Games, Local Rules*, pp. 86–7 for an overview of China's growing economic ties with Central Asia after 2000. The data presented here come from Cooley.

[128] See, for instance, Ibid., p. 91.

[129] Zhao, "Central Asia in Chinese Strategic Thinking," p. 178.

[130] Ibid., p. 179.

[131] Cooley, *Great Games, Local Rules*, p. 91 writes that some estimated that China controlled more than a quarter of Kazakhstan's oil by 2007. On Chinese energy interests in Central Asia, see also Karrar, *New Silk Road*, pp. 171–9.

of Xinjiang's foreign trade. As Zhao Huasheng emphasizes, "fostering economic development [in Xinjiang] through trade with Central Asia is considered an important way to alleviate the conditions that allow terrorism, separatism, and extremism to flourish."[132] Moreover, China's growing economic interests in the region gave the PRC more reason to be worried about the Russian unilateral option: a resurgent Russia in the early 2000s clearly hoped to keep Central Asia squarely in its sphere of influence, and Russia – as noted earlier – was constructing new institutions in the region (including EurAsEC) that excluded China. Indeed, some analysts have suggested that Russia, at the time, was worried about China's growing economic presence in the region, fearing this would, over time, translate into political and economic influence in what Russia saw as its backyard.[133] In this environment, with Russia both worried about the implications of growing Chinese economic interests in Central Asia and constructing regional institutions that excluded the PRC, Beijing had reason to doubt that a Russian-constructed regional order would protect Chinese economic stakes in Central Asia.

4.5.1.6 *Summary and Theoretical Expectations*

In summary, from China's perspective, the balance of outside options relating to the provision of stability in Central Asia was subject to competing influences in the years after the establishment of the SCO. Russian resurgence under Putin, for instance, changed the nature of Russia's unilateral option regarding order-provision in the region. Whereas in the 1990s Russian weakness meant that Beijing could not reliably depend on Moscow to provide stability in Central Asia, Russia's capacity to do so was improving in the 2000s. But Russia's desire to maintain a privileged position in what it saw as its backyard also served to diminish the attractiveness of the Russian unilateral option from Beijing's perspective, since a Russia-centric security order in the region would not necessarily accommodate Chinese interests in Central Asia. This was especially the case given China's rapidly growing energy and economic interests

[132] Zhao, "Central Asia in Chinese Strategic Thinking," p. 180. Zhao notes that Xinjiang's trade with Central Asia in 2012 represented about 70 percent of the XUAR's total trade that year.

[133] See for instance Wang Xiaoquan, "Eluosi dui Shanghai Hezuo Zuzhi de Zhengce Yanbian" [The evolution of Russia's policy toward the Shanghai Cooperation Organization], *Eluosi Zhongya Dongou Yanjiu*, 2007, no. 3, especially pp. 67–9. See also Liang Qiang, "Shanghai Zuzhi de Shuang Hexin Kunao" [The Two Core Troubles of the Shanghai Cooperation Organization], *Nanfeng Chuang*, June 2006 (2nd issue), p. 69; and Cooley, *Great Games, Local Rules*, p. 71.

in Central Asia, a factor that increased China's stakes in the region and, thus, reduced the attractiveness of its outside option ceteris paribus. Meanwhile, increased stability in Xinjiang (prior to 2009) improved China's outside options, while the Color Revolutions and the increased US military presence in Central Asia probably had a net negative impact on those options. In the aggregate, then, it is difficult to assess whether China's relative outside options – relating to stability provision in Central Asia – were net improving or worsening during the years after the SCO's establishment. At a minimum, there is little reason to think that China's outside options improved significantly over the course of the 2000s; as such, our theory would expect some continued Chinese willingness to invest in institution-building in the region to promote stability and continued Chinese engagement.

4.5.2 Continued (but Limited) Investment: China and the Evolution of the SCO after 2001

After establishing the SCO in 2001, the six member countries built an institutional structure for the organization over the next several years. The six states moved quickly to write the SCO Charter, which they formally signed during the 2002 Heads of State Summit in St. Petersburg. Building on the 2001 Declaration on the Creation of the SCO, the SCO Charter outlines the goals and tasks, principles, and areas of cooperation of the new organization.[134] Among the goals and tasks listed in the Charter are to "jointly counteract terrorism, separatism, and extremism in all their manifestations," to "strengthen mutual trust, friendship, and good-neighborliness between the member states," to cooperate in maintaining stability, and to seek cooperation in other areas. The principles outlined in the document include (among others) respect for sovereignty and non-interference, equality of member states, peaceful settlement of disputes, and "gradual implementation of joint activities in the spheres of mutual interest."[135] The Charter also lays out the institutional structure

[134] *Shanghai Cooperation Organization Charter*, posted online at The Official Webpage of Russia's Presidency to the Shanghai Cooperation Organization, 2014–2105: http://en.sco-russia.ru.

[135] In its areas of cooperation, the Charter first highlights maintaining peace and security in the region, "searching for common positions on foreign policy issues of mutual interest," and developing and implementing "measures aimed at jointly counteracting terrorism, separatism, and extremism," along with other non-traditional security threats in the region. Other areas of cooperation include promoting economic development, environmental management, among others.

and membership rules of the SCO. The Charter identifies the Council of Heads of State as the supreme body in the SCO, and summarizes the functions of several other bodies, including the Council of Heads of Government, the Council of Ministers of Foreign Affairs, the Council of National Coordinators, the Regional Anti-terrorist Structure, and the Secretariat.[136] The Charter further mandates that decisions in the various SCO bodies be made by consensus.

The member countries also signed a formal agreement at the 2002 summit to create the RATS in Bishkek (later moved to Tashkent), an idea which had been agreed to in principle several years earlier.[137] The agreement establishes RATS as a permanent body to be funded by the SCO, and outlines its primary functions and objectives. Key functions identified by the agreement include developing proposals and providing recommendations to SCO member states regarding "combating terrorism, separatism, and extremism," and the creation of a database on "international terrorist, separatist, and other extremist organizations, their structure, leaders, and members, other individuals associate with these organizations, as well as the financing sources and channels of these organizations." The SCO Council of Heads of State appoints the director of the RATS Executive Committee, which held its first meeting in October 2003.[138] Meanwhile, the SCO Secretariat opened its doors in January 2004. Chien-peng Chung writes that the body "works closely with the Council of National Coordinators in preparing draft documents, making suggestions, implementing resolutions, and exercising budgetary supervision for

[136] Briefly: the Council of Heads of Government would, like the Heads of State, meet annually. The Heads of Government would approve the budget and decide on mostly economic matters. The Foreign Ministers would also meet annually (before the Heads of State meeting, for which they would help prepare). The Council of National Coordinators would meet at least three times each year, and would manage routine affairs and help coordinate other Council meetings. The RATS is highlighted in the Charter, but details are left for a separate treaty (discussed later) also signed in St. Petersburg. The Secretariat would be a standing administrative body located in Beijing. The Charter also notes that meetings of other heads of ministries or agencies will take place according to the decisions of the Council of the Heads of State or the Council of the Heads of Government.

[137] An English translation of the agreement can be found on the Worldwide Movement for Human Rights webpage: www.fidh.org/en/issues/terrorism-surveillance-and-human-rights/Agreement-Between-the-Member.

[138] Chung, "China and the SCO," p. 7. Chung further notes that the 2004 Heads of State meeting created a Council of Permanent Representatives through which member states "exercise direct supervision over RATS." Note that the RATS headquarters ultimately opened in Tashkent in 2004, a point discussed at greater length below.

the" SCO.[139] The Secretariat has permanent offices located in Beijing, and has a staff of thirty officials who are seconded from SCO member countries.[140]

Along with the creation of a formal organizational structure, the SCO has also facilitated increased cooperation among member countries on security and economic issues. Perhaps most notably, SCO member countries have conducted regular security exercises under the organization's auspices since 2002. Many of these exercises are anti-terrorism drills that focus on a particular scenario, such as a 2008 exercise in Russia that involved a terrorist takeover of an oil tanker. Member countries also engage in larger-scale war game exercises (called "Peace Missions") that sometimes involve thousands of troops in activities such as amphibious landing drills and long-distance bombing simulations.[141] The scope of these sorts of cooperative exercises has continued to expand. In 2015, for instance, China hosted the SCO's first online anti-terrorism exercise, which was meant to improve cooperation in dealing with online activities of terrorist groups.[142] In the economic arena, the SCO has established a Business Council (headquartered in Moscow, founded in 2006) that aims to facilitate cooperation on trade and other economic issues, and an Interbank Association (created in 2005) that promotes cooperation among major banks in SCO member countries.[143]

Just as the PRC played a central role in the establishment of the Shanghai Five and the SCO, it continued to play a leading role in the further development of the SCO in the years after 2001. China's leading role is evident in the text of the SCO Charter, which – as was the case with the 2001 Declaration on the Establishment of the SCO, discussed earlier – clearly has PRC fingerprints all over it. The SCO principles identified in the Charter, for instance, echo PRC foreign policy principles: "mutual respect for sovereignty"; "territorial integrity"; "non-aggression";

139 Ibid., pp. 5–7.

140 Ibid., p. 7.

141 On SCO exercises, see Julie Boland, "Ten Years of the Shanghai Cooperation Organization: A Lost Decade? A Partner for the U.S.?" 21st Century Defense Initiative Policy Paper (Washington, DC: Brookings Institution, June 20, 2011), pp. 11–12. Boland (pp. 12–13) outlines other areas of security cooperation within the SCO, such as increased coordination with regard to Afghanistan (including hosting a 2009 Moscow conference on the topic) and increased cooperation on anti-narcotics efforts.

142 Ministry of National Defense, People's Republic of China, "SCO Hosts First Joint Online Counter-terrorism Exercise in China," October 15, 2015: http://eng.mod.gov.cn/Database/MOOTW/2015-10/15/content_4624404.htm.

143 Boland, "Ten Years of the Shanghai Cooperation Organization," p. 14.

"non-interference in internal affairs"; "non-use of force or threat of its use"; "equality of all member states"; "peaceful settlement of disputes"; and so forth.[144] As Chung notes, the decision to headquarter the SCO Secretariat in Beijing reflects China's central role in the organization; not surprisingly, a Chinese official – Zhang Deguang – served as the SCO's first secretary-general.[145] Henry Plater-Zyberk and Andrew Monaghan write that the creation of a RATS was initially promoted most forcefully by Moscow and that Beijing, fearing that the structure would be dominated by Russia, was at first cool to the idea.[146] But Chung notes that the PRC began to actively support an SCO anti-terrorism mechanism by 2002 "to avoid being sidelined by the post–9/11 US military presence in Central Asia"; China's advocacy, in turn, ultimately allowed the project to get off the ground.[147] Starting in 2003, China also pushed for further economic cooperation within the SCO.[148] And China's continued central role in the organization was again confirmed in 2009 when, during renewed instability in Xinjiang, Beijing drafted an SCO statement strongly supportive of PRC actions to restore order in the autonomous region; the SCO member countries immediately signed on to the communique.[149] In short, the

[144] *Shanghai Cooperation Organization Charter.*

[145] Chung, "China and the SCO," p. 10. Shambaugh notes that the headquarters were also "largely paid for by China." See David Shambaugh, "Return to the Middle Kingdom? China and Asia in the Early Twenty-First Century," in David Shambaugh, ed., *Power Shift: China and Asia's New Dynamics* (Berkeley, CA and Los Angeles, CA: University of California Press, 2005), p. 30.

[146] Henry Plater-Zyberk with Andrew Monaghan, *Strategic Implications of the Evolving Shanghai Cooperation Organization* (Carlisle, PA: Strategic Studies Institute and US Army War College Press, 2014), p. 21: www.strategicstudiesinstitute.army.mil/pdffiles/PUB1217.pdf.

[147] Chung, "China and the SCO," p. 10. Although Plater-Zyberk and Monaghan write that the initial planned location in Bishkek continued to be a source of contention (with China and Uzbekistan fearing that Russian influence in the Kyrgyzstan would enable Moscow to have too much influence over the organization). The authors suggest that instability in Kyrgyzstan provided a pretext for moving the planned headquarters to Tashkent, a decision made in 2003 and paving the way for the organization to start operating in 2004. See Plater-Zyberk and Monaghan, *Strategic Implications of the Evolving Shanghai Cooperation Organization*, p. 21.

[148] Shambaugh, "Return to the Middle Kingdom?" p. 31; See also Alexander Cooley, "Russia and the Recent Evolution of the SCO: Issues and Challenges for U.S. Policy," in Timothy J. Colton, Timothy Frye, and Robert Legvold, eds., *The Policy World Meets Academia: Designing U.S. Policy toward Russia* (Cambridge, MA: American Academy of Arts and Sciences, 2010), online at: www.amacad.org/content/publications/pubContent.aspx?d=1135. Some Chinese scholars explicitly advocated a stronger economic role for the SCO early on. See, for instance, Zhao, "Zhongya Xingzhi Bianhua," p. 59.

[149] See Cooley, "Russia and the Recent Evolution of the SCO." Cooley contrasts the 2009 Xinjiang case – rapid SCO backing for a Chinese position – with Russian failed efforts in 2008 to obtain SCO sanction for its policies in Georgia.

PRC continued to play a central role in the SCO in the years after 2001, and the further institutionalization of the organization during those years was largely a consequence of PRC efforts.

The SCO has also, over time, expanded its geographic scope. The organization began granting observer status to outside countries in 2004, with the admission of Mongolia to that status. The following year, India, Pakistan, and Iran were granted observer status,[150] and more recently Belarus and Afghanistan also became observers.[151] Several countries – such as Sri Lanka and Turkey – are formal dialogue partners of the SCO. In 2015, the SCO announced intentions to admit India and Pakistan as new members – the first expansion of full membership in the organization since its 2001 founding.[152] The two countries joined the organization in 2017, and Iran also appears likely to become a full member soon.[153]

In sum, in the decade and a half since its founding, the SCO has become more institutionalized, has facilitated some increased cooperation among members (especially on security issues), and has expanded its geographic scope. The RATS is widely seen – even among some skeptics of the SCO – as enhancing cooperation among SCO states on terrorism,[154] and the frequent high-level meetings held under the SCO umbrella have most likely contributed to improved diplomatic relations among its member countries.[155] Furthermore, the continued development of the SCO in the years after 2001 was, to a considerable degree, a consequence of continued PRC investment in the organization.

Still, we do not wish to overstate the depth of PRC investment in the Shanghai Cooperation Organization. The SCO remains a thinly

[150] See Chung, "China and the SCO," p. 12.

[151] "SCO Elevates Belarus as Observer, Admits Four New Dialogue Partners," *Xinhua*, July 10, 2015: http://news.xinhuanet.com/english/2015-07/10/c_134401676.htm; "SCO Accepts Afghanistan as Observer, Turkey Dialogue Partner," *Xinhua*, June 7, 2012: http://news.xinhuanet.com/english/china/2012-06/07/c_131637206.htm.

[152] See William Piekos and Elizabeth C. Economy, "The Risks and Rewards of SCO Expansion," Council on Foreign Relations Expert Brief, July 8, 2015: www.cfr.org/international-organizations-and-alliances/risks-rewards-sco-expansion/p36761.

[153] Russia, not China, is generally seen as the actor that has pushed the most for expansion of the SCO to South Asia. See, for instance, Meena Singh Roy, "Dynamics of Expanding the SCO," Institute for Defence Studies and Analyses, April 4, 2011: www.idsa.in/idsacomments/DynamicsofExpandingtheSCO_msroy_040411.

[154] See, for instance, Plater-Zyberk and Monaghan, *Strategic Implications of the Evolving Shanghai Cooperation Organization*.

[155] See, for example, Gisela Grieger, "The Shanghai Cooperation Organization," European Parliamentary Research Service, June 2015, p. 8: www.europarl.europa.eu/RegData/etudes/BRIE/2015/564368/EPRS_BRI(2015)564368_EN.pdf.

institutionalized organization with a small budget,[156] and the SCO's record in facilitating regional security and economic cooperation remains, at best, mixed. For instance, despite the organization's prioritization of regional stability, it has largely failed to become a significant player in Afghanistan, the primary source of instability in Central Asia.[157] Many analysts also point to the SCO's inefficacious response to 2010 instability in Kyrgyzstan as evidence of the organization's weakness.[158] And although the past fifteen years have witnessed increasing regional trade and major infrastructure projects (such as the energy pipelines extending to China), it is hard to attribute these achievements to the SCO. Chinese investments in the region, for instance, have been undertaken via bilateral agreements with the countries involved, and little progress has been made (despite PRC prodding) to move toward a regional free-trade bloc.[159] These limited achievements have led some observers to view the SCO as sometimes producing "more rhetoric than action";[160] one analyst goes so far as to suggest that the SCO more resembles a "politically motivated axis of convenience" than a fully-functioning international organization.[161]

Thus, China's approach to the SCO since 2001 is moderately consistent with our theory. Continued relatively poor outside options (on the issue of Central Asian stability) should have been pushing China to continue to invest in the construction of institutions that could facilitate second-order cooperation relating to stability-provision in the region. And, in fact, China did continue to invest in the organization, pushing for it to become more institutionalized and encouraging increased cooperation

[156] Current budgets are classified, but as of 2005 the SCO's budget was a mere US$3.8 billion. See Grieger, "The Shanghai Cooperation Organization," p. 6. Grieger notes that one issue concerning the budget has been "insufficient funds for SCO joint projects." She also observes that aside from the Secretariat, the RATS, and various ad hoc working groups, "no other permanent body has been created [in the SCO] to deepen formal cooperation in other fields of potential cooperation" (p. 6). China's contribution to the budget was set at 24 percent. See Wang, "China and the SCO," p. 112.

[157] See, for instance, Eleanor Albert, "The Shanghai Cooperation Organization," Council on Foreign Relations, *CFR Backgrounder*, October 14, 2015: www.cfr.org/china/shanghai-cooperation-organization/p10883.

[158] Matthew Crosston, "The Pluto of International Organizations: Micro-Agendas, IO Theory, and Dismissing the Shanghai Cooperation Organization," *Comparative Strategy*, Vol. 33, no. 2 (2013), pp. 283–94. See also Grieger, "The Shanghai Cooperation Organization," p. 9.

[159] See, for instance, Grieger, "The Shanghai Cooperation Organization," p. 8; Albert, "The Shanghai Cooperation Organization."

[160] Plater-Zyberk and Monaghan, *Strategic Implications of the Evolving Shanghai Cooperation Organization*, p. 18.

[161] Crosston, "The Pluto of International Organizations," p. 284.

in other areas – such as economics – that would further enhance PRC influence in the region and promote stability. Yet the SCO remains a relatively weak organization, with tangible – but limited – accomplishments. A key barrier to a more developed SCO, it appears, centers on competing interests among SCO members, including among the two poles of the organization, Russia and China. For instance, although Russia and China have a shared interest in regional stability, Russia remains wary of PRC efforts to increase Chinese influence in what Moscow continues to view as its backyard, and Moscow has in turn stymied initiatives promoted by China, such as an SCO free trade agreement.[162] On the other hand, though the organization remains relatively weak, China's continued efforts to invest in and promote the SCO – despite at times conflicting interests among member countries – underscore China's commitment to the organization and demonstrate a willingness to undertake costly investments to construct order-promoting institutions in Central Asia. We return to the issue of interest dissimilarity, and what it means for PRC second-order contributions to the provision of stability in Central Asia, in the conclusion to this chapter.

4.6 CONCLUSIONS

Broadly speaking, China's behavior in Central Asia since the 1990s is consistent with our theory. China's outside options relating to order-provision in Central Asia worsened during the 1990s, a consequence of growing unrest in Xinjiang and instability in Central Asia after the Soviet collapse. Moreover, China had little reason to expect that a weakened Moscow had the capacity to impose order in Central Asia unilaterally. In this environment, the PRC increasingly invested in building institutions that would include Russia and the Central Asian states, and that would facilitate regional stability. These efforts culminated with the establishment of the SCO, and extended after 2001 as the PRC continued to promote the new organization and to seek ways to enhance regional cooperation.

This is not to say that other factors haven't been important in shaping PRC behavior with regard to second-order cooperation in Central Asia. One straightforward alternative explanation centers on broader shifts in China's approach to international affairs. As Medeiros and

[162] See Piekos and Economy, "Risks and Rewards."

Fravel write, by the late 1990s and early 2000s China had "begun to take a less confrontational, more sophisticated, more confident, and, at times, more constructive approach toward regional and global affairs." This "new diplomacy" was reflected in increased PRC engagement with regional institutions (and Medeiros and Fravel include the establishment of the SCO as an example here), increased willingness to accept global non-proliferation norms, and increased pragmatism in dealing with territorial disputes with neighboring countries.[163] Medeiros and Fravel trace these shifts to a number of factors, some domestic (such as institutional reforms and aggressive foreign ministry training programs) and some international (such as socialization processes, as PRC scholars and analysts increasingly interacted with international experts).[164] We do not dispute that there were significant changes in PRC diplomacy starting in the late 1990s, and that these changes, as identified by Medeiros and Fravel, led Beijing to be more receptive toward an active role in second-order cooperation in Central Asia. Yet, as we emphasize throughout this book, it is important to recognize that there remained significant variation in the degree to which the PRC was willing to invest in second-order cooperative efforts, even after the late 1990s. As such, a general shift toward a more sophisticated and less confrontational diplomacy may have been a necessary condition for more investment in second-order cooperation, but it was not sufficient.

Moreover, although we have been careful to emphasize in this chapter that PRC investment in the SCO should not be exaggerated (and the organization remains fairly weak relative to other international organizations), China's continued willingness to invest in the SCO despite, at times, competing interests among member states also serves to underscore Beijing's willingness to engage in second-order cooperation in the region. By seeking to construct multilateral institutions that include both the PRC and Russia, along with the Central Asian states, China appears to be trying to accomplish two goals. First, as we have suggested in this chapter, Beijing wants to make sure that institutions constructed to provide stability in Central Asia do so in a way that also takes into account other Chinese interests, including China's economic interests and the PRC's hopes to intensify energy cooperation with Central Asia. As we

[163] Medeiros and Fravel, "China's New Diplomacy, p. 22. On these changes, see also Shirk, *China, Fragile Superpower*; Johnston, *Social States*; Fravel, *Strong Borders*; Evan S. Medeiros, *Reluctant Restraint: The Evolution of China's Nonproliferation Policies and Practices: 1980–2004* (Stanford, CA: Stanford University Press, 2007).

[164] On socialization, see also Johnston, *Social States*.

have explained, even though Russia's resurgence under Putin has meant a renewed Russian capacity to impose order in the region, Moscow has consistently preferred to do so via Russia-centric institutions that exclude China. It is not clear, however, how far these sorts of institutions would go to accommodate Chinese interests and, as such, the Russian unilateral option for order-provision in Central Asia has remained unfavorable from Beijing's perspective. Second, China hopes to reassure Russia that a China actively involved in Central Asia will not be a threat to core Russian interests; this may be a reason, in turn, that China has – to date – avoided countering Russian institutions by constructing its own competing institutions in the region that exclude Russia. By treating Russia and China as equal stakeholders and co-leaders of the organization, the SCO thus serves as a vehicle that both gives China a voice in the region and reassures Moscow that Beijing is not simply seeking to displace Russia in Central Asia.[165] Indeed, PRC scholars and officials have at times gone out of their way to highlight Russia's special interests in the region.[166]

Nevertheless, despite the success China has had in fostering the development of the SCO, the organization remains on shaky ground. China has found it difficult to gain traction on its economic initiatives in the organization, as both Russia and the Central Asian states fear PRC hegemony in the region. And the July 2017 expansion of the membership to include India and Pakistan will increase interest dissimilarity among member states, potentially making future accomplishments within the SCO even less likely.[167] Moreover, it is possible that China is becoming more confident in its ability to pursue its goals in Central Asia unilaterally. Clearly, given continued instability in China's western periphery and China's continued demand for imported energy, the stakes associated with maintaining stability in and good diplomatic relations with Central Asia remain high for the PRC. But as China's economic power has grown and its image as an economic juggernaut takes hold, Beijing

165 See, for instance, Zhao Huasheng, "Touxi Eluosi yu Shanghai Hezuo Zuzhi Guanxi" [Analyzing the Relationship between Russia and the Shanghai Cooperation Organization], *Guoji Guanxi Yanjiu*, 2011, issue 1, pp. 15–23. Zhao argues that the SCO plays a special role for Russia that differentiates it from other Russia-led institutions in the region, which are typically limited to former Soviet republics. The SCO, Zhao notes, is broader and more influential internationally, and it also gives Russia the opportunity to have some influence on China's engagement with the region. In this regard, the SCO is also quite useful for Moscow.

166 See, for instance, Zhao, "Central Asia in Chinese Strategic Thinking," pp. 183–4.

167 On this point, see Raffaello Pantucci, "Is SCO Expansion a Good Thing?" *The Diplomat*, July 12, 2016: http://thediplomat.com/2016/07/is-sco-expansion-a-good-thing.

appears to have more levers at its disposal through which to construct order in Central Asia unilaterally. The PRC's recent BRI initiative might be viewed – at least partially – in this light. We conclude this chapter with a brief consideration of BRI and its possible future implications for China's approach to second-order cooperation in Central Asia.

4.6.1 BRI and the Future of PRC Institution-building in Central Asia

Chinese President Xi Jinping first broached the idea of a Silk Road Economic Belt in 2013 as part of an effort to enhance cooperation with Central Asian countries. Later in the same year, in a speech to the Indonesian Parliament, Xi proposed the creation of a twenty-first century Maritime Silk Road in partnership with ASEAN nations.[168] The two concepts are now widely referred to as the BRI initiative. Although BRI remains somewhat vague, the initiative clearly entails a massive increase in infrastructure spending in developing Asia.[169] Beijing's goals in pursuing BRI are clearly diverse and, indeed, different observers point to different core motivating factors, ranging from the domestic political-economic to the geopolitical.[170] But Beijing's interest in the initiative (or,

[168] Speech by Chinese President Xi Jinping to Indonesian Parliament, October 2, 2013, online at ASEAN–China Center: www.asean-china-center.org/english/2013-10/03/c_133062675.htm.

[169] On the vagueness of the initiative, see Michael D. Swaine, "Chinese Views and Commentary on the 'One Belt, One Road' initiative," *China Leadership Monitor* 47 (summer 2015): www.hoover.org/research/chinese-views-and-commentary-one-belt-one-road. Swaine (p. 6) writes, for instance, that "few if any authoritative Chinese sources identify specific priorities among the many goals" of BRI. Swaine notes that financing for BRI's new infrastructure spending is expected to come from a variety of sources, including Chinese aid, private capital, as well as new China-led financial institutions, including the planned Silk Road Fund and the AIIB. China has already pledged to contribute US$40 billion to the new Silk Road Fund and nearly $30 billion to the AIIB. See "China to Establish $40 Billion Silk Road Infrastructure Fund," *Reuters*, November 8, 2015: www.reuters.com/article/2014/11/08/us-china-diplomacy-idUSKBN0IS0BQ20141108#sqFtftUhSB4iO1j8.97; and "Fifty Countries Sign up to China-led Asian Infrastructure Investment Bank, in Diplomatic Victory for Beijing," *International Business Times*, June 29, 2015: www.ibtimes.com/fifty-countries-sign-china-led-asian-infrastructure-investment-bank-diplomatic-1987459.

[170] For instance, at one end of the spectrum, some see BRI as (at least in part) a gambit to stimulate China's economy and to delay much-needed (but politically painful) structural reform by giving industries mired in overcapacity new export markets. See, for instance, Jiayi Zhou, Karl Hallding, and Guoyi Han, "The Trouble with China's 'One Belt, One Road' Strategy," *The Diplomat*, June 26, 2015: http://thediplomat.com/2015/06/the-trouble-with-the-chinese-marshall-plan-strategy; and David Dollar, "China's Rise as a Regional and Global Power: The AIIB and the 'One Belt, One Road,'" Brookings Research Paper, summer 2015: www.brookings.edu/research/papers/2015/07/

at least, the "belt" part of it) appears to be partly driven by the PRC's long-standing concerns over stability in Western China and, by extension, Central Asia. For instance, some analysts highlight the BRI's potential to facilitate economic development by increasing Xinjiang's linkages, both externally and internally, as new infrastructure projects pass through the region.[171] Likewise, Beijing appears to hope that the BRI will also spur economic development and stability within Central Asia, which in turn will help mitigate the potential for extremism to migrate into China's Western regions.[172] Furthermore, since the BRI entails investments in energy in Central Asia, it also advances PRC goals of energy diversification (and, in particular, reduced dependency on imports that must pass through the Strait of Malacca).[173] And, on a broader level, Beijing clearly hopes that the BRI will facilitate increased PRC influence in Central Asia. As Scott Kennedy and David Parker write, the economic resources at play in the BRI "will provide a major financial carrot to incentivize governments in Asia to pursue greater cooperation with Beijing."[174]

The BRI is not an obvious case of second-order cooperation as we saw with the SCO. Rather, to date, initiatives launched under the BRI's auspices are primarily a collection of bilateral investment projects "supported by both Chinese companies and the Chinese government."[175]

---

china-regional-global-power-dollar. On the other end of the spectrum, some observers see the initiative primarily through a geostrategic lens. One article quotes the US Naval War College's James Holmes, for instance, as suggesting that "the logic driving the enterprise" centers on increasing PRC influence and "[easing] America out of Asia over the long haul while weaning our allies away from us." See Wendell Minnick, "China's 'One Belt, One Road' Strategy," *Defense News*, April 12, 2015: www.defensenews.com/story/defense/2015/04/11/taiwan-china-one-belt-one-road-strategy/25353561.

[171] See, for instance, Jacob Stokes, "China's Road Rules: Beijing Looks West toward Eurasian Integration," *Foreign Affairs*, April 19, 2015: www.foreignaffairs.com/articles/asia/2015-04-19/chinas-road-rules. On the hopes that BRI will "improve connectivity" both within China and between China and countries along its periphery – hopefully jolting more balanced development within China – see Scott Kennedy and David A. Parker, "Building China's 'One Belt, One Road,'" Center for Strategic and Economic Studies *Critical Questions*, April 3, 2015: http://csis.org/publication/building-chinas-one-belt-one-road.

[172] See, for example, Nadege Rolland, "China's New Silk Road," National Bureau of Asian Research, February 12, 2015: www.nbr.org/research/activity.aspx?id=531; and William H. Overholt, "One Belt, One Road, One Pivot," *Global Asia*, Vol. 10, no. 3 (fall 2015).

[173] On this point, see Kennedy and Parker, "Building China's 'One Belt, One Road'"; and Rolland, "China's New Silk Road."

[174] Kennedy and Parker, "Building China's 'One Belt, One Road.'"

[175] The quote comes from Ariella Viehe, Aarthi Gunasekaran, Vivian Wang, and Stefanie Merchant, "Investments along China's Belt and Road Initiative," Center for American Progress, September 22, 2015: www.americanprogress.org/issues/security/

However, China's official Action Plan for the BRI suggests that the initiative aims to increase economic cooperation among participating countries. Though to some extent lacking in specifics, the blueprint emphasizes that the BRI will "help align and coordinate the development strategies of the countries along the Belt and Road, tap market potential in this region, promote investment and consumption, create demands and job opportunities," and "enhance people-to-people and cultural exchanges." Later, the document highlights several "cooperation priorities," including policy coordination, facilities connectivity, free trade, financial integration, and people-to-people exchanges.[176] If we take these objectives at face-value, they suggest that the Chinese government views the BRI as, ultimately, a vehicle through which to facilitate increased economic integration and cooperation.

Of course, lacking in specifics, it is not clear from the Action Plan how the PRC expects to achieve its objectives. For instance, will increased cooperation emerge from a network of mostly bilateral agreements, the revitalization of existing institutions like the SCO, or the creation of new multilateral institutions like the Asian Infrastructure Investment Bank? At this point, it is hard to say. But one way of thinking about the BRI relates to our discussion of dynamic conditions in Chapter 2. Here, BRI might represent, at least in part, a workaround that bypasses stalled efforts at increased economic cooperation within the SCO framework. More specifically, to the degree that the BRI succeeds in facilitating development and – ultimately – stability in both Western China and Central Asia, it improves China's outside options, relative to Russia, relating to cooperation over stability in the region (both because the stakes will become lower and because China will have cultivated a new – unilateral – option to help provide that stability). Moreover, to the degree that the PRC succeeds in making states in the region more dependent on the PRC economically, it increases the likelihood that those states will view China as an indispensable part of regional economic institutions – more so even than Russia. Our theory predicts, in turn, that a China with relatively strong outside options but that is nonetheless an indispensable part

news/2015/09/22/121689/investments-along-chinas-belt-and-road-initiative. The authors have compiled a useful list of BRI investments, including an interactive map.

176 "Vision and Actions on Jointly Building Silk Road Economic Belt and 21st Century Maritime Silk Road," issued by the National Development and Reform Commission, Ministry of Foreign Affairs, and Ministry of Commerce of the People's Republic of China, March 2015: http://en.ndrc.gov.cn/newsrelease/201503/t20150330_669367.html.

of institution-building in Central Asia will have the capacity to play a "hold-up" role – where, in this case, cooperation would increasingly take place on Beijing's terms.

Obviously, our discussion relating to the BRI and its implications is speculative, and we do not claim that our theory can predict future events in a deterministic fashion. Instead, we view our theory as providing a stylized framework through which to interpret and synthesize past events while also suggesting possible future scenarios. Here, we are simply suggesting one possible such scenario, in which the BRI over the long term – if successfully implemented – can serve as a means to jump-start institution-building in Central Asia in a way that more directly privileges PRC preferences, either through the SCO framework or via a new one.

5

Nuclear Nonproliferation

Accept, but Invest Selectively in the North Korea Issue

5.1 INTRODUCTION

Some of the concrete issues we consider in the empirical chapters in this book are handled by international regimes that predate China's rise; these regimes, in turn, typically have a legacy of underweighting China's influence in their decision-making procedures. So, for example, in international finance, until recently, China was treated as a peripheral state within the governance of the IMF and did not have as large a voice inside the institution as its material capabilities might have merited. The set of multilateral regimes around nuclear proliferation was different. Due to some fortunate (from China's perspective) timing, the NPT was negotiated by the United States and the Soviet Union in 1968 after the PRC had successfully tested a nuclear weapon. As the treaty prohibited the development of atomic weapons by states that did not already possess them, and grandfathered in those states (the United States, the Soviet Union, the United Kingdom, France, and China) that did possess them, China inherited a relatively privileged position within the regime (even though it was highly critical of the regime during the Maoist period).

So how has China approached the global nonproliferation regime? Our argument is that, in general, preventing nuclear proliferation has been a higher priority for the United States than it has been for China, and that, with few exceptions, the option of relying on US leadership has been generally good for Chinese interests. Furthermore, Chinese second-order cooperation has not been seen as indispensable for the maintenance of the regime. We therefore expect, and find, that (with one notable exception) the Chinese approach to global multilateralism on nuclear proliferation has been passive acceptance. Since the early 1990s, China has largely gone along with nonproliferation efforts (first-order cooperation) without making substantial efforts toward regime maintenance (second-order free-riding). This chapter therefore illustrates the logic of acceptance.

However, we find a divergence from the general pattern of acceptance in this regime, a divergence that also is consistent with our overall thesis. China faced relatively bad outside options, specifically with respect to the North Korean nuclear program, in the early 2000s, when concern about the US outside options led China to invest in a new set of institutions. This chapter therefore proceeds in two substantive sections. In the first, we trace the overall pattern of Chinese passive acceptance of the nuclear nonproliferation regime at the global level. In the second, we delve into substantially more detail about the North Korea case – as the exception from the overall pattern of acceptance – that, nonetheless, is consistent with our theory.

5.2 THE OVERALL PATTERN OF ACCEPTANCE

We predict that rising powers will invest in multilateral regimes when faced with a relatively poor balance of outside options; in the case of Central Asia, for instance, we saw that China became more willing to invest in regional institutions as its outside options worsened over the course of the 1990s. When the balance of outside options is more favorable from a rising power's perspective, however, its behavior will hinge on a second variable: the degree to which its contributions are generally seen as being indispensable to regime maintenance. So, when their outside options are favorable and they are generally viewed as indispensable, rising powers will tend to hold-up their own contributions, even at the risk of spoiling cooperation, in order to secure more benefits for themselves and push the costs of regime-building on to other states. When the balance of outside options is good for them but they are *not* indispensable, on the other hand, rising powers will passively accept existing regimes and, although they might follow the rules by engaging in first-order cooperation, they play little role in securing cooperation from other states.

Prior to the late 1980s, China's approach to second-order cooperation on nuclear nonproliferation was outside the scope of our theory, for three reasons. First, nuclear proliferation at this time was not an issue of common concern. The Maoist approach to foreign policy did not see nuclear proliferation as a bad thing and, early on, Deng saw no need to challenge that view. New proliferants were not threats to China; if anything, nuclear proliferation in South Asia seemed to contain Soviet influence (and was, therefore, possibly a net benefit to China), and proliferation elsewhere did not obviously implicate Chinese security interests. To the extent that the existing multilateral regime divided the world into nuclear "haves" and "have-nots," it was inconsistent with Beijing's public position on global inequality. Even though the system treated China as a privileged state, it was a privilege that Chinese leaders did not appear to value.[1]

This was true on the American side as well, since the United States and other established powers did not view proliferation as a highest-order foreign policy concern. Throughout the Cold War, both American and Soviet leaders were willing to let proliferation concerns fall in importance relative to their overall superpower competition. The United States, for instance, tacitly permitted at least two of its allies, Israel and Pakistan, to flout international nonproliferation norms even after the NPT was enacted.

Second, even though China did engage in some proliferation, China globally was not seen as an especially important power whose behavior would be highly relevant to a discussion of proliferation issues. This is not simply a question of China not being indispensable (it was not); rather, it was about China's relevance to the problem. Many other countries were selling unsafeguarded nuclear material and technology through the 1970s to a far greater extent than China was, and any sort of general agreement against unsafeguarded sales simply had not yet jelled. Chinese noncompliance with the kinds of nonproliferation norms that emerged only later was, therefore, a drop in the bucket. In terms of second-order cooperation, China's reluctance to play any sort of leadership role was also not unique. France, for instance, was not a member of the NPT, despite the fact that, like China, France was enshrined in the treaty as a nuclear state. So, not only did France not use any of its influence to promote a regime, France itself continued to make unsafeguarded transfers.[2]

[1] Mingquan Zhu, "The Evolution of China's Nuclear Nonproliferation Policy," *The Nonproliferation Review*, Vol. 4, no. 2 (1997), pp. 40–8; and Wendy Frieman, "New Members of the Club: Chinese Participation in Arms Control Regimes 1980–1995," *The Nonproliferation Review*, Vol. 3, no. 3 (1996), pp. 15–30.

[2] That France – a US military ally and a commercial and diplomatic partner – continued to sell nuclear technology outside of the commitments of the NPT through the early 1980s underscores both that nonproliferation was not a high priority among established states

In the language of our theory, China in this period was not a "rising state" with any unique influence.

Third, from the Chinese perspective, proliferation was not a foreign policy issue. The Chinese foreign ministry had neither a nonproliferation office nor an arms control office, and nuclear sales were handled entirely by commercially oriented entities operating without Beijing's approval.[3] It is therefore not the case that that China had a policy of, for instance, defying the West; China did not have a policy – and, in any case, the "West" barely had a policy to defy.

In turn, China into the 1980s sat at the fringes of the global nuclear nonproliferation regime. The PRC's basic compliance with existing international institutions (first-order cooperation) was minimal at best, and China only joined the International Atomic Energy Agency (IAEA) in 1984. Even then the move was mostly symbolic; because China was not a member of the NPT, it was not bound to adhere to any general proliferation safeguards. That is, China was not legally committed to require that all nuclear technology transfers out of China be "safeguarded," i.e., subject to IAEA inspection.[4]

By the late 1980s, the situation began to change. China started to see proliferation as both bad in general and bad for China. At the same time, the United States began treating proliferation as a major foreign policy

---

and that, in any case, China was in no way the weak link in the nonproliferation regime. See, for example, Lawrence Scheinman, *Atomic Energy Policy in France under the Fourth Republic* (Princeton, NJ: Princeton University Press, 2015).

[3] Even at lower levels, the PRC's foreign ministry did not have any specialized bureaus or experts focused on nonproliferation issues specifically. See Evan S. Medeiros, *Reluctant Restraint: The Evolution of China's Nonproliferation Policies and Practices, 1980–2004* (Stanford, CA: Stanford University Press, 2007), p. 49.

[4] The IAEA is, at its core, an international body tasked with verifying whether or not countries adhere to agreements involving nuclear technology. Those agreements, in turn, are largely made outside of the IAEA. When the agency was created in the 1950s, it was envisioned as a body that would verify bilateral agreements. For example, in a hypothetical United States–Pakistani deal in which an American firm would build a nuclear power plant in Pakistan, Pakistan would, as part of the bilateral deal, make a commitment to the United States not to divert material from the civilian plant to a military program. In this situation, the United States would ask the IAEA to verify, through inspections, that Pakistani authorities were living up to their end of the deal. IAEA inspections were, therefore, always voluntary, and monitoring happened at the discretion of the contracting states. Later, when the NPT (a separate treaty enacted in the 1970s, in which member states that did not already have nuclear weapons committed not to acquire them) needed a verification mechanism, the members turned to the IAEA. Thus, joining the IAEA without joining the NPT did not entail any actual commitments, since members of the IAEA were not bound to accept any particular inspections or limitations; they simply had the option of using the IAEA to verify any limitations they chose to accept on themselves.

concern and began to pressure other states, including China, to conform to a basic set of principles. From this point on, it makes sense to think about China in terms of our theory.[5] We divide our analysis here into two time periods: the late 1980s until the mid-1990s, and then the mid-1990s until today. In both of these periods, China faced relatively good outside options and Chinese second-order cooperation was not generally seen as being indispensable. Yet, beginning in the mid-1990s, nonproliferation became a more important priority for the United States, and the kind of strategic calculations Beijing faced began to change subtly (even though the eventual outcome was similar).

5.2.1 Chinese Behavior from the Late 1980s through Mid-1990s

During this first period, although the United States treated the proliferation of nuclear weapons as a serious issue, it was seldom at the top of the American global agenda. Chinese leaders, in general, understood that the United States would be likely to consistently pursue a policy of nonproliferation when it didn't contradict other American priorities and when the costs of pursuing such a policy were relatively low. At the same time, Chinese and American interests were generally aligned. So, from the Chinese perspective, China's outside options were good.

A number of individual incidents throughout the early 1980s made nuclear proliferation a more important agenda item than it had previously been. In the background, the United States and the Soviet Union made advances in arms control themselves. As the threat of a superpower arms race receded, however, the Iranian revolution and rising political instability in Pakistan and in other countries that had previously been recipients of nuclear technology transfers seemed to raise the stakes of global coordination on an inspections and monitoring regime. As a result, the United States began to exert more pressure on China to conform to an emerging norm of tighter controls, and China was more receptive as it began to see its own interests being aligned more with a tighter regime.[6] As Evan

[5] China, like France, did not sign the NPT until 1992. However, even though the PRC was not a party to the treaty, cooperation on nonproliferation issues could still conceivably have occurred. So, once the United States and China both believed that there was the potential for joint gains for cooperating on the nonproliferation issue, it became a situation that falls under the scope of our argument (on our scope conditions, see Section 2.1 in Chapter 2).

[6] On South Asia and Russia, see Susan Turner Haynes, *Chinese Nuclear Proliferation: How Global Politics Is Transforming China's Weapons Buildup and Modernization* (Lincoln: University of Nebraska Press, 2016), p. 110. On the general Chinese shift

Medeiros explains, there followed a series of individual cases throughout the 1980s involving nuclear energy agreements between China and various other countries, including Algeria, Israel, Pakistan, and South Africa. In each of these, the United States was able to convince China to change its behavior and restrict some of its technology transfers.[7]

By the end of the 1980s and the early 1990s, then, nonproliferation was an issue of mutual concern for the United States and China. As the issue became a priority for China, however, it became an even higher priority for the United States. In particular, it became clear to everyone that the United States was willing to go to great lengths to stop proliferation, including sacrificing other policy goals. The United States pressured allies (like Brazil and South Korea) and adversaries (like North Korea and Iraq) alike to observe norms of nuclear restraint. Here, noting the distinction between first-order indispensability and second-order indispensability is important. From a first-order perspective, traditional nuclear nonproliferation strategy is a "weakest link" public good – among those countries that have usable nuclear technology, a system of multilateral safeguards is generally only as good as the safeguards in whichever country is laxest. Among nuclear states, *every* country is indispensable. That is, every country needs to comply with the regime for it to work.[8]

around this period, see Stephanie Lieggi, "From Proliferator to Model Citizen? China's Recent Enforcement of Nonproliferation-related Trade Controls and Its Potential Positive Impact in the Region," *Strategic Studies*, Vol. 4, no. 2 (2010), pp. 39–62. See also Hongyu Zhang, "From Opponent to Proponent: The Rational Evolution of China's Nuclear Nonproliferation Policy," *Asian Politics & Policy*, Vol. 7, no. 2 (2015), pp. 283–301; and Rosemary Foot and Andrew Walter, *China, the United States, and Global Order* (New York: Cambridge University Press, 2010). On the precipitous drop in nuclear exports of concern by Chinese state-owned firms in particular, see Daniel Salisbury and Lucy Jones, "Exploring the Changing Role of Chinese Entities in WMD Proliferation," *The China Quarterly*, Vol. 225 (2016), pp. 50–72.

[7] Medeiros, *Reluctant Restraint*, pp. 61–72.

[8] On weakest-link public goods, see Simon Vicary and Todd Sandler, "Weakest-Link Public Goods: Giving In-kind or Transferring Money," *European Economic Review*, Vol. 46, no. 8 (2002), pp. 1501–20. Note that in this context we are referring to "nonproliferation" as a system designed to prevent countries from acquiring the technology and material to produce nuclear weapons. Policy analysts distinguish "nonproliferation" from "counterproliferation" – a policy of taking active, sometimes military measures to target and destroy a state's nuclear infrastructure or even destroy the regime itself; we return to this distinction later. Although nonproliferation is a weakest-link public good, counterproliferation is not; a counterproliferation strategy only requires one state that is willing, itself, to pay the costs of carrying out an attack. Thus, Chinese first-order cooperation would be necessary for a US–led program of *nonproliferation* but not for a US–led program of *counterproliferation*.

Consider, as an analogy, the citizens of a town stacking sandbags along the bank of a river whose waters are rising. Suppose each citizen stacks sandbags along a designated section of the riverbank. Here, the effectiveness of the makeshift levy will not depend on the average efforts of the citizens or on the efforts of the most productive citizen. Rather, whether their makeshift levy succeeds or fails depends on how effective it is at its weakest point, so that the efforts of the most ineffective citizen determine whether or not the entire town is flooded.[9] This is the situation with first-order cooperation to prevent nuclear proliferation. If a state seeks to divert nuclear technology to a military purpose, what matters is the supplier with the weakest safeguards – the break in the levy. So, from the 1980s on, China (like every other nuclear state) was *first-order indispensable.* Given that a regime existed, it could not meaningfully function without Chinese compliance.

China was not, however, *second-order indispensable.* That is, as long as China and other major states complied with the regime, the United States seemed to be fully capable of sustaining multilateralism through its own efforts. In the example of the townspeople building a levy, it only takes one sheriff to establish an expectation that underperformers will be punished and that future rewards will only go to stalwart cooperators. Even if the sheriff would ideally prefer deputies to help, no one deputy is strictly indispensable. For example, even in the case of Iraq, where diplomacy ultimately broke down, the United States was able to maintain a reasonably strong regime during the 1990s, to the point that, by the 2003 invasion of Iraq, there were few other states willing to side overtly with a country that had seemed to be defying the nonproliferation regime.

In summary, from the late-1980s through the mid-1990s, the balance of outside options generally favored China, and the PRC was not indispensable. Because it could count on the United States to enforce the nonproliferation regime by punishing defectors (like Iraq) and by coercing other states to take action to punish defectors (like those states that refused to join US–led efforts to impose economic sanctions on Iraq), China could abide by the basic norms of the regime without making any substantial efforts to enforce the regime itself, while maintaining some confidence that the basic contours of the regime would remain in place. We therefore expect, and find, that China adopted an approach of general

[9] Jack Hirshleifer, "From Weakest-Link to Best-Shot: The Voluntary Provision of Public Goods," *Public Choice*, Vol. 41, no. 3 (1983), pp. 371–86. For the riverbank metaphor, see Richard Comes, "Dyke Maintenance and Other Stories: Some Neglected Types of Public Goods," *The Quarterly Journal of Economics*, Vol. 108, no. 1 (1993), pp. 259–71.

acceptance of the regime; it complied with the basic set of norms and institutions but did not play a part in leading or reproducing the system.

5.2.2 Chinese Behavior from the Mid-1990s to the Present

After the 1991 Gulf War revealed that the Iraqi nuclear program had been further along than Americans had suspected, many within the United States foreign policy community began to treat the proliferation of nuclear weapons as a graver security threat than they had previously. In terms of our argument about second-order cooperation, two things changed as the 1990s progressed. First, the United States began to see nuclear proliferation as a higher priority than it had before; from the American perspective, the near miss in Iraq portended a future in which hostile regional powers might threaten the United States with a nuclear strike. Second, the end of the Cold War seemed to loosen the kinds of constraints the United States faced, so that there were fewer countervailing forces in place when the United States was inclined to discipline a hostile state for failing to adhere to the regime. Together, these changes meant that the United States began to adopt a more assertive posture toward those states that were generally not in compliance with the international nonproliferation regime.

Although the factors underlying the strategic setting of nonproliferation issues were changing, they combined together to produce the same result for China. As before, Beijing was left with a relatively favorable balance of outside options in which China was not indispensable (albeit for different reasons than before). As long as the more assertive US approach to stemming nuclear proliferation did not intrude on China's core regional interests, China was generally better off accepting the US–led regime without either trying to revise it through hold-up or to invest in the system itself. The one exception was with respect to North Korea, which of course did involve China's perceived sphere of influence. We return to this point later.

In the 1990s, there was a movement in American foreign policy circles to question the resilience of the existing nonproliferation regime in the face of seeming challenges from Iraq. This led to a detailed public discussion of moving from "nonproliferation" (inspections designed to prevent states from building nuclear programs in the first place, typically organized through multilateral regimes) to a more assertive "counterproliferation" (military actions to stop proliferation, which would ideally be done through large coalitions reminiscent of the 1991 Gulf War but, crucially, could be managed entirely unilaterally by the United States if necessary).[10] These discussions anticipated the 2003 Iraq war, for which the publicly stated rationale was to physically eradicate Iraq's ability to produce unconventional weapons, given that the nonproliferation regime, centered on inspections, had not been able to create confidence in Iraqi compliance.[11] Even if the United States was *not* actually moving toward a strategy of direct counterproliferation, the mere fact that the debate within the United States was taking place underscores the extent to which many policymakers, at least in Washington, were increasingly pessimistic that the existing institutional architecture of the nuclear nonproliferation regime would continue to function.

From the US perspective, to be sure, counterproliferation strikes were unappealing. Naturally, then, American foreign policy makers sought cheaper ways to prevent proliferation, and the United States doubled down on making continued investments in the nonproliferation regime. In 1995, the United States led the negotiations around the indefinite extension of the NPT, and it negotiated an extension to the agreements underlying the IAEA's mission with the creation of a new "model protocol," which would be used in situations where the IAEA might have a mandate to inspect an entire country's nuclear sector, rather than simply particular sites, when the country's commitment to transparency was suspect.[12] This feedback cycle further served to keep China on the path of passive acceptance – a set of outside options that were bad for the United States led the United States to make further investments in strengthening the regime, which further obviated the need for China (or any other power) to make costly investments on its behalf.[13]

10 See, for example, Barry R. Schneider, *Future War and Counterproliferation: US Military Responses to NBC Proliferation Threats* (Westport, CT: Greenwood Publishing Group, 1999); Harald Müller and Mitchell Reiss, "Counterproliferation: Putting New Wine in Old Bottles," *The Washington Quarterly*, Vol. 18, no. 2 (1995), pp. 143–54. For a strategic analysis of the ways in which the logic of counterproliferation can lead to mistaken wars, see Muhammet A. Bas and Andrew J. Coe, "A Dynamic Theory of Nuclear Proliferation and Preventive War," *International Organization*, Vol. 70, no. 4 (2016), pp. 655–85.

11 Iraq was revealed, in the end, not to have had a nuclear program by 2003. Still, the fear of an Iraqi nuclear program was a major contributor to the US decision to launch the attack.

12 Robert L. Brown, *Nuclear Authority: The IAEA and the Absolute Weapon* (Washington, DC: Georgetown University Press, 2015).

13 At the same time, however, there was a growing perception that the sensitive intelligence that states shared with the IAEA raised the stakes for which states had more influence in governance of the agency. Allison Carnegie and Austin Carson, "The Disclosure

The PRC, of course, was not entirely inert. China tacitly supported US efforts at the 1995 review conference and, prior to the later 2000 NPT review conference, Beijing made an exception to its ban on arms control talks with the United States (enacted in the wake of the US bombing of the Chinese embassy in Belgrade), allowing US and Chinese diplomats to present a joint slate of proposals for the conference – ultimately securing a rare joint statement from attendees.[14] After 2009, when the Obama administration inaugurated a series of "nuclear security summits" designed to elicit high-profile public commitments from heads of state on proliferation issues, China again tacitly supported the initiatives but without making any costly investments on its own.[15]

China's approach to the ongoing conflict between the United States (as the leader of the nonproliferation regime) and Iran is instructive. Throughout the late 1990s and early 2000s the United States grew increasingly suspicious that Iran was investing in a substantial secret nuclear program that would give it the ability to produce a weapon in violation of its commitment to the NPT. Upon discovering evidence that Iran was cheating (as a result of the kind of heightened IAEA inspections that emerged in the mid-1990s), the United States tried to induce China to join in sanctions. At first those inducements took the form of persuasion; later the United States threatened individual Chinese banks that did business in Iran. Although China had extensive and growing trade ties with Iran and saw Iran both as a potential source of energy and as a counterweight to US allies in the Middle East, Beijing eventually went along with the sanctions. China complied with sanctions on Iran but did not play a leadership role in negotiations or enforcement – in our language, this was an example solely of first-order cooperation but not second-order cooperation.[16]

Dilemma: Nuclear Intelligence and International Organizations," working paper (October 27, 2017). Available at SSRN: https://ssrn.com/abstract=3060677.

14 Medeiros, *Reluctant Restraint*, pp. 68–85.

15 Kelsey Davenport, "States Make New Nuclear Security Pledges," *Arms Control Today*, Vol. 42, no. 3 (2012), pp. 22. The purpose of Nuclear Security Summits was, effectively, to raise the international salience of existing commitments to regimes and to promote transparency in national commitments to regime compliance. The summits themselves were a clear example of US second-order regime provision. Given the overall effectiveness of the US effort relative to its goals, China has been generally supportive but has not played a leadership role. For an alternative view, that China has in fact been playing an important role in designing and upholding nonproliferation norms behind the scenes, see Nicola Horsburgh, *China and Global Nuclear Order: From Estrangement to Active Engagement* (London: Oxford University Press, 2015).

16 On the gradual moves in Beijing to agree to join international sanctions against Iran for its noncompliance with international nonproliferation norms, see Thomas J. Christensen,

Again, that China remained firmly in the "accept" approach to the issue is consistent with our theory. In principle, at least, China could have played hold-up, threatening to torpedo the international regime unless it won some sort of concessions on nuclear policy from the United States. This, however, was unlikely. China would have had very few demands to make in the first place. The option of allowing the United States to invest in and structure the regime to suit American preferences was, from China's perspective, not a bad outcome as, for the most part, American and Chinese interests were in line.[17] Consequently, a Chinese threat to hold out on cooperation would not have been credible. For similar reasons, China had no reason to go through the effort of constructing a multilateral solution to the Iran standoff, because there was little reason to think that a Chinese–led solution would have been better for China over the long run than a US–led solution.

North Korea's crisis with the nuclear regime, however, is an exception to this pattern; it is to this exception that we now turn.

5.3 NORTH KOREA'S NUCLEAR PROGRAM: INVESTING IN THE SIX PARTY TALKS

Since the 1990s, the North Korean nuclear weapons program has represented, arguably, the single greatest threat to stability in Northeast Asia. During the early 1990s, as the United States became increasingly convinced that North Korea (the Democratic People's Republic of Korea, or DPRK) was secretly developing nuclear weapons, a prolonged crisis

"Shaping the Choices of a Rising China: Recent Lessons for the Obama Administration," *The Washington Quarterly*, Vol. 32, no. 3 (2009), pp. 89–104. In a more recent study, while Christensen sees China as largely complying with UN sanctions against Iran, he also notes that China tried to water these sanctions down and that "most of the real international pressure on Iran" came from the United States and other leading economies. And although Christensen notes that China at times played a positive role in the run-up to the 2015 Iran nuclear agreement by, for instance, pushing Russia to be more willing to bargain, he is ambivalent about whether China's net role was constructive (facilitating an eventual agreement) or not. Thomas J. Christensen, *The China Challenge: Shaping the Choices of a Rising Power* (New York: W. W. Norton & Company), pp. 277–89, pp. 317–18. See also John W. Garver, "Is China Playing a Dual Game in Iran?" *The Washington Quarterly*, Vol. 34, no. 1 (2011), pp. 75–88; Joel Wuthnow, "Posing Problems without an Alliance: China–Iran Relations after the Nuclear Deal." *Strategic Forum*, no. 290 (Washington, DC: National Defense University Press, 2016).

17 Christensen, "Shaping the Choices of a Rising China," argues that this fundamental congruence of interests made eventual cooperation likely; despite some of its rhetoric, China fundamentally benefited from the set of international norms that Iran was violating.

erupted over the program and the terms of international inspections. As the crisis reached its climax in 1994, the Clinton administration considered the possibility of a military strike on North Korea to eliminate the program. Clinton ultimately decided against the strike because of the potentially devastating consequences of a new Korean war and, instead, pursued diplomacy that culminated in the 1994 Agreed Framework. By the early 2000s, the United States under the George W. Bush administration concluded that North Korea was again pursuing a clandestine nuclear program; this led to a renewed crisis on the Korean Peninsula. Fears of military conflict spiked as Pyongyang withdrew from the NPT in 2003, warning that efforts to punish the country's actions with sanctions would be viewed in North Korea as a "declaration of war."[18] North Korea first conducted a nuclear test in 2006, and has conducted several additional tests since then.

China's diplomatic behavior relating to international attempts to rein in North Korea's nuclear program has varied substantially since the 1990s. During the first nuclear crisis (1993–1994), although China at times played a helpful, behind-the-scenes role, Beijing for the most part was passive and emphasized that the United States and North Korea should find a bilateral solution to the nuclear issue. In the context of our theory, China's behavior was largely accepting of US leadership in constructing new institutions to manage the North Korean nuclear issue, and China's behavior in this regard was largely consistent with its approach to nonproliferation issues more generally. In 2003, however, Beijing began to play a more proactive, institution-building role, most notably by establishing the Six Party Talks as a forum for finding a solution to the issue. That is, whereas China's approach to nuclear nonproliferation has generally fallen squarely within our "accept" category, its approach to the North Korean nuclear issue, for a period of time during the 2000s, represents an exception, where Chinese behavior is more consistent with our "invest" category. More recently, however, China's behavior relating to the North Korean nuclear program has again become more passive (more resembling "accept"); since 2009, the 6PT mechanism has been moribund.

How can we explain this variation in China's willingness to show leadership in seeking a solution to the North Korean nuclear issue? In this section, we show that China's changing outside options – relative to

[18] "North Korea Warns against Act of War," *CNN Online*, January 22, 2003: www.cnn.com/2003/WORLD/asiapcf/east/01/22/koreas.un.

those of the United States – helped shape Chinese behavior relating to the DPRK. In the early 1990s, China's outside options were quite strong. Beijing doubted that Pyongyang possessed a robust nuclear weapons program and appeared to doubt that the United States would risk war over the issue. To the degree that Beijing believed the US unilateral option was likely to be a diplomatic one, it had reason to free-ride on US efforts. However, China's outside options worsened considerably during the 2002–2003 crisis, as Beijing appeared more worried (particularly in the lead-up to and early days of the Iraq War) that Washington might exercise a unilateral military option to address the problem. In this context, the PRC made the decision to invest in building institutions that would facilitate a diplomatic solution. After playing a proactive role within the 6PT, Beijing would later become more passive, especially during the Obama administration. We suggest that this shift back to more passive acceptance of the status quo in North Korea reflects both skepticism at the feasibility of a diplomatic solution and reduced fears of military conflict over the nuclear issue. Beijing's relative outside options, in other words, again improved.

5.3.1 The First Nuclear Crisis (1993–1994)

The first North Korean nuclear crisis evolved from tensions between the United States and North Korea over the questions of whether the North possessed nuclear weapons and whether the IAEA had the authority to carry out inspections. Encouraged by the United States, the two Koreas had agreed to a denuclearization declaration in 1992, and North Korea subsequently signed a safeguards agreement with the IAEA. Yet when IAEA inspections revealed significant discrepancies with North Korea's declaration, Pyongyang refused to grant inspectors access to additional sites and, shortly thereafter, announced its intention to withdraw from the NPT. The announcement triggered a crisis that appeared resolved with North Korea's decision to cancel its withdrawal and sign the 1994 Agreed Framework with the United States.[19]

The United States stood at the center of the largely informal regime seeking to resolve this crisis, and bargaining over the terms of an agreement took place primarily in bilateral negotiations between the United

[19] On the crisis, see Don Oberdorfer, *The Two Koreas: A Contemporary History* (New York: Basic Books, 2001); Scott Snyder, *China's Rise and the Two Koreas: Politics, Economics, Security* (Boulder, CO: Lynne Rienner Publishers, 2009).

States and North Korea. Three formal rounds of talks were held, supplemented by informal diplomatic contacts; the 1994 Agreed Framework was ultimately a product of bilateral United States–North Korea negotiations, though the United States coordinated its negotiating stance with its regional allies South Korea and Japan.[20] China stayed largely on the periphery of this regime, though (as noted earlier) it was represented in the organizations charged with enforcing the NPT, including the IAEA and the UNSC.

As we are focused on second-order cooperation, the balance of outside options in this case refers specifically to Beijing's expectations of what would happen, both to China and to the United States, if China declined to invest in institutions to manage North Korea's nuclear program. How bad would China's non-participation be for China relative to the outside options of the United States? Exit options for the United States appeared to be quite bad; US officials were alarmed that North Korea was moving rapidly to acquire nuclear weapons capabilities, the Clinton administration was under enormous domestic pressure to resolve the issue, and it was clear that a military option would be tremendously costly.[21] The United States, thus, had strong incentives to invest in the construction of new institutions to manage North Korea's nuclear program; these institutions ultimately took the form of the Agreed Framework. Given its preference for stability,[22] China certainly would have had reason to welcome

[20] For a good overview of the rounds, see Joel S. Wit, Daniel B. Poneman, and Robert L. Gallucci, *Going Critical: The First North Korean Nuclear Crisis* (Washington, DC: Brookings Institution Press, 2004).

[21] Oberdorfer, *The Two Koreas*; Wit, Poneman, and Gallucci, *Going Critical.*

[22] Most analysts view China's primary goal relating to North Korea as stability, meaning the absence of military conflict on the peninsula and the continued functioning of the North Korean regime. See, e.g., Avery Goldstein, "Across the Yalu: China's Interests and the Korean Peninsula in a Changing World," in *New Directions in the Study of China's Foreign Policy*, eds. Alastair Iain Johnston and Robert S. Ross (Stanford, CA: Stanford University Press, 2006), pp. 131–61; Jeremy Paltiel, "China and the North Korean Crisis: The Diplomacy of Great Power Transition," in *North Korea's Second Nuclear Crisis and Northeast Asian Security*, eds. Seung-Ho Joo and Tai-Hwan Kwak (Hampshire: Ashgate, 2007), pp. 94–109; John S. Park, "Inside Multilateralism: The Six-Party Talks," *The Washington Quarterly*, Vol. 28, no. 4 (Autumn 2005), p. 83; Andrew Scobell, *China and North Korea: From Comrades in Arms to Allies at Arms-Length* (Carlisle, PA: US Army War College Strategic Studies Institute, March 1, 2004), online at: www.strategicstudiesinstitute.army.mil/pubs/display.cfm?PubID=373, accessed August 10, 2010; Snyder, *China's Rise and the Two Koreas*; Anne Wu, "What China Whispers to North Korea," *The Washington Quarterly*, Vol. 28, no. 2 (Spring 2005), pp. 36–7; Zhu Feng, "Flawed Mediation and a Compelling Mission: Chinese Diplomacy in the Six-Party Talks to Denuclearise North Korea," *East Asia*, Vol. 28, no. 3 (September 2011), pp. 207, 214.

the creation of new institutions on the peninsula that would lead to a reduction of tensions. Nevertheless, there are at least two reasons to think that China's outside options during the first nuclear crisis were relatively favorable compared with the outside options of the United States.

First, unlike Washington, which viewed the North Korean nuclear program with considerable alarm, Chinese leaders and analysts appear to have doubted the seriousness of Pyongyang's nuclear ambitions. In public statements, PRC leaders at times expressed considerable uncertainty in this regard. Premier Li Peng, for example, in June 1994 emphasized that China needed more information as Beijing's "knowledge was incomplete."[23] Foreign Minister Qian Qichen had likewise noted, in April 1994, that China was "not well-informed" about North Korea's program.[24] And after meeting with Chinese officials that same month, Australian Foreign Minister Gareth Evans came away with the impression that "China does not think North Korea has developed the capability to build nuclear weapons."[25] Furthermore, numerous Chinese analysts and editorial writers were openly skeptical of US claims of a North Korean nuclear weapons program.[26] As Robert Sutter – a leading American expert on Chinese foreign policy – puts it, "[f]or many years after the Cold War, Chinese officials adopted a stance that assumed North Korean nuclear

[23] "Li Peng Seeks Data from IAEA on DPRK Nuclear Program," *Hong Kong Agence France Presse*, June 13, 1994 (in *FBIS-China*, June 13, 1994, p. 3).

[24] "Qian Qichen: China 'Not Well-Informed' on North Korean Nuclear Development," *Kyodo News Service*, April 30, 1994 (reported by *BBC Summary of World Broadcasts*, in *LexisNexis*, May 2, 1994).

[25] See "Australian FM: PRC Thinks DPRK Has No Nuclear Capability," *Melbourne Radio Australia*, April 2, 1994 (in *FBIS-China*, April 4, 1994). A Japanese news service also reported in July 1994 – based on an internal CCP document – that Chinese high-ranking officials believed North Korea's nuclear program did not constitute a significant threat. See "Beijing Reportedly Believes Pyongyang's Nuclear Programme Poses No Real Threat," *Kyodo News Service*, July 3, 1994 (reported by *BBC Summary of World Broadcasts*, in *LexisNexis*, July 4, 1994).

[26] See, for instance, Gao E, "Lengzhanhou de Chaoxian Bandao xingshi" [The Post–Cold War Situation on the Korean Peninsula], *Yafei Zongheng*, no. 3 (1994), pp. 12–14; Guo Wen, "Chao Mei hezhengduan de lailongqumai" [The Origins and Development of the United States–North Korea Nuclear Dispute], *Guoji Zhanwang*, no. 13 (1994), pp. 11–13; Tian Zhongqing, "Fengyun bianhuan de Chaoxian Bandao jushi" [The Constantly Changing Situation on the Korean Peninsula], *Guoji Zhanwang*, no. 7 (1993), pp. 9–11; "Delicate 'Nuclear Inspection' Diplomacy of [the] United States and North Korea," *Wen Wei Po*, July 13, 1993 (in *FBIS-China*, July 26, 1993, p. 1); Zhang Liangui, "Chaoxian Bandao Hewenti Zongheng Tan" [A Broad Discussion of the Korean Peninsula Nuclear Issue], *Guoji Shehui yu Jingji*, no. 9 (1994), pp. 1–5.

weapons development was unlikely or remote."[27] If Beijing doubted that North Korea had a serious nuclear weapons program, it suggests in turn that China viewed the stakes as being lower than they were viewed in Washington – which was more convinced that the North's nuclear program posed a significant threat.

Second, there are reasons to think that the PRC, at the time, would have doubted the likelihood of a military conflict on the Korean Peninsula, questioning in particular the resolve of the United States to undertake actions – such as a unilateral military strike against North Korea's nuclear facilities – that could trigger a wider war. Thomas Christensen, for instance, has written about the widespread prevalence of a "Somalia analogy" in Chinese strategic thinking about the United States in the late 1990s, observing that many Chinese strategic writings in the 1990s drew inferences from US behavior during its humanitarian intervention in Somalia in 1992–1994.[28] In particular, the Clinton administration's 1993 decision to withdraw US troops from combat operations after eighteen US service members lost their lives led many Chinese analysts to conclude that the United States was highly casualty-averse.[29] Christensen found similar sentiments in his own interviews with Chinese foreign policy elites during the second half of the 1990s; many of his interlocutors were skeptical in particular of US resolve to sustain significant casualties in the event of a conflict in the Taiwan Strait.[30] While Christensen's analysis focused on China's perceptions of the willingness of the United States to intervene in a Taiwan Strait conflict, some commentary reflects a similar sort of skepticism in the context of North Korea. For instance, an article in the PRC–affiliated Hong Kong daily *Hsin Wan Pao* discounted the possibility of war on the peninsula, noting that the DPRK "cannot afford a war" given its backward state, while emphasizing that the United States lacked resolve.[31] There are reasons to think, in short, that Beijing at the

[27] Robert G. Sutter, *Chinese Foreign Relations: Power and Policy since the Cold War* (Lanham, MD: Rowman and Littlefield, 2008), p. 249.

[28] Thomas J. Christensen, "Posing Problems without Catching Up: China's Rise and Challenges for U.S. Security Policy," *International Security*, Vol. 25, no. 4 (Spring 2001), pp. 5–40. See especially pp. 17–20.

[29] Christensen notes that other US interventions also contributed to this conclusion, such as the 1991 Gulf War (which involved relatively limited US casualties) and, later, the NATO decision to limit its actions in Yugoslavia to an air campaign.

[30] Christensen, "Posing Problems," pp. 17–20.

[31] The editorial notes: "Clinton is full of worries and dares not make any decision, even when thinking for a long time about dispatching troops to Haiti to deal with the 7,500-strong Haitian armed forces, who are equipped only with obsolete firearms dating back to World War II, so he certainly will not provoke the DPRK troops." See "Daily

time discounted the likelihood of the United States exercising a unilateral military option that could trigger war on the Korean Peninsula. This belief that the United States would be unlikely to unilaterally "solve" North Korea with an invasion that would run counter to China's interests, combined with Beijing's skepticism of the seriousness of North Korea's nuclear weapons program in the first place, made China's outside option, relative to the United States, seem quite strong.

Meanwhile, Chinese leaders appeared to believe that the United States had the ability to find a solution without extensive Chinese assistance. That is, Chinese leaders did not view extensive Chinese participation as indispensable for regime success in this case. Chinese officials, for instance, were insistent throughout the crisis that they saw it as a matter to be dealt with by the DPRK, the United States, the IAEA, and South Korea.[32] Beijing, moreover, seemed to believe that its influence over North Korea was relatively limited.[33]

Our theoretical framework thus predicts mostly passive Chinese behavior, which we term "accept." That is, Beijing, with a favorable balance of outside options and facing widely held expectations that China's participation was not indispensable for cooperation to succeed, would take a back seat to a country (the United States) with more to lose in the event cooperation failed. Broadly speaking, this prediction is consistent with actual Chinese behavior during the crisis.

This is not to suggest that Chinese behavior was counterproductive; indeed, at times it was supportive of US efforts. China, for instance, often served as a conduit for US messages to North Korea, and Chinese officials appear to have pressed North Korea to bargain in good faith with

Discounts War Possibilities in DPRK, Bosnia," *Hsin Wan Pao*, June 15, 1994 (in *FBIS-China*, June 15, 1994). Zhang Liangui, a leading Chinese expert on North Korea, also downplayed the likelihood of a US attack in 1994 (though the most intense phase of the crisis had already passed when he wrote the article). See Zhang, "Chaoxian Bandao Hewenti Zongheng Tan," p. 4. To be clear, these data points are only suggestive, and it is hard to know how widely shared these views were among PRC foreign policy elites.

32 See, for instance, comments made by Foreign Ministry spokesperson Wu Jianmin on May 13, 1993, in "On DPRK Nuclear Inspections," *Zhongguo Xinwen She*, May 13, 1993 (in *FBIS-China*, May 13, 1993, p. 2). See also remarks by Jiang Zemin in "China Opposes Sanctions on DPRK," *Tokyo NHK General Television Network*, June 10, 1994 (in *FBIS-China*, June 13, 1994, p. 1).

33 Snyder, *China's Rise and the Two Koreas*. See also Samuel S. Kim, "The Making of China's Korea Policy in the Era of Reform," in David M. Lampton, ed., *The Making of Chinese Foreign and Security Policy* (Stanford, CA: Stanford University Press, 2001), p. 393.

the United States.[34] More concretely, in March 1994 China agreed to support a UNSC presidential statement that called on North Korea to allow the IAEA to complete inspections in the country. The statement did not threaten sanctions, but it did warn of future UNSC consideration if needed.[35]

Still, despite some behind-the-scenes efforts to facilitate a solution during the crisis as an intermediary,[36] China's behavior was largely secondary to the more central bargaining occurring between the United States and North Korea.[37] China's reluctance to play a more central role was again confirmed when the United States and North Korea ultimately signed the Agreed Framework to end the crisis: Beijing declined to join the international consortium (the Korean Peninsula Energy Development Organization) charged with supplying North Korea with light-water reactors to replace its graphite reactors. China had less to lose than other key players – particularly the United States – if cooperation over the North's nuclear program fell apart. To be clear, in theory Beijing could have dealt (or tried to deal) with the crisis in other ways. For instance, the PRC might have taken a more active role in negotiations, leveraging its historical ties with North Korea to push the DPRK toward an agreement. China might also have contributed more actively to the construction of institutions that might help keep the peace on the Korea Peninsula after the crisis was defused in 1994, perhaps linking such efforts to US concessions on other issues like Taiwan (hold-up). But PRC policy during 1993–1994 most closely resembles our category of passive acceptance.

Because we cannot observe Chinese decision-making directly, it is admittedly difficult to determine decisively how important a factor outside options were in motivating China's behavior during the 1993–1994 crisis. We have provided evidence to suggest that China likely viewed its outside options as strong relative to the United States and did not view its contributions as indispensable to successful resolution; we then demonstrate that observed PRC behavior during the crisis is consistent with our

[34] See especially Wit, Poneman, and Gallucci, *Going Critical*, p. 198. The authors describe China's role as "nuanced – but ultimately helpful." China wanted to avoid siding too closely with North Korea, but also did not want to "openly 'gang up' on them."

[35] Wit, Poneman, and Gallucci, *Going Critical*, p. 159.

[36] As Snyder, *China's Rise and the Two Koreas*, p. 117, emphasizes, Beijing worried about further damaging its relationship with North Korea, already strained following China's diplomatic recognition of Seoul in 1992.

[37] For a similar characterization of PRC behavior in 1994 as largely "hands-off," see Park, "Inside Multilateralism," p. 81. Snyder, *China's Rise and the Two Koreas*, p. 117, also sees North Korea as playing a "passive role in managing the crisis."

theoretical expectations of the way China should have behaved given this configuration of strategic variables. But other factors outside of our theory were likely salient as well. For instance, China had only established diplomatic ties with South Korea in 1992, and Samuel Kim notes that normalization of relations with Seoul met considerable resistance from conservatives in Beijing.[38] This resistance, in turn, likely contributed to Beijing's pained efforts to appear balanced in its approach to the two Koreas in subsequent years – that is, to avoid any appearance of "ganging up" on North Korea.[39] We return to a consideration of alternative explanations in the conclusion to this chapter, but first we turn to the second nuclear crisis that erupted on the Korean Peninsula, in early 2003.

5.3.2 The Second Nuclear Crisis and the Establishment of the 6PT (2003)

As a new crisis over North Korea's nuclear program arose in early 2003, China's outside options (relative to the United States) had worsened considerably in comparison to the 1993–1994 crisis. In contrast to the early 1990s, by 2003 Chinese officials and analysts had become more convinced of the seriousness of North Korea's nuclear weapons program.[40] Particularly after North Korea announced in April 2003 that it had nuclear weapons,[41] some prominent Chinese analysts became increasingly worried about the implications of a nuclear North Korea for stability in the region. Yu Meihua, for instance, argued that the nuclear crisis had the potential to intensify arms races in the region and possibly lead to a "nuclear domino effect," as it would give "certain other countries in the region" an excuse to pursue nuclear weapons themselves.[42]

38 Kim, "The Making of China's Korea Policy in the Era of Reform."

39 Snyder, *China's Rise and the Two Koreas*, p. 117.

40 Sutter, *Chinese Foreign Relations*, p. 249, writes that "Beginning in late 2002, Chinese officials appeared more convinced by US and other evidence that North Korea had indeed developed nuclear weapons and was determined to build more." This view is reflected in the work of some Chinese analysts writing in 2003. See, for instance, Xu Weidi, "Chaoxian Bandao Heweiji de Huajie yu Bandao Zouchu Lengzhan" [Resolving the Korean Peninsula Nuclear Crisis and Moving beyond the Cold War on the Peninsula], *Shijie Jingji yu Zhengzhi*, no. 9 (2003), pp. 59–64; Zhang Liangui, "Chaohe Wenti Youyao Shengji?" [Will the Korean Nuclear Issue Intensify Once Again?], *Shijie Zhishi*, no. 12 (2003), pp. 22–23.

41 "North Korea Says It Now Possesses Nuclear Arsenal," *The New York Times*, April 25, 2003, p. 1 (in *LexisNexis*).

42 Luo Jie, "Zhongguo weishenme jiji cucheng liufang huitan: fang Chaoxian Bandao wenti zhuanjia Yu Meihua" [Why China Actively Facilitated the Six Party Talks: An

Moreover, the expected costs to China of US unilateralism were substantially higher than in 1993–1994, because this time a potentially highly destabilizing US military strike was seen as a significant possibility, with many Chinese analysts believing the crisis had the potential to escalate violently.[43] Some analysts pointed in particular to the hawkish views of certain officials within the Bush administration, along with the Bush administration's embrace of a doctrine of preventive war, as causes for concern.[44] While there was a general sense that the war in Iraq (beginning in March 2003) acted as a constraint on US actions in North Korea in the short run, some analysts worried that the United States would turn its attention to North Korea as military operations in Iraq drew to a close. Prominent international relations expert Shi Yinhong wrote, for instance, that "the rapid victory at low cost" the United States achieved in Iraq would likely encourage a somewhat more hawkish approach to

---

Interview with Korean Peninsula Expert Yu Meihua], *Shijie Zhishi*, no. 18 (2003), p. 25. Other accounts that emphasize Chinese worries about a nuclear North Korea triggering regional instability include Mike Chinoy, *Meltdown: The Inside Story of the North Korean Nuclear Crisis* (New York: St. Martins Press, 2008), p. 164; Scobell, *China and North Korea*, p. 12; Susan L. Shirk, *China: Fragile Superpower: How China's Internal Politics Could Derail Its Peaceful Rise* (New York: Oxford University Press, 2007), p. 123. Zhang Liangui likewise notes that North Korea's nuclear declaration had the potential to stimulate a regional arms race. See Zhang, "Chaohe Wenti Youyao Shengji," p. 22. Zhang highlighted similar concerns in the aftermath of North Korea's first nuclear test three years later. See Zhang Liangui, "Coping with a Nuclear North Korea," *China Security*, no. 4 (2006), pp. 2–18.

43 See, for example: Zhang, "Chaoxian Wenti Youyao Sheji"; Zhang Liangui, "Chaoxian de Hewuqi yu Meiguo de Jingcha Juese" [North Korea's Nuclear Weapons and America's Role as Policeman], *Zhanlue yu Guanli*, no. 5 (2003), pp. 65–77; Lu Yousheng, "Can the U.S. Win Two Wars Simultaneously?" *Liaowang*, January 27, 2003 (in *World News Connection*, February 14, 2003); Shi Yinhong, "Weixian he xiwang: Yilake Zhanzheng beijingxia de Chaoxian he wenti" [Danger and Hope: The North Korean Nuclear Issue against the Backdrop of the Iraq War], *Jiaoxue yu Yanjiu*, no. 5 (2003), pp. 50–53; Sun Cheng, "Dierci Chaoxian heweiji" [The Second North Korean Nuclear Crisis], *Guoji Wenti Yanjiu*, no. 3 (2003), pp. 15–19. Note that many analysts – even if highlighting the danger of US military action – also acknowledged some of the constraints on a US military strike (such as opposition from US allies in the region and high potential casualties). See, for example, Lu, "Can the U.S. Win Two Wars Simultaneously?" See also Zhu Feng, "Bushi zhengfu de bandao zhengce yu Chaoxian heweiji" [The Bush Administration's Peninsula Policy and the North Korean Nuclear Crisis], *Xiandai Guoji Guanxi*, no. 2 (2003), pp. 1–7. For a more skeptical view on the US willingness to escalate, see "The North Korean Nuclear Crisis Escalates Again," *Ta Kung Pao*, January 3, 2003 (in *World News Connection*, January 8, 2003). For a concurring view, see Snyder, *China's Rise and the Two Koreas*, p. 150.

44 See, e.g., Shi, "Weixian he xiwang," and Cheng, "Dierci Chaoxian heweiji." See also "If the Foreign Powers Neglect the Position of the DPRK, the DPRK Will Reveal Its Own Strength," *Wen Wei Po*, July 19, 2003 (in *World News Connection*, July 24, 2003).

North Korea.[45] Finally, China became more reliant on FDI to achieve its economic goals in the years after the first nuclear crisis; in turn, Chinese leaders were more sensitive to external instability – including instability on the Korean Peninsula – that could put FDI flows at risk.[46] In short, there is reason to think that the balance of outside options in 2003 was considerably worse for China than was the case during the 1993–1994 crisis.

China, of course, could conceivably have adopted a relatively hands-off approach to the 2003 nuclear crisis, as it had in 1993–1994. Yet this time, China instead pursued a policy of investing in institutions to manage the nuclear issue. After concluding that the Bush administration would continue to rule out the bilateral (United States–DPRK) talks demanded by North Korea to deal with the crisis, China – which had previously balked at the notion of a trilateral dialogue involving the PRC – coaxed North Korea to attend a trilateral meeting (United States, China, and North Korea) in Beijing in April 2003.[47] When talks went poorly and the United States insisted that future meetings include Japan and South Korea, China again took the lead in convincing North Korea to take part in a larger forum, the Six Party Talks, which commenced in August 2003 in Beijing.[48] Beijing's efforts in this regard carried significant risks: most importantly, Beijing risked harming the long-standing "lips and teeth" alliance with North Korea, undercutting Beijing's longer-term influence in the DPRK.

45 Shi, "Weixian he Xiwang," p. 51. See also Lu, "Can the U.S. Win Two Wars Simultaneously?" and "Ta Kung Pao Article Says DPRK to Go Nuclear if War Erupts with US," *Ta Kung Pao*, March 6, 2003 (in *World News Connection*, March 10, 2003). Zhu, "Bushi zhengfu de bandao zhengce yu Chaoxian heweiji," writing before the start of the Iraq war, saw the coming war in Iraq as something that would make military action on the Korean Peninsula much more difficult for the United States. But he also notes (p. 7), in conclusion, that the second nuclear crisis (compared to the 1993–1994 crisis) had a much greater chance of ending badly ("dierci Chao heweiji jiu qi xingzhi he keneng fasheng de xiaoji houguo er yan yijing yuanyuan chaoguole diyici"), and that the potential for military conflict could not be ruled out.

46 See especially Park, "Inside Multilateralism," pp. 81–2, on this point. See also John S. Park, "North Korean Crisis: China Shows the Way to Pyongyang," *International Herald Tribune*, May 14, 2004. Based on interviews in Beijing, Park argues that Chinese leaders analyzed the post–2002 nuclear crisis primarily from a "cost-benefit standpoint in terms of how the crisis" was impacting economic objectives.

47 Chinoy, *Meltdown*.

48 Chinoy, *Meltdown*, p. 179, writes that China promised North Korea that China would play a mediating role in talks, increase aid to North Korea, and encourage the United States to pledge nonaggression in exchange for nuclear disarmament.

In the years immediately after 2003, China's behavior as 6PT host continued to be proactive – at least to some extent. PRC officials often pushed the United States to be more flexible in its approach in the 6PT and sometimes offered solutions when the talks reached an impasse. Over the course of the various rounds, all adopted texts were drafted by Beijing.[49] China played an important role in facilitating the September 19 Declaration of 2005, as PRC officials drafted several different versions of the agreement and pushed North Korean and American officials to compromise.[50] And Chinese pressure on Pyongyang appears to have been decisive in restarting productive dialogue in the aftermath of North Korea's 2006 nuclear test, culminating in the February 2007 action plan.[51] In sum, by initiating the 6PT in 2003, Beijing played a central role in restructuring the basic institutional framework dealing with the North Korean nuclear issue, and China in the years thereafter continued to invest some effort in finding a lasting solution to the North Korean nuclear issue within the 6PT framework.

To be clear, many different factors likely contributed to Beijing's decision to invest in the creation of the Six Party Talks, ranging from a desire to improve China's image abroad to the desire to improve the relationship

[49] That China decided on procedures in the 6PT is significant, because at other times when playing "host," notably APEC meetings held in Shanghai in 2001, China left the agenda up to the United States.

[50] PRC officials also actively sought to narrow the gaps between the United States and North Korean positions by, for instance, crafting language that helped the two sides overcome disagreements about whether denuclearization should include peaceful nuclear programs in North Korea. Chinese officials likewise found a way to address last-minute US concerns about the use of the term "peaceful coexistence" in the declaration without losing North Korean support. Chinoy, *Meltdown*, pp. 243–9. A consistent analysis is Avery Goldstein, "Power Transitions, Institutions, and China's Rise in East Asia: Theoretical Expectations and Evidence," *Journal of Strategic Studies*, Vol. 30, no. 4–5 (2007), pp. 639–82.

[51] In addition to relatively harsh criticism of the North Korean nuclear test and support for UN sanctions imposed in the aftermath of the test, China also took behind-the-scenes steps, such as scaling back military-to-military cooperation with the North Korean regime. See Victor Cha, *The Impossible State: North Korea Past and Future* (New York: Harper Collins, 2013), p. 268. Thomas Christensen, who was present at the February 2007 session of the 6PT, likewise emphasizes Beijing's pressure on North Korea to negotiate in good faith (and cites Cha in this regard). See Christensen, *China Challenge*, p. 230. The February 2007 action plan laid out a series of steps the two sides would take to proceed with denuclearization of North Korea in line with the September 19 Agreement, and included, for instance, US shipments of fuel oil, and DPRK disclosures and shutting down of the Yongbyon facilities. As Cha and Christensen both note, the months following the February 2007 6PT session were the high point of the 6PT process. The text of the February 2007 agreement is available on the State Department webpage: https://2001-2009.state.gov/r/pa/prs/ps/2007/february/80479.htm.

with Washington following bilateral turbulence at the start of the George W. Bush administration.[52] But some PRC commentary at the time emphasized in particular the downside risks were China to stay on the sidelines; in other words, they stressed China's worsening outside options (noted earlier) as being a critical factor. Zhang Liangui, for instance, describes the establishment of the 6PT as a "crucial step in the process of solving the North Korean nuclear problem though the use of peaceful means" and as constituting "the last opportunity for avoiding war."[53] Korea expert Yu Meihua likewise emphasizes that China was motivated first and foremost by concerns about regional stability, and notes that since trouble on the Korean Peninsula would influence China's security, Beijing could not simply "sit back and watch."[54] Statements such as these suggest that Beijing's worsening outside options appear to have been an important factor influencing its decision to invest in the 6PT process.

5.3.3 China's Approach to the North Korean Nuclear Issue After the Six Party Talks

The February 2007 session of the 6PT sparked what was, in hindsight, the apogee of efforts to find a negotiated solution to the problem of North Korea's nuclear weapons program. By 2008, it appeared as though real progress was being made on the issue. Most notably, Pyongyang began

52 Paltiel, for instance, argues that a changed conception among PRC leaders of China's international role was critical; Chinese leaders increasingly embraced the notion of a "responsible great power," and North Korea served as a useful "test case of solving security problems through dialogue and through seeking 'win-win' solutions." See Paltiel, "China and the North Korean Crisis," p. 99. On the potential for the 6PT to improve China's image as a "responsible great power," see also Jiang Zhaijiu, "Zhongguo diqu duobian anquan hezuo de dongyin" [Motivations for China's Regional Multilateral Security Cooperation], *Guoji Zhengzhi Kexue*, no. 1 (2006), p. 21. On stable United States–China relations as a factor, see Gilbert Rozman, *Strategic Thinking about the Korean Nuclear Crisis: Four Parties Caught between North Korea and the United States* (New York: Palgrave, 2007), p. 104.

53 Zhang, "Chaoxian de hewuqi yu Meiguo de jingcha juese," p. 76.

54 Yu uses two idioms to emphasize this point, noting that China could not "fold its arms and look on" [xiushou pangguan] or "watch the fire from the other side of the river" [gean guanhuo], implying that China's outside options were bad. See Luo, "Zhongguo weishenme jiji cucheng liufang huitan." See also Jiang's ("Zhongguo diqu duobian anquan hezuo de dongyin," p. 18) analysis, which highlights the possibility of a US attack on North Korea and the instability and challenges it would generate as the primary factor leading China to invest in the 6PT. And see Shirk, *China*, p. 123, who quotes a Chinese America expert as suggesting that the United States or North Korea "might go crazy. This would cause big problems for China. So China had to do something."

to provide an account of its nuclear weapons program while also taking steps to dismantle the Yongbyon nuclear facility (including the destruction of the facility's cooling tower in June of that year). The Bush administration, meanwhile, removed North Korea from the US state sponsors of terrorism list later in 2008. This apparent progress, however, was short-lived. North Korea's nuclear declarations, for instance, did not explicitly reference the uranium enrichment program that Washington had long suspected the DPRK was pursuing. More importantly, the United States and North Korea could not reach agreement on how to verify North Korean compliance with its commitment to denuclearize. In late 2008, the 6PT collapsed as North Korea proved unwilling to submit to verification protocols that would satisfy US demands.[55] Further underscoring the return to a confrontational environment, North Korea in April 2009 tested a long-range missile, and in May conducted its second nuclear test.[56] Later in the year, it essentially admitted to the existence of a uranium enrichment program – an admission that was made more explicit in 2010 when Pyongyang showed Siegfried Hecker, an American nuclear scientist, a sophisticated and operational uranium enrichment facility.[57]

Broadly speaking, China's outside options regarding North Korea's nuclear program – relative to the United States – were significantly better during the Obama administration than they had been during the early George W. Bush administration. As the 2000s progressed, it became obvious that China had less reason to fear some of the worst-case scenarios that had worried Chinese analysts in the early 2000s. For instance, as the Iraq war turned into a prolonged debacle for Washington, the probability of a US military strike against North Korea appeared increasingly remote, especially after Washington seemed not to seriously consider a military strike after North Korea's 2006 nuclear test.[58] Meanwhile, North Korea's

[55] On progress in mid-2008, see "North Korea Destroys Tower at Nuclear Site," *The New York Times*, June 28, 2008: www.nytimes.com/2008/06/28/world/asia/28korea.html. On the collapse of the 6PT, see "In Setback for Bush, Korea Nuclear Talks Collapse," *The New York Times*, December 11, 2008: www.nytimes.com/2008/12/12/world/asia/12korea.html. See also Cha, *Impossible State*, pp. 270–1.

[56] See "North Korea Claims to Conduct 2nd Nuclear Test," *The New York Times*, May 24, 2009: www.nytimes.com/2009/05/25/world/asia/25nuke.html.

[57] See Cha, *Impossible State*, p. 274; "North Koreans Unveil New Plant for Nuclear Use," *The New York Times*, November 20, 2010: www.nytimes.com/2010/11/21/world/asia/21intel.html.

[58] On non-consideration of use of military force after the test, see Cha, *Impossible State*, p. 268. In a CRS report for Congress issued after the test, military force was placed near the bottom of US response options, with emphasis placed on the downside risks of a military strike. See Emma Chanlett-Avery and Sharon Squassoni, "North Korea's Nuclear

nuclear program and nuclear tests have not triggered a nuclear arms race in Northeast Asia.

The continued development of the DPRK's nuclear program does have some negative security consequences from Beijing's perspective. Certainly Pyongyang's nuclear and missile programs make it easier for the United States to sustain close security cooperation with Washington's Northeast Asian allies and a stronger presence in East Asia more broadly. Indeed, the United States in 2009 dispatched a group of officials to Beijing to warn Chinese leaders that continued development of the North Korean nuclear program would naturally lead to an increased US military presence in the region.[59] More recently, and in line with this warning, North Korea's weapons programs and nuclear tests have provided the rationale for the deployment of the Terminal High Altitude Area Defense (THAAD) anti-missile system in South Korea, which also poses a real security concern for China in that it might call into question China's ability to field a nuclear deterrent.[60] Given these consequences, Beijing would almost certainly prefer that North Korea abandon its nuclear program. Still, because the most dire potential consequences of allowing North Korea's nuclear program to fester did not materialize, Chinese stakes in resolving the problem were lower by the late 2000s than they were in the early 2000s.

Meanwhile, the Obama administration – shortly after coming into office in 2009 – settled on an approach to North Korea that was termed "strategic patience." Obama essentially conditioned a return to serious diplomacy with the DPRK on clear indications that North Korea was serious about abandoning its nuclear program and ending provocations like nuclear testing.[61] The administration was especially determined not

---

Test: Motivations, Implications, and U.S. Options," *CRS Report for Congress*, October 24, 2006: www.fas.org/sgp/crs/nuke/RL33709.pdf.

59 Jeffrey A. Bader, *Obama and China's Rise* (Washington, DC: Brookings, 2012), pp. 38–9.

60 See, for instance, "U.S. to Deploy THAAD Anti-Missile Battery in South Korea in 8–10 Months: Commander," *Reuters*, November 4, 2016: www.reuters.com/article/us-southkorea-usa-thaad-idUSKBN12Z028. THAAD deployment in South Korea is seen as troubling in Beijing because it can be used – potentially – against Chinese missiles as well, thereby undercutting PRC deterrence.

61 John Delury describes the Obama policy as one of "disengagement." See John Delury, "The Disappointments of Disengagement: Assessing Obama's North Korea Policy," *Asian Perspective*, Vol. 37 (2013), pp. 149–82. See also Cha, *Impossible State*, p. 274; Christensen, *China Challenge*, p. 272; and Jong Kun Choi, "The Perils of Strategic Patience with North Korea," *The Washington Quarterly*, Vol. 38, no. 4 (2015), pp. 57–72. Mann suggests that Obama administration policy could be more aptly described as

to reward Pyongyang for returning to denuclearization deals that had already been struck or, as Defense Secretary Robert Gates reportedly put it, the United States would stop "paying for the same horse three times."[62] Though some have argued that Obama's approach to North Korea amounted to wishful thinking – hoping for a regime change in Pyongyang – it is clear that the policy was grounded in a belief that North Korean leaders would never agree to a settlement that was also acceptable to the United States.[63] In other words, Washington did not view Beijing as especially indispensable, because it was deeply skeptical about North Korea's willingness to abandon its nuclear program under any circumstances, including pressure from China.[64] Given this skepticism, Beijing would have had little reason to think it had the leverage to pursue a hold-up strategy.

Our theory predicts that the combination of improved outside options and non-indispensability should lead to more passive PRC behavior relating to second-order cooperation on North Korea's nuclear program. Beijing's behavior after the late 2000s appears consistent with this prediction. After the 2009 missile and nuclear tests, for instance, it was the United States and allies that led efforts in the UNSC to respond to North Korea's actions. China went along with a strong condemnation of the missile test and with a new round of sanctions after the nuclear test, but in both cases it (along with Russia) was a stumbling block to stronger action. Indeed, China initially opposed any UN action in response to the missile test; it was only after US persuasion that Beijing supported a presidential statement (while still refusing to support a formal resolution

containment. See James Mann, *The Obamians: The Struggle Inside the White House to Redefine American Power* (New York: Viking, 2012), pp. 197–8.

62 Bader, *Obama and China's Rise*, p. 31.

63 That is, the Obama administration was deeply skeptical that North Korea would ever commit to a program of denuclearization on terms the United States could accept – as revealed by the failure of the 2007 action plan. Christensen (*China Challenge*, p. 228) writes, for instance, that the package the United States put on the table in late 2006, which ultimately led to the action plan, "was so generous in the diplomatic, economic, and security realms that any reasonable North Korean leadership not blinded by the desire to acquire a nuclear arsenal would have accepted it." See also Delury ("Disappointments of Disengagement") on the Obama administration's belief that North Korea would not give up its nuclear arsenal. For an analysis that paints strategic patience as amounting to wishful thinking, see Choi ("Perils of Strategic Patience"), who criticizes the policy for relying, ultimately, on the unlikely event of a regime change in North Korea.

64 On the Obama administration's skepticism about North Korea's willingness to abandon its nuclear program, see Bader, *Obama and China's Rise*, p. 29. Bader (p. 33) also notes, though, that Secretary of State Hillary Clinton believed that a more reserved approach might encourage Beijing to put more pressure on North Korea.

on the matter).[65] The sanctions imposed after the nuclear test were also weaker than those favored by Washington.[66] Indeed, Christensen suggests that China's willingness to go along with the sanctions was a "hiccup" in a broader pattern of enabling the North Korean regime by, for instance, continuing to engage with its government and being lax in enforcing sanctions.[67] In sum, after the late 2000s, while China did not actively undermine efforts to deal with the North Korean nuclear program, it was not willing to invest significant effort to help find a multilateral solution to the problem either. Instead, it pursued a strategy of "accept."

5.4 CONCLUSIONS

Our theory offers a good deal of leverage in explaining China's approach to second-order cooperation in the nuclear nonproliferation regime. Generally speaking, China's outside options have been favorable relative to other powers, principally the United States. At the same time, although nonproliferation's status as a weakest-link public good implied that China, like all nuclear-capable states, was necessarily first-order indispensible, Washington has generally not viewed China as indispensable on second-order issues. China, in turn, has generally complied with the regime since the late 1980s without investing significant resources in organizing or sustaining cooperation; that is, it has pursued a strategy of "accept." Its behavior toward Iran illustrates this general pattern: though China has generally complied with multilateral sanctions against Tehran, it has been the United States – with a much larger stake in regional stability and global nuclear nonproliferation more generally – that has invested the most effort to find a diplomatic solution to Iran's nuclear program and that has invested the most in inducing third countries to observe the sanctions regime targeting Iran.

The principal exception to this general pattern of acceptance was Beijing's willingness to invest in the 6PT in an effort to facilitate a diplomatic solution to North Korea's nuclear program. Here again, our theory proved useful in making sense of changes in Beijing's approach to Korea. During the 1990s, the strategic landscape on the Korean Peninsula, from

[65] Bader, *Obama and China's Rise*, pp. 32–3.

[66] See, for instance, "U.N. Security Council Pushes North Korea by Passing Sanctions," *The New York Times*, June 12, 2009: www.nytimes.com/2009/06/13/world/asia/13nations.html

[67] Christensen, *China Challenge*, p. 271.

Beijing's perspective, did not depart significantly from the landscape China faced regarding nonproliferation more generally. China's outside options were reasonably strong and the PRC did not appear to believe that Washington viewed active PRC participation as indispensable for cooperation to succeed. Our argument predicts passive behavior (accept) in such a case. In fact, Beijing mostly adopted a low profile at the time, though it did occasionally play a quietly constructive role in United States–North Korean negotiations. By 2003, China's relative outside options had worsened considerably; failure to find a credible negotiated settlement threatened to greatly destabilize the region. At this time, China played a more proactive role, most notably by choosing to invest in the construction of the 6PT mechanism. Beijing, that is, took the lead in reforming the institutional structure addressing the North Korean nuclear weapons issue. By the late 2000s, the balance of outside options had again shifted in Beijing's favor, and its behavior, in turn, became more passive.

To be sure, other factors have likely influenced PRC behavior toward North Korea, as we have highlighted, and we can point to alternative explanations that also provide some leverage in explaining, in particular, the shift in PRC behavior from passive acceptance during the 1993–1994 crisis to proactive investment during the 2002–2003 crisis. One straightforward alternative explanation centers on broader shifts in China's approach to foreign affairs – what Medeiros and Fravel refer to as "China's new diplomacy" (summarized briefly in Chapter 4). That is, China's more proactive approach to North Korea in 2003 may have been a reflection of a more general reorientation in the PRC's diplomatic behavior.[68] Still, our strategic focus on outside options offers some additional explanatory power to help make sense of shifting PRC policies relating to North Korea. Most importantly, China did not assume a proactive role until its outside options deteriorated precipitously in the spring of 2003; to paraphrase Christoph Bluth, it was Beijing's worsening outside options that served as the catalyst for China's more proactive approach in this instance.[69] Moreover, the shift to invest in Korea was

[68] Evan S. Medeiros and M. Taylor Fravel, "China's New Diplomacy," *Foreign Affairs*, Vol. 82 (2003), p. 22. In addition to Medeiros and Fravel, other scholars also view China's proactive role in setting up the 6PT as part of a more general pattern toward a more proactive, or "responsible", foreign policy. See, e.g., Shirk, *China*, chapter 5; and Christoph Bluth, *Crisis on the Korean Peninsula* (Washington, DC: Potomac Books, 2011), p. 181.

[69] More specifically, Bluth, *Crisis on the Korean Peninsula*, pp. 181–2, highlights the danger of instability that a unilateral US attack would provoke as being the catalyst behind the establishment of the 6PT, while emphasizing broader background conditions

not accompanied by a shift toward investments in multilateralism on a more global scale, even on issues directly related to nuclear proliferation (as we showed in the discussion of Iran). Finally, by later in the decade, the PRC appeared to be resuming a more passive approach to the North Korean nuclear issue, a shift that can be readily attributed to improving outside options as the likelihood of a unilateral US military strike declined sharply.

At the time of this writing, it appears as though Beijing's strategic incentives relating to the North Korean nuclear issue may be shifting again. The United States began to deploy the THAAD system in South Korea despite Beijing's strong protests.[70] North Korea has again (in September 2017) tested a nuclear device and has demonstrated further improvements in its long-range missile capabilities. US officials, meanwhile, have made strong statements hinting at the possibility of a unilateral US military strike.[71] At the same time, an American posture that suggests the potential for military disengagement over the long run has

like a more stable domestic environment in China and general shifts in PRC diplomacy around the turn of the century.

70 The dispute between China and South Korea over THAAD appeared to be resolved in late October 2017 when the two countries reached an understanding by which South Korea agreed not to allow additional launcher deployments or participate in regional networked missile defense efforts. China's opposition to THAAD derives primarily from the system's strong radar, which Beijing worries could be used to track Chinese missiles and undermine its deterrent threat. On China's opposition to THAAD, see "Why China is so Mad about THAAD, a Missile System Aimed at Deterring North Korea," *The Washington Post*, March 7, 2017: www.washingtonpost.com/news/worldviews/wp/2017/03/07/why-china-is-so-mad-about-thaad-a-missile-defense-system-aimed-at-deterring-north-korea. For an early analysis of the recent understanding between China and South Korea regarding THAAD, see Ankit Panda, "What China Gains with Its Détente with South Korea over THAAD," *The Diplomat*, November 7, 2017: https://thediplomat.com/2017/11/what-china-gains-with-its-detente-with-south-korea-over-thaad.

71 Consider, for instance, some recent statements by US President Donald Trump. In April 2017, he asserted in an interview that "if China is not going to solve North Korea, we will." More recently, Trump warned that the United States was prepared to unleash "fire and fury" on the DPRK. Though other US officials have sought to downplay some of Trump's most abrasive threats, they nevertheless have warned that military options remain on the table. US Secretary of Defense James Mattis, for instance, recently emphasized that "You have got to be ready to ensure that we have military options that our president can employ if needed." See "Trump Just Warned China to Rein in North Korea or the U.S. Would Go It Alone," *Vox.com*, April 3, 2017: www.vox.com/world/2017/4/3/15159904/trump-china-cooperate-north-korea; "Trump's 'Fire and Fury' Threat Raises Alarm in Asia," *The New York Times*, August 9, 2017: www.nytimes.com/2017/08/09/world/asia/north-korea-trump-threat-fire-and-fury.html; and "U.S. Military Must 'Be Ready' for North Korea Threat, Mattis Warns," *Newsweek*, October 9, 2017: www.newsweek.com/mattis-tells-army-it-has-got-be-ready-confront-north-korea-threat-680766.

led to more public debate within Japan and South Korea about exiting the NPT and building their own nuclear arms, which would run the risk of an accelerating regional arms race, to China's detriment.[72] In this environment, particularly if Chinese leaders conclude that recent US statements are not simply bluffs, Beijing is likely to conclude that the balance of outside options is again becoming less favorable. If so, our theory would predict a renewed willingness to invest in building multilateral institutions on the Korean Peninsula.[73]

72 David Sanger, Choe Sang-hun, and Motoko Rich, "North Korea Rouses Neighbors to Reconsider Nuclear Weapons," *The New York Times*, October 28, 2017: www.nytimes.com/2017/10/28/world/asia/north-korea-nuclear-weapons-japan-south-korea.html. On this point generally and on South Korea specifically, see Philipp C. Bleek and Eric B. Lorber, "Security Guarantees and Allied Nuclear Proliferation," *Journal of Conflict Resolution*, Vol. 58, no. 3 (2014), pp. 429–54. For an argument that the American system of alliances in East Asia is robust enough to survive the Trump administration, see Stephan Frühling and Andrew O'Neil, "Nuclear Weapons and Alliance Institutions in the Era of President Trump," *Contemporary Security Policy*, Vol. 38, no. 1 (2017), pp. 47–53.

73 As this book went to press, however, threats of US unilateral action have probably receded. Following a South Korean diplomatic initiative, President Trump and Kim Jong-un met in Singapore in June 2018. Just before and just after the summit Kim made visits to meet with Xi Jinping in Beijing, suggesting a heightened role for China in a process that may have led to a reduction in tensions (even if only temporarily). To the extent that China played a role, it has been outside of any formal institutional setting and has not involved the construction of a new regime. The speed with which the US declared the summit a success – even in the absence of concrete steps by the DPRK to abandon its nuclear program – suggests that Chinese outside options were probably not as bad as Chinese leaders seem to have thought in 2003.

6

Global Financial Governance

From Accept to Hold-Up

6.1 INTRODUCTION

China's behavior with regard to global financial governance issues has evolved markedly over the past two decades. The PRC was largely outside the system of international financial governance during the Maoist era. From reformer Deng Xiaoping's "opening to the outside world" in 1978 through the early 2000s, Beijing was a relatively passive actor and participated little in discussion of second-order issues. We interpret this tendency to take an acceptant stance as a function of China's perception that its outside options were favorable, its stake in the governance issues was relatively weak, and its participation was not indispensable for regime maintenance.[1]

Since the global financial crisis in 2008, in contrast, China has become a much more frequent (at times quite active) participant in discussions on rules governing global financial institutions. For instance, in 2009, prominent Chinese economist Li Daokui noted China's interest in becoming actively involved in the negotiations to rebuild the international financial

[1] A recent treatment of China's negotiations over IMF capital control policy is Jeffrey Chwieroth, "Controlling Capital: The International Monetary Fund and Transformative Incremental Change from within International Organizations," *New Political Economy*, Vol. 19, no. 3 (2014), pp. 445–69. On the global context surrounding renegotiations over influence within the IMF see Ayse Kaya, *Power and Global Economic Institutions* (Cambridge, Cambridge University Press, 2015), and Randall W. Stone, *Controlling Institutions: International Organizations and the Global Economy* (New York: Cambridge University Press, 2011).

system.[2] But even with this greater post-2008 activism – in contrast to China's proactive role in establishing the 6PT and SCO mechanisms and in addressing climate change – China did not invest heavily in the maintenance of existing institutions of global financial governance, nor in the construction of new institutions to wholly replace or supersede the existing institutions. (The PRC has indeed participated in building several parallel institutions related to multilateral development aid, notably the AIIB, as we discuss in our concluding chapter.) Rather, we show that in the case of participation in the IMF, China has pursued a hold-up strategy, made possible by its strong outside options relative to the established powers and by a growing sense among other key actors (principally the United States) that China's participation in global financial governance has become indispensable. China's indispensability – in terms of its sheer size, its importance in the global economy, and its symbolic ability to help legitimize the IMF in the eyes of the emerging economies – meant that China's participation was crucial, giving it leverage to request concessions. In short, Beijing held out for concessions on second-order issues in return for its cooperative participation in the organization. The most important concession that established powers made was to permit China a larger quota for contributions to the IMF, which gave it a larger vote share – a concession that Americans and Europeans had long been reluctant to make. China further made efforts to have its currency, the renminbi (RMB), included in the basket of currencies that make up the IMF's Special Drawing Right (SDR). In neither case was China's hold-up behavior characterized by extreme actions or rhetoric, as might be expected by dispositional arguments that focus exclusively on a rising power's dissatisfaction with the status quo. Instead, we argue that they played hold-up because such a posture would be likely to yield a favorable outcome. From China's perspective, its ability to make its support of the multilateral financial regime conditional allowed it to pursue, with eventual success, a change in the regime that made it more equitable and rolled back, to some degree, the legacy power position of the United States and the European nations. This chapter (after discussing the background for China's participation in the core institutions of global financial governance) examines closely two cases related to second-order decisions in the IMF in which China's behavior has moved, since the mid-2000s, from an

[2] Li Daokui, "Zuowei Yige Xinxing Daguo, Zhongguo Ying Jiji Canyu Guoji Jinrong Tixi Gaige" [China should Actively Participate in International Financial System Reform as an Emerging Power], *Zhongguo yu Shijie Guancha*, no. 1 (2009).

accepting stance to hold-up: (1) increasing developing countries' voice in the vote shares and (2) including the RMB in the SDR basket.

6.2 THE INSTITUTIONS OF GLOBAL FINANCIAL GOVERNANCE

The case studies that serve as the empirical focus of this chapter examine the most consequential multilateral institution of global economic governance: the IMF. The broader context for multilateral economic governance is worth understanding, however, as the group of players involved in negotiating second-order rules of financial governance has broadened over time. Moreover, China has begun to engage with a variety of other economic organizations that have been involved in decisions related to IMF governance.

The groundwork for a system to govern, to monitor, and especially to stabilize the international economy was laid in the Bretton Woods Conference of 1944. The major institutions created at Bretton Woods were the International Bank for Reconstruction and Development (known commonly as the World Bank) and the IMF.[3] Conferees designed these institutions to promote financial multilateralism as a means of addressing problems in international economic behavior that had become acute during the Depression of the 1930s: competitive devaluations, nonconvertibility of major currencies, imposition of trade barriers, and resultant decreased flows of international trade and investment. The IMF's formal purpose was to promote orderly currency exchange arrangements. The formation and operation of the IMF was, of course, heavily influenced by the world's major market economies (particularly the United States and Western Europe) and by market-oriented Keynesian principles. While membership in these organizations has expanded over time and staff have increasingly been drawn from a wide range of nationalities,

[3] The conference also recommended that countries reduce trade obstacles, a call that helped lead ultimately to the creation of the GATT in 1947. The GATT was succeeded in 1995 by the World Trade Organization. The WTO not only sought a further reduction in tariffs, but also to lower non-tariff barriers as well as provide a mechanism for resolution of disputes among contracting parties – features lacking in the GATT. The WTO also expanded the GATT agenda to include issues of trade in services, movement of peoples across borders, and protection of intellectual property. For basics on the WTO, see Craig VanGrasstek, *The History and Future of the World Trade Organization* (Geneva: World Trade Organization, 2013).

their leadership has been seen by many as reflecting the interests of the United States and of Western European nations.[4]

The landscape of multilateral economic governance broadened in the decades after Bretton Woods. Plurilateral heads-of-state cooperation emerged in response to the need for increased coordination, often after economic crisis. Important OECD countries – France, West Germany, the United States, Japan, the United Kingdom, and Italy – allied in 1975 over the economic shock of the first oil crisis and the collapse of the Bretton Woods fixed exchange rate system. When joined by Canada in 1976, the leaders' group came to be known as the Group of Seven. This G7 group broadened from liberal democracies when Russia joined in 1998, creating a Group of Eight (G8).[5] (Russia was excluded following its annexation of Crimea in 2014.) Although China and four other emerging economies began to attend the G8 meetings in 2005, leading to the informal moniker of "G8+5," the "+5" countries obviously were not equal participants and were unable to fully attend to their interests.

The Group of Twenty (G20) was formed in 1999 in the wake of growing recognition of the desirability of expanding dialogue to include emerging economies, especially in the wake of the perceived failure of the G8 and the IMF to adequately anticipate and address the 1997 Asian financial crisis. The G20 comprises 19 countries (including China) plus the European Union.[6] The managing director of the IMF and the president of the World Bank also participate in G20 meetings *ex officio*. Founders reasoned that inclusion of a broader range of countries – particularly those with growing weight in the world economy, such as India and China – would create a more representative and, hence, more legitimate forum for cooperation. The G20's influence has grown considerably, and meetings

[4] Domination by OECD countries is discussed in Kaya, *Power and Global Economic Institutions*, and in Bessma Momani, "IMF Staff: Missing Link in Fund Reform Proposal," *Review of International Organizations*, Vol. 2, no. 1 (2007), pp. 39–57.

[5] On the G7 and G8, see Peter I. Hajnal, *The G8 System and the G20: Evolution, Role and Documentation* (London: Routledge Press, 2016).

[6] The 19 member countries are Argentina, Australia, Brazil, Canada, China, France, Germany, India, Indonesia, Italy, Japan, the Republic of Korea, Mexico, the Russian Federation, Saudi Arabia, South Africa, Turkey, the United Kingdom, and the United States; the European Union is the 20th member. Together, these 20 economies are responsible for about 85 percent of global GNP and 80 percent of global trade. On the history and early years of the G20, see John Kirton, "What is the G20?" G20 Research Group, University of Toronto (November 20, 1999), online at: www.g20.utoronto.ca/g20whatisit.html, accessed April 3, 2010. On the G20, see Kaya, *Power and Global Economic Institutions*.

are taken quite seriously by IMF and World Bank staff.[7] The organization began in 1999 with meetings of member countries' finance ministers and central bank governors. It included an annual heads-of-state meeting for the first time in 2008 at the outset of the global financial crisis, and declared itself to formally supplant the G8 as the premier mechanism for cooperation among the major economies in 2009. The G20's scope has expanded from an early focus on international financial stability to include issues of the environment, employment, information, and terrorism, and it provides an arc over many levels of activity, ranging from meetings of leaders and ministers to working groups peopled by experts at multiple working levels.

The institutional landscape for discussions of global financial governance expanded further with the founding of a plurilateral grouping of the emerging-economy countries of Brazil, Russia, India, and China – the so-called "BRIC" group of nations. The formation of a separate forum for these new rising powers to consider their negotiating options vis-à-vis the established countries is not surprising. Following informal meetings initiated in 2006 on the sidelines of the annual UN opening summits, Russia hosted the first BRIC summit in 2009. The most coherent positions taken by the BRIC nations have surrounded security issues, notably the criticism of the NATO bombing of Libya in 2011.[8] Yet BRIC coordination has led to some pressure for IMF reform, as well as the launch in 2015 of a multilateral development bank: the New Development Bank.[9]

6.3 CHINA AND THE INSTITUTIONS OF GLOBAL FINANCIAL GOVERNANCE THROUGH THE EARLY 2000S: ACCEPT

From its founding in 1949 until 1971, when the PRC began to be recognized internationally as the legitimate regime of "China," the PRC did not participate in the IMF or the World Bank; as in the United Nations,

7 Author discussions with IMF and World Bank management make clear that they not only pay close attention to G20 meetings, but see them as setting important agendas and as important places for negotiating.

8 Bruce Jones, Emily O'Brien, and Richard Gowan, "The G8 and the Threat of Bloc Politics in the International System: A Managing Global Order Summitry Report" (Washington, DC: Brookings Institution, May 24, 2011): www.brookings.edu/research/the-g8-and-the-threat-of-bloc-politics-in-the-international-system.

9 On the problems and prospects of establishment by BRIC nations of a successful New Development Bank, see Michael Tierney, "Rising Powers and the Regime for Development Finance," *International Studies Review*, Vol. 16, no. 3 (2014), pp. 452–5.

the ROC (Taiwan) held the seat designated for "China." While some in the PRC government had an interest in the workings and policies of these institutions, Beijing's main interest in them was through the lens of its conflict with Taiwan.[10] Once the China seat at the United Nations was passed from Taipei to Beijing in 1971, and in the context of the Nixon administration's loosening of US constraints on trade with China, PRC economic leaders began to follow events at the global institutions more closely. Nevertheless, the domestic political environment in China toward the end of its Cultural Revolution dictated caution toward foreign "capitalist" institutions and, hence, delayed contact, as did US politics during the Vietnam War.[11] According to Harold Jacobson and Michel Oksenberg, the two PRC ministries tasked with considering entry to the institutions in the mid-1970s:

> were concerned that, because of the weighted-voting formula in the IMF and World Bank, the two institutions would not provide China with a suitable platform from which to pursue its broader foreign policy objectives. Already displaying sensitivity to the issue of Chinese voting power, the two ministries noted that were the People's Republic to inherit Taiwan's existing position, Beijing would have only 1.68 percent of the total votes in the IMF and 2.83 percent of those in the World Bank.[12]

Beijing's decision to apply to join the IMF, as well as the World Bank, came in early 1979, following Deng Xiaoping's ascendance to power and on the heels of PRC normalization of relations with the United States (and related termination of formal diplomatic relations between the United States and Taiwan).[13] Some in the PRC leadership were uneasy about

[10] On China's early integration into international financial regimes, see Harold K. Jacobson and Michel Oksenberg, *China's Participation in the IMF, the World Bank, and GATT: Toward a Global Economic Order* (Ann Arbor: University of Michigan Press, 1990), chapter 3. A recent discussion of these origins is Jue Wang, *The People's Republic of China and the IMF*, unpublished PhD Thesis, University of Warwick, Department of Politics and International Studies (September 2014): http://go.warwick.ac.uk/wrap.

[11] World Bank President Robert McNamara was quite supportive of having China join the World Bank, believing that China would benefit from development lending, that Chinese participation was important to upholding the global nature of the bank, and that China's participation could help the bank leverage additional resources. Jacobson and Oksenberg, *China's Participation*, pp. 63–4.

[12] Ibid., p. 64. Chinese officials also feared making the Chinese economy more vulnerable to international pressures and did not intend to borrow money from the IMF (while still being obliged to pay its quota).

[13] China's attitude toward integration into the IMF (focused on finance) and the World Bank (focused on development aid) bore important similarities, and Chinese leaders perceived integration in largely the same light. Yet there are important differences to

the need to submit data and to open China to missions from the IMF and the World Bank, as well as required future financial contributions. These were considered against the perceived benefits, the most important of which were unrelated to the core missions of the two organizations: diplomatic presence in key organizations (especially at the expense of Taiwan), reinforcement of bilateral relations, and information that might help its development program, with potential for future concessional loans and IMF drawing privileges.[14]

When the PRC took over the China seat in the IMF in 1980, membership in the organization required virtually no commitment of resources from Beijing. Nor, as noted, was China tempted to borrow funds, although it did respond favorably to extensive IMF advice on internal pricing matters in the 1980s and on current account convertibility in the 1990s.[15] China's role, at least symbolically, was not minimal, however. The quota negotiated upon its entry to the IMF was the ninth largest in the IMF and was designed to be higher than India's.[16] The size of the IMF Executive Board was also expanded, from twenty-one to twenty-two, to accommodate China's membership without needing to displace other members. Still, in light of the ability of the United States to dominate decisions through informal governance

---

be considered as well. We agree with Lipscy (*Renegotiating*) that the two institutions present China with different outside options; the World Bank's low network effects and barriers to entry have made it subject to greater competition – its member states have in general more favorable outside options – and so it has had to be much more flexible in renegotiating the status of members who are rising states. At the same time, although we theorize the ability of a member state's outside options to change over time, we emphasize that China's outside options vis-à-vis the IMF started out relatively favorable leading up to and remained so after the 2008 financial crisis.

14 As Jacobson and Oksenberg note regarding the PRC potential upon joining to draw on World Bank loans and IMF drawing privileges, "Our Chinese sources recall that [this consideration] was clearly the least important one" to those considering the decision. Jacobson and Oksenberg, *China's Participation*, pp. 70–1.

15 Nicholas R. Lardy, "China and the International Financial System," in Michel Oksenberg and Elizabeth Economy, eds., *China Joins the World: Progress and Prospects* (New York: Council on Foreign Relations Press, 1999), pp. 206–30. Lardy makes clear that the greatest international influence on the role of China's financial sector has come from market-based pressures rather than the IMF.

16 The eight countries with larger quotas were the United States, the United Kingdom, West Germany, France, Japan, Saudi Arabia, Canada, and Italy. Jacobson and Oksenberg, *China's Participation*, p. 76. Each member country of the IMF is assigned a quota, based broadly on its relative economic size. A country's quota determines its maximum financial commitment to the IMF and its voting power, and has a bearing on its access to IMF financing. See IMF Factsheet, April 2017: www.imf.org/About/Factsheets/Sheets/2016/07/14/12/21/IMF-Quotas?pdf=1.

processes, there could have been little expectation that China's entry foreshadowed a real shift in governance power.[17] Through the early 2000s, then, Beijing kept a low profile in the IMF, as well as in the World Bank, in terms of using its voting power in proceedings or on other second-order governance issues. While Beijing participated in the organization in terms of posting officials to IMF and World Bank headquarters in Washington, DC, it remained largely on the sidelines of policy debates. Jacobson and Oksenberg concluded, along similar lines, that "[a]lthough Chinese representatives have been fully engaged in the policy-making processes within these institutions [IMF, World Bank and GATT], as of mid-1989 they had not proposed major initiatives or sought a central role." In the early 2000s, a US Treasury Department official responsible for East Asian affairs indicated that there was little interaction between Chinese officials and IMF staff at the working level, and that at the Executive Board level the China representative "usually keeps quiet."[18] Gregory Chin agrees: "For the decade prior to the global crisis, the major emerging countries kept a low profile or minimized their engagement in the Bretton Woods institutions, did not bear significant costs in maintaining the global architecture, and could channel their resources instead to fostering hedging options."[19] It is true that in the early 2000s Beijing representatives to the IMF began to call for greater surveillance of the dollar and other advanced-economy currencies, just as the currencies of developing countries were monitored.[20] And, especially pertinent to our

[17] On informal IMF governance practices that are, in effect, dominated by the United States, see Stone, *Controlling Institutions*, chapter 4. In contrast, China was more active in the World Bank, which it joined in May 1980. Upon joining, as in the IMF, the PRC gained an executive board seat but also a voting power smaller than only a handful of countries. In 1993, China became the largest borrower from the World Bank, and retained that position throughout much of that decade. More generally, the PRC was widely perceived to be an ideal client. On China's role in the World Bank, see also Lardy, "China and the International Financial System," p. 209.

[18] When China's representatives did speak, this official noted, it was on behalf of first-order issues involving developing countries, such as increasing technical assistance. Author interview, August 20, 2002.

[19] Gregory T. Chin, "The Emerging Countries and China in the G20: Reshaping Global Economic Governance," *Studia Diplomatica*, Vol. 63, no. 2 (2010), p. 109.

[20] People's Bank of China (PBOC) Governor Dai Xianglong spoke in favor of more extensive surveillance of developed countries at the 2002 IMF annual meetings. See Statement by Mr. Dai Xianglong, Governor of the People's Bank of China, IMFC Meeting, Washington, DC" in IMF, International Monetary and Financial Committee, September 28, 2002: www.imf.org/external/am/2002/imfc/state/eng/chn.htm. On China's relative passivity on the surveillance issue until the mid-2000s, see Andrew Walter, "China's Engagement with International Macroeconomic Policy Surveillance," in Eric Helleiner

focus on second-order issues, Chinese officials began in the early 2000s to discuss with increasing seriousness the desirability of voting-share reforms to increase the voice of developing countries.[21] Yet for the most part Beijing's behavior on issues concerning global financial governance could best be described as passive acceptance, or free-riding; even into the 2000s China's participation lagged far behind its growing economic capabilities, and was focused on its own tangible first-order issues rather than second-order leadership or advocacy of developing country positions.[22]

How does our theory account for China's acceptant role? China's balance of outside options during this period appeared strong relative to the established powers. Key issues pertaining to international financial governance reform were low priorities in Beijing. China, more broadly, was content to seek deeper integration into the current system. Chinese leaders had worked hard to join the organization, believing that membership would impart both international and domestic legitimacy on the reform government.[23] Indeed, Beijing was quite supportive of global financial institutions generally, not the least because disrupting them would threaten the stability Beijing perceived it needed for its economic development program. Leading Chinese IR scholar Yu Yongding made China's support explicit in comments made in 2004:

> China has long regarded the International Monetary Fund (IMF), the World Bank (WB), and the World Trade Organization (WTO)/the General Agreement on Tariffs and Trade (GATT) as the three pillars of the world economic order. China has maintained a very good relationship with the IMF and the WB, especially with the latter, due to these two international organizations' sympathetic attitudes towards China's reform and opening up since the early 1980s.[24]

---

and Jonathan Kirshner, eds., *The Great Wall of Money: Power and Politics in China's International Monetary Relations* (Ithaca, NY: Cornell University Press, 2014), pp. 127–55. Walter states that, in 2007, China exhibited greater activity by blocking surveillance consultation procedures.

[21] These calls were made in concert with suggestions to increase staff from developing countries. They often were made in Chinese representatives' statements at the biannual IMFC meetings. Jue Wang indicates that the calls became louder in 2002, emphasizing the need to increase representation of African countries. See Wang, *The People's Republic of China and the IMF*, pp. 238–9.

[22] Hongying Wang and Erik French, "China in Global Economic Governance," *Asian Economic Policy Review*, Vol. 9, no. 2 (2014), pp. 254–71.

[23] See Jacobson and Oksenberg, *China's Participation*; and Robert G. Sutter, *Chinese Foreign Relations: Power and Policy since the Cold War* (Lanham, MD: Rowman and Littlefield, 2008), p. 114.

[24] Yu Yongding, "The G20 and China: A Chinese Perspective," *The G20 at Leaders' Level?* (Ottawa: International Development Research Centre, February 29, 2004): http://

Yu's comment does paper over some underlying dissatisfaction. The 1997 Asian financial crisis, in particular, had been the subject of biting internal criticisms. Overall, though, and despite some dissatisfaction, Beijing's leaders did not express serious disagreement with the United States over IMF governance policies, or with global financial governance systems in general, before about 2006. Thus, Beijing's stake was low relative to the established powers. With regard to a unilateral US option, Beijing had little reason to fear that the established powers would not continue to pay the costs of regime maintenance were China to fail to contribute; there was, for Beijing, little reason to worry that outcomes contrary to its interests would likely arise were it to decline to participate actively in governance issues within the IMF. At the same time, other established powers – principally the United States – did not see China's participation as indispensable for cooperation in the international financial governance regime. While China's economy was obviously growing at a strong pace, its participation was not yet seen as crucial for regime legitimacy. Given China's relatively strong outside options and the belief among the established powers that the value of China's active participation was marginal, Beijing adopted a passive role on second-order issues within the IMF.

6.4 MID-2000S THROUGH THE GLOBAL FINANCIAL CRISIS AND AFTER: THE MOVE TO HOLD-UP

This picture began to change after the mid-2000s; the period leading up to and through the global financial crisis of 2007–2008 was a formative time in leaders' attitudes toward global financial governance. Just prior to the onset of the crisis, China was becoming more active in global financial issues. A key venue for China's activity was the G20. While some observers have criticized the G20 as simply a larger version of the elitist G8 club, China – present at the organization's inception – has taken the organization very seriously.[25] As a result, China actively participated in the expansion of the G20 process. Both within and outside the G20, Chinese diplomats began to routinely raise the issue of expanding developing country representation (including that of China) in global financial

dspace.cigilibrary.org/jspui/bitstream/123456789/17390/1/The%20G20%20and%20China%20A%20Chinese%20Perspective.pdf?1.

[25] For a critique of the elitist nature of the G20, as with the G8, see Daniele Archibugi, "The G20 Ought to Be Increased to 6 Billion," *openDemocracy* (March 31, 2009): www.opendemocracy.net/article/email/the-g20-ought-to-be-increased-to-6-billion.

institutions, arguing that the percentage of vote shares assigned to these countries in the IMF vastly underrepresented their growing economic prowess.[26] This fed into general dissatisfaction in Beijing over the IMF, and over the US–dominated international financial system more generally. Chinese officials involved in international financial matters, as well as Chinese academicians, had become highly critical of the IMF's handling of the Asian financial crisis in 1997.[27] Officials and scholars also had begun, around 2006, to voice increasing criticism that loose US monetary and fiscal policy was creating instability in the world economy and, more generally, that a dollar-dominated international financial order allowed the United States too much power – and "exorbitant economic privilege" – over the global system. Criticisms of the IMF as a whole became especially pointed during the global financial crisis. Some of the most direct criticism came in comments by the PBOC's governor, Zhou Xiaochuan, in 2009: "A half century after its founding, it is clear that the IMF has failed in its mission."[28] Officials in the Chinese international finance policy community also made strong criticism of the inadequacies of the IMF's stability maintenance, including in late 2009 the deputy governor of the PBOC, Zhu Min, on the eve of his move several months later to the IMF as special advisor to the managing director.[29]

[26] China was insistent upon the elevation of the issue of its underrepresentation in the IMF in the Strategic and Economic Dialogue with the United States in 2009. Author interview, August 20, 2009.

[27] See, for example, the official statement of the governor of the PBOC, Dai Xianglong: "Statement by Mr. Dai Xianglong, Governor, People's Bank of China at the Fifty-Third Meeting of the Interim Committee of the Board of Governors of the International Monetary System," International Monetary Fund, September 26, 1999: www.imf.org/external/am/1999/icstate/chn.htm.

[28] Zhou is quoted in Ren Xiao, "A Reform Minded Status Quo Power?: China, the G20, and Changes in the International Monetary System," *RCCPB Initiative on China and Global Governance* (Bloomington: Indiana University Research Center for Chinese Politics and Business, 2012): www.indiana.edu/~rccpb/pdf/Ren%20RCCPB%2025%20G20%20Apr%202012.pdf.

[29] See, for example, Zhu Min, "Shijie Xuyao Zhongguo de Shengyin" [The World Needs China's Voice], *Jingji Huanjing Wang*, October 12, 2009: www.eeo.com.cn/observer/shijiao/2009/12/10/157756.shtml. Broad dissatisfaction was expressed in many articles in Chinese journals throughout the late 2000s. See, for instance, Li Xiangyang, "Guoji jingji guize de xingcheng jizhi" [The Formation Mechanism of International Economic Rules], *Shijie Jingji yu Zhengzhi* 2006, Issue 9, pp. 69–78; Pang Zhongying and Wang Ruiping, "Quanqiu Zhili: Zhongguo de Zhanlue Yingdui" [Global Governance: China's Strategic Response], *Guoji Wenti Yanjiu*, no. 41 (2013), pp. 57–68; and Su Changhe, "Zhongguo yu Quanqiu Zhili – Jincheng, Xingwei, Jiegou yu Zhishi" [China and Global Governance: Process, Actions, Structure, and Knowledge], *Guoji zhengzhi yanjiu*, no. 1 (2011). This trend in the academic literature is discussed in Wang Yong and Louis Pauly, "Chinese

Growing dissatisfaction with the global financial regime, in some respects, had the effect of raising the stakes for Beijing. Yet, in terms of our theory, we judge other trends as allowing China's balance of outside options to remain favorable relative to those of the established powers. The stakes for Beijing remained relatively low. For one, the PRC continued to be independent from the IMF for its financial security.[30] Second, the goals for inclusion of the RMB in the SDR basket were not related to core interests. As government economists acknowledged in 2015, though China's leadership and some in the PBOC very much wanted RMB inclusion in the SDR basket, it was largely for reasons of "face" rather than because it would have a real impact on global governance or China's economy.[31] In terms of concerns about the US unilateral option, although Beijing spoke favorably of a long-term reform of the system, it continued to have little reason to worry that outcomes contrary to its interests would arise in the near term were it to decline to participate actively in governance issues within the IMF. As we will discuss, there was broad acknowledgment in China that the IMF–led global financial system that privileged a role for the dollar was likely to persist for some time as the "basic framework" of global economic governance.[32] Thus, if China were to stay aloof, the outcome might be a less legitimate IMF (especially in the developing world) and, over time, a less effective organization. But it would not be an outcome that would deeply harm China. Indeed, an ineffective IMF would harm established powers much more than it

---

IPE Debates on (American) Hegemony," *Review of International Political Economy*, Vol. 20, no. 6 (December 2013), pp. 1165–88. A representative English-language article in China's official media is Chang Liu, "Commentary: U.S. Fiscal Failure Warrants a de-Americanized World," *Xinhuanet*, October 13, 2013: http://news.xinhuanet.com/english/indepth/2013-10/13/c_132794246.htm.

[30] China's lack of dependence on IMF reserves was related to its sizable reserve of foreign exchange.

[31] Author interviews with economists in the Chinese Academy of Social Sciences, Beijing, October 2015.

[32] For an official commentary, see PBOC Deputy Governor and soon-to-be IMF Deputy Managing Director Zhu Min, "Yanjiu "Weijihou de shijie jingji jinronggeju" de wuge wenti"' [Research the Five Problems of Post-Crisis World Economic and Financial Patterns], *Guoji Jingji Pinglun*, July–August 2009, pp. 25–7. For scholarly commentary, see, for example, Wang Guoxing and Cheng Jing, "G20 jizhihua yu quanqiu jingji zhili gaige" [Institutionalization of G20 and Global Economic Governance Reform], *Guoji Zhanwang*, no. 4 (2010), pp. 8–18. This view is similar to the idea that the international system of financial governance, though flawed, "worked" in the sense that it was not seen as in great danger of crashing. See Daniel Drezner, *The System Worked: How the World Stopped Another Great Depression* (New York: Oxford University Press, 2014).

would China, given China's low reliance on the institution for funds and the fact that the institution helps underpin the global authority of the established powers.

The broader context is important, moreover. By the late 2000s, Beijing had become enmeshed in a range of institutional arrangements that could potentially serve as an alternative to the existing global economic governance regime in future crises. The Asian financial crisis had deeply disturbed many governments in the region, and called into question IMF credibility.[33] Within Asia, this disenchantment, in turn, helped inspire the 2003 founding by the ASEAN Plus Three (APT)[34] of the Chiang Mai Initiative (CMI) – a network of bilateral swap arrangements to provide foreign currency reserves to ASEAN nations facing a reserve currency crisis.[35] Although, in its provisions for conditionality and surveillance, the CMI follows standards set by the IMF, it was designed explicitly to provide an alternative source of crisis funds to the IMF. As William Grimes states, it "creates the institutional basis for a more credible challenge to IMF management in the next regional crisis. Thus, it increases APT states' leverage over the IMF by creating a credible threat of regional exit from the global regime."[36] The 2008 crisis renewed discussion of the value of increased Asian regional monetary cooperation.[37] More particularly, from the point of view of our theory, these seem to be efforts to improve China's outside options. In a similar fashion, at the global level and later in the decade, China became involved in the BRIC forum, which took up inadequacies in global financial governance as a major topic. It would be an exaggeration to claim that the BRIC countries make a tight-knit unified advocacy group, as interests among the countries often

33 See William Grimes, *Currency and Contest in East Asia: The Great Power Politics of Financial Regionalism* (Ithaca, NY: Cornell University Press, 2008).

34 The APT includes the ten ASEAN countries plus China, Japan, and South Korea.

35 Most of the swaps have used dollar reserves, though increasingly they involve currencies of member countries, and China (alone) has insisted on exclusive use of local currencies in its bilateral agreements. See Grimes, *Currency and Contest in East Asia*, pp. 82, 85; Saori N. Katada and C. Randall Henning, "Currency and Exchange Rate Regimes in Asia," in Saadia Pekkanen, John Ravenhill, and Rosemary Foot, eds., *The Oxford Handbook of the International Relations of Asia* (Oxford: Oxford University Press, 2014); and Eswar Prasad and Lei Ye, *The Renminbi's Role in the Global Monetary System* (Washington, DC: Brookings Institution, 2012), p. 71.

36 Grimes, *Currency and Contest in East Asia*, p. 81.

37 See, e.g., Zhang Ming, "Quanqiu Huobi huhuan xianzhuang – gongneng ji guoji huobitixi gaige de qianzai fangxiang" [The Current Situation of Global Currency Swaps – Function and the Potential Direction of International Monetary System Reform], *Guoji Jingji Pinglun*, no. 6 (2012), pp. 65–88.

diverge considerably. Moreover, as with the CMI, China (for a while at least) remained reluctant to attempt to fully use this alternative emerging venue and, as we shall see, has softened other members' efforts to more openly challenge the IMF. Nevertheless, the BRIC meetings would become a key venue during the global financial crisis for pressuring the IMF to give a greater voice to BRIC countries.[38] On balance, the emergence of these alternative institutions helps enhance China's outside options by offering the prospect – if still remote – of bypassing existing regimes in the event of future crises. These alternative institutions did not immediately constitute viable options that could replace, for China, the IMF's value. However, Chinese initial investments in groups like the CMI and the BRIC countries can be viewed as down payments on the development of outside options over the long run. As such, they illustrate the potential for dynamic conditions underlying a state's outside options.

With the onset of the global financial crisis in 2008, then, China's outside options, on balance, remained favorable. Though the specifics changed, the favorable balance did not. What *did* change substantially was the perception of China's indispensability. It is clear that the United States, as well as the staff of the IMF, had come to see China's participation as indispensable for constructing a solution to the ongoing crisis. The established powers seemed unable to contemplate a China that was not "on board" with proposed actions to address the financial crisis – in part for legitimacy of the solutions backed by the IMF (given the erosion of legitimacy in the eyes of many) and in part because China's role in preventing its own economic collapse was seen as crucial to preventing a deeper global economic collapse. As the venue for addressing global financial issues shifted from the G8 to the G20, China was frequently singled out – along with the United States – as a critical actor that needed to be brought into, and assent to, a solution. The most obvious sign of the new attitude was the statement that the crisis needed to be resolved by a de facto "Group of Two," or "G2."[39] The view that China's cooperation had become indispensable has remained long after the immediate crisis.

[38] On China's approach to the BRIC grouping, see Joseph Y. S. Cheng, "China's Approach to BRICS," *Journal of Contemporary China*, Vol. 24, no. 92 (2015), pp. 357–75; and Michael A. Glosny, "China and the BRICs," *Polity*, Vol. 42, no. 1 (2010), pp. 100–29.

[39] The G2 concept was first floated by Washington-based economist C. Fred Bergsten. See C. Fred Bergsten, "Two's Company," *Foreign Affairs* (September/October 2009): www.foreignaffairs.com/articles/65232/c-fred-bergsten/twos-company. Although Beijing preferred to downplay this designation, the idea that China was the key (indispensable) player, along with the United States, in helping ward off global recession was clear in the G20 talks that took place surrounding the crisis. Another sign of China's growing

In short, China's cooperation in global financial governance through the IMF is seen as indispensable, not so much due to its immediate impact on second-order issues of governance, but on the operation of the system as a whole. China, in effect, was positioned to pursue a strategy whereby it could – by implicitly threatening to withhold its cooperation on global financial issues and, particularly in the late 2000s, on the global financial crisis – induce the established powers to shift the governance structure of the regime to better suit its preferences. As we shall see, moreover, Beijing's participation in IMF governance reform was significantly accommodated by the IMF staff itself, who would appear – at least implicitly – to have understood that Beijing now held the cards.[40]

In terms of specific actions, Beijing targeted two reforms that were centered not so much on the policy outputs of the IMF or the workings of the global system, however, as on two issues tied to status: China's underrepresentation in the IMF (given the size and importance of the Chinese economy) and, relatedly, the dominance of the dollar as a reserve currency (and the legacy benefits this brings to the US economy and government).[41]

6.4.1 Case 1: IMF Vote Shares

It was in the environment following the 2008 global financial crisis that China pressed the issue of IMF vote shares. As discussed, China's favorable outside options relative to the United States, combined with its and other nations' perceptions of its indispensability on issues of global financial governance, provided China with the wherewithal to pursue a hold-up strategy – a strategy by which China could make its cooperation on solutions to the ongoing global crisis conditional on concessions from other actors.

importance was the appointment in 2008 of Justin Yifu Lin, one of China's top academic economists, as chief economist at the IMF.

40 To be clear, the role of staff in international organizations is outside the scope of our theory. Nevertheless, regardless of whether or not accommodation by the IMF staff was itself consequential, the fact that they were trying to accommodate Beijing meant they understood China's indispensability, which itself can be taken as indirect evidence for the theory.

41 Typical expressions of dissatisfaction in Chinese journals include: Zhang Ming, "Cidai Weiji dui Dangqian Guoji Huobi Tixi de Chongji" [The Impact of Sub-prime Crisis to International Monetary System], *Shijie Jingji yu Zhengzhi*, no. 6 (2010), pp. 74–80; Shi Bin, "Zhixu Zhuanxing, Guoji Fenpei Zhengyi yu Xinxing Daguo de Lishi" [Order Transition, International Distributive Justice and Historical Responsibility of the Emerging Powers], *Shijie Jingji yu Zhengzhi*, no. 12 (2010), pp. 69–100.

Major decisions in the IMF require an 85 percent supermajority; the 16.7 percent voting share held by the United States during this period made it the only single country with effective veto power. The IMF adjusts voting share allocations periodically and conducts a scheduled review every five years.[42] Shares have been reallocated slightly several times in recent years, including in 2006 (at which time China's share was 2.98 percent), with further adjustments committed to in 2008 and 2010.[43] Beijing pursued several interrelated actions throughout 2009 with regard to redistribution of vote shares toward emerging economies. For one, Beijing officials pressured US officials to take a major lead in advocating China's reform agenda. Indeed, Chinese diplomats, possessing new leverage over the United States, spent significant energy behind the scenes to press for US support for its position. For example, US officials who have engaged with China in the G20 report that, in the May 2009 bilateral Sino–US Strategic and Economic Dialogue, Chinese diplomats repeatedly asked US negotiators to lobby the European Union about the vote shares issue on China's behalf.[44] Beijing also used its position in emerging-country meetings to lobby vocally for international monetary system reform, including reform of representation in the IMF. For example, the PRC representative at a summer 2009 meeting of five leading emerging economies called for increased representation of emerging economies in the IMF, a demand repeated at the first BRIC Leader's Summit in June 2009.[45]

[42] In its reviews, the IMF technically adjusts members' quota shares, which in turn determine each country's financial commitment (measured in SDRs) and voting power. Randall Stone describes the determination of vote shares as highly political:

"Voting in the IMF is based on the same quota system that determines member countries' financial contributions and credit access limits. The quotas of new members are determined by formulas based on national product, trade volumes, openness, and financial reserves, which are intended to reflect both the members' capacity to contribute and likely need to draw on Fund resources. The formulas are essentially arbitrary, however, have been adjusted over the years, and are periodically subject to renegotiation, which underscores their political origin. The original quota formulas arise from an American effort at Bretton Woods to cloak in technocratic calculations its political judgments about what share of control it was necessary to cede to each of the major powers in order to secure their participation." Stone, *Controlling Institutions*, p. 53.

[43] Under these reforms, the allocation of voting shares among member countries in the IMF was as follows: the EU countries held approximately 32 percent (individual EU member countries hold shares but tend to vote as a block), the United States 16.7 percent, and Japan 6 percent, compared with China's 3.7 percent and India's 1.9 percent. See IMF 2011, *Quota and Voting Shares*, p. 1: www.imf.org/external/np/sec/pr/2011/pdfs/quota_tbl.pdf.

[44] Author interview with US Treasury official, Washington, DC, June 26, 2009.

[45] Reported in "China Urges Actions to Reform Global Financial System," *Xinhua News Agency*, July 9, 2009: http://news.xinhuanet.com/english/2009-07/09/content_11681665.

Most important, perhaps, were Beijing's direct calls in the G20 for greater developing country representation in the IMF; this demand became a central thread throughout the September 2009 G20 Leader's Summit in Pittsburgh. Zhu Guangyao, the PRC's assistant finance minister at the time, called for the transfer of IMF voting weight from the developed to developing countries, such that emerging-market economies would gain an additional 7 percent of vote shares.[46] A central outcome of the summit was the directive to the IMF (also a G20 member) to accelerate its quota shares review process to give greater voice to emerging-economy countries and, concretely, shift at least 5 percent (though not the requested 7 percent) of shares from overrepresented to underrepresented countries. This review and reform was completed ahead of schedule, in 2010, resulting in the "2010 Quota and Governance Reforms." The reforms were designed, upon passage by sufficient member legislatures, to shift more than 6 percent of total shares to emerging economies and developing countries, with the bulk of the vote shares coming at the expense of shares held by European countries. Most significant, the proposed reforms allocated China 6.071 percent of IMF vote shares, still quite a bit less than the slightly reduced US share of 16.5 percent, but surpassing those held by Germany, France, and the United Kingdom, all of whose shares were to be cut.[47] A similar reform was made in the World Bank in 2010, increasing China's voting share to the third highest in the bank and ahead of major European nations.[48] The reallocation of shares

htm; was and in Andrew E. Kramer, "Emerging Economies Meet in Russia," *The New York Times*, June 16, 2009: www.nytimes.com/2009/06/17/world/europe/17bric.html.

46 Bessma Momani, "China at the IMF," in Domenico Lombardi and Hongying Wang, eds., *Enter the Dragon: China in the International Financial System* (Waterloo, Canada: Centre for International Governance Innovation, 2015), p. 271. See also Wang, *The People's Republic of China and the IMF*, pp. 239–40.

47 These changes were made in the "14th General Review" in December 2010. The four BRIC countries each were to be elevated to among the ten largest shareholders in the IMF. See IMF, *Quota and Voting Shares*; and IMF Factsheet 2011.

48 These reforms also included agreement to review International Bank for Reconstruction and Development (IBRD) and International Finance Corporation (IFC) shareholdings every five years with a commitment to equitable voting power between developed and developing countries over time. World Bank, "World Bank Group Voice Reform: Enhancing Voice and Participation of Developing and Transition Countries in 2010 and Beyond," Report of the Development Committee Meeting April 2010: http://siteresources.worldbank.org/DEVCOMMINT/Documentation/22553921/DC2010-006(E)Voice.pdf. See analysis of these reforms in Gregory T. Chin, "The World Bank and China: The Long Decade of Realignment," in Carla P. Freeman, ed., *Handbook on China and Developing Countries* (Cheltenham: Edward Elgar Publishing, 2015), pp. 169–92.

to Beijing would make it the third largest holder of vote shares and would enhance its status in the institution to a considerable degree. The hold-up strategy worked, as suggested by Bessma Momani: "China and other like-minded states used the growing international consensus around the need to facilitate coordinated action that could restore global economic stability, as an opportunity to push for reforms that would reconfigure IMF quotas to better reflect emerging market economies' contribution to the world economy."[49]

With its IMF quota share raised, China of course was required to increase its subscription commitment of funds (as also was true in the World Bank reforms). It also gained increased access to IMF funds, though Beijing has little need to draw on them. These requirements, and Beijing's willingness to fulfill them, might seem to suggest that China was actually engaged in behavior similar to "invest." Yet it is clear from statements in Beijing, as cited earlier, that the prize was not to be the provision of a well-funded IMF but, rather, an adjustment of the rules of – and power within – the institution. The fact that the enhanced voting weight for China was widely seen in the United States and Europe as a concession to Chinese interests, rather than a sacrifice that China made for the sake of effective global governance, shows that the added financial costs to China of making the higher contributions were far less consequential – to China or to anyone else – than the voting shares they came with.

The actual implementation of the 2010 reforms took five years, as the domestic political approval of the largest member nation, the United States, was needed to bring them into force. Under US law, specific congressional authorization is required for the United States representatives to the IMF to consent to change the US quota and, hence, US voting power. Moreover, new US contributions to the IMF require Congressional approval. Some Republican members of Congress were reluctant to increase the vote share of emerging countries, fearing these countries were not fully aligned with the IMF mission.[50] A favorable vote

Chin's analysis emphasizes the accommodative nature of the World Bank staff, given China's growing economic position and its increasing importance as a donor to the bank. Nevertheless, negotiations with member countries were reported to be contentious. See Lesley Wroughton, "China Gains Clout in World Bank Vote Shift," Reuters, April 25, 2010: www.reuters.com/article/us-worldbank-idUSTRE63O1RQ20100425.

49 Momani, "China at the IMF," p. 271.

50 The reform bill also doubled the IMF's capital and, therefore, raised opposition to "reckless" spending. On the role of the US Congress, see Rebecca N. Nelson and Martin L. Weiss, *IMF Reforms: Issues for Congress* (Washington, DC: Congressional Research Service, April 9, 2015): https://fas.org/sgp/crs/misc/R42844.pdf.

finally occurred in December 2015, and this turnaround was commonly attributed to fear that China was beginning to flex its muscles for setting up alternative institutions (even though these did not, by and large, compete with the IMF).[51] As the IMF managing director said of this "early Christmas gift": "The United States Congress approval of these reforms is a welcome and crucial step forward that will strengthen the IMF in its role of supporting global financial stability."[52] China's strategy, though delayed in bearing fruit, was effective.

6.4.2 Case 2: Inclusion of the RMB in the SDR Basket of Currencies

Over the course of the 2000s, the PRC pressured to have its currency, the renminbi, included in the basket of currencies that makes up the IMF's Special Drawing Rights (SDR). As we have argued, before the mid-2000s, China's outside options in the arena of global financial governance were relatively favorable, and yet its position was not viewed as indispensable. Its position, consistent with our theory, was relatively passive and acceptant. By the onset of the global financial crisis, China's cooperation came to be seen as indispensable. While Beijing became more dissatisfied with the global order, in our assessment its outside options remained favorable relative to those of the other major powers, especially the United States. As a result, the PRC was able to threaten, albeit implicitly, to withhold cooperation if its desire for RMB inclusion was not met. In 2015, the IMF announced that it would expand the basket of SDR currencies to include the RMB.

The international context of the SDR issue bears many similarities to the vote shares issue. On the second-order global financial governance questions, Beijing wished to move away from what it considered overreliance of the global system on the dollar as an international reserve currency (a currency that is used broadly outside of one country to carry out economic transactions). (As we will discuss, Chinese statements at the same time indicate Beijing did not advocate ousting the dollar from its dominant position, but rather reducing "overreliance.") Beijing advocated a two-pronged approach: expansion of global liquidity through increased

[51] See, for example, *The New York Times* Editorial Board, "Congress Gets Out of IMF's Way," *The New York Times*, December 22, 2015: www.nytimes.com/2015/12/22/opinion/congress-gets-out-of-the-imfs-way.html.

[52] "IMF Managing Director Christine Lagarde Welcomes U.S. Congressional Approval of the 2010 Quota and Governance Reforms" (Washington, DC: IMF, December 18, 2015): www.imf.org/en/News/Articles/2015/09/14/01/49/pr15573.

usage of SDRs and inclusion of the renminbi in the basket of currencies on which the SDR is based. China and other emerging-economy countries also stated they preferred that the SDR basket itself be made more representative through inclusion of the RMB in that basket. The question of RMB inclusion in SDRs admittedly occupies fuzzy ground with regard to second-order cooperation. The inclusion does not directly increase China's say in actual governance. Moreover, as is laid out later, Beijing's pressure on the SDR was linked to its desire for broader internationalization of its currency. Still, we argue that the question of SDR inclusion is a second-order issue insofar as it was a symbolic ratification of the view that China is a global financial leader and, as important, diversifies representation of this instrument of global financial governance through inclusion of an emerging-market currency.

Under the status quo norms that held at the time of the global financial crisis, RMB inclusion would be considered only if the currency could be deemed "freely usable."[53] Although being named part of the SDR basket by the IMF would be a valuable imprimatur, it was presumed that inclusion would follow only once Beijing laid the groundwork for extensive international usage.[54] Indeed, RMB internationalization such that it would be freely usable and, eventually, convertible had been Beijing's stated long-term goal for many years, and the country had taken many concrete steps toward internationalization. It was clear at the time of the global financial crisis, however, that the RMB's "free usability" was not imminent. Nevertheless, the IMF revised its norms such that, in November 2015, it committed to China's inclusion in the SDR basket based on the idea that the RMB was on the road to being fully usable, that the PRC government had committed to make further changes for convertibility, and that inclusion was symbolically important. We expand on this thumbnail description and indicate the ways in which the dynamics are broadly supportive of "hold-up."

By way of background, SDRs are distributed among IMF members in line with each member's quota subscriptions in the IMF. The SDR was created by the IMF as a reserve asset in 1969. It is not usable in transactions as a currency *per se*, nor is it a claim on the IMF, but rather can (in

[53] The definition of "freely usable" has been flexible, but in general it has meant that a currency is widely used outside of its home country to make payments for international transactions and is widely traded on the major exchange markets. The term is discussed more fully later.

[54] Eswar Prasad, *Gaining Currency: The Rise of the Renminbi* (New York, NY: Oxford University Press, 2016), chapter 6.

principle) be exchanged by its holders for freely usable currencies and, as such, can potentially help stabilize the global economy in the face of liquidity problems. The overall importance of the SDR is more symbolic, with less of a practical impact in global finance. As of March 2016, the stock of SDRs was less than 3 percent of international reserves held by all countries.[55] Prior to the RMB's inclusion, the SDR basket was constituted by the four major reserve currencies: the US dollar, the euro, the Japanese yen, and the pound sterling. Though the US dollar is the most commonly used reserve currency, all are freely and readily convertible. A currency's importance in global transactions can be measured by the share of global foreign currency reserves that are held in financial instruments denominated in that currency. In turn, a currency's use in transactions is facilitated by open capital accounts, a flexible exchange rate, and the development of financial markets in a country, as well as a country's role in global trade and overall macroeconomic policies.[56]

Along with its efforts with the SDR, China's government has engaged in a long-term and multistage strategy to "internationalize" the RMB.[57] This issue is conceptually separate from the SDR issue, but has an impact on it and is worth discussing briefly. A reserve currency serves several functions: it is a store of value (allowing transactions over distance and time), a medium of instant exchange, and a broadly used unit of account. In order to expand the usability of the RMB across these functions,

55 On SDRs, see Prasad, *Gaining Currency*, chapter 6.

56 While many focus on the benefits to the United States of being the world's main reserve currency, there are both benefits and costs. On this "balance sheet," as well as the main functions of reserve currencies, see Arvind Subramanian, "Renminbi Rules: The Conditional Imminence of the Reserve Currency Transition," *Peterson Institute for International Economics Working Paper* 11–14 (Washington, DC: Peterson Institute for International Economics, September 2011).

57 For various perspectives on the process and prospects of RMB internationalization, see Prasad, *Gaining Currency*; Gregory T. Chin, "True Revisionist: China and the Global Monetary System" in Jacques deLisle and Avery Goldstein, eds., *China's Global Engagement: Cooperation, Competition, and Influence in the 21st Century* (Washington, DC: Brookings Press, 2017); Gregory T. Chin, "China's Rising Monetary Power," in Eric Helleiner and Jonathan Kirshner, eds., *The Great Wall of Money: Power and Politics in China's International Monetary Relations* (Ithaca, NY: Cornell University Press, 2014), pp. 184–212; Barry Eichengreen, *Exorbitant Privilege: The Rise and Fall of the Dollar and the Future of the International Monetary System* (New York: Oxford University Press, 2011); Steven Liao and Daniel McDowell, "No Reservations: International Order and Demand for the Renminbi as a Reserve Currency," *International Studies Quarterly*, Vol. 60, no. 2 (2016), pp. 272–93; David A. Steinberg, *Demanding Devaluation: Exchange Rate Politics in the Developing World* (Ithaca, NY: Cornell University Press, 2015); and Subramanian, "Renminbi Rules."

Beijing has built a number of institutional and market facilitators. It has opened several RMB bond markets (offshore and onshore) and encouraged central banks to invest in its currency bonds. It also has negotiated bilateral swap arrangements in which trading partners can settle accounts in RMB. It has opened offshore trading hubs in Singapore, London, and elsewhere in which foreign banks have become "clearing banks" for the RMB.[58] In addition to establishing new venues where use of the RMB might occur, Beijing's policies have increased somewhat the flexibility of the RMB exchange rate and eased restrictions on the inflow and outflow of capital. Still, the PBOC continues to closely manage and sometimes intervene in the exchange rate, and retains significant capital controls. Indeed, capital controls remain a major tool of the PBOC, as evident in their use to slow down capital flight that became a major problem for the regime after 2015.

It is within this broader context of RMB internationalization that China engaged an international discussion about an expanded role for the SDR and inclusion of the renminbi in the SDR basket as a means of diversifying the basket. As with the issue of IMF voting share, as early as 2002 China's PBOC governor, Dai Xianglong, stated (at the IMF) that China's interest in expanding the use of SDRs was a move toward multipolarity and away from reliance on the dollar.[59] Yet, as with the vote share issue and China's overall behavior at the IMF (and World Bank), Beijing displayed a behavior consistent with "accept."

China become more active on this issue over the course of the decade, capped by a widely quoted essay by PBOC Governor Zhou Xiaochuan that was published on the eve of the April 2009 G20 Leader's Summit in London. In the wake of much domestic and international criticism of the role of US monetary policy in spurring the global financial crisis, Zhou made a much-publicized call for a move toward increased use of SDRs.[60] The timing of the comments made certain the issue would be on the minds of participants in London. Though the statement did not mentioned RMB inclusion explicitly, the comments were interpreted to signal that China wished it. Some PRC diplomats quickly suggested that Zhou was merely expressing his private views, and Subramanian

[58] These steps are detailed in Gregory T. Chin, *The Political Economy of Renminbi Internationalization* (unpublished manuscript).

[59] See Chin, "China's Rising Monetary Power," and Momani, "China and the IMF," p. 282. Dai's successor, Zhou Xiaochuan, repeated similar sentiments at the IMF in 2006.

[60] Zhou Xiaochuan, *Reform the International Monetary System*, March 23, 2009: www.bis.org/review/r090402c.pdf.

discounts Zhou's comments as "an aberration."[61] While the 2009 speech may have been a trial balloon, preference for a move away from dollar reliance went beyond Zhou Xiaochuan. It was given further credibility a few weeks later at talks involving the G8 and four emerging economies at L'Aquila, when State Councilor Dai Bingguo, in even more harsh terms, raised the criticism of the dollar as a global reserve currency, indicating PRC displeasure with China's vulnerability to US deficits and monetary policy.[62] This view was echoed by prominent government officials.[63]

Intriguingly, although the SDR commentary timing is unlikely to have been coincidental, China chose not to pursue the issue in the G20 context. Indeed, China did not raise the issue at all at the London summit that followed immediately on Zhou's comments and did not attempt to build a coalition around the proposal.[64] PRC officials also did not follow through in other venues where a sympathetic audience awaited and were, presumably, ripe for coalition-building. At a meeting of BRIC countries held in late July 2009, *other* members – notably India and Brazil – favored using the group's closing declaration to make a strong statement about the need to reduce reliance on the dollar. Chinese officials are reported to have argued *against* including such a statement – indeed, they unilaterally blocked such a statement at both a planning meeting and the formal meeting of BRIC heads of state in Moscow later in the summer. Vice Foreign Minister He Yafei noted that movement away from reliance on the dollar was "not the position of the Chinese government" and reassured that the dollar remained "the most important major international reserve currency of the day, and for years to come ... That's the reality."[65] His comments also appeared to be representative of a view, broadly held, that while the PRC sought to gradually reduce the dominance of the dollar, it did not foresee overturning the system as a whole or denying a lead role for the dollar.[66]

61 Subramanian, "Renminbi Rules," p. 18.

62 George Parker, Guy Dinmore, Krishna Guha, and Justine Lau, "China Attacks Dollar's Dominance," *Financial Times*, July 9, 2009: www.ft.com/cms/s/0/81f3125a-6cae-11de-af56-00144feabdc0.html. Dai was then Beijing's top foreign policy official and director of the Foreign Affairs Leading Small Group.

63 Zhang Ming, "Guoji Huobi Tixi Gaige: Beijing, Yuanyin, Cuoshi ji Zhongguo de Canyu" [International Currency System Reform: Background, Reasons, Measures, and China's Participation], *Guoji Jingji Pinglun*, no. 1 (2010), pp. 114–17.

64 Glosny, "China and the BRICs." On Beijing's avoidance of the issue in direct contacts with US officials, see Daniel W. Drezner, "Bad Debts: Assessing China's Financial Influence in Great Power Politics," *International Security*, Vol. 34, no. 2 (2009), pp. 7–45.

65 Glosny, "China and the BRICs."

66 On this reformist position, see Chin, "True Revisionist."

PBOC Governor Zhou's own step back from his proposal perhaps anticipated rejection by the IMF, which in 2010 was clear: "The Chinese RMB does not currently meet the criteria to be a freely usable currency and it would therefore not be included in the SDR basket at this time."[67] Still, the cause had gained an ally. French President Nicholas Sarkozy announced, at the January 2010 World Economic Forum in Davos, that France would use its spot as G20 chair in 2011 to press for a move away from the dollar.[68] Sarkozy made good on his word at subsequent G20 meetings, including a G20 conference in Nanjing in March 2011. There, Sarkozy called explicitly for inclusion of the RMB in the SDR basket: "Isn't it the time today to reach agreement on the timetable for enlarging the basket of SDRs to include new emerging currencies, such as the yuan? Who could deny the major role the yuan plays in the international monetary system?"[69] The G20 Leader's Summit communiqué that year endorsed broader representation in the SDR basket. This directive to the IMF reportedly was made by G20 leaders in response to Chinese pressure, with the hope that if Beijing was satisfied on this issue China might be more forthcoming on exchange rate appreciation or capital account liberalization – though this concession did not occur at the meetings.[70] As with the vote shares case, in the early discussions other countries carried some of the weight of the argument.

In subsequent years, the use of the RMB around the world expanded along a broad range of indicators, albeit from a base of zero and still well below that of the dollar. According to the Brussels-based Society for the Worldwide Interbank Financial Telecommunication (SWIFT), among countries whose currency is used in international payments, the RMB rose from twenty-fourth place in 2012 to a peak of fourth in 2015, or 2.79 percent of total global payments. (It fell back to sixth in 2016.)[71] Gregory Chin reports that, by 2011, Chinese officials were frustrated that their push for an expanded role for the SDR was "falling on deaf ears,"

67 Quoted in Prasad, *Gaining Currency*, p. 142.

68 Katrin Bennhold, "Sarkozy Calls for Global Monetary System, without Dollar as Top Reserve Currency," *The New York Times*, January 28, 2010.

69 Quoted in Prasad, *Gaining Currency*. "Renminbi" is the official name of the currency, whereas "yuan" denotes a unit of the renminbi currency.

70 Edwin M. Truman, "G-20 Reforms of the International Monetary System: An Evaluation," *Peterson Institute for International Economics Policy Brief PB11-19* (Washington, DC: Peterson Institute for International Economics, November 2011).

71 SWIFT tracks use of the RMB on a monthly basis. Reports are available at: www.swift.com/our-solutions/compliance-and-shared-services/business-intelligence/renminbi/rmb-tracker.

and they "reoriented to putting more emphasis on promoting the international use of the RMB."[72] In 2015, PBOC Governor Zhou Xiaochuan once again began a major push for RMB inclusion. This effort involved lobbying the IMF, but also – in April – committing to a series of reforms in capital account liberalization that was designed to meet the criteria for a freely usable currency.[73] Apparently reacting favorably to the increased use of the RMB and to China's commitments and policy changes, the IMF leadership, particularly Managing Director Christine Lagarde, indicated support for inclusion of China's currency in the SDR basket. Importantly, the IMF gave signals that, in defining a freely usable currency, it would focus on use and not on institutional underpinnings in a home economy. In the words of an IMF official, "The concept of a freely usable currency concerns the actual international use and trading of currencies, and it is distinct from whether a currency is either freely floating or fully convertible. In other words, a currency can be widely used and widely traded even if it is subject to some capital account restrictions."[74]

On the heels of the IMF's SDR report in August 2015, Beijing announced steps to liberalize controls on the RMB exchange rate. At the same time, however, it announced a nearly 2 percent devaluation relative to the dollar. These moves created expectations (particularly in offshore RMB markets) for continued devaluation, leading to significant further downward pressure.[75] This interlude led to much international commentary questioning the competence of the PBOC's handling of these issues, as well as China's intentions. There also was considerable debate within Chinese policy circles about the importance of pushing for SDR inclusion and, relatedly, the speed for continued RMB internationalization, especially given the ongoing downturn in the Chinese economy.[76] Despite

72 Chin, "True Revisionist." Chin quotes China Development Bank Chairman Chen Yuan.

73 Prasad, *Gaining Currency*, chapter 5.

74 Interview with Siddharth Tiwari, director of the IMF's Strategy, Policy, and Review Department, "IMF Work Progresses on 2015 SDR Basket Review," August 4, 2015: www.imf.org/en/News/Articles/2015/09/28/04/53/sopol080415a, accessed January 19, 2017. Prasad, *Gaining Currency*, p. 145, references "intense political jockeying."

75 Prasad, *Gaining Currency*, chapter 4. Prasad emphasizes the IMF's concerns with a relatively sustained gap between onshore and offshore rates.

76 Interviewees indicated that many in the Chinese Academy of Social Sciences believed China should move cautiously with RMB internationalization and capital account liberalization, and hence had come to believe that China should not pressure the IMF hard for inclusion in the SDR basket. They reported that the PBOC economists were more interested in moving forward with liberalization and with SDR inclusion. Moreover, they suggested that Xi Jinping wanted inclusion of the RMB in the SDR mainly for "face" (status) reasons. Author interviews, Beijing, October 2015. Caution is expressed

debate, PBOC officials continued to press hard at the IMF. During IMF annual meetings in Lima in October 2015, PBOC Deputy Governor Yi Gang made the case that China already carried out reforms and would continue with further reforms to address remaining concerns.[77] Xi Jinping further lobbied in his G20 statement at Antalya, Turkey, in November.

Beijing's lobbying, in concert with evolving views of IMF staff, paid off. Renminbi inclusion in the SDR basket of currencies was announced formally on November 30, 2015, and took effect October 1, 2016. The RMB made up 10.9 percent of the basket, compared to a nearly unchanged 41.7 percent for the US dollar, 30.9 percent for the euro, 8.3 percent for the yen, and 8.1 percent for the pound sterling.[78] The formal IMF rationale for the inclusion was based on the increased international usage of the RMB, on past steps taken by Beijing to reform its financial and currency systems, and on expectations that China would continue in the future to liberalize its own financial regulations and banking sector. Not only was the IMF staff encouraged by Beijing's promises, but they were also convinced that SDR inclusion would further those domestic reforms. Liberalizing-minded Chinese officials often have argued that international commitments bind the hands of potential opponents and further the cause of the reform agenda.[79] (This argument was made frequently during the negotiations for China's entry into the WTO, for example.) Until such reforms are made, allowing more actual transactions to be made using the renminbi, the consensus of external economists is that the impact of the RMB's inclusion in the SDR basket will remain largely symbolic. Yet underlying the formal rationale was the perceived need to placate Chinese dissatisfaction.

---

in Zheng Liansheng and Zhang Ming, "Zhongguo Zhengfu Yinggai Qiangli Tuidong Renminbi Jiaru SDR me? [Should the Chinese Government Strongly Push for the RMB to Enter the SDR?], *Guoji Jinrong*, July 2015, pp. 3–6.

[77] Statement by the Honorable Yi Gang, Alternate Governor of the International Monetary Fund for China to the Thirty-Second Meeting of the International Monetary and Financial Committee, Lima, October 9, 2015: www.imf.org/External/AM/2015/imfc/statement/eng/chn.pdf.

[78] IMF Factsheet, "Q&As on the New SDR Basket that Comes into Effect October 1, 2016," July 25, 2016: www.imf.org/external/np/exr/faq/sdrbsktfaq.htm#one.

[79] See, for example, Liu Dongmin and He Fan, "Zhong-Mei Jinrong Hezuo: Jinzhan, Tezheng, Tiaozhan yu Celue" [China–US Financial Cooperation: Progress, Characteristics, Challenges, and Strategies], *Guoji Jingji Pinglun*, March 2014, pp. 81–83. This reasoning was also expressed by US government officials. See, for example, comments by Caroline Atkinson, former Deputy National Security Advisor (2013–2016), at Brookings Institution, September 23, 2016.

Chinese officials were poised to read the IMF staff signals as meaning they did not want to harm Chinese interests. Eswar Prasad, who for over fifteen years served as an economist at the IMF, notes that in the face of the intensive lobbying by PRC leaders, "the IMF was cornered, for [Managing Director Christine] Lagarde had no desire to incur the wrath of the Chinese government."[80] After all, Beijing did not have a lot to lose from non-cooperation in the IMF and did not have strong worries that the IMF would take unilateral actions harmful to Beijing. At the same time, China could see that its cooperation was deemed indispensable to the IMF and the established powers, notably the US, which concurred with the inclusion of the SDR.[81] In this context, China was able to play hold-up, i.e., condition its cooperation on the IMF improving the status of the currency and improving the environment for internationalization of its currency.

6.5 CONCLUSIONS ON CHINESE HOLD-UP IN GLOBAL FINANCIAL GOVERNANCE

In both cases of global financial governance in the IMF – increasing China's vote share and inclusion of the RMB in the IMF's SDR basket – China's position evolved from accepting the status quo to hold-up. In both situations, China's outside options remained favorable relative to those of the United States. Over the course of the period examined, however, what changed significantly in the strategic context were perceptions by other major powers of China's indispensability – and Beijing's understanding of such changed perceptions. Much as Poland's indispensability to Germany in negotiations over the 2007 Lisbon Treaty allowed it to block agreement on the new voting system until its demands were met, China was able to use its favorable outside options and post-2008 US perceptions of PRC indispensability to pursue a hold-up strategy on issues of global financial governance. China had the option of continuing to acquiesce in the existing voting rules and SDR makeup – in other words, continuing to accept its underrepresentation. But instead, Beijing used its increased leverage to ramp up pressure for changes at the IMF by implicitly threatening to withhold its cooperation in the G20 process that

80 Prasad, *Gaining Currency*, p. 145.

81 Keith Bradsher, "China's Renminbi is Approved by IMF as a Main World Currency," *The New York Times*, November 30, 2015, p. A1.

was at the center of solving the global crisis. Beijing made its willingness to cooperate on second-order issues relating to international finance conditional on an increased voice in decision-making and pushed the IMF to consider issues that address long-term Chinese concerns (like the global role of the dollar).

Unlike the Lisbon Treaty and the example of Poland's hold-up strategy, China's pursuit of a hold-up in the IMF was not explicit or obstreperous. In international negotiations, Chinese officials often are cognizant of image concerns and – as we have seen in the vote share case – hope other countries might make the case on their behalf. Beijing was helped by sympathetic and accommodating positions by IMF staff and some member countries (recall the position of Sarkozy). Such accommodation is consistent with hold-up, or fear of it, but accommodation can be – and in this case obviously was – driven by broader questions of legitimacy of the institution.[82]

Our analysis of China's hold-up posture with regard to IMF voting and SDR inclusion is contrary to behavior that would be predicted by theories emphasizing China's socialization into international regimes. Although theories of China's socialization into the organization seem a potent explanation for China's acceptant behavior toward the IMF up through the mid-2000s, a unidirectional socialization process does not account for China's challenge to the IMF following the global financial crisis. Stone suggested that a combination of socialization, institutional power dynamics, and shifting interests might lead to changes in China's behavior (and that of other emerging economies). He argues that developing countries, because they are net borrowers, would participate cooperatively despite underrepresentation, but that "when countries have shifted from net borrower to net creditor status in the past, their interests have generally aligned more closely with that of the United States, ensuring that is was relatively easy to maintain a consensus among the states that were powerful enough to change the rules."[83] This line of reasoning would

[82] The argument that IMF staff accommodation has been useful is made in Mikko Huotari and Thilo Hanemann, "Emerging Powers and Change in the Global Financial Order," *Global Policy*, Vol. 5, no. 3 (2014), pp. 298–310. A similar argument about World Bank reforms is made in Chin, "The World Bank and China." Still, World Bank reform negotiations of 2010 were contentious. See www.reuters.com/article/us-worldbank-idUSTRE63O1RQ20100425.

[83] Stone, *Controlling Institutions*, 79. He suggests developing countries, as borrowers dependent upon IMF disbursements, did not have the leverage to counter the established practices.

predict that when emerging countries gain voting shares, they would tend to remain aligned with the established powers. This explanation does not predict hold-up.

However, our explanation based on strategic considerations is not inconsistent with (and, indeed, in the previous discussion to some degree incorporates) alternative explanations emphasizing domestic trends. The mid-2000s saw a pronounced turn among intellectuals and the Chinese populace toward greater skepticism about Western countries' control of the global financial system, although dissatisfaction had been sparked by the Asian financial crisis in the late 1990s. This increased dissatisfaction was accompanied by the view that China's government should stand up for Chinese interests against American "hegemony," including in the international financial system. The onset of the global financial crisis, which in China was largely blamed on US excesses and advantages of a dollar-dominated monetary regime, furthered the view that China should "stand up."[84] However, despite the importance of these domestic trends, we show that any nascent desire for change in China's actual policy toward its representation in the IMF was not acted on until perceptions of China's indispensability to a solution were transformed during the global financial crisis. In other words, while domestic trends toward nationalism are important, we gain significant additional leverage from analysis of Beijing's assessment of its strategic context, as provided by our theory.

Interestingly, operating outside the established institutions, Beijing has been enhancing its outside options to be able to carry out a hold-up strategy more effectively. In other words, as foreshadowed by our discussion of dynamic conditions in Chapter 2, China's leaders appear to have been attempting to improve their outside options in global finance through investment in new institutions. Beijing in 2014–2015 established two new global financial bodies that exclude US participation: the New (formerly BRICS) Development Bank and the Asian Infrastructure Investment Bank. The NDB – established in 2014, headquartered in Shanghai, and whose main aim is to fund large infrastructure projects – gained substantial commitments of funding and established voting rules for members that contrast with those of the World Bank and IMF: one country–one vote and no veto. The AIIB – headquartered in Beijing and driven strongly by China's actions and funds – was founded by a pan-Asian membership in

84 Wang and Pauly, "Chinese IPE Debates."

October 2014 to fund infrastructure projects in Asia. The establishment of these two organizations appears to be a more robust attempt than has been made with the CMI to construct alternatives to the US–created global financial institutions.[85] We return in our concluding chapter to the case of AIIB, which we note may be partly motivated by China's desire to enhance its outside options.

[85] For representative commentary on these new institutions from a US perspective, see Evan A. Feigenbaum, "The New Asian Order and How the United States Fits In," *Foreign Affairs* (February 2015): www.foreignaffairs.com/articles/142843/evan-a-feigenbaum/the-new-asian-order; and Ellen L. Frost, "Rival Regionalisms and Regional Order: A Slow Crisis of Legitimacy," *NBR Special Report # 48* (Seattle, WA: National Bureau of Asian Research, 2014).

7

Climate Change Negotiations

From Hold-Up to Invest

7.1 INTRODUCTION

International negotiations to address climate change have continued for nearly half a century, ever since the 1972 United Nations Conference on the Human Environment held in Stockholm. The PRC has been a participant in these talks from the beginning. In recent years, China's participation in negotiations to limit the emission and impact of greenhouse gases has received intense scrutiny, particularly as both China's leaders and outside observers have recognized the country's rapidly increasing contribution to the problem. Since the turn of the century, Beijing's outlook on international cooperation over climate change issues has evolved: at first, China's leaders preferred a framework that relied on "historical emitters" from industrialized countries paying the costs of addressing climate change, but more recently Beijing has shown considerable willingness to undertake greater cooperation with the developed world.[1] Most explanations of China's evolving behavior have put China's domestic politics at center stage, arguing that Chinese leaders' emphasis on domestic "dirty" growth at the expense of curbing GHG emissions (and pollution in general) has given way to their growing perception that

[1] We take no position on whether the agreements in which China has increasingly invested will be effective at addressing climate change, any more than we take a position on whether US–led agreements will be effective. As will become clear in this chapter, moreover, despite identifying China's position in the late-2000s as one of "hold-up," Beijing engaged in considerable cooperation with other developing countries. We also note that the United States engaged in long periods of intransigence against a cooperative outcome, specifically during most of the George W. Bush administration. During these times, "Western" leadership was the purview of the European Union.

climate change is a domestic social, economic, and political threat. These accounts often point to social pressure on China's leaders to address climate change.[2] Although the discussion in this chapter does not deny the considerable importance of domestic factors, we show that our structural theory can shed new light on explanations of China's behavior that have been based primarily on its domestic politics.

The case of climate negotiations also provides a lens through which to observe the evolution in Beijing's behavior from hold-up to invest. At the December 2009 climate summit in Copenhagen, in particular, Beijing's strategy was widely perceived outside of China as preventing a negotiated solution and, as a result, a key reason the resultant nonbinding Copenhagen Accord was relatively weak.[3] This perception is not quite correct, in the sense that Beijing had begun to move toward a strategy of investment in the period prior to Copenhagen.[4] Nevertheless, to view China's behavior at these crucial meetings as hold-up *is* correct insofar as Beijing's core positions were designed to induce the established powers – the United States and Europe – to pay the costs of a cooperative solution.[5] Stated in terms of our theory, China's bargaining power during this period derived from its favorable outside options and the perception of its indispensability, meaning that China could bargain hard and hold up support as a way to extract concessions from the other major powers. Moreover, as the meetings themselves unfolded and events

[2] Discussions that highlight domestic drivers of China's participation in the international climate change negotiations include: Thomas J. Christensen, *The China Challenge: Shaping the Choices of a Rising Power* (New York, NY: W. W. Norton, 2015); and Bran Buijs, *China, Copenhagen, and Beyond: The Global Necessity of a Global Sustainable Energy Future for China* (The Hague: Clingendael International Energy Program, 2009): www.clingendael.nl/publications/2009/20090900_ciep_report_buijs_china_copenhagen_beyond.pdf. A discussion that relies mainly on domestic drivers but also emphasizes international norms (though not structural factors) is Rosemary Foot and Andrew Walter, *China, the United States, and Global Order* (Cambridge: Cambridge University Press, 2011), chapter 5.

[3] Jonathan Watts, Damian Carrington, and Suzanne Goldenberg, "Mark Lynas: How China Wrecked Chances of Copenhagen Deal," *The Guardian* (February 11, 2010): www.guardian.co.uk/.../11/chinese-thinktank-copenhagen-document.

[4] As in all our case studies in this book, the timing of movement between outcomes (e.g., hold-up to invest) cannot be attributed to a precise moment.

[5] Note that in the case of climate negotiations – unlike the other cases in this book – the identity of the status quo powers (and, thus, who China interacted with) shifts; the US and EU positions at Bali (2007) and after were relatively divided. We conceptualize the United States and the European Union as trading off leadership at different moments, but given that we are attempting to understand China's behavior, the question of which power is leading at a given moment is secondary.

became unpredictable, Beijing's negotiators defaulted to a hold-up position on some issues for which cooperation might have occurred and, as was widely reported, attempted to scuttle a cooperative outcome.

China's hold-up strategy in the Copenhagen meetings is well predicted by our theory, which says hold-up will emerge if an indispensable rising power perceives its balance of outside options as strong relative to the other major players. The Hu-Wen administration, which held power from 2002 to 2012, paid increasing attention to the seriousness of global climate change and to the damage it was wreaking, and would continue to wreak, on the domestic environment and the Chinese economy. The government undertook many domestic steps to address it, ranging from the promotion of clean energy technology as a core initiative of the eleventh and twelfth Five Year Plans, to subjecting local governments to targets for energy intensity. Yet this domestic urgency did not translate into second-order multilateral cooperation. Indeed, China's stake in international cooperation remained low relative to that of the United States and the European Union. On the one hand, there was rising optimism about regime leadership coming from Europe and the United States. In particular, the European Union placed the Kyoto targets as a central plank of its participation in the common market, suggesting that a deal crafted by the United States–European Union would not leave China worse off. For its part, on the other hand, Beijing continued its longstanding position that the country's economic development, which would of necessity remain coal-dependent for a long time, took precedence over protecting global resources. This viewpoint was, furthermore, consistent with China's longstanding emphasis that the United States and the developed world are historically responsible for the buildup of GHGs in the atmosphere and should take primary responsibility for remediation. Chinese policy-makers further argued that, since developed countries that signed onto the Kyoto Protocol were unlikely to meet their committed targets, developing countries could not be expected to accept new targets. Thus, Beijing appeared to be quite tolerant of noncooperation toward a post-Kyoto framework and comfortable with the default Kyoto status quo.

As the UN process unfolded over the late 1990s and 2000s, moreover, China's participation in a cooperative solution came to be perceived by the established powers as indispensable. This assessment was based primarily on an evolving understanding of China's technical contribution to the problem of climate change (that is, its rising carbon emissions). China's indispensability from a first-order technical perspective translated into growing indispensability from a second-order perspective: to construct an agreement that dealt with the first-order issue of Chinese GHG emissions without active Chinese participation seemed implausible. Without China's participation, any new agreement to reduce GHGs would exclude a major source of emissions. China's technical contributions to the problem were also linked to its political indispensability. The United States, as well as some other wealthy countries, had already defected from the 1997 Kyoto Protocol based on the view that major developing country emitters were not treated symmetrically. At the same time, China was not "on the hook" because of its categorization as a developing country. Governments in wealthy countries saw that they could not make a new agreement credible to their home audiences without strong commitments from China. Increasingly, moreover, those poor countries most vulnerable to climate change – such as small island nations – also came to see China's active cooperation as indispensable to a credible agreement.

Despite China's willingness to submit unilateral plans to reduce carbon emissions, Beijing (at least through the 2009 Copenhagen talks) made its participation in a post-Kyoto treaty strictly conditional on gaining concessions on issues about which it was particularly sensitive: the maintenance of a firewall between the responsibilities of developed versus developing nations ("common but differential responsibilities"), the ability of developing countries to avoid binding treaty commitments and set their own targets, and a desire for wealthy countries to pay for mitigation costs incurred by poor countries. In short, the government was well positioned to adopt a hold-up posture.

In the period following the Copenhagen summit, China's balance of outside options worsened relative to the major powers (particularly the United States), and Beijing was no longer in a position to walk away. Specifically, we demonstrate China's growing interest in addressing climate change and that this translated into a serious interest in global cooperation on climate issues. Meanwhile, the fact that China had become the major emitter of greenhouse gases – a position Beijing acknowledged – made it difficult for China to opt out of global negotiations that would increase its contributions to a solution. In short, while Beijing's participation continued to be perceived as indispensable, the worsening of its outside options incentivized Beijing to invest in cooperation with the United States.[6] What followed was significantly more extensive cooperation between presidents Xi Jinping and Barack Obama in their

[6] By the time of the Copenhagen meetings in 2009, China's failure to participate would mean there was no agreement or, even worse for China, the prospect of EU unilateralism.

autumn 2014 meeting on the sidelines of the Beijing APEC summit, a process that continued and strongly shaped the outcome of the much heralded December 2015 Paris Agreement. The worsening of China's outside options was primarily a result of its increasing stake, a shift driven, in turn, by domestic politics. We stress that these changes – culminating in a posture of "invest" – did not occur overnight. As noted, climate issues had been on the government's agenda for years, and citizen activism had been prominent. The issue took on new urgency particularly following the infamous "airpocalypse" of January 2013. Over a span of several days, the air in dozens of Chinese cities hit pollution levels over twenty-five times that which is seen as safe in the United States. The problem of toxic particulates at the surface level is not coterminous with climate change, but these two issues came to be linked; addressing climate change was framed as a co-benefit of reducing air pollution. China's leaders came under substantial pressure at home – from local governments and citizens – and abroad to be seen as substantially helping mitigate climate change. The sting to China's status resulting from the negative perception in the West of China's intransigence at Copenhagen also seems to have pressed Beijing toward cooperation with the United States.

At the same time, in global negotiations following Copenhagen, Beijing's negotiators found it difficult to maintain key positions about which they and US negotiators had long disagreed. Primary among these was the sharp distinction between the "two camps" of the developed and developing world and the placement of the PRC in the "developing" camp. Even before Copenhagen, deep cracks had occurred in the BRIC and Group of Seventy-seven (G77) coalitions of developing countries, moreover.[7] Although the coalition of emerging economies had never been very solid, Beijing faced the prospect that both Brazil and India could defect toward greater cooperation with the United States. The G77 coalition that China aspired to lead exhibited new divisions that pressured Beijing to pay much greater costs of cooperation.

7.2 BACKGROUND: UNDERSTANDING THE INTERNATIONAL CLIMATE ARENA AND CHINA'S PLACE IN IT

The evolution of the global regime on greenhouse gas emissions provides a good case for examining China's behavior with regard to second-order

7 The G77 is a UN-based coalition of developing countries. It was established in 1967 by 77 countries, but now represents 134 member countries.

cooperation. While in the future we may be able to look back and examine China's first-order cooperation – how well it complied with the terms of its commitments to influence climate change – the past decades have already provided much evidence about how Beijing contributes to the creation of new rules as to how countries collectively should address the problem. At the same time, China's participation in global climate negotiations differs in some important ways from the other cases of second-order cooperation considered in this book, both in terms of the regime itself and China's participation in it. It is useful to consider these circumstances before turning to discussion of the evolution of China's participation in the UN climate regime.

7.2.1 The UN Climate Regime: A Complex of Issues and Actors

International discussions about mitigation and adaptation to climate change take place in many different venues. As Robert Keohane and David Victor point out, there is not just one regime but a set of "complexes," with participation by not just states and international organizations but a broad set of nongovernmental and subnational actors.[8] Our discussion in this book focuses on the most prominent of these complexes: negotiations under the rubric of the United Nations Framework Convention on Climate Change (UNFCCC), the UN-based organization established in Rio in 1992. China's leaders have viewed the UNFCCC as the most legitimate venue for global talks and, indeed, in position papers, always refer to the UN talks as the locus of their efforts. Even within this narrowed focus on the UN legal process, both technical and political factors render the negotiations highly complex.

On the technical side, negotiations cover many second-order issues related to climate change. To simplify, the issues can be categorized according to (i) the physical problem to be addressed, (ii) who will pay the costs of addressing the problem, and (iii) the form an agreement will

8 Other venues for negotiation over global climate issues include in "clubs" such as the G20, in bodies designed for expert assessment (especially the Intergovernmental Panel on Climate Change), trade and investment agreements (e.g., border tariff measures and intellectual property agreements in the WTO), multilateral development banks (e.g., environmental standards incorporated in World Bank loans), and bilateral agreements. Robert O. Keohane and David G. Victor, "The Regime Complex for Climate Change," *Perspectives on Politics*, Vol. 9, no. 1 (2011), pp. 7–23. On the influence of nongovernmental actors, particularly at the Copenhagen meetings in 2009, see Jennifer Hadden, *Networks in Contention: The Divisive Politics of Climate Change* (New York, NY: Cambridge University Press, 2015).

take. First, the subject most central to international talks (though not always most controversial) has been how to *mitigate* (reduce) the absolute quantity of GHGs being emitted into the atmosphere. Other subjects related to the physical problem include: steps countries might take to *adapt* to the expected results of climate change (e.g., flood control projects), and the diffusion of technology for climate mitigation and adaptation. Second, discussions surround the issue of which countries (and more recently, which other actors, including subnational and private actors) will *pay the costs* of change. Many attempts to address this issue revolve around the categorizations of countries ("differentiation" or "bifurcation") into "payers" and "receivers." We might think of this as discussions over who bears the greatest burden of physical cuts to emissions (with the trade-off often characterized as opportunity costs for economic development), and who pays for projects to help poorer countries mitigate, adapt and acquire technology. Third, many disagreements between countries concern the format of an agreement: How specific will an agreement be (e.g., will it contain fixed numeric targets or more general intentions)? How long will the terms of an agreement be and using what metrics as a baseline? Will it be a legal agreement or a political one?[9] Will it be binding and, if so, to all or to just a subset of countries? Will implementation and outcomes be verified by actors outside the country taking actions (inclusive of mechanisms for verification and transparency)? Our chapter focuses primarily on mitigation-related subjects of quantity of and payment for emissions, but this focus entails attention to the distributional and agreement format matters as well.

In addition to the expanse of issues subject to negotiation, important socio-political dynamics related to the issue of climate change, and the viewpoints of actors, have changed over time. Not only has the concept of human-induced and deleterious climate change become widely accepted as fact throughout most of the world, but the perceived urgency of the problem has intensified dramatically. Nevertheless, the distribution of responsibility across countries remains controversial. The countries that have been emitting GHGs for many decades are "historic emitters"; among these, the United States was the top emitter until 2005, responsible

[9] The concept of "legal instrument" means that an agreement will have the force of a treaty (even if not technically in the form of a treaty) and will have legal status under international law. In the climate negotiations, "legality" has meant that signatories "deposit" their commitments with the United Nations. A legal agreement can vary according to how much and how specifically it binds signatories, however.

for approximately 27 percent of cumulative historic emissions.[10] The ranking of countries with highest total emissions has evolved from the historic emitters to include the emerging economies of India and, especially, China. China became the biggest contemporary emitter of GHGs in 2005, and by 2014 India was ranked fourth after China, the United States, and the European Union. China ranks third of all countries in total emissions over the period 1850–2011.[11] When *per capita* emissions are considered, however, China and India fall away from the top countries, and the list is dominated by (in order) Canada, the United States, the Russian Federation, Japan, and the European Union. Complexities also arise when we consider countries' ability to address climate change. While the OECD countries continue to be most able on an absolute and per capita basis to pay the costs and harness the technology to address the problem, China's rapid growth over the past several decades and its position as the first or second largest economy in the world (depending on the method of measurement) has also moved it onto the list of countries most capable of addressing the problem, despite its lower per capita income. As China has taken center stage in these ways, its indispensability – what we might consider "technical indispensability" to resolving the problem of climate change – has become obvious to observers inside and outside of the country; it has become an unquestioned tenet of negotiations that any meaningful climate stabilization will be impossible without China.

A final issue is that addressing climate change involves complex technological and economic considerations inherent in all countries' energy systems.[12] GHG emissions have been a function of development, increasing as societies grow in population, in urbanization, in the use of energy for industrialization, heating, and cooling, and in other factors related to improving living standards. Yet countries vary as to how difficult it is to substitute "clean" energy technologies for carbon-intensive ones. China and the United States alike have enormous industrial economies built on the use of fossil fuels. The incorporation of new technology to an

[10] Figures on historic emitters are reported in Ben Adler, "Trump Can't Do Much to Worsen Climate Change," *The Washington Post*, April 2, 2017, B1; and Johannes Friedrich and Thomas Damassa, "The History of Carbon Dioxide Emissions," World Resources Institute blog (May 21, 2014): www.wri.org/blog/2014/05/history-carbon-dioxide-emissions.

[11] On the list of top emitters by absolute GHG emissions and per capita GHG emissions, see the online resource from World Resources Institute (July 5, 2016): www.wri.org/blog/2014/11/6-graphs-explain-world%E2%80%99s-top-10-emitters.

[12] See Sergey Paltsev, Jennifer Morris, Yongxia Cai, Valerie Karplus, and Henry Jacoby, "The Role of China in Mitigating Climate Change," MIT Joint Program on the Science and Policy of Global Change, Report no. 215 (Cambridge, MA: JPSPCG, April 2012).

extent that can have a substantial mitigation impact, effectively creating an entirely new energy system, is both logistically challenging and costly. Unlike most of the other issues considered in this book, which involve either diplomacy or narrow interests that can be relatively isolated from the rest of the economy, mobilization involves many actors and many deep interests. Moreover, enforceability of climate policy is arguably more difficult than in other realms (such as IMF practices), as mitigation and adaptation tools depend on a host of factors outside the direct policy domain.

Also unlike other issues considered in this volume, as the perceived urgency of climate change has deepened, so too have the numbers of actors involved and the amount of attention negotiations have received. In part, this is related to the economy-wide impacts of GHG mitigation and adaptation. But expansion of the number of actors also is due to the often contentious involvement of societal actors and networks.[13] At the same time, the UNFCCC framework requires that decisions be made by consensus among all 197 (as of 2018) participating parties. These factors create high hurdles for a meaningful agreement. Perhaps, then, finding a wide variety of coalitions – formal and informal – attempting to influence the negotiations is no surprise. Coalitions have also evolved over time. An early divide between, primarily, the OECD countries and the G77 has evolved into a split within the OECD, as the United States defected from negotiations (2001–2007) and finds weaker domestic support than the European Union. Fissures also have emerged within the developing world – notably the emerging economies versus the poorest countries versus the nations most existentially vulnerable to climate change (small island nations and countries with densely populated, low-lying coastal areas). These different groupings are fluid, and interests shift depending on the specific subject of negotiation.[14] As we shall see, the shifting of alliances and groupings has been quite influential on China's position in negotiations, and has altered the balance of outside options. Most importantly, and reflecting the return of the United States to negotiations in Bali in 2007 and China's changed status in terms of both raw emissions and mitigation capabilities, a United States–China G2 emerged after Copenhagen (2009) as the lead parties in negotiations. This reflection of China's "political indispensability" made sense given that without

[13] On networks involved in climate change politics, see Hadden, *Networks in Contention*.

[14] Some of these groupings are usefully illustrated at: www.carbonbrief.org/infographic-mapping-country-alliances-at-the-international-climate-talks; and at: www.carbonbrief.org/why-more-political-rifts-could-be-good-for-international-climate-negotiations.

these two actors taking major steps the actions taken by other countries would have a much diminished impact, reducing the incentives for other countries to bear significant costs.

Finally, the PRC has been a participant in UN-sponsored negotiations over climate issues since their inception: first at the 1972 Stockholm meetings that led to the founding one year later of the UN Environmental Program, then at the founding meeting for the UNFCCC in Rio in 1992.[15] Unlike some other issue areas we consider in this volume, then, China helped set the original rules of the dominant regime.

7.3 CHINA AND CLIMATE NEGOTIATIONS FROM BALI TO COPENHAGEN: INDISPENSABILITY AND FAVORABLE OUTSIDE OPTIONS LEAD TO HOLD-UP

Our theory predicts that a favorable balance of outside options and China's growing understanding that China is perceived as indispensable to cooperation will lead to hold-up in second-order cooperation. Hold-up is, for all intents and purposes, what occurred in the defining Conference of the Parties (COP) meetings held in Copenhagen in 2009. As with all COP events, these meetings were preceded by months of negotiations in different fora. Before examining the Copenhagen meetings, we offer some background on early climate agreements and China's participation in climate negotiations up to and through the meetings at Bali in 2007.

7.3.1 Negotiations in the Lead-up to Bali

The founding treaty of the UNFCCC in Rio in 1992, signed by 154 countries and the European Commission, established several baseline norms that strongly affected subsequent negotiations.[16] First, it called for only

[15] On China's long history of participation in environmental regimes more generally, see Lester Ross, "China and Environmental Protection," in Michel Oksenberg and Elizabeth Economy, eds., *China Joins the World: Progress and Prospects* (New York, NY: Council on Foreign Relations Press, 1999), pp. 296–325; Elizabeth Economy, "The Impact of International Regimes on Chinese Foreign Policy-Making: Broadening Perspectives and Policies ... But Only to a Point," in David M. Lampton, ed., *The Making of Chinese Foreign and Security Policy in the Era of Reform*, (Stanford, CA: Stanford University Press, 2001); and Foot and Walter, *China, the United States, and Global Order*.

[16] This discussion is based on Foot and Walter, *China, the United States, and Global Order*, pp. 179–81. An additional norm, problematic mainly in the United States, was use of the "precautionary principle," which stated that action should be taken to avoid the possibility of harm, even if scientific evidence was inconclusive.

voluntary provisions and for flexibility in implementation, rather than legally binding commitments. Second, signatories agreed to set ("from above") collective goals for climate mitigation, but without specifying how implementation responsibilities would be divided among specific countries. Rather, a general agreement emerged such that developed countries would, by 2000, stabilize GHG emissions at 1990 levels. Third, norms about the distribution of burdens for resolving problems *according to capability* were set: the principles that "the polluter pays" and countries would be assigned "common but differentiated responsibility" meant that remediation tasks could be assigned differentially to rich and poor countries. Finally, it was established that governments should regularly report on their current and projected emissions, injecting the possibility of greater transparency than often appeared in other agreements. The PRC, still widely considered a developing country despite being a decade into its economic reforms, strongly supported the first three of these norms. It was less comfortable with the norm concerning transparency.

Within a few short years, the principle of nonbinding targets, while retained in the case of developing countries, was eroded for developed countries. The UNFCCC COP meetings in Berlin in 1995 settled a mandate for developed countries to act first, whereas rights to economic development would remain the overriding priority for developing countries. This mandate carried into the 1997 Kyoto Protocol, which set a collective target for a group of wealthy countries (called "Annex I" countries) to reduce emissions levels by 5.2 percent below 1990 levels prior to 2012.[17] In addition to the collective figure of 5.2 percent, individual countries were assigned targets. For example, the United States was to reduce emissions by 7 percent. Based on arguments of historical responsibility, per capita emissions, and source of demand for products creating GHG emissions (since production facilities responding to demand from wealthy countries were increasingly outsourced to poor countries), China and India were not assigned targets. Despite the endorsement at Kyoto of market-oriented emissions trading schemes that reflected preferences of the US government, the absence of binding targets for major emitters from the developing world led to strong opposition in the US government.[18] In 2001, the Bush administration announced the United States

[17] On the Kyoto Protocol, see the UN statement at: http://unfccc.int/kyoto_protocol/items/2830.php.

[18] The Byrd–Hagel resolution of 1997 foreshadowed the Bush administration position, declaring the United States should not sign an agreement that mandated new

would drop out of the Kyoto Protocol because it was a legally binding instrument under which the costs for mitigating damage fell on a small and defined number of developed nations. When the Bush administration decided to rejoin discussions at Bali in 2007, many of these original Kyoto principles remained influential.

With the clock ticking on the need to negotiate a replacement agreement in light of the scheduled close of the Kyoto Protocol's first commitment period in 2012, China (with a long record of arguing that primary responsibility for the climate crisis lay at the doorsteps of the developed West) argued that the developing world should be protected from bearing the costs of mitigation.[19] Peking University's Zhang Haibin has emphasized the continuity in China's position on key elements of second-order cooperation over the period from 1991 to 2005. Under the rubric of a "principle of fairness" [*gongping yuanze*], China maintained a strong commitment to the principle of common but differentiated responsibilities [*gongtong de danyou qubie de zeren*] reflecting varying national capabilities [*benxian guojia butong nengli*] and equitable per capita "rights" [*renjun pingdeng quanli*]. On issues of both mitigation commitments and finance, then, China argued that developed countries should bear the greatest costs. China also consistently opposed the idea that developing countries should have to submit binding commitments to reduce emissions [*fou chengnuo jianpai*], and – as we shall see in China's position in Copenhagen in 2009 – sometimes even opposed binding commitments by developed countries.[20]

Whereas China exhibited fundamental continuities in the principles underlying its negotiating position, other important changes were taking place. In particular, domestic assessments of China's vulnerability to climate change were evolving. By the mid-2000s, Chinese leaders acknowledged that the country was on track to quickly become the world's largest

commitments to limit or reduce GHG emissions for the Annex I parties unless that agreement also mandated new specific scheduled commitments to limit or reduce GHG emissions for developing countries within the same compliance period.

[19] Joanna I. Lewis, "China's Strategic Priorities in International Climate Change Negotiations," *The Washington Quarterly*, Vol. 31, no. 1 (2007), pp. 155–74.

[20] Zhang Haibin asserts the continuity between 1991 and 2005 of China's insistence on fairness and nonbinding commitments for developing countries, but states that China's position became more flexible on financing mechanisms, particularly to include cap and trade schemes. Zhang Haibin, "Zhongguo zai Guoji Qihou Bianhua Tanpan zhong de Lichang: Lianxuxing yu Bianhua jiqi Yuanyin Tanxi" [China's Positions in International Climate Change Negotiations: Continuity and Change and Analysis of its Causes], *Shijie Jingji yu Zhengzhi*, no. 10 (2006), pp. 36–43.

emitter. In tandem, leaders recognized that the domestic impact of climate change was likely substantial, threatening growth and livelihood.[21] Domestic scholars also made cost-benefit analyses that pointed to the declining monetary costs of emissions reduction technologies relative to the vulnerability of the environment.[22] These pressures, and the felt need by China's leaders that the country must respond, were evident in several key party and government documents. Most important, because it was the most authoritative statement of national policy, was the State Council's eleventh Five Year Plan covering the years 2006–2010, which set a goal of 20 percent reduction in energy intensity and a target to have non-fossil fuels account for 10 percent of China's primary energy consumption.[23] Chinese leaders' growing recognition that climate change posed serious domestic challenges suggested that Beijing's stake in the issue had begun to increase. Nevertheless, the legacy development agenda that saw economic growth as the key to national rejuvenation and security underlay China's consistent negotiating position. Addressing climate change competed with economic growth as a priority for Chinese leaders. Chinese Premier Wen Jiabao, during a speech in Singapore in November 2007, rejected the idea that addressing climate change should come at the expense of economic growth: "Efforts to fight climate change should promote, not block, economic development."[24] Similar high-profile statements suggesting a willingness to pursue unilateral actions to address climate change included "China's National Climate Change Program" issued by the National Development and Reform Commission (NDRC) – the lead agency for China's climate policy – several months before the Bali meetings in June 2007:

> Mitigating greenhouse gas emissions is one of the important components in addressing climate change. According to the principle of "common but differentiated responsibilities" of the UNFCCC, the Parties included in Annex I to the Convention should take the lead in reducing greenhouse gas emissions. For developing countries with less historical emission and current low per capita

[21] See the excellent summary in Buijs, *China, Copenhagen, and Beyond*.

[22] Zhang Haibin argued that China's position in climate negotiations was based on three elements: the cost of emission reduction, the cost of environmental fragility, and – as considered later – the international principle of fairness. See Zhang Haibin, "Zhongguo zai Guoji Qihou Bianhua Tanpan."

[23] On the mechanisms set forth in the eleventh Five Year Plan to address climate change, see Paltsev et al., "The Role of China in Mitigating Climate Change."

[24] Wen Jiabao speech at the East Asia Summit, Singapore, November 2007, quoted at: http://uk.reuters.com/article/environment-asean-dc/asian-leaders-sign-vague-climate-pact-idUKSP77652200711 21.

emission, their priority is to achieve sustainable development. As a developing country, China will stick to its sustainable development strategy and take such measures as energy efficiency improvement, energy conservation, development of renewable energy, ecological preservation and construction, as well as large-scale tree planting and afforestation, to control its greenhouse gas emissions and make further contribution to the protection of global climate system.[25]

Thus, despite significant growing concern about climate change, Beijing remained consistent in the view that historical responsibility for climate emissions and the "right to development" must be protected, even as China pursued a sustainable development model. The government also continued to strongly advocate a bifurcation "firewall" between developed and developing countries, letting others – the previously identified wealthy countries – pay the costs of cooperation by making binding commitments to reduce carbon emissions and to finance mitigation efforts (and required technology) for the developing world. Beijing, always sensitive to sovereignty issues, also resisted what it saw as an intrusive verification system. China's leaders thus appear to have expected that cooperating with the established powers on a new agreement would not leave China any better off than not cooperating. Beijing's position upholding the basic terms of the Kyoto Protocol as the status quo had for years been facilitated by the international coalitional politics of the mid-2000s. Up to and through the Bali meetings, Beijing remained ensconced in a G77+China grouping. Indeed, its position within the G77 served to deflect attention from its growing status as an emitter.[26] The G77 remained a relatively cohesive grouping during this period, despite some defection (as when Argentina broke away in 1998 to set its own mitigation commitments).[27]

At the international level, meanwhile, assessments of China's indispensability were becoming commonplace. While recognition of China's role as a major emitter had existed since the 1990s, it was front and center by the mid-2000s. China's rapidly growing GHG emissions pointed to its

[25] Quoted at: www.china.org.cn/english/environment/213624.htm#21. See also Gorild Heggelund, "China's Climate Change Policy: Domestic and International Developments," *Perspective*, Vol. 31, no. 2 (2007), pp. 155–91. China's National Climate Change Program, issued June 4, 2007 by the NDRC, was China's first major domestic climate change policy initiative. The document recognizes the impact of climate change on China, and it commits the government to adopting laws and economic and technology policies for reducing GHG emissions and to initiating a "flexible" approach to climate change: www.china-un.org/eng/chinaandun/economicdevelopment/climatechange/t626117.htm.

[26] Lewis, "China's Strategic Priorities," p. 162.

[27] Elizabeth Economy, "The Impact of International Regimes."

technical indispensability – that effectively addressing the problem would ultimately require active Chinese efforts at mitigation. Models from the International Energy Administration, for example, argued that whereas Annex I countries had accounted for 60 percent of global emissions when the UNFCCC was signed in 1992, they were expected to account for only 3 percent of global emissions growth after about 2010.[28]

7.3.2 The Bali Conference of the Parties Meetings, 2007

These factors – rapidly increasing developing world emissions and the US return to negotiations – set the context for the 2007 Bali Conference of the Parties, attended by representatives of 180 countries and multitudes of NGOs. The Bali meetings were to provide a path beyond Kyoto's first commitment period, setting a roadmap for a new "agreed outcome" to be adopted in 2009 at the COP meetings in Copenhagen. Thus, while perhaps not the landmark meeting that was anticipated for Copenhagen, the Bali meetings deserve attention because they set the tone for what would transpire with the US government's return to the negotiations. The United States agreed to rejoin the UN process, despite remaining a non-signatory to the Kyoto Protocol, in exchange for agreement from the European Union to participate in the Bush administration's newly created Major Economies Meeting (later, Major Economies Forum). With the return of the United States, then, the strongest voice in favor of reworking the principles of Kyoto reappeared. Unlike the European Union, the United States was highly unlikely to agree to a continuation of Kyoto – which protected large emerging economies – as the main instrument for addressing climate change.[29] China, not a member of that small group of Annex I countries despite Beijing's increased recognition that it would take stronger mitigation steps, had no desire to submit to binding obligations. The Kyoto legacy provided plausible legitimacy for this position and, thus, China repeatedly embraced Kyoto's continuation.[30]

[28] Cited in Trevor Houser, *Copenhagen, the Accord, and the Way Forward*, Peterson Institute for International Economics Policy Brief PB10-5 (Washington, DC: PIIE, 2010), p. 2. Note that Houser was a member of the US negotiating team at Copenhagen.

[29] A continued bifurcation between Annex I and non-Annex I countries that kept China, in particular, from committing to firm mitigation targets was not politically acceptable to the George W. Bush administration and was untenable in the context of US legislative politics.

[30] The singling out of Annex I countries as the only countries subject to binding international targets protected emerging countries (such as China and India) from submitting binding targets. They thus favored continuing talks along two tracks after Bali: the

In short, the United States wanted a legal instrument with symmetry between actors, whereas China did not want a legal instrument, at least for non-Annex I countries.[31]

Given the cohesive G77 position, China was relatively insulated at Bali. The United States, in contrast, was on the defensive and isolated. The United States attempted to push developing countries toward more stringent commitments, but also sought to avoid EU pressure to impose numeric targets based on scientific recommendations from the Intergovernmental Panel on Climate Change.[32] Nevertheless, through intense end-stage negotiations and under pressure, the United States relented on some objections, and a consensus text emerged as the Bali Action Plan. The text showed compromise from the G77+China, as the plan called on developing countries to take heavier action to reduce their emissions than required under the Kyoto Protocol in exchange for developed nations continuing to take a major role on mitigation, as well as funding and facilitating the process of clean technology transfer. The Bali Action Plan also reaffirmed economic development as the overriding priority for developing countries. The developing countries avoided binding reductions, favored by the United States, moreover. Rather, those developing countries whose national circumstances enabled emissions reductions were to work out the details of their reductions over the next two years, prior to Copenhagen.[33] (Although China suggested it would contribute more unilaterally to mitigation "actions," it did not agree that it should make binding commitments in a new agreement.[34]) Most basically, then, the sharp distinction between developed and developing obligations remained ensconced in the language of Bali, though the move to a distinction based on "developed" versus "developing" removed some of the rigidity of the Kyoto "Annex I/non-Annex I" categories. At the same

---

Kyoto process and the Bali Long-term Cooperative Action (LCA) process. A succinct discussion of the post-Bali and Copenhagen positions of the major actors and blocs is found in Houser, "Copenhagen." The EU position favored a binding agreement that included the United States but was willing to continue the legal asymmetry of Kyoto.

[31] See above note. 9 on the significance of legal instruments.

[32] See Raymond Clémençon, "The Bali Road Map: A First Step on the Difficult Journey to a Post-Kyoto Protocol Agreement," *The Journal of Environment Development*, Vol. 17, no. 1 (2008), pp. 70–94; and: www.asil.org/insights/volume/12/issue/4/bali-climate-change-conference.

[33] Elizabeth Burleson, "The Bali Climate Change Conference," *Insights* (American Society for International Law), Vol. 12, no. 4 (2008): www.asil.org/insights/volume/12/issue/4/bali-climate-change-conference.

[34] See: www.globalbioenergy.org/uploads/media/0809_UNDP_-_The_Bali_action_plan_key_issues_in_the_climate_negotiations.pdf.

time, because the Kyoto Protocol did not expire, China and India, in particular, strongly favored the continuation of negotiations geared toward a second commitment period.[35] Two tracks in negotiations thus emerged: a new one pursuant to Bali that included the United States (the Long-term Cooperative Action track charged with implementing the Bali Action Plan) and one continuing to seek an agreement under Kyoto.[36] With the United States out of Kyoto (other countries, such as Canada and Japan, also had dropped out), it was unclear how effective the Kyoto track preferred by China could be. However, by preserving Kyoto, the reference point of Annex I/non-Annex I bifurcation, with binding commitments by the former only, remained. Bifurcation of responsibilities, with China primarily on the developing-country side – though with increasing willingness to contribute nationally to mitigation efforts – continued front and center.[37]

One additional, and little noticed at the time, result from Bali was new activism from small and especially vulnerable Pacific island nations that formed the Alliance of Small Island States (AOSIS). This group had been founded in 1990, and generally aligned with the G77. As the impact of climate change on these countries became clearer, AOSIS began more forcefully to express both the need for a strong mitigation regime and concerns that emerging economies (such as China and India) were too weakly committed to a strong mitigation regime.

35 Houser ("Copenhagen," p. 5) explains a common misperception about the legal force of Kyoto: While most press accounts described the Bali Action Plan as a roadmap for a new legally binding international agreement to replace the Kyoto Protocol, the Kyoto Protocol does not actually expire. While the Kyoto Protocol specified emission reductions only for 2008–12 (known as the first commitment period), its calls for Annex I countries to agree to further emission reductions from 2013, and for negotiations over this 'second commitment period' to begin in 2005.

36 In 2005, on the entry into force of the Kyoto Protocol, parties established an Ad Hoc Working Group to negotiate binding post-2012 emission targets for developed countries (except the United States, which is not a party to Kyoto). Recognizing that the countries with Kyoto emission targets would not accept a second commitment period without some corresponding commitment from the United States and the major emerging economies, parties adopted the Bali Action Plan in 2007, launching a second Ad Hoc Working Group under the UNFCCC with the aim of an "agreed outcome" two years later in Copenhagen. The resulting LCA thus emerged in 2007, primarily as a forum for discussing a new climate agreement that would bring parties that were not bound (especially the United States and China) to reduce their emissions under the Kyoto Protocol.

37 The Bali Action Plan also took steps toward meaningful financial assistance to help poor countries mitigate emissions and adapt to changes in the earth's climate. These financing provisions, which had been weakly addressed in the Kyoto Protocol, in the future would prove an important tool to bring the poorest countries on board with a more stringent agreement.

7.3.3 Hold-up at Copenhagen, 2009

Against the backdrop of the Bali negotiations and China's growing emissions, we can trace how China's position at Copenhagen became characterized by hold-up. In the months leading up to the meetings in Copenhagen in December, 2009, Beijing continued to express considerable concern over the domestic impact of climate change, as seen in a government white paper issued in 2008.[38] Along with the significant evolution of policy at home, Beijing's positions on some key issues related to an international agreement were also evolving, at least somewhat. Most notably, there seemed to be a deepening understanding that the impact of climate issues on China's domestic welfare would depend on an agreement to which developed countries could commit. Moreover, the Hu-Wen administration was also feeling the shift in expectations about its contributions to climate change and its potential role in addressing it – in other words, about its indispensability. External pressure on China to acknowledge its role was strong.[39] The outcome was Beijing's unilateral offer – several days in advance of the Copenhagen meetings and shortly after a comparable US public commitment – as a sign of "initiative and good example,"[40] a nonbinding yet "unconditional" commitment. The offer targeted a 40- to 45-percent reduction in domestic carbon intensity by 2020, from 2005 levels. In addition, China pledged to increase the share of non-fossil fuels in primary energy consumption to around 15 percent by 2020.[41] As we will discuss, Beijing's offer represented a potentially profound shift in favor of cooperation with the developed world, although it ultimately did not have the desired impact in Copenhagen itself. At the Copenhagen meetings, moreover, Beijing also sought means for alternative and flexible mitigation mechanisms (such as emissions

[38] State Council Information Office (Beijing: SCIO, 2008): www.ccchina.gov.cn/WebSite/CCChina/UpFile/File419.pdf.

[39] Zhongxiang Zhang, "Breaking the Impasse in International Climate Negotiations: A New Direction for Currently Flawed Negotiations and a Roadmap for China till 2050," in Mingjiang Li, ed., *China Joins Global Governance: Cooperation and Contentions* (Lexington, MA: Lexington Books, 2015), pp. 173–86.

[40] Pan Jiahua, "Gebenhagen qihou Huiyi de Zhengxi Jiaodian he Fansi" [Focal Points and Revisiting of the Copenhagen Controversy], *Renmin Ribao* (March 19, 2010).

[41] "Carbon intensity" is a measure of carbon dioxide emissions per unit of GDP. On the commitments submitted, see Su Wei (2010), "Letter Including Autonomous Domestic Mitigation Actions," letter to Executive Secretary Yvo De Boer, January 28, 2010, UNFCCC: https://unfccc.int/files/meetings/cop_15/copenhagen_accord/application/pdf/chinacphaccord_app2.pdf.

trading schemes)[42] and accepted a role, albeit limited, for international verification. Finally, some speculated that Chinese negotiators, especially experienced negotiators from the NDRC (notably Xie Zhenhua and Su Wei) who had been in numerous bilateral and multilateral climate negotiations over the years, might be ready for further compromise with the United States and the European Union.[43]

Yet, in important ways, coming in to the negotiations, China's core positions hewed to the past.[44] The domestic priority on economic development remained. Indeed, China's leaders often were quite blunt about this priority. Yu Qingtai, China's lead climate negotiator from the Ministry of Foreign Affairs between 2007 and 2010, argued even in 2010 that "China is bound to be dependent on coal for energy ... Many problems can only be solved through development. We cannot blindly accept that protecting the climate is humanity's common interest – national interests should come first."[45] Along with the other emerging economy countries, moreover, China continued to insist on bifurcation (common and differentiated responsibilities) and that only developed countries should submit binding commitments.[46]

The distance between China's position and that of the Obama administration was substantial. The United States emphasized that countries of different capacities could make different types of commitments. For example, wealthy countries could commit to specific emissions reduction targets, while developing countries could commit to the implementation of policies intended to reduce emissions in developing countries. Commitments did not need to be uniform. But – in contrast to the EU position, which tolerated a continuation of the Kyoto bifurcation – the

42 Lewis, "China's Strategic Priorities," pp. 163–4.

43 Björn Conrad, "China in Copenhagen: Reconciling the 'Beijing Climate Revolution' and the 'Copenhagen Climate Obstinacy,'" *The China Quarterly*, no. 210 (2012), pp. 435–55.

44 Conrad emphasizes the puzzling contrast between extensive steps taken at home and the seeming rigidity of positions in negotiations. See Conrad, "China in Copenhagen."

45 Quoted in Andrew C. Revkin, "China Sustains Blunt 'You First' Message on CO_2," *The New York Times*, September 2, 2010: http://dotearth.blogs.nytimes.com/2010/09/02/china-sustains-blunt-you-first-message-on-co2.

46 See, for example, Wen Jiabao, "Jiaqiang Guoji Jishu Hezuo Jiji Ying Dui Qihou Bianhua" [Strengthen International Technical Cooperation in Tackling Climate Change], *Xin Shijie Lingdaozhe*, Vol. 11, no. 6 (2008), pp. 55–6; *China's Position on the Copenhagen Climate Change Conference*, posted May 20, 2009 on the PRC UN website: www.china-un.org/eng/chinaandun/economicdevelopment/climatechange/t568959.htm; and Wang Xiaogang, "Gongtong dan you Qubie de Zeren Yuanze de Shiyong jiqi Xianzhi" [Application and Limits of the Principle of Common but Differentiated Responsibility], *Shehui Kexue*, no. 7 (2010), pp. 80–9.

United States insisted on a legally "symmetric" agreement that was binding for major developing countries and developed countries alike, with "binding" indicating a requirement to make *some* commitment, and to have transparency and accountability in implementation. The United States also insisted on a mechanism to adjust levels of obligation in light of evolving circumstances and capacity, and hence an end to the fixed set of Annex I countries.[47] China, and the emerging economy countries more generally, resisted relinquishing their protected status as non-Annex I countries. They wished to retain, in any new agreement, the Kyoto Protocol definitions that focused responsibility for the problem and rectification on developed countries.[48] In addition, they were reluctant to have their own mitigation actions internationally bound or scrutinized. China's constant reification of bifurcated responsibilities seemed to have hardened. US negotiators note that, in discussions preparing for Copenhagen, compromise proposals in which China might submit to binding international obligations were repeatedly rejected.[49] Verification and transparency were particular concerns of the new Obama administration, and flew in the face of China's long-held concerns about international scrutiny of its actions. The energy and climate arena posed particular challenges for a verification regime, as many of the policies and mechanisms (such as the replacement of carbon-emitting energy sources by renewable energy), as well as their implementation, were as yet unproven.

Thus, as the Copenhagen meetings loomed, on issues of international verification, on transparency of mitigation actions, and on "internationalization" of the commitments, Chinese and US negotiators were firmly split, suggesting cooperation was unlikely. While some aspects of China's participation at Copenhagen are murky, it was clear that the hope for Premier Wen Jiabao – to present China's unilateral offer to great appreciation and then sign an agreement – did not unfold as anticipated. The negotiating dynamics that emerged proved difficult for all, but especially

47 Todd Stern, speech to the Center for American Progress, June 4, 2009: http://thinkprogress.org/climate/2009/06/03/174345/todd-stern-transcript.

48 As Houser ("Copenhagen," p. 7) explains: Because of the highly preferential legal structure of the Kyoto Protocol, reluctance to be bound to emission reduction results during a period of policy formation and experimentation [in China and emerging economies], and concerns about opening the door to further obligations, BASIC countries sought two Copenhagen agreements: a second commitment period under the Kyoto Protocol with legally binding commitments for developed countries, and a new agreement with economy-wide emission reduction commitments from the United States and nonbinding mitigation actions from developing countries.

49 Author interview with a former US climate negotiator, May 20, 2016.

for the Chinese delegation and leadership. A major reason for such difficulty was the complexity of overlapping negotiating blocs. Many meetings among different subgroups had been held in the months ahead of Copenhagen, including bilaterals and meetings among developing (G77), developed (G7), and mixed (Major Economies Forum) groupings. Important for China was the BASIC (Brazil, South Africa, India, and China) group of emerging economies, organized formally in the months prior to Copenhagen.[50] The Danish hosts to the summit also held a series of confidential meetings beginning in the summer of 2009, first with developed countries, and then including some emerging economy participants (such as China and India). Days before the December summit was to begin, a draft text that had been circulated in the Danish forum was leaked (by China or India, US negotiators believe). The report that the developed countries had been meeting secretly led to an uproar about the "exclusive club" that was engaged in deal-making and attempting to eliminate the Kyoto Protocol as the basis for climate negotiations.[51] Chinese negotiators did not publicly acknowledge their involvement in the meetings and sided with the G77 pronouncements of anger, which were expressed with particular vehemence by Sudan's representative. In the wake of this controversy, the summit got off on a very bad foot. While it had been evident for some months that a strong accord was not likely to emerge from the summit, it now looked as though little would be salvaged.

A last-ditch negotiating effort between Obama and the leaders of the BASIC group (Wen, Zuma, Singh, and Lula) was widely viewed in the West as having resurrected the prospects for an agreement, leading to the political accord that eventually emerged.[52] The Copenhagen Accord was hammered out in the last hours of the summit by leaders of about

50 Of the emerging countries, Russia is an Annex I country under the Kyoto Protocol and was not included in BASIC. For an assessment of BASIC grouping positions, see Kathryn Hochstetler and Manjana Milkoreit, "Responsibilities in Transition: Emerging Powers in the Climate Change Negotiations," *Global Governance*, Vol. 21, no. 2 (2015), pp. 205–26.

51 John Vidal, "Copenhagen Climate Summit in Disarray after 'Danish Text' Leak," *The Guardian* (December 8, 2009): www.theguardian.com/environment/2009/dec/08/copenhagen-climate-summit-disarray-danish-text.

52 See, for example, Henry D. Jacoby and Y.-H. Henry Chen, "Launching a New Climate Regime," MIT Joint Program on the Science and Policy of Global Change, Report no. 215 (Cambridge, MA: JPSPCG, November 2015).

thirty countries,[53] representatives of all the main coalitions.[54] When submitted to the parties for consensus adoption, six countries refused to agree, preventing the accord from being adopted as a COP decision.[55] The conferees agreed only to "take note" of the agreement in their closing document.[56]

The contents of the Copenhagen Accord are roughly as follows. It was a political, i.e. "nonlegal," instrument. It called for nations to limit global warming to within two degrees Celsius, and it provided for developed countries to fund new climate adaptation mechanisms for the developing world. It also set up a procedure by which all countries could "associate" with the accord – in other words, submit to the UNFCCC secretariat their respective plans for reducing GHG emissions. Most countries did in fact "associate" by the deadline, which was set as the end of January 2010.[57] The format for these commitments listed Annex I countries separately and called on them to give "quantified economy-wide emissions targets for 2020." Non-Annex I countries – thus including China – were asked to submit Nationally Appropriate Mitigation Actions (NAMAs). Least developed countries and small island developing states were allowed to undertake actions "voluntarily and on the basis of support" provided internationally. Despite maintaining a distinction in submissions between Annex I and non-Annex I countries, the accord did have the advantage (from the US perspective) of providing greater symmetry, because all countries were called on to act according to their capabilities, not rigidly divided into two sets, only one of which had any responsibility.[58] By calling for submissions from countries, the accord also marked the end of the line for a Kyoto-style, top-down binding agreement in which

53 See the text of the Copenhagen Accord at: http://unfccc.int/resource/docs/2009/cop15/eng/11a01.pdf.

54 John Vidal and Jonathan Watts, "Copenhagen: The Last-ditch Drama that Saved the Deal from Collapse," *The Guardian*, December 20, 2009.

55 These six countries were Sudan, Venezuela, Cuba, Bolivia, Nicaragua, and Tuvalu. Sudan's representative equated the accord to the Holocaust.

56 The US and UK delegates pushed hard to have the agreement "noted." Though many were disappointed that the accord was merely a "political" document and, thereby, possessed no formal standing in the UN negotiations, having the accord noted set it up to become the basis for subsequent adoption at the COP meeting the following year in Cancun.

57 See associated commitments of developed (Annex I) countries at: http://unfccc.int/meetings/copenhagen_dec_2009/items/5264.php; and of developing (non–Annex I) countries at: http://unfccc.int/home/items/5265.php.

58 In this sense, the Copenhagen Accord followed the formulation originally envisioned in the Bali Action Plan.

countries collectively agree to a target. It opened a less ambitious but, perhaps, more politically feasible bottom-up path by which countries would voluntarily set their own targets for emissions reduction, based on their own assessments of national capabilities. In sum, the negotiations resulted in a "least common denominator" approach: the accord was a nonlegal instrument (a "political" accord) that, although allowing for different contributions based on national capabilities, applied symmetrically with the same force – neither were bound – to developed and emerging economies.

As noted, China was widely perceived as playing a negative role in the Copenhagen negotiations, particularly at the summit meetings in December 2009.[59] We have seen ways in which this is not quite true. The Chinese government had taken a new approach on first-order issues to demonstrate willingness to contribute to climate mitigation – offering unilateral mitigation proposals in the 2007–2008 timeframe, and again, with more specific targets, just before the Copenhagen summit commenced in December. Moreover, to the extent that China's behavior was deemed obstructionist on second-order issues, it may have been due in part to unexpected real-time negotiating dynamics – particularly insofar as the disarray in negotiations led Premier Wen Jiabao's announcements to garner much less positive attention than hoped and put him in the unanticipated position of bargaining, face-to-face and without scripts, with other world leaders.[60] Yet China played a substantial part in, first, getting

59 Reports in *The Guardian* and *Der Spiegel* were particularly harsh. See Ed Miliband, "China Tried to Hijack Copenhagen Climate Deal," *The Guardian*, December 20, 2009; Mark Lynas, "How Do I Know China Wrecked the Copenhagen Deal? I Was In the Room," *The Guardian*, December 22, 2009: www.theguardian.com/environment/2009/dec/22/copenhagen-climate-change-mark-lynas; Watts et al., "Mark Lynas: How China Wrecked"; Tobias Rapp, Christian Schwägerl, and Gerald Traufetter, "The Copenhagen Protocol: How China and India Sabotaged the UN Climate Summit, *Der Spiegel*, May 5, 2010: www.spiegel.de/international/world/the-copenhagen-protocol-how-china-and-india-sabotaged-the-un-climate-summit-a-692861.html. The latter article is also critical of President Obama for holding private meetings with the BASIC countries and "stabbing the EU in the back." *Der Spiegel* Online posted a video with audio of the meetings purporting to show stalling by representatives from China (He Yafei) and India (www.youtube.com/watch?v=-ybecKdwj2c, June 8, 2016). Chinese media presented its own picture of Western hold-up, e.g., Xin Benjian, "Ge Hui Pi Fada de Guojia Bi Zhi Shibai Bianyuan" [Developed Countries bring the Copenhagen Meetings to the Brink of Failure], *Renmin Ribao*, December 20, 2009.

60 That China's leaders were unprepared for these kinds of fluid negotiations is suggested in Francois Godement," Does China Have a Real Climate Change Policy?" *Climate Policies after Copenhagen*, ECFR China Analysis, no. 27 (2010): www.css.ethz.ch/en/services/digital-library/publications/publication.html/118292.

wealthy nations to pay the costs of climate technology and finance. More important for our purposes, China played a role in keeping a stronger accord from being presented to the plenary body. As Björn Conrad states, whether or not there had been some room for flexibility on China's part coming in, "not to relinquish any ground became the simple and overriding goal during these last two days ... At a point when US President Obama and the EU leaders supposedly thought now is the time to push through and forge at least a somewhat acceptable accord, the actual Chinese negotiators had already left the table."[61] Earlier clauses of draft versions of the Copenhagen agreement included a timeline for reaching a *binding* agreement by the end of 2010, a clause China and India insisted be taken out.[62] A key turning point occurred in the context of a negotiating draft offer made by developed countries (originally presented at the G8 meetings in July 2009) for global long-term targets of a global 50 percent reduction by 2050, with the developed world reducing their emissions by 80 percent over this time period (the 50–80 proposal). The concrete goals were strongly supported by the European Union, but China rejected them by referring, as in the past, to arguments based on historical responsibility. China's representative rejected the 80 percent offer for binding reductions by *developed* countries.[63] This action led to the much publicized outrage expressed by German Chancellor Angela Merkel and French President Nicholas Sarkozy that China was obstructing rich countries' attempts to bind themselves. On this and other points, Mark Lynas gives an eyewitness account:

[61] Conrad, "China in Copenhagen." Conrad, whose detailed account is less critical of the Chinese actions in Copenhagen than most, is referring to the fact that the NDRC's expert climate negotiators Xie Zhenhua and Su Wei were replaced by the senior generalist diplomat He Yafei, who in turn had the job to protect Premier Wen from damage that could result from his being pressured into costly concessions.

[62] Gary Clyde Hufbauer and Jisun Kim, "After the Flop in Copenhagen," Peterson Institute of International Economics PB10-4 (March 2010), pp. 1–11: https://piie.com/sites/default/files/publications/pb/pb10-04.pdf. Houser ("Copenhagen," p. 5) reports that EU negotiators were willing to allow developing countries to submit nonbinding strategies.

[63] Reported in Lynas, "How Do I Know China Wrecked." See also Andrew Ward and Bertrand Benoit, "Deadlock Threatens Copenhagen Climate Deal," *Financial Times*, December 14, 2009: www.ft.com/cms/s/0/9bc43ba0-e8af-11de-9c1f-00144feab49a.html#axzz4ApTsl2Dw. China alone was not represented at the summit by its top leader, Wen Jiabao, but rather by He Yafei of the Ministry of Foreign Affairs. Wen claimed that he had never been invited to the meeting. Conrad ("China in Copenhagen"), while not arguing that China did not veto this proposal, takes the more sympathetic position that China, through He Yafei, did not veto the proposal to be destructive but, instead, knew that an 80 percent commitment could only be achieved if Chinese participation was included – and implicitly did not wish to pay the costs required of this proposal.

> "Why can't we even mention our own targets?" demanded a furious Angela Merkel. Australia's prime minister, Kevin Rudd, was annoyed enough to bang his microphone. Brazil's representative too pointed out the illogicality of China's position. Why should rich countries not announce even this unilateral cut? The Chinese delegate said no, and I watched, aghast, as Merkel threw up her hands in despair and conceded the point ... China, backed at times by India, then proceeded to take out all the numbers that mattered. A 2020 peaking year in global emissions, essential to restrain temperatures to 2C, was removed and replaced by woolly language suggesting that emissions should peak "as soon as possible." The long-term target, of global 50% cuts by 2050, was also excised. No one else, perhaps with the exceptions of India and Saudi Arabia, wanted this to happen.[64]

China's negotiators also did not wish to subject the country to new norms and rules for external verification of its mitigation actions. The strength of this preference was revealed when faced with trading off one of the key demands about climate aid China was making on behalf of the G77. US Secretary of State Clinton pledged the US contribution to a $100 billion annual climate fund by 2020, meeting the demands of G77 nations. The announcement was linked, though, with the quid pro quo containing what had become a hallmark of the US position, that "all major economies [would] stand behind meaningful mitigation actions and provide full transparency as to their implementation."[65] The US offer also came with the proviso that China would not be one of the beneficiaries of aid, meaning an offer that had high value to many G77 countries had especially little value to China. Chinese negotiators would look bad for turning down a financing offer they had been advocating, and yet they continued to be deeply opposed to submitting implementation of their agreements to independent international evaluation – measuring, reporting, and verification (MRV) was the terminology used at the time. Despite the threat to the aid offer, Chinese negotiators objected to MRV as "intrusive." In the end, negotiators accepted a provision calling for "national" verification except where international funds (which would not go to China anyway) were involved.[66]

[64] Quoted from Lynas, "How Do I Know China Wrecked." Consistent accounts were offered in interviews, and in Hufbauer and Kim ("After the Flop in Copenhagen," p. 3) and Conrad ("China in Copenhagen"). These meetings were suspended and not resumed; instead, the United States and BASIC countries met to agree on the final accord.

[65] Hillary Clinton, remarks at the UNFCCC, December 17, 2009.

[66] On Chinese support at Copenhagen for national MRV, as opposed to more intrusive international mechanisms, see Wang Xiaogang, "'Gongtong dan you Qubie de Zeren' Yuanze."

In sum, as scholar Zhongxiang Zhang notes, China "took full advantage of being the world's largest carbon emitter, and attempted to secure a deal to its advantage. It was widely reported that China walked away 'happy'... Officially, China was backed by allies like India and Brazil, but they admitted in private that this was mainly China's battle."[67]

Even beyond the striking negotiating dynamics, our theory's explanation for why China would engage in hold-up fits the outcome at Copenhagen well. It is true that China was engaging in first-order cooperation by making extensive domestic efforts to curtail pollution. Yet, at Copenhagen, China did not cooperate on second-order issues regarding allocation of the costs of the regime and of cooperation. First, Beijing made clear that it preferred unilateral actions rather than cooperative international mitigation actions that would make it accountable to others. Views such as expressed in Yu Qingtai's comment noted earlier indicate that the PRC government preferred to take unilateral steps that would not harm its economic development goals, and that determination of any trade-offs China would make would be done domestically.[68] That China should still be treated as a developing country with a right to increase its emissions also was expressed by scholars.[69]

Second, China's negotiating stances suggest it did not want to bear deep financial costs for domestic mitigation that might harm development or costs for aid to the poorer countries. Models by Paltsev et al. show that the Copenhagen commitments made by China could be reached "at modest cost," and did not go beyond what was proposed in the eleventh Five Year Plan.[70] Conrad concurs that the carbon intensity targets would not be as costly to China as some had assumed: they equaled "the emissions savings 'automatically' achieved through the restructuring of China's economic model. Reductions that go beyond this level might be harmful to the restructuring efforts by putting an additional strain on the economic system ... China's government will carefully avoid committing

67 Zhang, "Breaking the Impasse," p. 178.

68 The question of trade-offs was in fact being debated domestically, as some influential voices in China argued that China should take a greater responsibility than was being proposed in the lead-up to Copenhagen. See Hu Angang, "Tong Xiang Gebenhagen zhi Lu de Quanqiu Jian Pai Luxian Tu" [The Road to Copenhagen's Roadmap for Global Emissions Reduction], *Dangdai Ya Tai*, no. 6 (2008), pp. 22–38.

69 See, for example, Zhang Shengzhang and Li Chunlin, "Gebanhegen Qihou Bianhua Huiyishang Wo Guo Mianlin de Tiaozhang ji Yingdui" [Challenges Faced by Our Country at the Copenhagen Climate Change Meetings and Responses], *Kunming Ligong Daxue Xuebao* [Shehui Kexue Ban], Vol. 9, no. 11 (2009), pp. 11–16.

70 Paltsev et al., "The Role of China in Mitigating Climate Change."

to emission reduction obligations that clearly go beyond the amount of 'no regrets' reduction, neither in the domestic nor in the international arena."[71] Moreover, with regard to the 50–80 offer by developed countries, Chinese analysts calculated that this formula would require more substantial reductions in China's carbon emissions than the government was ready to make. [72]

We can probe this issue further by considering what Beijing thought would be the results for China if they did not bear the costs of cooperation with the established powers. As shown in the Copenhagen negotiations, they strongly preferred the default position as set by the Kyoto Protocol: no binding commitments by developing countries and payment of financial costs by developed countries. The need to preserve the Kyoto Protocol as a viable legal instrument was reiterated multiple times by top leaders (e.g., Wen Jiabao) and negotiators (e.g., Xie Zhenhua) in the lead-up to Copenhagen.[73] The official PRC position at Copenhagen continued to press for a second commitment period under the Kyoto Protocol,[74] and was consistent with efforts backed by China to undermine progress on the second LCA/Bali track (as described earlier). China's alliance with the G77, and India in particular, as well as the consensus rules of the UNFCCC, meant China could feel protected from the danger of the United States and Europe moving against it. Thus, the costs of noncooperation with the terms preferred by the United States and Europe appeared to be acceptable to China's leaders, at least at this critical juncture. In contrast, US and EU outside options worsened leading up to the meetings at Copenhagen, given increasingly dire scientific reports on climate change and rising climate justice activism.[75] The specter of weak agreement that did not contain

[71] Conrad, "China in Copenhagen," p. 10.

[72] Ibid. A similar assessment, that Beijing's offers have required little sacrifice on the country's part, is found in Christensen, *The China Challenge*, p. 282.

[73] See Wen Jiabao, "Jiaqiang Guoji Jishu Hezuo," and Xie Zhenhua, "Yingdui Qihou Bianhua Wenti Zhongguo Zhen Zhua Shigan" [China Grasps Hard Work to Tackle the Problem of Climate Change], *WTO Jingji Daokan*, no. 11 (2008), pp. 53–4 (published by PRC Ministry of Commerce). On China and India's staunch defense of the Kyoto Protocol as the sole legal and normative reference for negotiations, see Fuzuo Wu, "Sino-Indian Climate Cooperation: Implications for the International Climate Change Regime," *Journal of Contemporary China*, Vol. 21, no. 77 (2012), pp. 827–43.

[74] See the statement about the importance of a second commitment period for Kyoto, posted May 20, 2009 on the PRC UN website, entitled "China's Position on the Copenhagen Climate Change Conference": www.china-un.org/eng/chinaandun/economicdevelopment/climatechange/t568959.htm.

[75] On climate justice activism, see Hadden, *Networks of Contention*.

stringent commitments from China spelled special trouble for the Obama administration in particular, already hamstrung in its ability to sell any such agreement at home. Leaders in the Obama administration and in EU countries thus had viewed a cooperative outcome as a high priority;[76] the disappointment at the inability to come to agreement with an indispensable China was evident during and following the meetings.

Finally, as previously noted, China's participation was viewed as indispensable by the United States and Europe, something well understood by the Chinese leadership. Indeed, 2009 cemented the centrality of United States–China negotiations to progress in the climate regime.[77] In short, Beijing was in a position to induce the United States (and wealthy countries) to pay a greater share of the costs of regime establishment and maintenance but, by its actions, showed it would trigger the risk of regime collapse if it could not.

It is useful to note that, in addition to producing what was perceived as a disappointing accord, the Copenhagen meetings had a further result that would greatly affect China's position – and its outside options – in subsequent years: the corrosion of the negotiating coalition it had been a part of since the 1990s. The coalescence of BASIC into a formal group before Copenhagen of course made much sense in terms of their current and expected contributions to the problem of climate change. But the optics of a deal being hashed out between the United States and the BASIC countries were not good, because it was perceived as a defection by China (and the other emerging economies) on its previous commitment to negotiate only within the G77+China group. Moreover, Copenhagen amplified the pressure by the AOSIS group of island nations, along with some other less-developing nations, to speak up for a stringent binding and universal restrictions on carbon emissions by both developed and emerging economies.[78] A proposal from Tuvalu – backed by AOSIS, some African countries, and most members of the G77 – called for binding commitments from major developing (BASIC) countries (including China, India, and Brazil), bringing to the fore an idea that had been percolating: "common but differentiated responsibilities" would be interpreted differently for major and minor emitters among developing nations. As Gary Hufbauer and Jisun Kim note, "Taukiei Kitara, head

[76] See, for example, Tom Zeller Jr., "Climate Talks Open with Calls for Urgent Action," *The New York Times* (December 7, 2009): www.nytimes.com/2009/12/08/science/earth/08climate.html.

[77] Foot and Walter, *China, the United States, and Global Order*, p. 186.

[78] On these perceptions of China's role, ibid., pp. 194, 200.

of Tuvalu's delegation, acknowledged that the proposal marked the first serious rift in the previously united front between the G-77 and China."[79] A report commissioned by China's environment ministry claimed this interlude was a conspiracy by developed countries to divide the G77 nations.[80] Conspiracy or not, China's position among the broader group of developing nations was diminished. The crumbling of the G77 coalition would prove important to the context in which China moved toward greater cooperation with the United States in the years before the 2015 COP meeting in Paris.

7.4 TOWARD INVEST: WORSENING OUTSIDE OPTIONS AND THE POST-COPENHAGEN NEGOTIATIONS

In Paris, in December 2015, 190 countries agreed to what was widely hailed as a landmark agreement on climate change.[81] The Paris meetings, entered into with much more confidence than the Copenhagen summit six years earlier, followed not only annual COP and other UN-sponsored meetings and meetings of allied groupings, but also numerous sessions between US and Chinese negotiators. Bilateral meetings had produced a major agreement between Chinese President Xi Jinping and US President Barack Obama in November 2014. This bilateral agreement laid the groundwork for the conclusion of a more robust agreement at Paris. In contrast to the brief political agreement that emerged from Copenhagen, the 2015 Paris agreement was long. It consisted of a twelve-page "Paris Agreement," which set out new commitments for climate action beyond 2020 (and potentially through the end of the century) and a twenty-page "decision," which described what signatories must do before the agreement would enter into force. Partly due to pressure from the most vulnerable nations and a new so-called "high ambition coalition," the declared goals were more ambitious than in the past. The long-term goal

79 Hufbauer and Kim, "After the Flop in Copenhagen," p. 3.

80 Comments to this effect were leaked, and reported in Jonathan Watts, Damian Carrington, and Suzanne Goldenberg, "China's Fears of Rich Nations 'Climate Conspiracy' at Copenhagen Revealed," *The Guardian* (February 11, 2010): www.theguardian.com/environment/2010/feb/11/chinese-thinktank-copenhagen-document.

81 The agreement came into force on November 4, 2016, thirty days after a threshold of fifty-five countries representing 55 percent of total GHG emissions deposited their instruments of ratification, acceptance, approval, or accession with the UN depository. See: https://treaties.un.org/pages/ViewDetails.aspx?src=TREATY&mtdsg_no=XXVII-7-d&chapter=27&lang=en.

of the agreement was set as *phasing out* GHG emissions, and participants would "aim to reach global peaking of greenhouse gas emissions as soon as possible." Further, the agreement called for limiting global average warming to "well below" two degrees Celsius (2C) above pre-industrial levels, with an aim "to pursue efforts to limit the temperature increase to 1.5C."[82]

Several outcomes of the agreement are important for our analysis of Chinese second-order cooperation:

- The agreement is legally binding at the international level, using the critical language, "entry into force," which signals that countries consent to be bound by it under international law, and asserts it is "subject to ratification, acceptance, or approval" by governments. This contravened Chinese negotiators' longstanding position that they did not wish any binding agreement at the international level that was inconsistent with the Kyoto Protocol.[83]
- The Paris Agreement has no reference to Annex I countries. It calls for sharing of responsibilities "in the light of different national circumstances" (Article 2.2). While different responsibilities for rich and poor still pervade the agreement, there is no reference to a fixed group of countries. Instead, "all parties are to undertake and communicate ambitious efforts." This stipulation effectively ends the core bifurcation of Kyoto, which China had long attempted to retain.
- All signatories are *required* to submit national mitigation targets – called nationally determined contributions (NDCs) – to the United Nations, and they are to prepare policies to achieve these targets. All countries are to communicate new NDCs every five years, with developed countries taking the lead. Each round of NDCs is to be more ambitious than the last. This stipulation, continuing efforts that began in Copenhagen, helped satisfy the US concern for symmetry.
- Goals specified within each country's NDCs are separate from the Paris agreement, and are not internationally legally binding to countries. The European Union preferred these targets to be binding, but the United States did not, in part because that would have

[82] The 1.5C language was inserted, reportedly, under pressure from small island nations and other vulnerable countries. See: https://newrepublic.com/article/125662/wants-final-climate-deal.

[83] Author interview with US negotiator, June 2016.

made the agreement subject to US Senate ratification. China, too, continued to prefer nonbinding specific commitments.[84]

- On climate finance, developed countries were to take the lead in supplying finance beyond previous efforts. Large finance packages were agreed to by developed countries.
- On transparency, the agreement contains an "enhanced transparency framework" for both mitigation and financial support. Under this framework, almost all countries would "regularly" measure their emissions and would report progress against their NDCs at least every two years. Prior to Paris, while developed countries already reported emissions annually and reported progress towards their emissions targets every two years, developing countries were not required to do so.

In terms of our theory, the agreement constituted investment in second-order cooperation by the United States and China. Some clarification, in the context of 2015, is important. The agreement was quite a bit weaker than many EU governments had wanted: a binding, top-down agreement. China and the United States, agreeing on bottom-up determinations of commitments and nonbinding specific commitments, took the lead in negotiating a less ambitious agreement, although one that, perhaps, ensured more participation. China acquiesced to the US vision for a legally binding ("internationally deposited") agreement that would, in essence, replace the Kyoto Protocol and its asymmetrical treatment of a small group of nations. China appeared to agree to mechanisms that would enforce greater transparency as to how well commitments were working, though details remained to be worked out after Paris.

What, then, led the PRC government to choose to invest in a climate cooperation strategy with the United States? As our theory predicts, China's investment followed a worsening balance of China's outside options, a worsening that began before Copenhagen but became much more acute in the aftermath of those meetings. During this time, the PRC's stake in reducing GHG emissions increased as a consequence, primarily, of the urgency of the threat to China's environment and economy posed by climate change, as well as the emergence of climate issues in the popular consciousness. At the same time, however, China's ability – with other developing countries – to manage the UN process toward

[84] This hybrid between binding requirement for submission (and some review) but not binding specific targets was credited to New Zealand.

agreements that allowed China to avoid being held responsible began to crumble. We should note that, unlike cases considered in this volume in which other major powers may have a unilateral option, in climate negotiations no single power could act alone. The PRC thus had to consider which coalitions could act together to create a highly unfavorable deal that the PRC would then have to either accept or veto, both at considerable cost. Investment in cooperation with the United States would prevent China from being isolated in the face of a strong agreement shaped by other powers – primarily the European Union, perhaps in concert with the United States – that might enforce costs China was not prepared to accept. The following discussion details how and why China's position evolved from hold-up at Copenhagen to invest, six years later, at Paris.

7.4.1 Copenhagen's Immediate Aftermath and Evolving Steps toward a Xi–Obama Deal

Progress on various core issues of climate talks came, in fits and starts, across the multiple venues in which parties interacted. With the exception of the Xi–Obama deal in November 2014, our focus post-Copenhagen is on the annual COP meetings, held in December of each year, where we can trace the major changes on issues of second-order cooperation.

At COP 16, held in Cancún in 2010, a major goal of both the UN and the Mexican leadership was to produce some positive outcome, after the disappointment of the previous year's meetings in Copenhagen.[85] In Cancún, the Copenhagen Accord was adopted, officially, as a UNFCCC document. Beyond this, much attention was focused on having developed countries pledge financing for mitigation efforts and technology transfer in the developing world – specifically, agreement to establish a new Green Climate Fund (GCF). In general, however, the balancing acts of earlier agreements continued. On the tough issue of whether symmetrical (not identical) mitigation efforts should be made, developing countries were able to retain references to differentiation, and salience for the Kyoto Annex divisions. That developing countries should take NAMAs also was retained, further moving away from the top-down model of commitments, which was preferred by the European Union but increasingly less

[85] The Cancún meeting results are well summarized in Eliot Diringer, *Sixteenth Session of the Conference of the Parties to the United Nations Framework Convention on Climate Change and Sixth Session of the Meeting of the Parties to the Kyoto Protocol* (Arlington, VA: Pew Center on Global Climate Change, 2010): www.c2es.org/docUploads/cancun-climate-conference-cop16-summary.pdf.

important to the United States. Another contentious issue concerned verification. Soon after Copenhagen, it appeared as though the Copenhagen compromise – whereby one system of MRV would be used for mitigation actions by developing countries supported by outside financial support, and another for actions that were not supported – had evaporated.[86] Although MRV issues would remain unsettled, with agreements being renegotiated at nearly every COP to follow, the Cancún Accord followed India's proposal that biennial reports would be submitted by all countries, hewing to the US insistence on symmetry but avoiding international monitors or penalties for failure to meet goals.

The 2011 COP meetings in Durban, South Africa, were perhaps the most important of the meetings in the interim between Copenhagen and Paris. In Durban, negotiators pressed forth with implementation of many of the Cancún Accord's provisions, including transparency mechanisms, technology and adaptation cooperation, and the establishment of the GCF. But Durban was most significant, perhaps, insofar as the underlying mandate for the successor agreement to the Kyoto Protocol (to be agreed at Paris in 2015 and to take effect in 2020) was fleshed out. On the one hand, under pressure from developing countries, the Durban COP formally kept the Kyoto process alive on a limited basis by initiating negotiations for a second commitment period to the Kyoto Protocol. In that track, with the first commitment period set to expire a year later, new binding commitments by developed Annex I countries were to be worked out. By the start of the meetings, a number of developed countries – Japan, Canada, Russia, Australia, New Zealand, and (at first) the European Union – declared they would not sign on to a second Kyoto commitment period. (The US view was not relevant, as it had withdrawn from the Kyoto Protocol.) Strong objections from developing countries led the European Union to back down, and a second commitment period was worked out the following year. (As of December 2017, it had not gained the signatories needed to come into force.)[87]

[86] Andrew Light, "The Cancun Compromise: Masterful Diplomacy Ends with Agreement," Center for American Progress (2010): www.americanprogress.org/issues/green/news/2010/12/13/8751/the-cancun-compromise.

[87] A second commitment period for the Kyoto Protocol was adopted at the following year's 2012 COP in Doha (see the UN statement at: http://unfccc.int/kyoto_protocol/doha_amendment/items/7362.php). As of July 2016, sixty-six countries had ratified the 2012 Doha COP agreement setting forth the second commitment period, China of course among them and Europe not. Because 144 "instruments of acceptance" are required for the "entry into force," the amendment preserving the Kyoto track remains "not in force" after a number of years. The US withdrawal from the Kyoto Protocol obviates the issue

On the other hand, in exchange for agreeing to a second Kyoto period, the European Union – with support from island nations and least developed countries – extracted commitments to another negotiating track that would carry the mandate for an internationally binding legal commitment.[88] The United States, with support from Japan, Russia, and Canada, insisted on a symmetrical agreement that would include commitments from major developing countries. This new track – known as the Durban Platform[89] – lay the groundwork for a system of voluntary pledges from below (the "pledge-and-review" approach) and applicable to all. Agreed language, worked out "in an impromptu 3 a.m. huddle on the plenary floor in full view of observers and the press" pledged to "launch a process to develop a protocol, another legal instrument or an agreed outcome with legal force under the Convention applicable to all parties."[90] According to negotiators who developed this language, China's negotiators agreed. China and India did not insist on reference to "common but differentiated responsibilities" in this text, and no reference was made to other core principles from Kyoto – the right to development and per capita emissions. The precise legal nature of a new agreement, and the manner of symmetry, would still need to be determined, but it would not contain a Kyoto-style bifurcation. As scholar Bo Yan observed, China therefore agreed with evolution of the climate framework "from the asymmetric distribution of responsibilities between developed and developing countries to a common framework for all countries to reduce emissions."[91] In short, Durban created yet another track that would ulti-

of its signature. Canada announced its withdrawal from the Kyoto Protocol shortly after the Durban conference ended.

88 Houser states that, "The Kyoto Protocol extension was ... very important in one regard – it was the leverage used by the European Union and supported by the United States to win a pretty good post-2020 negotiating mandate." See Trevor Houser, "Dissecting Durban: A Fighting Chance for Progress on Climate Change" (Washington, DC: Peterson Institute for International Economics, 2011): http://blogs.piie.com/realtime/?p=2595.

89 The text is found at: http://unfccc.int/2860.php. Durban established the Ad Hoc Working Group on the Durban Platform, which would conduct ongoing multilateral negotiations in the lead-up to the Paris meetings. The new negotiations were meant to be concluded in 2015 (bringing Paris into the spotlight) and to cover the period from 2020 forward. Durban also saw increased attention to adaptation measures.

90 "Outcomes of the UN Climate Change Conference in Durban, South Africa," December 2011, Center for Climate and Energy Solutions: www.c2es.org/docUploads/COP17_Summary.pdf.

91 Yan Bo, "China's Role in the Transformation of the Global Climate Change Regime," speech at University of Nottingham, April 5, 2013: http://blogs.nottingham.ac.uk/chinapolicyinstitute/2013/04/15/chinas-role-in-the-transformation-of-global-climate-change-regime.

mately move the regime away from Kyoto's top-down and asymmetrical norms and began to solidify a process that would overshadow the Kyoto track.[92]

7.4.2 Toward "Invest"

US President Obama and Chinese President Xi made a surprise announcement following bilateral meetings on the sidelines of APEC in November 2014. The agreement set new, more stringent targets for carbon emission reductions by the United States, setting emissions at 26 percent to 28 percent less in 2025 than in 2005 (and hence doubling the pace of reduction it targeted for the 2005–2020 period). It also contained a commitment by China to peak its emissions by around 2030, to be achieved, in part, by having 20 percent of China's energy production supplied by "clean" sources by that year. In addition to reiterating language of differentiation – the two countries stated commitments to a Paris agreement that "reflects the principle of common but differentiated responsibilities and respective capabilities, in light of different national circumstances"[93] – Chinese negotiators were reportedly happy for the clear statement favoring nationally-determined contributions, which effectively scuttled the European Union hope for a more top-down agreement.[94] At the same time, it was fully clear that Beijing no longer viewed China as one of the countries that warranted substantial protection from making specific commitments.[95] More importantly, perhaps, the agreement was designed to demonstrate resolve to other countries prior to the Paris agreement, and thereby pressure other countries to put forth commitments as well. US negotiators gambled that if they could get

[92] On the 2013 COP held in Warsaw, generally considered the least important of the Copenhagen–Paris interim COP meetings, see the analysis at: www.c2es.org/docUploads/c2es-cop-19-summary.pdf.

[93] See the announcement text at: www.whitehouse.gov/the-press-office/2014/11/11/us-china-joint-announcement-climate-change. This language was continued into the COP held the following month in Lima, Peru.

[94] François Godement, "China: Taking Stock before the Paris Climate Conference," *China Analysis* (September 2015): www.css.ethz.ch/en/services/digital-library/publications/publication.html/194229.

[95] Beijing did continue to support some efforts to retain the Kyoto Annex construct, though. In particular, a month after the Xi–Obama announcement, in the 2014 COP in Lima, China seemed supportive of efforts (primarily from India) to have explicit differentiation between Annex I (developed) and non-Annex I (developing) countries throughout the decision. The compromise language that emerged echoed the language of the bilateral agreement: www.c2es.org/docUploads/cop-20-summary.pdf.

China in concert with the United States to announce commitments early, other countries would be pulled along. US negotiators also suspected that China would feel protection from public criticism of the type they faced after Copenhagen if Washington could be viewed as giving Beijing its imprimatur.[96] And a joint agreement protected both countries from being pushed by others, especially the European Union and island nations, for deeper commitments.

The Paris climate summit was set to be the apex of Chinese investment in climate cooperation. And yet cracks in cooperation remained, as we can see from two examples. First, Beijing announced a major contribution to climate finance at a nuclear cooperation summit in Washington, held just weeks before the Paris meetings. The $3.1 billion to facilitate mitigation and adaptation efforts by developing countries was slightly more than the $3 billion pledged by the United States, and would seem to symbolize China's acknowledgment that it could not be considered a developing country for issues related to climate. However, Beijing set up this financing tool to be run unilaterally by China, rather than contributing these funds to the multilateral GCF. Interviewees in Beijing indicated that China's contributions remained outside the GCF because the GCF is a mandatory commitment for developed countries and China did not wish to take on a mandatory international funding commitment as a developed country.[97] Second, Chinese negotiators appeared caught off guard by successful efforts from a self-proclaimed "High Ambition Coalition" to formulate a more ambitious agreement, introducing a 1.5C temperature goal as well as binding commitments. This coalition, made up primarily of representatives of European, island, and most vulnerable nations, had met quietly for many months before Paris. Neither US nor Chinese negotiators were involved in these meetings, though both sides reportedly were aware of them. During the Paris meetings, the United States allowed itself to be associated with the coalition, though not with the specific issues – especially the goal of binding specific commitments, given that such a goal

96 This surprise bilateral agreement, made at the APEC summit in Beijing, was worked out in months of secret talks between Chinese and US negotiators. The US negotiators ran the idea behind other key actors, including Ban Ki Moon and European leaders, but did not speak with other BASIC country members. A Chinese scientist with knowledge of the negotiations stated, in an interview, that he was quite certain the Obama team also had approached India. Chinese negotiators had extensive internal discussions about the technical aspects of their commitments, but news of these internal consultations did not leak (author interview).

97 Author interview with university-based climate scientists involved in negotiations, October 2015.

would be politically unfeasible in the United States. Beijing's negotiators, who were communicating intensively with the United States throughout the Paris meetings, privately expressed their upset with the United States. Beijing publicly was very dismissive of the coalition's announcements, with Vice Minister Liu Jianmin saying, "It is a kind of performance, it makes no difference."[98]

7.4.3 China's Increased Stake

Governments in China, the European Union, and the United States (under Obama) were all under pressure from segments of society that saw action on climate change as ever more urgent and demanded multilateral cooperation. Yet, compared to the United States, several factors made the possibility of multilateral action on climate change more politically pressing in China.[99] In terms of elite politics, it remained well accepted in China that climate change would greatly harm China's environment and economy. For example, many studies warned of the huge anticipated cost to the major metropolis and financial center of Shanghai from an expected rise in sea level, as well a more general harm to the industrialized coastal areas (including Tianjin and Guangzhou).[100] China's twelfth Five Year Plan (2011–2015) reflected this sense of urgency, as it set ever more ambitious national targets, including increasing the share of non-fossil fuels used in primary energy consumption, reductions in energy intensity (energy use per unit of GDP), and reductions in carbon intensity.[101] Public consciousness of GHG emissions also became intertwined with public consciousness of toxic air caused by ground level particulate matter. In the span of a few days in January 2013, eastern China, including the capital, Beijing, was blanketed with the worst smog ever

[98] James Crisp, "China Pours Cold Water on EU's Ambition Coalition at COP21," *Euractive* (December 11, 2015): www.euractiv.com/section/climate-environment/news/china-pours-cold-water-on-eu-s-ambition-coalition-at-cop21.

[99] On the continued skepticism of climate change science in the United States in the lead-up to the Paris meetings, see: www.npr.org/2015/12/01/457939497/paris-climate-talks-face-a-familiar-hurdle-american-politics.

[100] These harms and others, such as the increase in extreme weather, had been referenced in the 2008 White Paper cited earlier. In 2015, China's top meteorological official warned of the impending disasters to China from climate change. See "Climate Change: China Official Warns of 'Huge Impact,'" March 15, 2015: www.bbc.com/news/world-asia-china-32006972.

[101] These targets were consistent with those which had been submitted to the UNFCCC at Copenhagen. Paltsev et al., "The Role of China in Mitigating Climate Change." Inclusion in the plan provided the institutional means for reaching these goals.

seen. Moreover, while the Beijing area and northeast China in general had suffered from poor air quality for many years, dense particulate matter began to settle over previously less affected "clean" areas in the south (including Hong Kong) and southwest, as well as Shanghai. Previous steps used to clean up the air before the 2008 Olympic Games – e.g., moving or temporarily shuttering coal-burning factories and seeding rain clouds – no longer seemed sufficient, and obviously were not a long-term solution. Reports produced both inside and outside of China about the excess number of lives lost and cases of pollution-causing diseases, and the impact on the elderly and the young, received widespread coverage in China.[102] Although ground level particulate matter and GHG emissions are technically different issues,[103] it became widely accepted in China that actions to reduce GHG emissions often reduce air pollutants, bringing co-benefits for air quality and human health.[104] Polls taken in the spring of 2015, several months before the Paris climate conference, showed the political salience of this issue, as air pollution in China was seen as a "very big" or "moderately big" problem by three-quarters of those surveyed, second only to corruption.[105] If stake alone were the driver of China's actions, we can imagine that Beijing could have chosen to spend more on remediation and adaptation measures within China rather than invest in cooperative measures. Imagining Beijing making a choice to forego costly investments in multilateralism, given its historical reluctance on this and other issues to "go it alone" or to invest in a regional solution, is not difficult. Yet the unilateral option was less feasible for several reasons. First, as discussed, the domestic political, economic, and social consequences for China of other countries' contributions to cli-

[102] The film "Under the Dome: Investigating China's Smog," by independent filmmaker Chai Jing, was at first praised by Chinese authorities, then subsequently banned, but nevertheless was reportedly widely viewed. A study in mid-2015 by Berkeley Earth estimated that air pollution causes 4,400 deaths in China every day. Robert Rhode and Richard Muller, *Air Pollution in China: Mapping of Concentrations and Sources*, 2015: http://berkeleyearth.org/wp-content/uploads/2015/08/China-Air-Quality-Paper-July-2015.pdf.

[103] Some scientists argue that particulates provide a "parasol effect" that reflects the sun's rays, reducing the impact of global warming at ground level.

[104] Author interview with university climate scientist, Beijing, June 9, 2015.

[105] See: www.pewglobal.org/2015/09/24/corruption-pollution-inequality-are-top-concerns-in-china. The political salience of climate change was much less in the United States, despite commitments by President Obama and Secretary of State Kerry. Polls also taken in the spring of 2015 reported that "among the nations we surveyed, the U.S. has the highest carbon emissions per capita, but it is among the least concerned about climate change and its potential impact." See also: www.pewresearch.org/fact-tank/2016/04/18/what-the-world-thinks-about-climate-change-in-7-charts.

mate change were clearly rising, and with it the costs of unilateral action by Beijing. Second, the optics of the situation had changed, as had the potency of the US position that emerging economies could not be exempt from paying the costs of cooperation, making it unlikely that the United States and the European Union – if acting without China – would fashion a cooperative agreement that would suit China's interests, much less allow China to free-ride upon efforts of others. Third, China's ability to forestall an agreement contrary to many of its previously held positions (such as avoiding a binding mechanism) was increasingly undermined by weakness in its coalition, including the G77 and the BASIC group. We discuss the further deterioration of the coalition in the following section.

7.4.4 China's Coalitional Options

In the months after Copenhagen, China's ability to rely on its position in the developing world to protect core interests had seriously eroded. In large part, this reflected China's changed status as a major emitter, as discussed earlier. The corrosion of the developing country coalition was evident in two ways. First, the relevance of the Kyoto track of negotiations – putting together and ratifying a second commitment period – significantly diminished for China. Recall that the Kyoto track would maintain China's position in the non-Annex I countries, thereby protecting it from binding commitments. But the "annex" distinctions were losing relevance for actually addressing climate change. A rejection by many poorer countries of the Kyoto "annex" system reflected assessments that the Annex I countries had come to account for less than 30 percent of global emissions, making binding commitments by this group insufficient.[106] Thus, it was clear that even the most ambitious mitigation targets in a second commitment period would not sufficiently reduce emissions.

The second, and perhaps more significant, source of corrosion of the China-led coalition was a continuation of the splintering that began seriously in Copenhagen. Many of those countries that saw a coalition with China as protecting them from commitments began to see a binding commitment from China as necessary to addressing the problem of climate change. The small island nations and most vulnerable nations

[106] See Light, "The Cancun Compromise." Also see Houser's ("Dissecting Durban") discussion of post-2009 projections that Annex I countries would only account for 3 percent of global growth going forward.

became quite articulate in their favor for a binding agreement that included large emitters such as China and India. Among the BASIC countries, Brazil had largely defected (presenting its own program, without broader consultation within BASIC) at the Lima COP in 2014. South Africa also began to question the position of unilateral and nonbinding commitments that had been core to India and China. Long-standing security tensions between India and China also hampered the ability of those countries to work together over the long term; whereas Indian negotiators in the past had relied upon China to "carry the water," following Copenhagen, India became concerned that China could not be depended on to protect the interests of "development." In the view of an Indian climate policy specialist, India was expressing more and more that they "might have to go it alone, without China."[107]

It also appears that the US strategy in the lead-up to Paris was to try to exploit these divisions among the BASIC countries. US negotiators hoped, when pursuing the bilateral China–United States agreement signed in 2014 (as previously discussed), to give Beijing "cover" to make more aggressive commitments there and at Paris. It was hoped that, in light of China's sensitivity to avoid the criticism to which it was subject following Copenhagen, a strong co-commitment by the United States and China would deflect unilateral attention away from China, while at the same time creating momentum for commitments by other countries.[108] But at a deeper level, the very idea that China would be attracted to such an agreement was dependent upon its isolation from the earlier developing country coalition, especially when – after the mid-1990s – China's technical status within that group was being questioned.

The upshot of the splintering of the developing country coalition was, in terms of our theory, a worsening of China's outside options. There was growing recognition in China that it was no longer feasible to leverage its position in the developing world to push for rules favorable to it. That is, holding out would lead to the failure of the regime to address climate change, and that would be bad for China. Not only would this be politically unpopular in China, but it could isolate China diplomatically and render it subject, potentially, to a more stringent set of international rules, imposed by the European Union. The desire to avoid international

107 Author interview, May 26, 2015, Washington, DC.

108 Author interviews with US negotiators, 2016. Chinese negotiators, reportedly, repeatedly stated that the post-Copenhagen criticisms of China (such as by the United Kingdom's Ed Miliband) irritated them, and that the United States and China should not criticize each other.

diplomatic isolation and avoid losing allies in the developing world was captured in the idea of a "new framework for cooperation" that emerged in scholarly writings and in interviews with climate policy academics in the PRC.[109] As scholar Yu Hongyuan noted in 2014, the international struggle between developed countries and the G77 on climate issues evolved as developing countries' positions started to divide, and Pacific island, African, and some Latin American countries began to ask big developing countries (including China) to bear more responsibility for emission reduction.[110] Scholar Zhang Haibin alludes to the fragility of the developing country coalition, urging the PRC government to strengthen south-south and BASIC group cooperation.[111] This advice would seem prescient in light of the formation of the high-ambition coalition at Paris (noted earlier) and, particularly, Brazil's participation in that group.[112]

7.5 CONCLUSION AND ALTERNATIVE EXPLANATIONS ON CONSTRUCTING A CLIMATE CHANGE AGREEMENT

For China, while remaining indispensable to an agreement in the eyes of the rest of the world, its outside options – the alternatives to jointly investing in an agreement – had decreasing appeal. Most important,

109 See, for example, Yu Hongyuan, "Zhongguo Ying Jiji Canyu Guoji Qihou Tanpan" [China Should Positively Participate in International Climate Negotiations], *Shehui Guancha*, no. 11 (2014), pp. 13–16; Zhangyao Zong, Zhang Bo, Liu Yanyan, and Zhang Yong, "Zhongguo Yingdui Qihou Bianhua yu Qihua Bianhua Waijiao" ["China's Response to Climate Change and Climate Change Diplomacy"], *Zhongguo Ruan Kexue*, no. 11 (2014), pp. 9–16; and Bo Yan, "Hezuo Yiyuan yu Hezuo Nengli yi zhong Fenxi Zhongguo Canyu Quanqiu Qihou Bianhua Zhili de Xin Kuangjia" ["Willingness to Cooperate with the New Framework for Cooperation Capacity – China's Participation in Global Climate Change, a Governance Analysis"], *Shijie Jingji yu Zhengzhi*, no. 1, (2013), pp. 135–55. According to Bo, the most common area for a "new willingness to cooperate" would be in further developing funding mechanisms for developing countries and meeting the two-degree collective target.

110 Yu Hongyuan, "Zhongguo Ying Jiji Canyu Guoji Qihou Tanpan." On increasingly differentiated negotiating blocs and positions within G77, especially after Copenhagen, see also J. Brunnée and C. Streck, "The UNFCCC as a Negotiation Forum: Towards Common but More Differentiated Responsibilities," *Climate Policy*, Vol. 13, no. 5 (2013), pp. 589–607.

111 Nevertheless, Zhang Haibin, "Zhongguo zai Guoji Qihou Bianhua Tanpan" concludes that China should absolutely not "lead" in climate change (though it should be a constructive participant), and urges China to maintain its refusal to enact medium-term (2020) quantified binding commitments and to maintain basic "development rights."

112 Alex Pashley, "Brazil Backs 'High Ambition Coalition' to Break Paris Deadlock," *Climatehome*, December 11, 2015: www.climatechangenews.com/2015/12/11/brazil-backs-high-ambition-coalition-to-break-paris-deadlock.

China's stake in a solution to the problem of increasing GHGs had taken a sharp turn with domestic attention to China's air pollution and climate vulnerability. The alternative to investing with the United States was further pressure from the European Union – now joined by island and vulnerable nations – on a top-down agreement that would press them for specific (numeric) binding international commitments on the one hand or, on the other hand, no agreement at all, which would expose them further to the reputation as spoiler. By taking cover with the proposals worked out with the United States, they avoided this outcome.

As in our other chapters, while we believe that our theory of strategic influences on China's choices sheds light on the shift in China's position on climate negotiations, we cannot discount fully the utility of other approaches. The most straightforward alternative would be to explain all Chinese behavior as a function of the change in domestic attentiveness to the need for remediation of climate change, especially insofar as it would be perceived domestically in China as addressing air pollution. The role of domestic politics – and the genuinely felt efforts to address climate change for domestic reasons – is important and is incorporated into our theory via its influence on China's stake. An influential PRC climate scientist, for example, highlighted the Chinese government's desire to respond to domestic unhappiness about air pollution over the previous three to five years, particularly after the January 2013 "airpocalypse." He noted the shift from a time that climate negotiations were perceived as a constraint on growth to the current view that pollution is also a challenge to growth, and so China must face the challenge of the need to move to a low-carbon economy.[113] Nevertheless, although domestic factors undoubtedly played an important role, China might have chosen to continue to invest only in unilateral actions, many of which could ameliorate air pollution (and thus deal with the biggest domestic concern). Moreover, although there had been a growing sense of concern about climate change for some time within China, it was only in the years after Copenhagen that China's approach to second-order issues changed dramatically. This timing suggests that other factors were at play. Our approach shows how China's growing stake in the issue – driven largely by domestic factors – interacted with international-level factors (like

[113] Author interview, June 2015, Beijing. Other works highlighting the role of domestic politics surrounding climate policy per se include: Christensen *The China Challenge*; Foot and Walter, *China, the United States, and Global Order*; and Björn Conrad, "Bureaucratic Land Rush – China's Administrative Battles in the Arena of Climate Change Policy," *Harvard Asia Quarterly* (spring 2010).

shifting coalitions on climate change) to alter China's outside options relative to other major stakeholders, thereby triggering a change in PRC strategy.

We have discussed the broad shift in China's "new diplomacy" in international affairs, as analyzed by Medeiros and Fravel.[114] Yet such a long-term, more confident, and often constructive approach to international affairs, as traced by Medeiros and Fravel, was evident by the late 1990s. In the climate change case, however, this greater tendency toward cooperation was not evident even a decade later in Bali or Copenhagen.

Socialization arguments also do not fit well for the climate change case. For one, there was no dominant regime that had been constructed by the major powers for China to be socialized *into*.[115] China was an important player in the construction of norms on climate, particularly arguments for common but differentiated treatment of developed and developing countries. Moreover, a change in socialization is not consistent in the change in Chinese behavior from hold-up to invest. Chinese policy-makers were, in fact, very well incorporated into the international scientific community that was central to the climate negotiations during the period leading to Copenhagen, and also were well socialized during the period leading to Paris. In short, socialization theory cannot easily explain the shift between incorporation into the developing world coalition to significant abdication from that position.[116]

An alternative explanation that perhaps has the most plausibility concerns change in China's status-seeking behavior. This argument focuses on the reasons Chinese President Xi Jinping, who came to official power in late 2012 (as party secretary) and early 2013 (as president), was willing to engage in high-profile diplomacy with US President Obama. These diplomatic efforts culminated in the November 2014 announcement of a bilateral agreement at APEC in Beijing and the Paris Agreement a year later. A status-seeking argument focuses on Xi's responsiveness to Chinese citizens' desire not only for cleaner air, but also for PRC to take on more

114 See our more extended discussion of Medeiros and Fravel's "new diplomacy" approach, focusing on domestic factors and international socialization, in the chapters on nonproliferation and Central Asian stability; and Medeiros and Fravel, "China's New Diplomacy," p. 22.

115 See Johnston, *Social States*.

116 Moreover, the lack of convergence between the United States and the European Union on the rules for a framework (e.g., different views about the importance of binding commitments) demonstrates that there was *not* an emerging norm about climate. Absent a common, shared understanding, we would not expect this to be a case in which there is meaningful socialization.

responsibility for global governance. As discussed by the aforementioned climate scientist, Chinese citizens were not comfortable with Xi "leading" the effort unilaterally, but to demonstrate "more responsibility" on a par with the United States and Europe. This desire became more acute after the perceived failure of the previous Hu Jintao–Wen Jiabao administration in Copenhagen. Indeed, an interviewee involved in climate negotiations at Copenhagen and Paris noted that following Copenhagen, top Chinese negotiators stated repeatedly that the two countries should not in the future disagree publicly, reportedly saying "We won't criticize you in public, you don't criticize us. We can disagree in meetings but let's agree not to criticize each other."[117] Such arguments are consistent with the idea that China lacked diplomatic capacity to act alone, a problem that was particularly acute in the lead-up to Copenhagen; China was seen to lack the diplomatic and bureaucratic capacity to put forward its own proposals, and was left with a default option of hold-up.[118]

Speculation as to China's continued role in climate change negotiations was rife after the election of Donald Trump in 2016. At the next COP meetings in Marrakech, there was a strong expectation that China would continue to play a leading cooperative role, an impression China's leaders fostered. The withdrawal of any plausible source of US leadership after 2017 will render the main dynamic as between the European Union and China. This, and the absence of a US inclination to bear costs of cooperation, together, we suggest, will worsen China's outside options while it remains an indispensable player. We come back to the implications of our theory for US abdication of leadership in climate cooperation in the concluding chapter.

[117] Author interview, May 20, 2015. This participant also reiterated that the Chinese negotiators generally demonstrated sensitivity to the way China was portrayed internationally after those meetings. A related argument focuses on bilateral optics: in the face of deteriorating Sino–US relations, climate change was one issue for which cooperation with the United States might be possible, especially given its importance to US Secretary of State John Kerry. This point was raised by interviewees in both US and Chinese climate communities.

[118] See, for example, Bo Yan, "China's Role in the Transformation."

8

Conclusions

China's behavior in international regimes has exhibited considerable variation, both over time and across cases. To help make sense of this variation, we developed a general theoretical framework that considers how emerging great powers like China will approach international governance institutions in a particular issue area. Some of these issue areas have been governed by regimes that were put in place by established great powers that excluded China at the outset, while others included China from the beginning. Our argument focuses on two variables: the balance of outside options and the perceived indispensability of the emerging power's participation in a particular institutional setting. We hypothesize that the rising power will be most likely to contribute actively to second-order cooperation – to invest in the maintenance of existing regimes and the creation of new ones – when the rising power's outside options are unfavorable relative to those of established powers. But if the rising power's outside options are more favorable relative to those of the established powers, then its behavior will hinge on whether established great powers view the rising power's participation in a particular institutional setting as critical to regime success. If established powers see the rising power as indispensable, then it will have considerable bargaining power and, hence, the capacity to "hold-up" cooperative efforts – that is, to make its cooperation conditional on a restructuring of regimes to better reflect the rising power's interests. If the rising power is not viewed as indispensable, on the other hand, it will lack bargaining power and will tend to adopt a more passive approach to regime maintenance, an approach we term "accept."

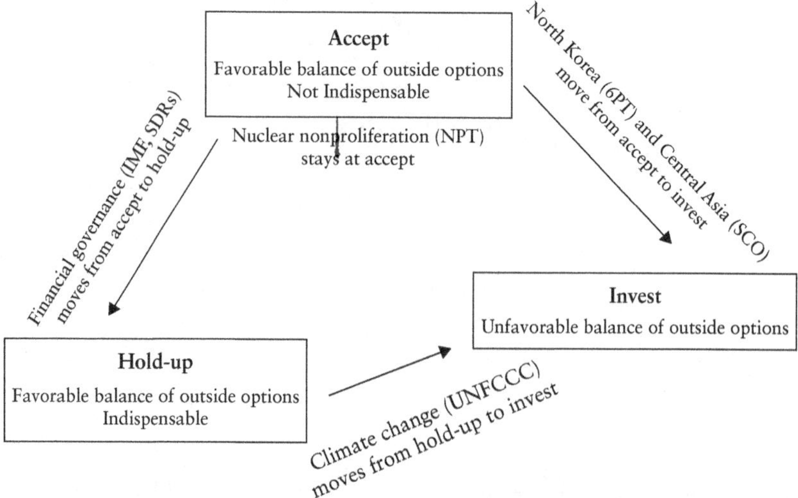

FIGURE 8.1. *Three stable outcomes: accept, hold-up, and invest*

The cases explored in this volume, taken as a whole, increase our confidence in the value of our theoretical framework. Figure 8.1 offers a simplified overview of the way we characterized Chinese second-order cooperative behavior (invest, hold-up, or accept) in our main cases and how this behavior varied over time.

In our first case study, which examined China's role in Central Asia, we saw a shift in Chinese behavior over time from an "accept" role at the end of the Cold War to more proactive investment in regional institutional architecture by the late 1990s and early 2000s. We argued that this shift in behavior was driven, at least in part, by China's worsening outside options during the 1990s. Instability in Xinjiang in the 1990s meant that China had a growing stake in stability in Central Asia. Meanwhile, the collapse of Russian power at the time meant that Beijing could not pass the buck on this issue. In turn, Beijing invested in new regional institutions: first the Shanghai Five forum and, later, the Shanghai Cooperation Organization. In the years after the establishment of the SCO, China faced a more ambiguous set of constraints in the region, though we suggested that continued concerns about regional instability, combined with doubts about the degree to which Russian unilateralism would accommodate China's interests in the region, meant that Beijing's outside options remained relatively unfavorable. Our theory thus predicts continuing Chinese investment in second-order cooperation in the region, a prediction that is moderately supported by the empirical record of some continued proactive investment in the SCO – though the effectiveness of the SCO has remained fairly limited.

Among our cases, China's behavior in the global nuclear nonproliferation regime has exhibited the least variation over time. Broadly speaking, China has accepted existing institutions, neither actively seeking to revise the NPT nor contributing substantial resources to the regime's maintenance. We argued that this relative stasis could be explained, in part, by consistently favorable outside options combined with limited perceived indispensability. One key exception to this general pattern of acceptance on the issue of nonproliferation is the North Korea case, where China's behavior has exhibited more substantial variation over time. During the 1993–1994 crisis on the Korean Peninsula, though playing a helpful behind-the-scenes role, Beijing's behavior was largely passive – consistent with China's broader approach to nuclear nonproliferation. But we argued that worsening outside options led to a shift to "invest" during the second nuclear crisis, in 2002–2003. At this time, just as PRC leaders were becoming more convinced of the seriousness of North Korea's weapons program, they worried more about the possibility of a US unilateral approach, which could lead to considerable instability on the peninsula. In turn, the PRC took the lead in setting up the Six Party Talks to help find a cooperative solution to the crisis. Later, as the risks of a US unilateral military operation waned, and as the feared Northeast Asian nuclear arms race failed to materialize, Beijing saw its outside options improve, but it did not become indispensable and, as a result, it shifted again to a more passive "accept" posture in its approach to the issue. Beijing's eventual lack of vigor in pursuing negotiation through the 6PT (the institution it founded) is consistent with our predictions.

Our third case study, on global financial governance, saw a shift in PRC strategy from passive acceptance through the early 2000s to more proactive participation in discussions on second-order rules governing the global financial system, in particular after the 2008 financial crisis. But even with this greater post-2008 activism – and in contrast to China's proactive role in establishing the 6PT and SCO – China did not actively invest in the construction and maintenance of the existing global financial institutions. Indeed, China's increased activism often was the result of prodding from other actors, principally the United States. Rather, we argue that China pursued a hold-up strategy, made possible by strong outside options and a growing sense among other key actors, primarily the United States, that China's participation in global financial governance had become indispensable after the financial crisis. Beijing demanded significant concessions in return for its increased participation, including concessions related to increasing developing countries' voices, through increasing their vote shares, within the IMF. In 2015, China pursued a similar strategy to have its currency, the renminbi, included among the basket of currencies that constitute the IMF's Special Drawing Rights.

Finally, in the case of China's approach to global climate change negotiations, we saw a shift from a strategy that could be broadly classified as hold-up in the years prior to 2009 to a more proactive "invest" strategy since then. Prior to 2009, China's stake in international climate change cooperation was low relative to that of the United States and the European Union. At the time, Beijing maintained its longstanding position that the country's economic development, which would of necessity remain coal-dependent for a long time, took precedence over the long-term damage from carbon emissions. This viewpoint was consistent with China's long-stated position that the United States and the developed world are historically responsible for the buildup of greenhouse gases in the atmosphere and should take primary responsibility for paying the costs of remediation. Beijing, overall, appeared to be quite tolerant of noncooperation toward a post-Kyoto framework and comfortable with the default Kyoto status quo. While Beijing had participated in climate talks from the start, China's leaders also remained relatively committed to centering their response to climate change on unilateral domestic activities. PRC outside options, in short, appeared quite strong; moreover, as the UN process unfolded over the late 1990s and 2000s, China's participation in a cooperative solution had come to be perceived by the major players as indispensable. Governments in wealthy countries saw that they could not make a new agreement palatable to their home audiences without strong commitments from China. Beijing, in turn, pursued a hold-up strategy, making its participation in a post-Kyoto treaty strictly conditional on gaining concessions on issues about which it is particularly sensitive: the firewall between the responsibilities of developed versus developing nations ("common but differential responsibilities"), the ability of developing countries to avoid binding treaty commitments and set their own targets, and a commitment from wealthy countries to pay for mitigation costs incurred by poor countries as they address their own emissions. In the period following the 2009 Copenhagen summit, however, China's outside options worsened, partly as a result of an increasing stake in the issue – a shift, in turn, driven by domestic politics. In particular, the issue took on new urgency following the infamous "airpocalypse" of January 2013. Shifting coalitional dynamics at the international level further undermined China's outside options. While Beijing's participation continued to be perceived as indispensable, the worsening of its outside options incentivized Beijing to invest in cooperation with the United States. The result was extensive cooperation between presidents Xi Jinping and Barack Obama in their fall 2014 meeting on the sidelines of the Beijing APEC summit, a cooperation that continued and strongly shaped the outcome of the much-heralded December 2015 Paris Agreement.

In sum, our theory offers considerable leverage in the cases explored in this book. To be sure, as we have emphasized throughout, a multitude of factors undoubtedly influence Chinese multilateral behavior in any given issue area. In each chapter, we considered various alternative explanations for Chinese behavior and showed that these, at times, offer important insight and explanatory power. For instance, socialization processes were an important factor driving Chinese engagement with, and accepting behavior toward, the IMF in the years before the mid-2000s.[1] Likewise, China's willingness to invest in the SCO was made possible, in part, by broader changes in Beijing's approach to diplomacy after the late 1990s.[2] And concerns about its international image have almost certainly affected Beijing's calculations on climate change issues.[3] Our aim in this project has not been to debunk these alternative explanations, since these explanations point to factors that have clearly helped shape Chinese behavior. Rather, our goal has been to construct a theory that could provide an explanatory lens that helps make sense of broad patterns of behavior over time and across issue areas. In this regard, we believe that our theory performs quite well. For instance, it helps explain why China invested in multilateral institutions (the 6PT) to facilitate resolution of the North Korean nuclear issue in the early 2000s, but then later reverted to more of an "accept" posture. It helps explain both China's accepting approach to the IMF in the early 2000s and its shift to a hold-up posture after the global financial crisis. And it helps explain why China has been, at the same point in time, more willing to invest in some regimes but not

[1] Alastair Iain Johnston, *Social States: China in International Institutions, 1980–2000* (Princeton, NJ: Princeton University Press, 2008).

[2] Evan S. Medeiros and M. Taylor Fravel, "China's New Diplomacy," *Foreign Affairs* Vol. 82 (2003), p. 22.

[3] On the role of status, see Xiaoyu Pu, "China's International Leadership: Regional Activism vs. Global Reluctance," *Chinese Political Science Review*, Vol. 3, issue 1 (2018), pp. 48–61.

others (compare, for instance, China's current behavior on climate versus nuclear nonproliferation).

In the remainder of this chapter, we first consider some of the broader implications of our theory for the international relations literature. We then speculate about how much guidance our theory might offer concerning China's very recent institution-building initiatives, including most prominently the Asian Infrastructure Investment Bank. Finally, we consider (again, speculatively) the way Beijing is likely to react should the United States and Europe begin to abdicate leadership in the contemporary global order – a real possibility in an age of spreading nationalist populism in North America and Europe (exemplified by the British referendum on exiting the European Union), the strong showings by anti-globalization parties throughout Europe, and the Donald Trump administration in the United States.

8.1 IMPLICATIONS FOR THE INTERNATIONAL RELATIONS LITERATURE

Within the study of international organizations and regimes, there is considerable debate about how multilateral regimes develop and change. Scholars have developed this research question against the backdrop of theories of hegemonic stability, which come in many varieties but which, in general, posit that states enjoying primacy in the international system will be driven to structure the world order in ways that produce public goods (such as mutually beneficial trading regimes or financial orders), because these leading states will themselves stand to gain the most from the benefits of these goods. Leading states have an incentive to work at maintaining regimes even if it means giving up on other priorities, where "maintaining" implies ensuring the regimes remain functional and relevant by incorporating other powerful states as necessary.[4]

Our thesis in this book is rooted in this approach as well. We argue analytically and show empirically that when a rising state like China has more to lose from a failure of multilateralism than it has to lose by jumping into the fray to try to build international order, it is perfectly willing

[4] For contemporary versions of this type of argument, see, for example, David A. Deese, *World Trade Politics: Power, Principles and Leadership* (New York: Routledge, 2007); and Sandra Destradi, "Regional Powers and Their Strategies: Empire, Hegemony, and Leadership," *Review of International Studies*, Vol. 36, no. 4 (2010), pp. 903–30.

to adopt a policy of investing in a regime. The unique contribution we make to this research project is threefold.

First, we explore the strategic logic of investing in regimes in greater detail than many prior studies have, by distinguishing between first- and second-order cooperation and by showing that the strategic setting of second-order cooperation is critical. Whether China has high or low overall stakes in the particular issue (the outside option with respect to first-order cooperation) is less important than what the outside options are for regime maintenance generally. So, for example, in Chapter 5 we argued that even though China benefits from the nuclear nonproliferation regime and, itself, plays a crucial role in the regime as a nuclear weapons state and therefore as a potential nuclear supplier, its outside options in its *second-order* interaction with the United States are relatively favorable. China can have confidence that the United States will continue to invest heavily in the regime and that China can, therefore, free-ride on regime production.

Second, by introducing the importance of perceived indispensability we are able to describe the interplay between the balance of outside options and the technology of regime production. That is, when the rising state's outside options are good, its approach to multilateralism will depend on whether or not it is seen as indispensable to the creation of a regime. Consider the contrast between nuclear nonproliferation and global finance. In both cases, China in the 1990s was in a position where it had a favorable balance of outside options and was not seen as indispensable. That is, in both instances the United States was clearly able and willing to continue investing in the global regime. As the issues diverged, however, with China becoming indispensable in finance but not in nonproliferation, China adopted a different approach to the two issues by bargaining hard for a renegotiation to the regime governing finance, even while it continued to accept the basic outlines of the nonproliferation regime both in general (the NPT) and in specifics (sanctions on Iran, for example). Uniquely, we show how differences in the values of different kinds of inputs into the production of a regime are critical variables.[5]

[5] Randall Stone's argument (*Controlling Institutions*, p. 14) is instructive here. He argues that, during normal times, international institutions operate in accordance with their formal decision rules, but that, during times of unusual stress or attention, states control institutions using informal leverage, which in turn derives from their outside options. Where our analysis differs is in how regimes get built or maintained. Stone does not assume, in his model of regime production, that any one state can be indispensable (that it can have a monopoly on some critical component for the success of the regime); for

Third, we advance the scholarly agenda by showing, empirically, how one rising state's approach to multilateralism differs across different issue areas, even as broader international and domestic factors are held constant. While we acknowledge that domestic political factors can play an important role in shaping China's approach to global governance, at a minimum our argument provides a language for the way those domestic factors affect strategy at the international level. For example, while on one level it should not be surprising that a public outcry about rising pollution levels in major Chinese cities was followed by a greater Chinese investment in international cooperation to address climate change, putting the domestic political pressure to do something in terms of "worsening outside options" allows us to show how that kind of pressure alone is likely sufficient to tip China from playing hold-up to acting as a major global investor in a new climate regime.

Our approach to the question of China's behavior toward international regimes is consciously rationalist; we describe the opportunities and constraints that rising states face as being primarily shaped by the strategic setting of an issue, so that it is the rising state's expectation of the way established states will react to its actions that matters. Also, we describe the goals motivating Chinese leaders as rooted in a calculation of their interests that emerges independently of the institutional setting. That is, the international system matters (in that each state's interests and abilities come together to shape outside options and indispensability) but the rules of each regime are, themselves, products of the strategic setting; those rules are not, themselves, the prime movers of the way regimes function. Our approach contrasts with explanations of changes in regimes that highlight the role of prior institutional features of regimes. Ayse Kaya, for example, argues that both the broader purposes and the shared understanding of what regimes are for, as well as the formal funding mechanisms and internal points of control within existing institutions, determine how regimes adapt to changing circumstances as new powers emerge.[6] Ultimately, the extent to which representation within

him, these are simply functions of the state's outside option. However, being indispensable does not necessarily mean that the state's outside option is strong. China was not made obviously better off by being indispensable to the production of a climate regime leading up to the Copenhagen summit, and (as we note at the end of the current chapter) we are skeptical that the rise in Chinese indispensability that might follow populist nationalist turns in the United States and Europe is necessarily good for China. We feel there is a strong case for thinking of indispensability and strong outside options as being distinct.

6 Ayse Kaya, *Power and Global Economic Institutions* (Cambridge: Cambridge University Press, 2015), p. 8. For a similar argument about institutional change at the IMF and

existing institutions conditions the way regimes accommodate change is an empirical one; at the very least, Chinese leaders and other members of Beijing's foreign policy establishment *seemed* to act on the basis of the structural factors we identify.

Phillip Lipscy's argument begins from a similar starting point as ours: he asks why some institutions are quicker to change than others to accommodate rising states, and argues that the characteristics of the issues themselves give existing institutions more or less monopoly power. When starting up a new, rival institution is costly due to some combination of start-up costs (developing expertise and credibility in the issue area is expensive and time-consuming) and network externalities (the issue is one where it pays to work through the same institution as most other states), existing institutions will persist and survive whether or not they adapt to a changing distribution of capabilities in the world, and so established states will know they can get away with preventing reform. However, if starting up new regimes to compete with old ones is easy, then established states will allow existing regimes to quickly accommodate rising states in order to stave off competing institutions.[7]

While Lipscy's argument and findings are an important advance in the study of institutional change – in particular because he shows, with an extremely parsimonious theory, that the issue area alone can lead to important differences in the way institutions adapt, quite apart from the specific interests of the member states – our argument nevertheless makes a contribution in a different direction. Lipscy's analysis is systemic; he assumes that all of the public goods that regimes produce lead to shared benefits that have distributive consequences, but that otherwise all states have similar stakes in the regime overall. It is not entirely clear that this is true of all regimes, however. The potential for political instability in Central Asia, for arms races in East Asia, and for climate change will affect different states differently, and some states may be better prepared to face climate change or financial crises alone, either due to innate differences (having a geography and human ecology less exposed to drought or rising sea levels) or due to conscious investments (currency reserves or swap agreements). In particular, different states may have outside

the World Bank, see Catherine Weaver and Manuela Moschella, "Bounded Reform in Global Economic Governance at the International Monetary Fund and the World Bank," in Orfeo Fioretos, ed., *International Politics and Institutions in Time* (London: Oxford University Press, 2017), pp. 274–92.

7 Phillip Y. Lipscy, *Renegotiating the World Order: Institutional Change in International Relations* (New York: Cambridge University Press, 2017).

options that address problems in ways entirely different from the ways that a multilateral regime would have – nuclear proliferation, for example, could be addressed via a nonproliferation regime focused on denial or via a unilateral regime based on a combination of counterproliferation strikes and missile defenses. Furthermore, these stakes and outside options may change over time in ways that would be entirely unpredictable at the systemic level but that can be explained at the state level, as we do, using the language of outside options and indispensability as they apply to specific policy choices.

8.2 CHINA INVESTS IN DEVELOPMENT FINANCE: THE ASIAN INFRASTRUCTURE INVESTMENT BANK

China has recently undertaken several high-profile initiatives relating to development finance, including the creation of the Asian Infrastructure Investment Bank, the launch of the Belt and Road Initiative, and participation in the creation of the New Development Bank. The PRC has been investing substantial resources in these new endeavors – both financial and, perhaps more importantly, reputational. These initiatives have generated a great deal of interest abroad, with some analysts viewing them as a major challenge to established global financial institutions – or even "a fundamental challenge to the U.S.-centered world order" more broadly.[8] To what degree, then, does our theory offer useful insight into China's decision to launch these new development finance institutions? We already speculated on BRI to some degree in the conclusions to Chapter 4. Here, we focus our attention on the most high profile of these initiatives, the AIIB.

Chinese President Xi Jinping first publically proposed the creation of an Asian Infrastructure Investment Bank during a 2013 visit to Indonesia. In a speech in which he also called for the establishment of a maritime Silk Road (the "road" of the BRI initiative), Xi emphasized that China hoped to provide support for infrastructure investment and

[8] This quote is from Yun-han Chu in "Should Washington Fear the AIIB?" *Foreign Affairs* snapshot, June 11, 2015: www.foreignaffairs.com/articles/china/2015-06-11/should-washington-fear-aiib. For a view that the new institutions potentially represent a challenge to the Bretton Woods institutions, see, for instance, Robert Wihtol, "Beijing's Challenge to the Global Financial Architecture," *Georgetown Journal of Asian Affairs*, Spring/Summer 2015, pp. 7–15: https://asianstudies.georgetown.edu/sites/asianstudies/files/GJAA%202.1%20Wihtol,%20Robert_0.pdf.

increased connectivity in Asia.[9] The AIIB was generally well received in the region,[10] and China moved quickly to make the proposed bank a reality. In October 2014, a total of twenty-one Asian countries signed a memorandum of understanding to establish the AIIB, agreeing that the new bank would be headquartered in Beijing.[11] Even though the United States, fearing the AIIB would undercut established development finance institutions, openly opposed Beijing's initiative, the number of countries expressing interest continued to grow.[12] In early 2015, several key US allies (starting with the United Kingdom and soon including Germany, Italy, Australia, and South Korea) announced their intention to join the AIIB despite Washington's opposition.[13] Fifty-seven countries ultimately signed the 2015 Articles of Agreement establishing the AIIB, charging the new organization with promoting development and infrastructure connectivity in Asia, while also promoting "regional cooperation and partnership in addressing development challenges by working in close collaboration with other multilateral and bilateral development institutions."[14] The founding members of the AIIB included most major

[9] Mike Callaghan and Paul Hubbard, "The Asian Infrastructure Investment Bank: Multilateralism on the Silk Road," *China Economic Journal*, Vol. 9, no. 2 (2016), p. 121. For the text of the speech, see Speech by Chinese President Xi Jinping to Indonesian Parliament, October 2, 2013, at ASEAN-China Center: www.asean-china-center.org/english/2013-10/03/c_133062675.htm.

[10] See ibid.

[11] See Ming Wan, *The Asian Infrastructure Investment Bank: The Construction of Power and the Struggle for the East Asian International Order* (New York: Palgrave Macmillan, 2016), p. 47.

[12] That the United States chose to oppose AIIB so strongly, even to the point of creating rifts with key allies, is puzzling. Clearly Washington had concerns about good governance issues, yet (as we note later) the new bank has appeared to align itself with key international norms on these issues. We suspect that this opposition is rooted in a belief that the AIIB and the BRI are – at least in part – motivated by a desire to increase China's regional influence (at the expense of the United States). Consider, for instance, a hearing in the Senate Armed Services Committee in which US Secretary of Defense James Mattis and Chairman of the Joint Chiefs of Staff Joseph Dunford both testified. During questioning, Senator Gary Peters stated that "we are well aware that the 'One Belt, One Road' strategy seeks to secure China's control over both continental and the maritime interests, in their eventual hope, I think, of dominating Eurasia and exploiting natural resources there, things that are certainly at odds with U.S. policy." Mattis responded that "in a globalized world, there are many belts and many roads, and no one nation should put itself into a position of dictating One Belt, One Road." See committee transcript at: www.armed-services.senate.gov/imo/media/doc/17-82_10-03-17.pdf.

[13] Ibid., p. 48. For a discussion of US and Japanese strategic concerns about the AIIB, see Callaghan and Hubbard, "The Asian Infrastructure Investment Bank," pp. 123–125.

[14] See Gregory T. Chin, "Asian Infrastructure Investment Bank: Governance Innovation and Prospects," *Global Governance*, Vol. 22 (2016), p. 11.

stakeholders in the global economy, though governments of a number of key economies – including especially the United States and Japan – remained outside the new institution.[15]

We believe that China's decision to launch the AIIB should be characterized as investing in second-order cooperation for two reasons. First, China is clearly devoting considerable resources to this new endeavor. Most obviously, China is by far the largest financial contributor to the AIIB: of the bank's initial capitalization of US$100 billion, China's share was nearly US$30 billion (India, the second largest contributor, pledged US$8.36 billion).[16] Perhaps more importantly, China has made the AIIB a major diplomatic priority; its rapid progression from concept in 2013 to reality in 2015 is almost entirely a function of PRC leadership – including extensive bilateral diplomacy to expand the bank's initial membership.[17] The AIIB is entirely a Chinese initiative and is headquartered in Beijing; as such, China will earn respect and praise to the degree the bank succeeds and will inevitably bear most of the blame for any failures. Thus, because it has been such a high-profile endeavor, China will have to show competence and restraint in running the organization in order to maintain its credibility.[18]

Second, the AIIB appears to be consistent with – and indeed in many ways contributing to – the current global development finance regime. Perhaps most importantly, the new bank is addressing an area – infrastructure spending in Asia – with extensive needs: more than US$8 trillion over the next decade, according to the Asian Development Bank.[19] Yet current funding for infrastructure in Asia does not come close to financing these needs and, as Raj Desal and James Vreeland write, established development finance institutions "cannot hope to fill this hole." Even if they focused exclusively on Asian infrastructure finance (which they obviously do not), the World Bank and the Asian Development Bank lack a sufficient capital base to meet regional needs.[20] Although the AIIB

15 For a full list of AIIB founding members, and how those compare with the founding members of the Asian Development Bank, see Wan, *The Asian Infrastructure Investment Bank*, pp. 45–7.

16 Ibid., pp. 49–50.

17 On PRC leadership in constructing the AIIB, see Wan, *The Asian Infrastructure Investment Bank*, pp. 44–51.

18 Similar to Lipscy (*Renegotiating*, p. 289), we conceive of these factors as part of the costs of investment.

19 Raj M. Desal and James Raymond Vreeland, "How to Stop Worrying and Love the Asian Infrastructure Investment Bank," *Monkey Cage [The Washington Post]*, April 6, 2015.

20 Ibid.

itself will only provide a fraction of Asian infrastructure finance needs, it certainly helps fill an important gap in development finance,[21] and PRC officials have stressed that filling this gap is the principle purpose of the AIIB.[22]

Meanwhile, initial AIIB operations appear consistent with key norms – such as good governance and environmental safeguards – of the global development finance regime. For instance, the appointment of Jin Liqun as the first president of the AIIB appeared to signal a commitment to working with, rather than at cross-purposes to, the current regime. Jin has extensive personal experience working within established development finance institutions: early in his career, he worked in Washington for the executive director for China offices at the World Bank and, later, he served as vice-president of the Asian Development Bank. A strong advocate for good governance, Jin is a vocal proponent of environmentally responsible development and emphasizes no tolerance for corruption.[23]

Moreover, the structure of the AIIB shares many similarities with the major established development banks. Gregory Chin highlights a number of key continuities with incumbent institutions, including in terms of representation (membership is not limited to Asian countries, with China actively seeking wide participation) and authority structure (China holds veto power on important decisions, and each country's voting power is based on criteria such as capital contribution and economic size).[24] To be sure, the AIIB also differs in important ways from the main established banks; for instance, the new bank has a dual board structure (a board of governors and a board of directors), and neither the governors nor the directors are in residence in Beijing.[25] Chin notes that although some are skeptical of a nonresident board of directors, fearing this will result in increased Chinese control over the bank, other prominent observers view this innovation in a more positive light, believing that a nonresident board will contribute to efficiency and reduce waste. Indeed, some

21 For another argument along similar lines, see "The Infrastructure of Power," *The Economist*, June 30, 2016: www.economist.com/news/finance-and-economics/21701494-reasons-be-enthusiastic-about-chinas-answer-world-bank-infrastructure.

22 For examples in this regard, see Hai Yang, "The Asian Infrastructure Investment Bank and Status-Seeking: China's Foray into Global Economic Governance," *Chinese Political Science Review*, Vol. 1 (2016), pp. 769–70.

23 See, for instance, "A Banker Inspired by Western Novelists Seeks to Build Asia," *The New York Times*, January 14, 2017, p. A8.

24 Chin, "Asian Infrastructure Investment Bank," pp. 13–14.

25 Ibid., p. 15.

of these observers have called for similar reforms at the World Bank.[26] It is worth noting here, as well, that China was apparently willing to sacrifice veto power if either the United States or Japan had joined the AIIB,[27] suggesting to us that Beijing is motivated by a desire to create a bank that has broad buy-in from key stakeholders in the current global development finance regime, even if it means sacrificing control over the new institution.

Finally, as Hai Yang observes, both the World Bank and the Asian Development Bank have viewed the AIIB as filling an important role that contributes to, rather than competes with, the current regime. Both institutions signed co-financing framework agreements with the new bank,[28] and the AIIB has already pursued several co-financing projects with them. Of the nine projects approved by the AIIB in 2016, at least three (including a pipeline project in Azerbaijan, a hydropower project in Pakistan, and a slum upgrading project in Indonesia) are co-financed with the World Bank, and a fourth (a motorway project in Pakistan) is co-financed with the Asian Development Bank.[29] Early reports suggest that the AIIB has been careful to undertake detailed background investigations concerning the environmental and social implications of its projects.[30]

At the time of this writing, then, it seems more accurate to describe the AIIB as contributing to the existing international development finance regime, rather than as competing with it. China's behavior, then, falls under our "invest" category. Our theory expects investment in second-order cooperation to occur when China's outside options, relative to other established powers, are weak. Is that the case here?

Some evidence suggests that China's outside options relating to development finance under the incumbent regime have indeed been relatively poor. As we noted in our chapter on China's efforts to promote stability in Central Asia, Beijing has good reason to want to see more development finance in Asia, particularly in its immediate periphery. Efforts to increase connectivity and infrastructure development will benefit China economically, of course, but will also enhance China's regional influence

[26] David Dollar, for instance, has made these sorts of arguments. See Chin, "Asian Infrastructure Investment Bank," p. 16.

[27] Ibid., p. 13.

[28] Yang, "Asian Infrastructure Investment Bank and Status-Seeking," p. 756.

[29] A list of approved projects is available on the AIIB webpage at: www.aiib.org/en/projects/approved.

[30] See, for instance, Sara Hsu, "How China's Asian Infrastructure Investment Bank Fared in its First Year," *Forbes Online*, January 14, 2017.

as other states become more integrated with it. And perhaps even more importantly from China's perspective, development has the potential to enhance regional stability. These benefits from infrastructure development would accrue to China regardless of who funded them, yet, as noted earlier, Asia's infrastructure investment needs have been woefully underfunded, and established development banks lack the financial capacity to address the gap.

China, with its massive foreign reserves and burgeoning economic power, certainly has unilateral options: it can pursue (and has pursued) bilateral development assistance, most notably via the massive BRI initiative. Yet as Ho-fung Hung notes, bilateral initiatives have their own drawbacks – including the risk of backlash against perceived Chinese imperialism and the lack of shared risk should investments go bad.[31] Investing in the AIIB offers China a way to pursue its goals in a manner that helps mitigate this risk. As Hung puts it, constructing the AIIB "is not Beijing's attempt at world domination; it is a self-imposed constraint, and a retreat from more than a decade of aggressive bilateral initiatives."[32] Seen in this light, China's decision to invest in the AIIB reflects somewhat weak outside options (relative to the United States), which arise from a combination of a recognized need for more development finance in the region, the limited capacity of established development banks to meet this need, the downside risks of relying purely on bilateral investment deals, and the simple reality that China likely has a larger stake in the issue than the United States since it stands to benefit more directly (in terms of both security and economics) from Eurasian regional development.

Factors outside our theory have undoubtedly contributed to China's decision to invest in the AIIB. For instance, Hai Yang describes the bank as a "quintessential status-seeking initiative" that advances Beijing's goal of being widely recognized as having attained great power status.[33] Domestic political-economy factors are likely salient as well: some observers have noted, for instance, that Beijing's interest in increased infrastructure investment in Asia may be partially rooted in China's efforts to deal with persistent overcapacity problems in heavy industries

[31] Ho-Fung Hung, "China Steps Back," *International New York Times*, April 6, 2015.

[32] Ibid.

[33] Yang, "Asian Infrastructure Investment Bank and Status Seeking," p. 773. On China's status-seeking behavior more generally, see also Xiaoyu Pu and Randall Schweller, "Status Signaling, Multiple Audiences, and China's Blue-Water Naval Ambition," in T. V. Paul, Deborah Welch Larson, and William C. Wohlforth, eds., *Status in World Politics* (Cambridge: Cambridge University Press, 2014), pp. 141–63.

such as steel.[34] And some analysts view the decision to launch the AIIB as part of a broader effort to challenge, or to find a "route around," the US-led international order.[35] One useful way to think about the possibility of a "route around" established institutions – that is also consistent with our theory – is to explore the implications of the AIIB (and other recent PRC initiatives like the New Development Bank, the BRI, and Renminbi internationalization) for China's long-term outside options relating to the global financial system (see our discussion in Chapter 2 on dynamic conditions). To the degree that these new initiatives make it easier for China to pursue its financial interests outside established institutions, they enhance the PRC's bargaining power within those institutions and facilitate China's ability to play a hold-up strategy – where it can use its bargaining power to reshape global institutions more to its liking. In other words, outside options can actually become endogenous, over the long-term, to Chinese strategy. We are agnostic about whether China in fact aims, over the long-term, to challenge the US-led order. Rather, we simply note that a focus on the way new institutional initiatives affect China's long-term outside options offers a potentially useful way to assess the degree to which Beijing could be successful in this regard in the future, while noting that the sacrifices Beijing has already had to make to ensure the credibility of the AIIB (such as shared governance and a commitment to follow existing norms concerning development assistance) suggest that even a world in which China exercises institutions such as the AIIB as outside options would still be a world in which China is nonetheless relatively constrained.

In sum, China's decision to invest in the AIIB appears driven in part by relatively unfavorable outside options, a consequence of China's desire to see increased infrastructure spending in Asia combined with the inability of established development finance institutions to meet this need and the

34 See, for instance, the discussion on the BRI in Jiayi Zhou, Karl Hallding, and Guoyi Han, "The Trouble with China's 'One Belt, One Road' Strategy," *The Diplomat*, June 26, 2015: http://thediplomat.com/2015/06/the-trouble-with-the-chinese-marshall-plan-strategy/. For a broader discussion of some of the domestic economic motivations underpinning BRI (and, given its similar aim of promoting infrastructure investment in Asia, presumably AIIB as well), see Scott Kennedy and David A. Parker, "Building China's 'One Belt, One Road,'" Center for Strategic and Economic Studies *Critical Questions*, April 3, 2015: http://csis.org/publication/building-chinas-one-belt-one-road. See also Hong Yu, "Motivation behind China's 'One Belt, One Road' Initiatives and Establishment of the Asian Infrastructure Investment Bank," *Journal of Contemporary China*, Vol. 26, no. 105 (2017), pp. 353–68.

35 See, for instance, Naazneen Barma, Ely Ratner, and Steven Weber, "Welcome to the World without the West," *National Interest*, November 12, 2014.

downside risks Beijing faces in dealing with the issue unilaterally. In this light, China's creation of the AIIB can be seen as investing in a public good that will disproportionately benefit China, though it also will face significant constraints if the organization is to be credible. Of course, as with all the cases examined in this study, other factors have also been salient, including Beijing's desire for increased international status and domestic political and economic conditions. But our short sketch suggests that our theory is likely to prove useful in helping make sense of this important and still-unfolding case.

8.3 LOOKING TOWARD THE FUTURE: THE IMPLICATIONS OF POPULIST NATIONALISM IN THE UNITED STATES AND THE EUROPEAN UNION

As we write this conclusion, world politics are in flux. The election of Donald Trump as US president has called US global leadership more into question than it has been since the end of World War II. In the few months after Trump entered office, he withdrew the United States from the Trans-Pacific Partnership, signaled his intention to withdraw from the Paris climate change agreement, signaled lukewarm support for NATO, and called into question Washington's broader commitment to the global trade regime (including even the WTO).[36] In Europe, meanwhile, the United Kingdom voted to leave the European Union, and the rise of right-wing populism across Europe raises questions about the long-term viability of the European Union itself. In short, the commitment of key stakeholders to the current global order is increasingly in doubt.

There is a tendency among some observers to view the possible abdication of leadership by Washington as an opportunity for China. Consider, for instance, a recent article by leading Chinese international relations expert Yan Xuetong published in *The New York Times*. Yan argues that "Trump's scrapping of the Trans-Pacific Partnership is a chance for Beijing to strengthen its position as the economic leader of East Asia"; that Trump's confrontational approach on Taiwan offers China the opportunity to construct a regional alliance system of its own; that Trump's anti-immigration stance offers China the opportunity to lead by

[36] Consider, for instance, the Trump administration's refusal to accept anti-protectionist language in a 2017 G20 statement on trade. See "Trump Admin Rejects Anti-Protectionism Language in G20 Free Trade Statement," *The Hill online*, March 18, 2017.

becoming more open to immigrants; and that US abdication of leadership on climate change opens the door for China to assume such a role.[37]

Meanwhile, in his January 2017 speech to the World Economic Forum in Davos, Switzerland, Chinese President Xi Jinping suggested that China was indeed prepared to assume such a leadership role, strongly defending economic globalization (even as the West increasingly appears to reject it) and endorsing the Paris climate accord (despite Trump's pledge to walk away from it).[38] Beijing, it seems, is prepared to lead if need be and, from the perspective of many, this would be a good thing for China.[39]

Should the United States and its Western allies come to reject a leadership role in sustaining the liberal world order, however, a tremendous burden would be placed on China, despite the opportunities. China might indeed be called on to salvage what is left of the international order if populist nationalism prevails in the West, but this is because Beijing has a lot riding on that order. In fact, China arguably has benefited more from economic openness in the West than any other country.[40] In other words, the opportunity for China to lead in Washington's absence also implies the loss of an opportunity to passively accept a functioning regime – that is, the loss of the ability to free-ride on the second-order cooperative efforts of others. Being the architect of international order is not cheap. In the case of the United States, it has meant being a lender of last resort and having a market that – while not totally open – is nonetheless sufficiently open to support export-led growth in China and elsewhere. It has meant having a global reserve currency that offers substantial privileges, but that also comes at high cost in terms of economic competiveness over the long term.[41] At the time, the United States in the twentieth century and the United Kingdom in the nineteenth century accepted this role, as they were already the most advanced economies in the world. For Beijing

[37] Yan Xuetong, "China Can Thrive in the Trump Era," *The New York Times*, January 25, 2017, p. A25.

[38] See "Xi Cast China as Champion of Openness," *The New York Times*, January 18, 2017, p. A1.

[39] To be clear, there is considerable disagreement among scholars and analysts in China about whether Beijing should adopt a much broader leadership role in global governance. For a discussion, see Angela Poh and Mingjiang Li, "A China in Transition: the Rhetoric and Substance of Chinese Foreign Policy under Xi Jinping," *Asian Security*, Vol. 13, no. 2 (2017), pp. 84–97.

[40] See G. John Ikenberry, "The Rise of China and the Future of the West: Can the Liberal System Survive?" *Foreign Affairs*, Vol. 87, no. 1 (2008), pp. 23–37.

[41] On the benefits and costs of maintaining a global reserve currency, see Benjamin J. Cohen, "The Benefits and Costs of an International Currency: Getting the Calculus Right," *Open Economies Review*, Vol. 23 (2012), pp. 13–31. DOI: 10.1007/s11079-011-9216-2.

to take on this role now would place enormous economic burdens on the country before China has truly become rich. Indeed, it is far from clear that China even has the capacity to play such a role in the near term.[42] Even on an issue in which China has invested considerably – addressing climate change – we observe in China an awareness of the costs to China and a reluctance to assume them. As one commentary notes:

> China should have a clear and thorough understanding of the cost, benefits, as well as feasibility of taking over of the leadership. On one hand, it is necessary to clearly understand that "leadership" is not a free lunch and leading the global climate governance would require not just political momentum and the provision of some free public goods, but more importantly it demands much greater responsibility in terms of emission reductions and financing obligations. It is largely in question that if it is wise to focus on the leadership debate at the current timing whereas China's industry, economy, and diplomacy may not benefit as much as the price we pay for taking that leadership. On the other hand, China should be fully aware that the leadership is never self-given and cannot be an overnight achievement, which needs careful cost-benefit analysis and feasibility assessment.[43]

Viewing Trumpism and the possible retreat of the United States as an opportunity for China would be akin to viewing the 1993–1994 crisis on the Korean Peninsula as an opportunity for the United States. During that crisis, the United States would ideally have leaned on China – North Korea's key remaining patron – to rein in Pyongyang, but China, as we saw, was happy to maintain a relatively passive posture. Having no good outside options (the military option would have been disastrous), the United States ultimately "invested" in new regional security architecture, most notably the 1994 Agreed Framework with the DPRK. Yet the Agreed Framework was, in many ways, an albatross around the Clinton administration's neck: not only was it of dubious efficacy, but it also created unending domestic political difficulties for Clinton. Far from an

42 To give one obvious example, the renminbi remains far removed from being a major global reserve currency on par with the dollar. In early 2017, less than 2 percent of all international trade was settled in renminbi, for instance. For a succinct discussion of other factors undermining the capacity of China to assume the role of global leader (at least in the near term), see Yanzhong Huang, "A Superpower, but Not yet a Global Leader," *Asia Unbound (blog)*, Council on Foreign Relations, April 20, 2017: www.cfr.org/blog/superpower-not-yet-global-leader.

43 Qimin Chai, Sha Fu, Huaqing Xu, Weiran Li, and Yan Zhong, "The Gap Report of Global Climate Change Mitigation, Finance, and Governance after the United States Declared Its Withdrawal from the Paris Agreement," *Chinese Journal of Population Resources and Environment*, Vol. 15, no. 3 (2017), pp. 196–208 (quote is p. 206).

opportunity, the 1994 agreement was a costly burden for Washington, one that it pursued only because the alternatives were worse. A retreat from global leadership by the United States and the European Union would present China with a similar set of unattractive alternatives: the triumph of populist nationalism would, in our view, be an ominous development for China, a development we hope might still be avoided.

References

English Language References

Adger, W. Niel, ed., *Fairness in Adaptation to Climate Change* (Cambridge, MA: MIT press, 2006).

Adler, Ben, "Trump Can't Do Much to Worsen Climate Change," *The Washington Post*, April 2, 2017, B1.

Albert, Eleanor, "The Shanghai Cooperation Organization," Council on Foreign Relations, *CFR Backgrounder*, October 14, 2015: www.cfr.org/china/shanghai-cooperation-organization/p10883.

Alesina, Alberto, Reza Baqir, and William Easterly, "Public Goods and Ethnic Divisions," *The Quarterly Journal of Economics*, Vol. 114, no. 4 (1999), pp. 1243–84.

Archibugi, Daniele, "The G20 Ought to Be Increased to 6 Billion," *openDemocracy* (March 31, 2009): www.opendemocracy.net/article/email/the-g20-ought-to-be-increased-to-6-billion.

Aslund, Anders, *Russia's Capitalist Revolution: Why Market Reform Succeeded and Democracy Failed* (Washington, DC: Peterson Institute for International Economics, 2007).

Avant, Deborah D., Martha Finnemore, and Susan K. Sell, eds., *Who Governs the Globe?* (London: Cambridge University Press, 2010).

Bader, Jeffrey A., *Obama and China's Rise* (Washington, DC: Brookings, 2012).

Bailer, Stefanie, "Bargaining Success in the European Union: The Impact of Exogenous and Endogenous Power Resources," *European Union Politics*, Vol. 5, no. 1 (2004), pp. 99–123.

Bakshi, Jyotsna, "Shanghai Cooperation Organization (SCO) before and after September 11," *Strategic Analysis*, Vol. 26, no. 2 (2002), pp. 265–76.

Barfield, Thomas J., *The Perilous Frontier: Nomadic Empires and China* (Cambridge, MA: Blackwell, 1989).

"The Hsiung-nu Imperial Confederacy: Organization and Foreign Policy, *Journal of Asian Studies*, Vol. 41, no. 1 (1981), pp. 45–61.

Barma, Naazneen, Ely Ratner, and Steven Weber, "Welcome to the World without the West," *National Interest*, November 12, 2014.

Barrett, Scott, *Why Cooperate? The Incentive to Supply Global Public Goods* (London: Oxford University Press, 2007).

Bas, Muhammet A. and Andrew J. Coe, "A Dynamic Theory of Nuclear Proliferation and Preventive War," *International Organization*, Vol. 70, no. 4 (2016), pp. 655–85.

Bearce, David. H. and Stacy Bondanella, "Intergovernmental Organizations, Socialization, and Member-State Interest Convergence," *International Organization*, Vol. 61, no. 4 (2007), pp. 703–733.

Becquelin, Nicolas, "Staged Development in Xinjiang," in David S. Goodman, ed., *China's Campaign to "Open up the West": National, Provincial, and Local Perspectives* (Cambridge: Cambridge University Press, 2004).

Bennhold, Katrin, "Sarkozy Calls for Global Monetary System, without Dollar as Top Reserve Currency," *The New York Times*, January 28, 2010.

Bergsten, C. Fred, "Two's Company," *Foreign Affairs* (September/October 2009): www.foreignaffairs.com/articles/65232/c-fred-bergsten/twos-company.

Bitzinger, Richard, "Modernizing China's Military, 1997–2012," *China Perspectives*, no. 4 (88) (2011), pp. 7–15.

Blasko, Dennis J., *The Chinese Army Today: Tradition and Transformation for the Twenty-First Century* (London: Routledge, 2012).

Bleek, Philipp C. and Eric B. Lorber, "Security Guarantees and Allied Nuclear Proliferation," *Journal of Conflict Resolution*, Vol. 58, no. 3 (2014), pp. 429–54.

Bluth, Christoph, *Crisis on the Korean Peninsula* (Washington, DC: Potomac Books, 2011).

Bo, Yan, "China's Role in the Transformation of the Global Climate Change Regime," speech at University of Nottingham, April 5, 2013: http://blogs.nottingham.ac.uk/chinapolicyinstitute/2013/04/15/chinas-role-in-the-transformation-of-global-climate-change-regime/.

Boland, Julie, *"Ten Years of the Shanghai Cooperation Organization: A Lost Decade? A Partner for the U.S.?" 21st Century Defense Initiative Policy Paper* (Washington: Brookings, 20 June 2011).

Bovingdon, Gardner, *Uyghurs: Strangers in their Own Land* (New York: Columbia University Press, 2010).

Brandt, Loren, Debin Ma and Thomas G. Rawski, "Industrialization in China," in Kevin O'Rourke and Jeffrey Williamson, eds., *The Spread of Modern Industry to the Global Periphery Since 1871* (Oxford: Oxford University Press, 2017), pp. 197–228.

Branstetter, Lee and Nicholas Lardy, "China's Embrace of Globalization," in Loren Brandt and Thomas G. Rawski, eds., *China's Great Economic Transformation* (New York: Cambridge University Press, 2008), pp. 633–82.

Brown, Robert L., *Nuclear Authority: The IAEA and the Absolute Weapon* (Washington, DC: Georgetown University Press, 2015).

Brunnée, Jutta and Charlotte Streck, "The UNFCCC as a Negotiation Forum: Towards Common but More Differentiated Responsibilities," *Climate Policy*, Vol. 13, no. 5 (2013), pp. 589–607.

Buijs, Bran, *China, Copenhagen, and Beyond: The Global Necessity of a Global Sustainable Energy Future for China* (The Hague: Clingendael International

Energy Program, 2009): www.clingendael.nl/publications/2009/20090900_ciep_report_buijs_china_copenhagen_beyond.pdf.

Burcu, Bayram, A. and Erin R. Graham, "Financing the United Nations: Explaining Variation in How Donors Provide Funding to the UN," *The Review of International Organizations*, Vol. 12, no. 3 (2017), pp. 421–59.

Burleson, Elizabeth, "The Bali Climate Change Conference," *Insights (American Society for International Law)*, Vol. 12, no. 4 (2008): www.asil.org/insights/volume/12/issue/4/bali-climate-change-conference.

Callaghan, Mike and Paul Hubbard, "The Asian Infrastructure Investment Bank: Multilateralism on the Silk Road," *China Economic Journal*, vol. 9, no. 2 (2016), pp. 116–39.

Carlson, Allen, "More than Just Saying No: China's Evolving Approach to Sovereignty and Intervention since Tiananmen," in Alastair Iain Johnston and Robert S. Ross, eds., *New Directions in the Study of China's Foreign Policy* (Palo Alto, CA: Stanford University Press, 2006), pp. 217–41.

Carnegie, Allison, "States Held Hostage: Political Hold-up Problems and the Effects of International Institutions," *American Political Science Review*, Vol. 108, no. 1 (2014), pp. 54–70.

Power Plays: How International Institutions Reshape Coercive Diplomacy (Cambridge: Cambridge University Press, 2015).

Carnegie, Allison and Austin Carson, "The Disclosure Dilemma: Nuclear Intelligence and International Organizations," working paper (October 27, 2017). SSRN: https://ssrn.com/abstract=3060677.

Casadesus-Masanell, Ramon and Daniel F. Spulber, "The Fable of Fisher Body," *The Journal of Law and Economics*, Vol. 43, no. 1 (2000), pp. 67–104.

Cha, Victor, *The Impossible State: North Korea Past and Future* (New York: Harper Collins, 2013).

Chai, Qimin, Sha Fu, Huaqing Xu, Weiran Li, and Yan Zhong, "The Gap Report of Global Climate Change Mitigation, Finance, and Governance after the United States Declared Its Withdrawal from the Paris Agreement," *Chinese Journal of Population Resources and Environment*, Vol. 15, no. 3 (2017), pp. 196–208.

Chan, Gerald, Pak K. Lee, and Lai-Ha Chan, *China Engages Global Governance: A New Order in the Making?* (UK: Routledge Press, 2012).

Chan, Lai-Ha, *China Engages Global Health Governance: Responsible Stakeholder or System-transformer?* (London: Springer, 2011).

Chan, Steve, *China, the U.S., and the Power Transition Theory: A Critique* (New York: Routledge Press, 2008).

Chang, Felix K., "China's Central Asian Power and Problems," *Orbis*, Vol. 41, No. 3 (1997), pp. 401–25.

Chang, Liu, "Commentary: U.S. Fiscal Failure Warrants a de-Americanized World." Xinhuanet, October 13, 2013: http://news.xinhuanet.com/english/indepth/2013-10/13/c_132794246.htm.

Chanlett-Avery, Emma and Sharon Squassoni, "North Korea's Nuclear Test: Motivations, Implications, and U.S. Options," *CRS Report for Congress*, October 24, 2006: www.fas.org/sgp/crs/nuke/RL33709.pdf.

Chen, Dingding, Xiaoyu Pu, and Alastair Iain Johnston, "Debating China's Assertiveness," *International Security*, Vol. 38 no. 3 (2013/2014), pp. 176–83.

Chen, Titus C., "China's Reaction to the Color Revolutions: Adaptive Authoritarianism in Full Swing," *Asian Perspective*, Vol. 34, no. 2 (2010), pp. 5–51.

Cheng, Joseph Y. S., "China's Approach to BRICS," *Journal of Contemporary China*, Vol. 24, no. 92 (2015), pp. 357–75.

Chin, Gregory T., "The Emerging Countries and China in the G20: Reshaping Global Economic Governance," *Studia Diplomatica*, Vol. 63, no. 2 (2010), pp. 105–23.

"China's Rising Monetary Power," in Eric Helleiner and Jonathan Kirshner, eds., *The Great Wall of Money: Power and Politics in China's International Monetary Relations* (Ithaca, NY: Cornell University Press, 2014) pp. 184–212.

"The World Bank and China: The Long Decade of Realignment," in Carla P. Freeman, ed., *Handbook on China and Developing Countries* (Cheltenham: Edward Elgar Publishing, 2015), pp. 169–92.

"Asian Infrastructure Investment Bank: Governance Innovation and Prospects," *Global Governance*, Vol. 22 (2016), pp. 11–26.

"True Revisionist: China and the Global Monetary System" in Jacques deLisle and Avery Goldstein, eds., *China's Global Engagement: Cooperation, Competition, and Influence in the 21st Century* (Washington, DC: Brookings Press, 2017).

The Political Economy of Renminbi Internationalization (unpublished manuscript).

"Chinese Communist Party Central Committee Document No. 7 (1996): Record of the Meeting of the Standing Committee of the Politburo of the Chinese Communist Party Concerning the Maintenance of Stability in Xinjiang;" translated in full in *China: State Control of Religion, Update Number 1*, Human Rights Watch, Vol. 10, No. 01(C) (March 1998), pp. 10–14.

Chinoy, Mike, *Meltdown: The Inside Story of the North Korean Nuclear Crisis* (New York: St. Martins Press, 2008).

Choi, Jong Kun, "The Perils of Strategic Patience with North Korea," *The Washington Quarterly*, Vol. 38, no. 4 (2015), pp. 57–72.

Chwieroth, Jeffrey, "Controlling Capital: The International Monetary Fund and Transformative Incremental Change from within International Organisations," *New Political Economy*, Vol. 19, no. 3 (2014), pp. 445–469.

Chung, Chien-peng, "The Shanghai Co-operation Organization: China's Changing Influence in Central Asia," *The China Quarterly*, Vol. 180 (December 2004), pp. 989–1009.

"China and the Institutionalization of the Shanghai Cooperation Organization," *Problems of Post-Communism*, Vol. 53, no. 5 (2006), pp. 3–14.

China's Multilateral Cooperation in Asia and the Pacific: Institutionalizing Beijing's "Good Neighbor Policy" (London and New York: Routledge, 2010).

Christensen, Thomas J., "Posing Problems without Catching Up: China's Rise and Challenges for U.S. Security Policy," *International Security*, Vol. 25, no. 4 (Spring 2001), pp. 5–40.

"Shaping the Choices of a Rising China: Recent Lessons for the Obama Administration," *The Washington Quarterly*, Vol. 32, no. 3 (2009), pp. 89–104.

The China Challenge: Shaping the Choices of a Rising Power (New York: W. W. Norton & Company, 2015).

Clémençon, Raymond, "The Bali Road Map: A First Step on the Difficult Journey to a Post-Kyoto Protocol Agreement," *The Journal of Environment Development*, Vol. 17, no. 1 (2008), pp. 70–94.

Cohen, Benjamin J., "The Benefits and Costs of an International Currency: Getting the Calculus Right," *Open Economies Review*, Vol. 23 (2012), pp. 13–31.

Comes, Richard, "Dyke Maintenance and Other Stories: Some Neglected Types of Public Goods," *The Quarterly Journal of Economics*, Vol. 108, no. 1 (1993), pp. 259–71.

Conrad, Björn, "Bureaucratic Land Rush – China's Administrative Battles in the Arena of Climate Change Policy," *Harvard Asia Quarterly*, Vol. 12 (Spring 2010), pp. 52–64.

"China in Copenhagen: Reconciling the "Beijing Climate Revolution" and the "Copenhagen Climate Obstinacy," *The China Quarterly*, Vol. 210 (2012), pp. 435–55.

Cooley, Alexander, "Russia and the Recent Evolution of the SCO: Issues and Challenges for U.S. Policy," in Colton, Timothy J., Timothy Frye, and Robert Legvold, eds., *The Policy World Meets Academia: Designing U.S. Policy toward Russia* (Cambridge, MA: American Academy of Arts and Sciences, 2010).

Great Games, Local Rules: The New Great Power Contest in Central Asia (Oxford: Oxford University Press, 2012).

Crawford, Vincent P., *Thomas Schelling and the Analysis of Strategic Behavior* (Cambridge, MA: MIT Press, 1991).

Crisp, James, "China Pours Cold Water on EU's Ambition Coalition at COP21," *Euractive* (December 11, 2015): www.euractiv.com/section/climate-environment/news/china-pours-cold-water-on-eu-s-ambition-coalition-at-cop21/.

Crosston, Matthew, "The Pluto of International Organizations: Micro-Agendas, IO Theory, and Dismissing the Shanghai Cooperation Organization," *Comparative Strategy*, Vol. 33, no. 2 (2013), pp. 283–94.

Davenport, Kelsey, "States Make New Nuclear Security Pledges," *Arms Control Today*, Vol. 42, no. 3 (2012), pp. 22–24.

Davignon, Etienne, "The Empty Chair Crisis and the Luxembourg Compromise," in Jean Marie Palayret, Helen S. Wallace, and Pascaline Winand, eds., *Visions, Votes and Vetoes. The Empty Chair Crisis and the Luxembourg Compromise Forty Years On* (Brussels: P. I. E.-Peter Lang, 2006).

Debs, Alexandre and Nuno P. Monteiro, "Known Unknowns: Power Shifts, Uncertainty, and War," *International Organization*, Vol. 68, no. 1 (2014), pp. 1–31.

Dechezleprêtre, Antoine, Matthieu Glachanty, Ivan Hascic, Nick Johnstone, and Yann Meniere "Invention and Transfer of Climate Change–mitigation Technologies: A Global Analysis," *Review of Environmental Economics and Policy*, Vol. 5, no .1 (2011), pp. 109–30.

Deese, David A., *World Trade Politics: Power, Principles and Leadership.* (New York: Routledge, 2007).

Delury, John, "The Disappointments of Disengagement: Assessing Obama's North Korea Policy," *Asian Perspective*, Vol. 37 (2013), pp. 149–82.

Desal, Raj M. and James Raymond Vreeland, "How to Stop Worrying and Love the Asian Infrastructure Investment Bank," Monkey Cage [*The Washington Post*], April 6, 2015.

Destradi, Sandra, "Regional Powers and Their Strategies: Empire, Hegemony, and Leadership," *Review of International Studies*, Vol. 36, no. 4 (2010), pp. 903–30.

Dillon, Michael, *Xinjiang: China's Muslim Far Northwest* (London and New York: Routledge, 2004).

Diringer, Eliot, *Sixteenth Session of the Conference of the Parties to the United Nations Framework Convention on Climate Change and Sixth Session of the Meeting of the Parties to the Kyoto Protocol* (Arlington, VA: Pew Center on Global Climate Change, 2010): www.c2es.org/docUploads/cancun-climate-conference-cop16-summary.pdf.

Dollar, David, "China's Rise as a Regional and Global Power: The AIIB and the 'One Belt, One Road,'" *Brookings Research Paper*, Summer 2015: www.brookings.edu/research/papers/2015/07/china-regional-global-power-dollar.

Doyle, Michael W., *Empires* (Ithaca, NY: Cornell University Press, 1986).

Drezner, Daniel W., "Bad Debts: Assessing China's Financial Influence in Great Power Politics." *International Security*, Vol. 34, no. 2 (2009), pp. 7–45.

The System Worked: How the World Stopped Another Great Depression (New York: Oxford University Press, 2014).

Early, Bryan R., "Sleeping with Your Friends' Enemies: An Explanation of Sanctions-Busting Trade," *International Studies Quarterly*, Vol. 53, no. 1 (2009), pp. 49–71.

"Acquiring Foreign Nuclear Assistance in the Middle East: Strategic Lessons from the United Arab Emirates," *Nonproliferation Review*, Vol. 17, no. 2 (2010), pp. 259–280.

Busted Sanctions: Explaining Why Economic Sanctions Fail (Palo Alto, CA: Stanford University Press, 2015).

Economy, Elizabeth, "The Impact of International Regimes on Chinese Foreign Policy-Making: Broadening Perspectives and Policies ... But Only to a Point," in David M. Lampton, ed., *The Making of Chinese Foreign and Security Policy in the Era of Reform* (Stanford, CA: Stanford University Press, 2001).

Economy, Elizabeth and Michel Oksenberg (eds.), *China Joins the World: Progress and Prospects* (New York: Council on Foreign Relations, 1999).

Eichengreen, Barry, *Exorbitant Privilege: The Rise and Fall of the Dollar and the Future of the International Monetary System* (New York: Oxford University Press, 2011).

Enders, Walter and Todd Sandler, *The Political Economy of Terrorism* (New York: Cambridge University Press, 2011).

Fairbank, John King, *China: A New History* (Cambridge, MA: Harvard University Press, 1992).

Fang, Songying and Kristopher W. Ramsay, "Outside Options and Burden Sharing in Nonbinding Alliances," *Political Research Quarterly*, Vol. 63, no. 1 (2010), pp. 188–202.

Fearon, James D., "Bargaining, Enforcement, and International Cooperation," *International Organization*, Vol. 52, no. 2 (1998), pp. 269–305.

Fehr, Ernst and Simon Gächter, "Fairness and Retaliation: The Economics of Reciprocity," *The Journal of Economic Perspectives*, Vol. 14, no. 3 (2000), pp. 159–81.

Feigenbaum, Evan A., "The New Asian Order and How the United States Fits In," *Foreign Affairs* (February 2015): www.foreignaffairs.com/articles/east-asia/2015-02-02/new-asian-order.

Fewsmith, Joseph, *China since Tiananmen: The Politics of Transition* (New York: Cambridge University Press, 2001).

Fioretos, Orfeo, "Historical Institutionalism in International Relations," *International Organization*, Vol. 65, no. 2 (2011), pp. 367–99.

Fisher, Roger and William Ury, *Getting to Yes: Negotiating Agreement without Giving In* (New York: Penguin Books, 1981).

Fleurant, Aude, Pieter D. Wezeman, Siemon T. Wezeman, and Nan Tian, *Trends in World Military Expenditure, 2016* (Stockholm: SIPRI, 2017): www.sipri.org/sites/default/files/Trends-world-military-expenditure-2016.pdf.

Foot, Rosemary, "China in the ASEAN Regional Forum: Organizational Processes and Domestic Modes of Thought," *Asian Survey*, Vol. 38, no. 5 (1998), pp. 425–40.

"Selective or Effective Multilateralism? The Bush Administration's Proliferation Security Initiative and China's Response," in Jochen Prantl, ed., *Effective Multilateralism: Through the Looking Glass of East Asia* (London: Palgrave Macmillan UK, 2013), pp. 215–31.

Foot, Rosemary and Andrew Walter, *China, the United States, and Global Order* (New York: Cambridge University Press, 2011).

Fravel, M. Taylor, *Strong Borders Secure Nation: Cooperation and Conflict in China's Territorial Disputes* (Princeton, NJ: Princeton University Press, 2008).

Friedrich, Johannes and Thomas Damassa, "The History of Carbon Dioxide Emissions," World Resources Institute blog (May 21, 2014): www.wri.org/blog/2014/05/history-carbon-dioxide-emissions.

Frieman, Wendy, "New Members of the Club: Chinese Participation in Arms Control Regimes 1980–1995," *The Nonproliferation Review*, Vol. 3, no. 3 (1996), pp. 15–30.

Frost, Ellen L., "Rival Regionalisms and Regional Order: A Slow Crisis of Legitimacy," *NBR Special Report # 48* (Seattle, WA: National Bureau of Asian Research, 2014).

Frühling, Stephan and Andrew O'Neil, "Nuclear Weapons and Alliance Institutions in the Era of President Trump," *Contemporary Security Policy*, Vol. 38, no. 1 (2017), pp. 47–53.

Garver, John W., "Is China Playing a Dual Game in Iran?" *The Washington Quarterly*, Vol. 34, no. 1 (2011), pp. 75–88.

Gill, Bates and Matthew Oresman, *China's New Journey to the West: China's Emergence in Central Asia and Implications for U.S. Interests*, Center for Strategic and International Studies, CSIS Report, 2003.

Glosny, Michael A., "China and the BRICs," *Polity*, Vol. 42, no. 1 (2010), pp. 100–29.

Godehardt, Nadine, *The Chinese Constitution of Central Asia: Regions and Intertwined Actors in International Relations* (New York: Palgrave MacMillan, 2014).

Godement, François, "China: Taking Stock before the Paris Climate Conference," *China Analysis* (September, 2015): www.css.ethz.ch/en/services/digital-library/publications/publication.html/194229.

"Does China have a Real Climate Change Policy?" *Climate Policies after Copenhagen*, ECFR *China Analysis* No. 27 (2010): www.css.ethz.ch/en/services/digital-library/publications/publication.html/118292.

Goldstein, Avery, "Across the Yalu: China's Interests and the Korean Peninsula in a Changing World," in *New Directions in the Study of China's Foreign Policy*, eds. Alastair Iain Johnston and Robert S. Ross (Stanford, CA: Stanford University Press, 2006), pp. 131–61.

"Power Transitions, Institutions, and China's Rise in East Asia: Theoretical Expectations and Evidence," *Journal of Strategic Studies*, Vol. 30, no. 4–5 (2007), pp. 639–82.

Goncharov, Sergei N., John W. Lewis, and Xue Litai, *Uncertain Partners: Stalin, Mao, and the Korean War* (Stanford, CA: Stanford University Press, 1993).

Gray, Julia and Jonathan B. Slapin, "Exit Options and the Effectiveness of Regional Economic Organizations," *Political Science Research and Methods*, Vol. 1, no. 2 (2013), pp. 281–303.

Grieger, Gisela, "The Shanghai Cooperation Organization," *European Parliamentary Research Service*, June 2015, PE 564.368: www.europarl.europa.eu/RegData/etudes/BRIE/2015/564368/EPRS_BRI(2015)564368_EN.pdf.

Grimes, William, *Currency and Contest in East Asia: The Great Power Politics of Financial Regionalism* (Ithaca, NY: Cornell University Press, 2008).

Gruber, Lloyd, *Ruling the World: Power Politics and the Rise of Supranational Institutions* (Princeton, NJ: Princeton University Press, 2000).

Grynaviski, Eric and Amy Hsieh, "Hierarchy and Judicial Institutions: Arbitration and Ideology in the Hellenistic World," *International Organization*, Vol. 69, no. 3 (2015), pp. 697–729.

Hadden, Jennifer, *Networks in Contention: The Divisive Politics of Climate Change* (New York: Cambridge University Press, 2015).

Hafner-Burton, Emilie, Brad L. LeVeck, and David G. Victor, "No False Promises: How The Prospect of Non-Compliance Affects Elite Preferences for International Cooperation," *International Studies Quarterly*, Vol. 61, no. 1 (2016), pp. 1–13.

Hajnal, Peter I., *The G8 System and the G20: Evolution, Role and Documentation* (London: Routledge Press, 2016).

Haynes, Susan Turner, *Chinese Nuclear Proliferation: How Global Politics Is Transforming China's Weapons Buildup and Modernization* (Lincoln: University of Nebraska Press, 2016).

Heckathorn, Douglas D., "Collective Action and the Second-Order Free-Rider Problem," *Rationality and Society*, Vol. 1, no. 1 (July 1989), pp. 78–100.

Heggelund, Gorild, "China's Climate Change Policy: Domestic and International Developments," *Perspective*, Vol. 31, no. 2 (2007), pp. 155–91.

Heilmann, Sebastian, "Maximum Tinkering under Uncertainty: Unorthodox Lessons from China." *Modern China*, Vol. 35, no. 4 (2009), pp. 450–62.

Hiro, Dilip, *Inside Central Asia: A Political and Cultural History of Uzbekistan, Turkmenistan, Kazakhstan, Kyrgyzstan, Tajikistan, Turkey, and Iran* (New York and London: Overlook Duckworth, 2009).

Hirshleifer, Jack, "From Weakest-Link to Best-Shot: The Voluntary Provision of Public Goods," *Public Choice*, Vol. 41, no. 3 (1983), pp.371–86.

Hirschman Alfred O., *Exit, Voice, and Loyalty: Responses to Decline in Firms, Organizations, and States* (Cambridge: Harvard University Press, 1970).

Hochstetler, Kathryn and Manjana Milkoreit, "Responsibilities in Transition: Emerging Powers in the Climate Change Negotiations," *Global Governance*, Vol. 21, no. 2 (2015), pp. 205–26.

Holzer, Kateryna, "Proposals on Carbon-Related Border Adjustments: Prospects for WTO Compliance," *Carbon & Climate Law Review*, Vol. 4, no. 1 (2010), pp. 51–64.

Horne, Christine, *The Rewards of Punishment: A Relational Theory of Norm Enforcement* (Palo Alto, CA: Stanford University Press, 2009).

Horsburgh, Nicola, *China and Global Nuclear Order: From Estrangement to Active Engagement* (London: Oxford University Press, 2015).

Houser, Trevor, *Copenhagen, the Accord, and the Way Forward*, Peterson Institute for International Economics Policy Brief PB10-5 (Washington, DC: Peterson Institute for International Economics, 2010).

"*Dissecting Durban: A Fighting Chance for Progress on Climate Change*," (Washington, DC, Peterson Institute for International Economics, 2011).

Huang, Yanzhong, "A Superpower, but Not yet a Global Leader," *Asia Unbound (blog)*, Council on Foreign Relations, April 20, 2017: www.cfr.org/blog/superpower-not-yet-global-leader.

Hufbauer, Gary Clyde and Jisun Kim, "*After the Flop in Copenhagen*," Peterson Institute of International Economics PB10-4 (Washington, DC, March 2010): https://piie.com/sites/default/files/publications/pb/pb10-04.pdf.

Huotari, Mikko and Thilo Hanemann, "Emerging Powers and Change in the Global Financial Order," *Global Policy*, Vol. 5, no. 3 (2014), pp. 298–310.

Ikenberry, G. John, "The Rise of China and the Future of the West: Can the Liberal System Survive?" *Foreign Affairs*, Vol. 87, no. 1 (2008), pp. 23–37.

After Victory: Institutions, Strategic Restraint, and the Rebuilding of Order after Major Wars (Princeton, NJ: Princeton University Press, 2009).

IMF 2011, *Quota and Voting Shares*, p. 1: www.imf.org/external/np/sec/pr/2011/pdfs/quota_tbl.pdf.

Jackson, Patrick Thaddeus, *The Conduct of Inquiry in International Relations: Philosophy of Science and Its Implications for the Study of World Politics* (New York: Routledge, 2010).

Jacobson, Harold K. and Michel Oksenberg, *China's Participation in the IMF, the World Bank, and GATT: Toward a Global Economic Order* (Ann Arbor: University of Michigan Press, 1990).

Jacoby, Henry D. and Y.-H. Henry Chen, "Launching a New Climate Regime," MIT Joint Program on the Science and Policy of Global Change, Report No. 215 (Cambridge, MA: JPSPCG, November 2015).

Jagchid, Sechin and Van Jay Symons, *Peace, War, and Trade along the Great Wall: Nomadic-Chinese Interaction through Two Millennia* (Bloomington, IN: Indiana University Press, 1989).

Jensen, Keith, Josep Call, and Michael Tomasello, "Chimpanzees are Vengeful but Not Spiteful," *Proceedings of the National Academy of Sciences*, Vol. 104, no. 32 (2007), pp. 13046–50.

Jesse, Neal G., Steven E. Lobell, Galia Press-Barnathan, and Kristen P. Williams, "The Leader Can't Lead when the Followers Won't Follow: The Limitations of Hegemony," in Neal G. Jesse, Steven E. Lobell, Galia Press-Barnathan, and Kristen P. Williams, eds., *Beyond Great Powers and Hegemons: Why Secondary States Support, Follow, or Challenge* (Palo Alto, CA: Stanford University Press, 2012).

Johns, Leslie, "A Servant of Two Masters: Communication and the Selection of International Bureaucrats," *International Organization*, Vol. 61, no. 2 (2007), pp. 245–75.

Johnson, Rob, *Oil, Islam, and Conflict: Central Asia since 1945* (London: Reaktion Press, 2007).

Johnson, Tana, *Organizational Progeny: Why Governments are Losing Control over the Proliferating Structures of Global Governance* (New York: Oxford University Press, 2014).

Johnston, Alastair Iain, "Is China a Status Quo Power?" *International Security*, Vol. 27, no. 4 (2003), pp. 5–56.

Social States: China in International Institutions, 1980–2000 (Princeton, NJ: Princeton University Press, 2008).

"How Assertive Is China's New Assertiveness?" *International Security*, Vol. 37, no. 4 (2012), pp. 7–48.

Cultural Realism: Strategic Culture and Grand Strategy in Chinese History (Princeton, NJ: Princeton University Press, 1995).

Johnston, Alastair Iain and Robert Ross, eds., *Engaging China: The Management of an Emerging Power* (New York: Routledge Press, 1999).

Jones, Bruce, Emily O'Brien and Richard Gowan, "*The G8 and the Threat of Bloc Politics in the International System: A Managing Global Order Summitry Report*" (Washington, DC: Brookings Institution, May 24, 2011): www.brookings.edu/research/the-g8-and-the-threat-of-bloc-politics-in-the-international-system.

Jonson, Lena, *Vladimir Putin and Central Asia: The Shaping of Russian Foreign Policy* (London and New York: I. B. Tauris, 2004).

Joronen, Sanna, Markku Oksanen, and Timo Vuorisalo, "Towards Weather Ethics: From Chance to Choice with Weather Modification," *Ethics, Policy and Environment*, Vol. 14, no. 1 (2011), pp. 55–67.

Kahler, Miles, "Rising Powers and Global Governance: Negotiating Change in a Resilient Status Quo," *International Affairs*, Vol. 89, no. 3 (2013), pp. 711–729.

Kaplan, Lawrence S., *NATO Divided, NATO United: The Evolution of an Alliance* (New York: Greenwood Publishing Group, 2004).

Karrar, Hasan H., *The New Silk Road Diplomacy: China's Central Asian Foreign Policy since the Cold War* (Vancouver: University of British Columbia Press, 2009).

Kastner, Scott L. and Phillip C. Saunders, "Is China a Status Quo or Revisionist State? Leadership Travel as an Empirical Indicator of Foreign Policy Priorities," *International Studies Quarterly*, Vol. 56, no. 1 (March 2012), pp. 163–77.

Kastner, Scott L., Margaret M. Pearson, and Chad Rector, ""Invest, Hold-Up or Accept? China in Multilateral Governance," *Security Studies*, 25, no. 1 (2016), pp. 142–79.

Katada, Saori N. and C. Randall Henning. "Currency and Exchange Rate Regimes in Asia," in Saadia Pekkanen, John Ravenhill, and Rosemary Foot, eds., *The Oxford Handbook of the International Relations of Asia* (Oxford: Oxford University Press, 2014).

Katzenstein, Peter J., Robert O. Keohane, and Stephen D. Krasner, "International Organization and the Study of World Politics," *International Organization*, Vol. 52, no. 4 (1998): 645–85.

Kaya, Ayse, *Power and Global Economic Institutions* (Cambridge: Cambridge University Press, 2015).

Kelley, Judith, "International Actors on the Domestic Scene: Membership Conditionality and Socialization by International Institutions," *International Organization*, Vol. 58, no. 3 (2004), pp. 425–57.

Kennedy, Andrew B., "China and the Free-Rider Problem: Exploring the Case of Energy Security," *Political Science Quarterly*, Vol. 130, no. 1 (2015), pp. 27–50.

Kennedy, Scott, "The Myth of the Beijing Consensus," *Journal of Contemporary China*, Vol. 19, no. 65 (2010), pp. 41–62.

Kennedy, Scott and David A. Parker, "Building China's 'One Belt, One Road,'" Center for Strategic and Economic Studies *Critical Questions*, April 3, 2015: http://csis.org/publication/building-chinas-one-belt-one-road.

Kent, Ann, *Beyond Compliance: China, International Organizations, and Global Security* (Stanford, CA: Stanford University Press, 2007).

Keohane, Robert O., *After Hegemony: Cooperation and Discord in the World Political Economy* (Princeton, NJ: Princeton University Press, 1984).

Keohane, Robert O. and David G. Victor, "The Regime Complex for Climate Change," *Perspectives on Politics*, Vol. 9, no. 1 (2011), pp. 7–23.

Kerr, David and Laura C. Swinton, "China, Xinjiang, and the Transnational Security of Central Asia," *Critical Asian Studies*, Vol. 40, no. 1 (2008), pp. 113–42.

Kim, Samuel, *China, The United Nations and World Order* (Princeton, NJ: Princeton University Press, 1979).

"China and the United Nations," in Michel Oksenberg and Elizabeth Economy, eds., *China Joins the World: Progress and Prospects* (New York: Council on Foreign Relations Press, 1999), pp. 42–89.

Kirton, John, "What Is the G20?" G20 Research Group, University of Toronto (November 20, 1999), online at www.g20.utoronto.ca/g20whatisit.html.

Klein, Benjamin, Robert G. Crawford, and Armen A. Alchian, "Vertical Integration, Appropriable Rents, and the Competitive Contracting Process," *The Journal of Law and Economics*, Vol. 21, no. 2 (1978), pp. 297–326.

Klein-Ahlbrandt, Stephanie, "China: Global Free-Rider," Foreign Policy (November 12, 2009): http://foreignpolicy.com/2009/11/12/beijing-global-free-rider/.

Kong, Bo, *China's International Petroleum Policy* (Santa Barbara, CA: Praeger, 2010).

Konstantinidis, Nikitas, "Gradualism and Uncertainty in International Union Formation: The European Community's First Enlargement," *The Review of International Organizations*, Vol. 3, no.4 (2008), pp. 399–433.

Koremenos, Barbara, Charles Lipson, and Duncan Snidal, "The Rational Design of International Institutions," *International Organization*, Vol. 55, no. 4 (2001), pp. 761–99.

Kroeber, Arthur R., *China's Economy: What Everyone Needs to Know* (New York: Oxford University Press, 2016).

Kurlantzick, Joshua, *Charm Offensive: How China's Soft Power Is Transforming the World* (New Haven, CT: Yale University Press, 2007).

Lake, David A., *Power, Protection, and Free Trade: International Sources of US Commercial Strategy, 1887–1939* (Ithaca, NY: Cornell University Press, 1988).

Hierarchy in International Relations (Ithaca, NY: Cornell University Press, 2009).

"Rightful Rules: Authority, Order, and the Foundations of Global Governance," *International Studies Quarterly*, Vol. 54, no. 3 (2010), pp. 587–613.

Lampton, David M., ed., *The Making of Chinese Foreign and Security Policy in the Era of Reform, 1978–2000* (Palo Alto, CA: Stanford University Press, 2001).

Lanteigne, Marc, *China and International Institutions: Alternate Paths to Global Power* (London: Taylor and Francis, 2005).

Lardy, Nicholas R., *Foreign Trade and Economic Reform in China, 1978–1991* (New York, Cambridge University Press, 1993).

"China and the International Financial System," in Michel Oksenberg and Elizabeth Economy, eds., *China Joins the World: Progress and Prospects* (New York: Council on Foreign Relations Press, 1999), pp. 206–230.

Integrating China into the Global Economy (Washington, DC: Brookings Institution Press, 2002).

Lewis, Joanna I., "China's Strategic Priorities in International Climate Change Negotiations," *The Washington Quarterly*, Vol. 31, no. 1 (2007), pp. 155–74.

Liao, Steven and Daniel McDowell, "No Reservations: International Order and Demand for the Renminbi as a Reserve Currency," *International Studies Quarterly*, Vol. 60, no. 2 (2016), pp. 272–93.

Lieggi, Stephanie, "From Proliferator to Model Citizen? China's Recent Enforcement of Nonproliferation-related Trade Controls and Its Potential Positive Impact in the Region," *Strategic Studies*, Vol 4, no. 2, 2010, pp. 39–62.

Light, Andrew, "The Cancun Compromise: Masterful Diplomacy Ends with Agreement," Center for American Progress (2010): www.americanprogress.org/issues/green/news/2010/12/13/8751/the-cancun-compromise/.

Lipscy, Phillip Y., "Explaining Institutional Change: Policy Areas, Outside Options, and the Bretton Woods Institutions," *American Journal of Political Science*, Vol. 59, no. 2 (2015), pp. 341–56.

Renegotiating the World Order: Institutional Change in International Relations (New York: Cambridge University Press, 2017).

Lobell, Steven E., *The Challenge of Hegemony: Grand Strategy, Trade, and Domestic Politics* (Ann Arbor: University of Michigan Press, 2003).

Ludlow, N. Piers, "Challenging French Leadership in Europe: Germany, Italy, the Netherlands and the Outbreak of the Empty Chair Crisis of 1965–1966," *Contemporary European History*, Vol. 8, no. 2 (1999), pp. 231–48.

McKibben, Heather Elko, *State Strategies in International Bargaining: Play by the Rules or Change Them?* (London: Cambridge University Press, 2015).

Maddison, Angus, *The World Economy* (Paris: OECD, 2007).

Mann, James, *The Obamians: The Struggle Inside the White House to Redefine American Power* (New York: Viking, 2012).
Medeiros, Evan S., *Reluctant Restraint: The Evolution of China's Nonproliferation Policies and Practices, 1980–2004* (Stanford, CA: Stanford University Press, 2007).
Medeiros, Evan S. and M. Taylor Fravel, "China's New Diplomacy," *Foreign Affairs*, Vol. 82 (2003), pp. 22–35.
Meisels, Greer A., "Lessons Learned in China from the Collapse of the Soviet Union," The University of Sydney China Studies Centre, Policy Paper Series, Paper No. 3 (2013).
Melville, Andrei and Tatiana Shakleina, eds., *Russian Foreign Policy in Transition: Concepts and Realities* (Budapest and New York: Central European University Press, 2005).
Millward, James A., *Violent Separatism in Xinjiang: A Critical Assessment* (Washington, DC: East-West Center, 2004).
Eurasian Crossroads: A History of Xinjiang (New York: Columbia University Press, 2007).
Momani, Bessma, "IMF Staff: Missing Link in Fund Reform Proposal," *Review of International Organizations*, Vol. 2, no. 1 (2007), pp. 39–57.
"China at the IMF," in Domenico Lombardi and Hongying Wang, eds., *Enter the Dragon: China in the International Financial System* (Waterloo, Canada: Centre for International Governance Innovation, 2015).
Moravcsik, Andrew, "De Gaulle between Grain and Grandeur: The Political Economy of French EC Policy, 1958–1970 (Part 2)," *Journal of Cold War Studies*, Vol. 2, no. 3 (2000), pp. 4–68.
Müller, Harald and Mitchell Reiss, "Counterproliferation: Putting New Wine in Old Bottles," *The Washington Quarterly*, Vol. 18, no. 2 (1995), pp. 143–54.
Naughton, Barry, *Growing Out of the Plan: Chinese Economic Reform, 1978–1993* (New York: Cambridge University Press, 1995).
The Chinese Economy: Transitions and Growth (Cambridge, MA: MIT Press, 2007).
Naughton, Barry and Kellee Tsai (eds.), *State Capitalism, Institutional Adaptation, and the Chinese Miracle* (Cambridge: Cambridge University Press, 2015).
Nelson, Rebecca N. and Martin L. Weiss, *IMF Reforms: Issues for Congress* (Washington, DC: Congressional Research Service, April 9, 2015): https://fas.org/sgp/crs/misc/R42844.pdf.
Newsom, David D., *The Imperial Mantle: The United States, Decolonization, and the Third World* (Bloomington, IN: Indiana University Press, 2001).
Nexon, Daniel H. and Thomas Wright, "What's at Stake in the American Empire Debate," *American Political Science Review*, Vol. 101, no. 2 (2007), pp. 384–97.
Oberdorfer, Don, *The Two Koreas: A Contemporary History* (New York: Basic Books, 2001).
Overholt, William H., "One Belt, One Road, One Pivot," *GlobalAsia*, Vol. 10, no. 3 (Fall 2015).
Paltiel, Jeremy, "China and the North Korean Crisis: The Diplomacy of Great Power Transition," in Seung-Ho Joo and Tai-Hwan Kwak, eds., *North*

Korea's Second Nuclear Crisis and Northeast Asian Security (Hampshire: Ashgate, 2007), pp. 94–109.

Paltsev, Sergey, Jennifer Morris, Yongxia Cai, Valerie Karplus, and Henry Jacoby, "The Role of China in Mitigating Climate Change," MIT Joint Program on the Science and Policy of Global Change, Report No. 215 (Cambridge, MA: JPSPCG, April 2012).

Panda, Ankit, "What China Gains with Its Détente with South Korea over THAAD," *The Diplomat*, November 7, 2017: https://thediplomat.com/2017/11/what-china-gains-with-its-detente-with-south-korea-over-thaad/.

Pantucci, Raffaello, "Is SCO Expansion a Good Thing?" *The Diplomat*, 12 July 2016: http://thediplomat.com/2016/07/is-sco-expansion-a-good-thing/.

Park. John S., "North Korean Crisis: China Shows the Way to Pyongyang." *International Herald Tribune*, May 14, 2004.

"Inside Multilateralism: The Six-Party Talks," *The Washington Quarterly*, Vol. 28, no. 4 (Autumn 2005), pp. 73–91.

Parker, George, Guy Dinmore, Krishna Guha, and Justine Lau, "China Attacks Dollar's Dominance," *Financial Times*, July 9, 2009: www.ft.com/cms/s/o/81f3125a-6cae-11de-af56-00144feabdco.html.

Pashley, Alex, "Brazil Backs 'High Ambition Coalition' to Break Paris Deadlock," Climatehome (December 11, 2015): www.climatechangenews.com/2015/12/11/brazil-backs-high-ambition-coalition-to-break-paris-deadlock/.

Paterson, William E., "The Reluctant Hegemon? Germany Moves Centre Stage in the European Union," *Journal of Common Market Studies*, Vol. 49, no. 1 (2011), pp. 57–75.

Pearson, Margaret M., "China in Geneva: Lessons from China's Early Years in the World Trade Organization," in Alastair Iain Johnston and Robert Ross, eds., *New Directions in the Study of China's Foreign Policy* (Stanford, CA: Stanford University Press, 2006), pp. 587–644.

"China's Foreign Economic Relations and Policies," in Saadia Pekkanen, John Ravenhill and Rosemary Foot, eds., *Oxford Handbook on the International Relations of Asia* (Oxford: Oxford University Press, 2015), pp. 160–78.

Piekos, William and Elizabeth C. Economy, "The Risks and Rewards of SCO Expansion," Council on Foreign Relations Expert Brief (July 8, 2015): www.cfr.org/international-organizations-and-alliances/risks-rewards-sco-expansion/p36761.

Pilat, Joseph F. and Robert E. Pendley, eds., *1995: A New Beginning for the NPT?* (New York: Springer Science and Business Media, 2012).

Plater-Zyberk, Henry with Andrew Monaghan, *Strategic Implications of the Evolving Shanghai Cooperation Organization* (Carlisle, PA: Strategic Studies Institute and U.S. Army War College Press, 2014).

Poh, Angela and Mingjiang Li, "A China in Transition: The Rhetoric and Substance of Chinese Foreign Policy under Xi Jinping," *Asian Security*, Vol. 13, no. 2 (2017), pp. 84–97.

Prasad, Eswar, *Gaining Currency: The Rise of the Renminbi* (New York: Oxford University Press, 2016).

Prasad, Eswar and Lei Ye, *The Renminbi's Role in the Global Monetary System* (Washington, DC: Brookings Institution, 2012).

Pu, Xiaoyu, "Ambivalent Accommodation: Status Signaling of a Rising India and China's Response," *International Affairs*, Vol. 93, no. 1 (2017), 147–63.

"China's International Leadership: Regional Activism vs. Global Reluctance," *Chinese Political Science Review*, Vol. 3, no 1 (March 2018), pp 48–61.

Pu, Xiaoyu and Randall Schweller, "Status Signaling, Multiple Audiences, and China's Blue-Water Naval Ambition," In T. V. Paul, Deborah Welch Larson and William C. Wohlforth, eds., *Status in World Politics* (Cambridge: Cambridge University Press, 2014), pp. 141–63.

Qin Yaqing, "Development of International Relations Theory in China," *International Studies*, Vol. 46, no. 1–2, pp. 185–201.

Rapp, Tobias, Christian Schwägerl and Gerald Traufetter, "The Copenhagen Protocol: How China and India Sabotaged the UN Climate Summit," *Der Spiegel* May 5, 2010: www.spiegel.de/international/world/the-copenhagen-protocol-how-china-and-india-sabotaged-the-un-climate-summit-a-692861.html

Rector, Chad, *Federations: The Political Dynamics of Cooperation.* (Ithaca, NY: Cornell University Press, 2009).

Ren, Xiao, "A Reform Minded Status Quo Power?: China, the G20, and Changes in the International Monetary System," *RCCPB Initiative on China and Global Governance* (Bloomington: Indiana University RCCPB, 2012): www.indiana.edu/~rccpb/pdf/Ren%20RCCPB%2025%20G20%20Apr%202012.pdf.

Rhode, Robert and Richard Muller, *Air Pollution in China: Mapping of Concentrations and Sources*, 2015: http://berkeleyearth.org/wp-content/uploads/2015/08/China-Air-Quality-Paper-July-2015.pdf.

Richardson, Philip, *Economic Change in China, c. 1800–1950* (Cambridge: Cambridge University Press, 1999).

Rolland, Nadege, "China's New Silk Road," National Bureau of Asian Research, February 12, 2015: www.nbr.org/research/activity.aspx?id=531.

Rosefielde, Steven, *The Russian Economy: From Lenin to Putin* (Malden, MA: Blackwell, 2007).

Ross, Lester, "China and Environmental Protection," in Michel Oksenberg and Elizabeth Economy, eds., *China Joins the World: Progress and Prospects* (New York: Council on Foreign Relations Press, 1999), pp. 296–325.

Roy, Meena Singh, "Dynamics of Expanding the SCO," Institute for Defence Studies and Analyses, April 4, 2011: www.idsa.in/idsacomments/DynamicsofExpandingtheSCO_msroy_040411.

Rozman, Gilbert, *Strategic Thinking about the Korean Nuclear Crisis: Four Parties Caught between North Korea and the United States* (New York: Palgrave, 2007).

Salisbury, Daniel and Lucy Jones, "Exploring the Changing Role of Chinese Entities in WMD Proliferation," *The China Quarterly*, Vol. 225 (2016), pp. 50–72.

Sandler, Todd, *Global Collective Action* (New York, NY: Cambridge University Press, 2004).

Scheinman, Lawrence, *Atomic Energy Policy in France under the Fourth Republic* (Princeton, NJ: Princeton University Press, 2015).

Schneider, Barry R., *Future War and Counterproliferation: US Military Responses to NBC Proliferation Threats* (Westport, CT: Greenwood Publishing Group, 1999).

Schneider, Christina J., "Weak States and Institutionalized Bargaining Power in International Organizations," *International Studies Quarterly*, Vol. 55, no. 2 (2011), pp. 331–55.

Schneider, Christina J. and Johannes Urpelainen, "Distributional Conflict between Powerful States and International Treaty Ratification," *International Studies Quarterly*, Vol. 57, no. 1 (2013), pp. 13–27.

Schweller, Randall L. and Xiaoyu Pu, "After Unipolarity: China's Visions of International Order in an Era of US Decline," *International Security*, Vol. 36, no. 1 (2011), pp. 41–72.

Scobell, Andrew, *China and North Korea: From Comrades in Arms to Allies at Arms-Length* (Carlisle, PA: US Army War College Strategic Studies Institute, March 1, 2004).

Shambaugh, David, "Return to the Middle Kingdom? China and Asia in the Early Twenty-First Century," in David Shambaugh, ed., *Power Shift: China and Asia's New Dynamics* (Berkeley and Los Angeles: University of California Press, 2005).

China's Communist Party: Atrophy and Adaptation (Berkeley: University of California Press, 2009).

China Goes Global: The Partial Power (New York: Oxford University Press, 2013).

Shinada, Mizuho, Toshio Yamagishi, and Yu Ohmura, "False Friends are Worse than Bitter Enemies: 'Altruistic' Punishment of In-group Members," *Evolution and Human Behavior*, Vol. 25, no. 6 (2004), pp. 379–93.

Shirk, Susan L., *China: Fragile Superpower: How China's Internal Politics Could Derail Its Peaceful Rise* (New York: Oxford University Press, 2007).

"The Domestic Context of Chinese Foreign Security Policies," in Saadia Pekkanen, John Ravenhill, and Rosemary Foot, eds., *Oxford Handbook on the International Relations of Asia* (Oxford: Oxford University Press, 2015), pp. 390–410.

How China Opened Its Door: The Political Success of the PRC's Foreign Trade and Investment Reforms (Washington, DC: Brookings, 1994).

Shleifer, Andrei, *A Normal Country: Russia after Communism* (Cambridge, MA: Harvard University Press, 2005).

Tiwari, Siddharth, "IMF Work Progresses on 2015 SDR Basket Review," August 4, 2015: www.imf.org/en/News/Articles/2015/09/28/04/53/sopol080415a.

Slapin, Jonathan, "Bargaining Power at Europe's Intergovernmental Conferences: Testing Institutional and Intergovernmental Theories," *International Organization*, Vol. 62, no.1 (2008), pp. 131–162.

Snyder, Scott, *China's Rise and the Two Koreas: Politics, Economics, Security* (Boulder, CO: Lynne Rienner Publishers, 2009).

Steinberg, David A., *Demanding Devaluation: Exchange Rate Politics in the Developing World* (Ithaca, NY: Cornell University Press, 2015).

Stokes, Jacob, "China's Road Rules: Beijing Looks West toward Eurasian Integration," Foreign Affairs, April 19, 2015: www.foreignaffairs.com/articles/asia/2015-04-19/chinas-road-rules.

Stone, Randall, *Controlling Institutions: International Organizations and the Global Economy* (New York: Cambridge University Press, 2011).

Stone, Randall W., Branislav L. Slantchev, and Tamar R. London, "Choosing How to Cooperate: A Repeated Public-Goods Model of International Relations," *International Studies Quarterly*, Vol. 52, no. 2 (2008), pp. 335–62.

Su, Wei (2010), "Letter Including Autonomous Domestic Mitigation Actions." Letter to Executive Secretary Yvo De Boer. January 28, 2010, UNFCCC: https://unfccc.int/files/meetings/cop_15/copenhagen_accord/application/pdf/chinacphaccord_app2.pdf.

Subramanian, Arvind, "Renminbi Rules: The Conditional Imminence of the Reserve Currency Transition," *Peterson Institute for International Economics Working Paper 11-14* (Washington, DC: Peterson Institute for International Economics, September 2011).

Sutter, Robert G., *Chinese Foreign Relations: Power and Policy since the Cold War* (Lanham, MD: Rowman and Littlefield, 2008).

Sutter, Robert G., Michael E. Brown, and Timothy J. A. Adamson, "*Balancing Acts: The U.S. Rebalance and Asia-Pacific Stability*," (Elliot School of International Affairs, George Washington University, August 2013): www2.gwu.edu/~sigur/assets/docs/BalancingActs_Compiled1.pdf.

Swaine, Michael D., "Chinese Leadership and Elite Responses to the US Pivot," *China Leadership Monitor*, no. 38 (2012): http://media.hoover.org/sites/default/files/documents/CLM38MS.pdf.

"Chinese Views and Commentary on the 'One Belt, One Road' Initiative," *China Leadership Monitor*, no. 47 (summer 2015): www.hoover.org/research/chinese-views-and-commentary-one-belt-one-road.

Swaine, Michael D. and Ashley J. Tellis, *Interpreting China's Grant Strategy: Past, Present and Future* (Santa Monica and Washington, DC: RAND, 2000).

Thomas, Daniel C., "Beyond Identity: Membership Norms and Regional Organization," *European Journal of International Relations*, Vol. 23, no. 1 (2016), pp. 217–40.

Thompson, Robert, *Resolving Controversy in the European Union: Legislative Decision-Making before and after Enlargement* (Cambridge: Cambridge University Press, 2011).

Tierney, Michael, "Rising Powers and the Regime for Development Finance," *International Studies Review*, Vol. 16, no. 3 (2014), pp. 452–55.

Truman, Edwin M., "G-20 Reforms of the International Monetary System: An Evaluation," *Peterson Institute for International Economics Policy Brief PB11-19* (Washington, DC: Peterson Institute for International Economics, November 2011).

Urpelainen, Johannes and Thijs Van de Graaf, "Your Place or Mine? Institutional Capture and the Creation of Overlapping International Institutions," *British Journal of Political Science*, Vol. 45, no. 4 (2015), pp. 799–827.

VanGrasstek, Craig, *The History and Future of the World Trade Organization* (Geneva: World Trade Organization, 2013).

Verdier, Daniel, "The Dilemma of Informal Governance with Outside Option as Solution," *International Theory*, Vol. 7, no. 1 (2015), pp. 195–229.

Vicary, Simon and Todd Sandler, "Weakest-Link Public Goods: Giving In-kind or Transferring Money," *European Economic Review*, Vol. 46, no. 8 (2002), pp. 1501–20.

Victor, David G., *The Collapse of the Kyoto Protocol and the Struggle to Slow Global Warming* (Princeton, NJ: Princeton University Press, 2004).

Viehe, Ariella, Aarthi Gunasekaran, Vivian Wang, and Stefanie Merchant, "Investments along China's Belt and Road Initiative," Center for American Progress, September 22, 2015: www.americanprogress.org/issues/security/news/2015/09/22/121689/investments-along-chinas-belt-and-road-initiative/.

Vinokurov, Evgeny and Alexander Libman, *Re-Evaluating Regional Organizations: Behind the Smokescreen of Official Mandates* (London: Springer, 2017).

Voeten, Erik, "Outside Options and the Logic of Security Council Action," *American Political Science Review*, Vol. 95, no. 4 (December 2001), pp. 845–58.

"Competition and Complementarity between Global and Regional Human Rights Institutions," *Global Policy*, Vol. 8, no. 1 (2017), pp. 119–23.

von Stein, Jana, "The International Law and Politics of Climate Change: Ratification of the United Nations Framework Convention and the Kyoto Protocol," *Journal of Conflict Resolution*, Vol. 52, no. 2 (2008), pp. 243–68.

Walter, Andrew, "China's Engagement with International Macroeconomic Policy Surveillance," in Eric Helleiner and Jonathan Kirshner, eds., *The Great Wall of Money: Power and Politics in China's International Monetary Relations* (Ithaca, NY: Cornell University Press, 2014), pp. 127–55.

Wang, Hongying and Erik French, "China in Global Economic Governance," *Asian Economic Policy Review*, Vol. 9, no. 2 (2014), pp. 254–71.

Wang, Jianwei, "China and the SCO: Towards a New Type of Interstate Relations," in Guoguang Wu and Helen Lansdowne, eds., *China Turns to Multilateralism: Foreign Policy and Regional Security* (London and New York: Routledge, 2008).

Wan, Ming, *The Asian Infrastructure Investment Bank: The Construction of Power and the Struggle for the East Asian International Order* (New York: Palgrave Macmillan, 2016).

Wang, Jue, "The People's Republic of China and the IMF," unpublished PhD Thesis, University of Warwick, Department of Politics and International Studies (September 2014): http://go.warwick.ac.uk/wrap.

Wang, Yong and Louis Pauly, "Chinese IPE Debates on (American) Hegemony," *Review of International Political Economy*, Vol. 20, no. 6 (December 2013), pp. 1165–88.

Ward, Andrew and Bertrand Benoit, "Deadlock Threatens Copenhagen Climate Deal," *Financial Times*, December 14, 2009: www.ft.com/cms/s/0/9bc43ba0-e8af-11de-9c1f-00144feab49a.html#axzz4ApTsl2Dw.

Weaver, Catherine and Manuela Moschella, "Bounded Reform in Global Economic Governance at the International Monetary Fund and the World Bank," in Orfeo Fioretos, ed., *International Politics and Institutions in Time* (London: Oxford University Press, 2017), pp. 274–92.

Weiss, Jessica Chen, *Powerful Patriots: Nationalist Protest in China's Foreign Relations* (New York: Oxford University Press, 2014).

Wit, Joel S., Daniel B. Poneman, and Robert L. Gallucci, *Going Critical: The First North Korean Nuclear Crisis* (Washington, DC: Brookings Institution Press, 2004).

Wihtol, Robert, "Beijing's Challenge to the Global Financial Architecture," *Georgetown Journal of Asian Affairs*, Spring/Summer 2015, pp. 7–15: https://asianstudies.georgetown.edu/sites/asianstudies/files/GJAA%20 2.1%20Wihtol,%20Robert_0.pdf.

World Bank, "World Bank Group Voice Reform: Enhancing Voice and Participation of Developing and Transition Countries in 2010 and Beyond, Report of the Development Committee Meeting" (April 2010): http:// siteresources.worldbank.org/DEVCOMMINT/Documentation/22553921/ DC2010-006(E)Voice.pdf.

Wu, Anne, "What China Whispers to North Korea," *The Washington Quarterly*, Vol. 28, no. 2 (Spring 2005), pp. 5–48.

Wu, Fuzuo, "Sino-Indian Climate Cooperation: Implications for the International Climate Change Regime," *Journal of Contemporary China*, Vol. 21, no. 77 (2012), pp. 827–43.

Wuthnow, Joel, "Posing Problems without an Alliance: China-Iran Relations after the Nuclear Deal." *Strategic Forum*, no. 290 (Washington, DC: National Defense University Press, 2016).

Yan, Xuetong, "China Can Thrive in the Trump Era," *The New York Times*, January 25, 2017, p. A25.

Yang, Hai, "The Asian Infrastructure Investment Bank and Status-Seeking: China's Foray into Global Economic Governance," *Chinese Political Science Review*, Vol. 1 (2016), pp. 754–78.

Yu, Hong, "Motivation behind China's 'One Belt, One Road' Initiatives and Establishment of the Asian Infrastructure Investment Bank," *Journal of Contemporary China*, Vol. 26, no. 105 (2017), pp. 353–68.

Yu, Yongding, "The G20 and China: A Chinese Perspective," *The G20 at Leaders' Level?* (Ottawa: International Development Research Centre, February 29, 2004): http://dspace.cigilibrary.org/jspui/bitstream/123456789/17390/1/ The%20G20%20and%20China%20A%20Chinese%20Perspective.pdf?1.

Yuan, Jing-Dong, "China's Role in Establishing and Building the Shanghai Cooperation Organization (SCO)," *Journal of Contemporary China*, Vol. 19, no. 67 (2010), pp. 855–69.

Zhang, Hongyu, "From Opponent to Proponent: The Rational Evolution of China's Nuclear Nonproliferation Policy," *Asian Politics & Policy*, Vol. 7, no. 2 (2015), pp. 283–301.

Zhang, Liangui, "Coping with a Nuclear North Korea," *China Security*, no. 4 (2006), pp. 2–18.

Zhang, Zhongxiang, "Breaking the Impasse in International Climate Negotiations: A New Direction for Currently Flawed Negotiations and a Roadmap for China till 2050," in Mingjiang Li, ed., *China Joins Global Governance: Cooperation and Contentions* (Lexington, MA: Lexington Books, 2015), pp. 173–86.

Zhao, Huasheng, "Central Asia in Chinese Strategic Thinking," in Thomas Fingar, ed., *The New Great Game: China and South and Central Asia in the Era of Reform* (Stanford, CA: Stanford University Press, 2016).

Zhou, Jiayi, Karl Hallding, and Guoyi Han, "The Trouble with China's 'One Belt, One Road' Strategy," *The Diplomat*, June 26, 2015: http://thediplomat .com/2015/06/the-trouble-with-the-chinese-marshall-plan-strategy/.

Zhu, Feng, "Flawed Mediation and a Compelling Mission: Chinese Diplomacy in the Six-Party Talks to Denuclearise North Korea," *East Asia*, Vol. 28, no. 3 (September 2011), pp. 191–218.

Zhu, Mingquan, "The Evolution of China's Nuclear Nonproliferation Policy," *The Nonproliferation Review*, Vol. 4, no. 2 (1997), pp. 40–8.

Chinese Language Sources

Bo, Yan, "Hezuo Yiyuan yu Hezuo Nengli yi zhong Fenxi Zhongguo Canyu Quanqiu Qihou Bianhua Zhili de Xin Kuangjia," ["Willingness to Cooperate with the New Framework for Cooperation Capacity --- China's Participation in Global Climate Change, a Governance Analysis"], *Shijie Jingji yu Zhengzhi*, no. 1 (2013), pp. 135–55.

Gao, E, "Lengzhanhou de Chaoxian Bandao xingshi" [The Post-Cold War Situation on the Korean Peninsula], *Yafei Zongheng*, no. 3 (1994), pp. 12–14.

Guo, Wen, "Chao Mei hezhengduan de lailongqumai" [The Origins and Development of the United States –North Korea Nuclear Dispute], *Guoji Zhanwang*, no. 13 (1994), pp. 11–13.

He, Zhilong and Zhao Xinggang, "Zhongya 'Yanse Geming' de Genyuan ji qi dui Zhongguo de Yingxiang" [The Root Causes of Central Asia's 'Color Revolutions' and their Impact on China], *Gansu Qingnian Guanli Ganbu Xueyuan Xuebao*, Vol. 18, no. 2 (2005).

Hu, Angang, "Tong Xiang Gebenhegen zhi Lu de Quanqiu Jian Pai Luxian Tu," [The Road to Copenhagen's Roadmap for Global Emissions Reduction], *Dangdai Ya Tai*, no. 6 (2008).

Jiang, Zhaijiu, "Zhongguo diqu duobian anquan hezuo de dongyin" [Motivations for China's Regional Multilateral Security Cooperation], *Guoji Zhengzhi Kexue*, no. 1 (2006), pp. 1–21.

Li, Baozhen, *Shanghai Hezuo Zuzhi yu Zhongguo de Heping Fazhan* [The Shanghai Cooperation Organization and China's Peaceful Development] (Beijing: Xinhua Chubanshe, 2011).

Li, Daokui, "Zuowei Yige Xinxing Daguo, Zhongguo Ying Jiji Canyu Guoji Jinrong Tixi Gaige" [China should Actively Participate in International Financial System Reform as an Emerging Power], *Zhongguo yu Shijie Guancha*, no. 1 (2009), pp. 57–60.

Li, Minlun, "Zhongguo "Xin Anquanguan" Yu Shanghai Hezuo Zuzhi Yanjiu" [Research on China's "New Security Concept" and the Shanghai Cooperation Organization] (Beijing: Renmin Chubanshe, 2007).

Li, Peng, "Zhongguo de Nengyuan Zhengce" (China's Energy Policy), *Qiu Shi*, no.11 (1997), pp. 524–32.

Li, Xiangyang, "Guoji jingji guize de xingcheng jizhi" [The Formation Mechanism of International Economic Rules], *Shijie Jingji yu Zhengzhi*, no. 9 (2006), pp. 69–78.

Liang, Qiang, "Shanghe Zuzhi de Shuang Hexin Kunao" [The Two Core Troubles of the Shanghai Cooperation Organization], *Nanfeng Chuang*, no. 12 (June 2006), pp. 68–70.

Liu, Dongmin and He Fan, "Zhong-Mei Jinrong Hezuo: Jinzhan, Tezheng, Tiaozhan yu Celue" [China - US Financial Cooperation: Progress, Characteristics, Challenges and Strategies], *Guoji Jingji Pinglun* (March 2014), pp. 81–3.

Liu, Fenghua, "Zhongguo zai Zhongya: Zhengce de Yanbian" (China in Central Asia: Policy Evolution), *Eluosi Zhongya Dongou Yanjiu*, no. 6 (2007), pp. 63–72.

Lu, Yousheng, "Can the U.S. Win Two Wars Simultaneously?" *Liaowang*, January 27, 2003 (in *World News Connection*, February 14, 2003).

Luo, Jie, "Zhongguo weishenme jiji cucheng liufang huitan: fang Chaoxian Bandao wenti zhuanjia Yu Meihua" [Why China Actively Facilitated the Six Party Talks: An Interview with Korean Peninsula Expert Yu Meihua], *Shijie Zhishi*, no. 18 (2003) p. 25.

Ma, Hong, "Jiakuai Zhongguo Shiyou Gongye Fazhan de Guanjian shi Shenru Gaige Kuada Kaifa" (The Key to Speeding up the Development of China's Petroleum Industry Is to Deepen Reform and Expand Openness), *Shiyou Qiye Guanli*, no. 5 (1995), pp. 3–7.

Pan, Guang, "Cong 'Shanghai Wuguo' Dao Shanghai Hezuo Zuzhi" [From the 'Shanghai Five' to the Shanghai Cooperation Organization], *Eluosi Yanjiu*, No. 124, no. 2 (2002), pp. 31–4.

Pan, Jiahua, "Gebenhagen qihou Huiyi de Zhengxi Jiaodian he Fansi" [Focal Points and Revisiting of the Copenhagen Controversy], *Renmin Ribao* (March 19, 2010).

Pang, Zhongying and Wang Ruiping, "Quanqiu Zhili: Zhongguo de Zhanlue Yingdui" [Global Governance: China's Strategic Response], *Guoji Wenti Yanjiu*, no. 4 (2013), pp. 57–68.

Shi, Bin, "Zhixu Zhuanxing, Guoji Fenpei Zhengyi yu Xinxing Daguo de Lishi" [Order Transition, International Distributive Justice and Historical Responsibility of the Emerging Powers], *Shijie Jingji yu Zhengzhi*, no. 12 (2010), pp. 69–100.

Shi, Yinhong, "Weixian he xiwang: Yilake Zhanzheng beijingxia de Chaoxian he wenti" [Danger and Hope: The North Korean Nuclear Issue against the Backdrop of the Iraq War], *Jiaoxue yu Yanjiu*, no. 5 (2003), pp. 50–3.

Su, Changhe, "Zhongguo yu Quanqiu Zhili – Jincheng, Xingwei, Jiegou yu Zhishi" [China and Global Governance: Process, Actions, Structure and Knowledge], *Guoji zhengzhi yanjiu*, no. 1 (2011), pp. 35–45.

Sun, Cheng, "Dierci Chaoxian heweiji" [The Second North Korean Nuclear Crisis], *Guoji Wenti Yanjiu*, no. 3 (2003) pp. 15–19.

Tian, Zhongqing, "Fengyun bianhuan de Chaoxian Bandao jushi" [The Constantly Changing Situation on the Korean Peninsula], *Guoji Zhanwang*, no. 7 (1993), pp. 9–11.

Wang, Guifang, "'Shanghai Five' Mechanism: Testimony of the Elevation of China's International Status," *Jiefangjun Bao*, June 15, 2001, in *World News Connection* ("JFJB Article Views on China's Unique Role in Developing 'Shanghai Five' Mechanism"), June 19, 2001.

Wang, Guoxing and Cheng Jing, "G20 jizhihua yu quanqiu jingji zhili gaige" [Institutionalization of G20 and Global Economic Governance Reform] *Guoji Zhanwang*, no. 4 (2010), pp. 8–18.

Wang, Jiayin, "Sulian Jietihou de Zhongya yu Zhongguo" (Central Asia and China after the Disintegration of the Soviet Union), *Guoji Zhengzhi Yanjiu*, no. 4 (1995), pp. 3–27.

Wang, Weimin, "Qianxi Shijiezhijiao de Shiyou Zhengduozhan" [An Analysis of the Battle for Oil at the Turn of the Century, *Xiandai Guoji Guanxi*, no. 3 (1998), pp. 19–23.

Wang, Xiaogang, "'Gongtong dan you Qubie de Zeren' Yuanze de Shiyong jiqi Xianzhi," [Application and Limits of the Principle of "Common but Differentiated Responsibility], *Shehui Kexue*, no. 7 (2010), pp. 80–9.

Wang, Xiaoquan, "Eluosi dui Shanghai Hezuo Zuzhi de Zhengce Yanbian" [The evolution of Russia's policy toward the Shanghai Cooperation Organization], *Eluosi Zhongya Dongou Yanjiu*, no. 3, (2007), pp. 67–75.

Wen, Jiabao, "Jiaqiang Guoji Jishu Hezuo Jiji Ying Dui Qihou Bianhua," [Strengthen International Technical Cooperation in Tackling Climate Change], *Xin Shijie Lingdaozhe* Vol. 11, no. 6 (2008), pp. 55–56.

Xia, Yishan, "'Shanghai Hezuo Zuzhi' de Tedian ji qi Fazhan Qianjing" (The Characteristics and Development Prospects for the "Shanghai Cooperation Organization"), *Heping yu Fanzhan*, no. 3 (2001), pp. 22–4.

Xie, Zhenhua. "Yingdui Qihou Bianhua Wenti Zhongguo Zhen Zhua Shigan," [China Grasps Hard Work to Tackle the Problem of Climate Change] *WTO Jingji Daokan*, no. 11 (2008), pp. 53–4 (published by PRC Ministry of Commerce).

Xin, Benjian, "Ge Hui Pi Fada Da Guojia Bi Zhi Shibai Bianyuan," [Developed Countries bring the Copenhagen Meetings to the Brink of Failure], *Renmin Ribao* (December 20, 2009), p. 1.

Xing, Guangcheng and Sun Zhuangzhi, *Shanghai Hezuo Zuzhi Yanjiu [A Study of the Shanghai Cooperation Organization]* Changchun: Changchun Chuban She, 2007).

Xu, Weidi, "Chaoxian Bandao Heweiji de Huajie yu Bandao Zouchu Lengzhan" [Resolving the Korean Peninsula Nuclear Crisis and Moving beyond the Cold War on the Peninsula], *Shijie Jingji yu Zhengzhi*, no. 9 (2003), pp. 59–64.

Xu, Tongkai, *Shanghai Hezuo Zuzhi Quyu Jingji Hezuo* [The Shanghai Cooperation Organization's Regional Economic Cooperation] (Beijing: Renmin Chubanshi, 2009).

Yang, Xiqian, "Sulian Jietihou de Zhongya Xingshi" (The Situation in Central Asia after the Soviet Disintegration), *Sulian Yanjiu*, no. 4 (September 1992), pp. 1–5.

Yu, Hongyuan, "Zhongguo Ying Jiji Canyu Guoji Qihou Tanpan" [China Should Positively Participate in International Climate Negotiations], *Shehui Guancha*, no. 11 (2014), pp. 13–16.

Yu, Jianhua, *Shanghai Hezuo Zuzhi Feichuantong Anquan Yanjiu [Shanghai Cooperation Organization Nontraditional Security Research]* (Shanghai: Shanghai Shehui Kexueyuan Chubanshe, 2009).

Zhang, Haibin, "Zhongguo zai Guoji Qihou Bianhua Tanpan zhong de Lichang: Lianxuxing yu Bianhua jiqi Yuanyin Tanxi" [China's Positions in International Climate Change Negotiations: Continuity and Change and Analysis of Its Causes], *Shijie Jingji yu Zhengzhi*, no. 10 (2006), pp. 36–43.

Zhang, Liangui, "Chaohe Wenti Youyao Shengji?" [Will the Korean Nuclear Issue Intensify Once Again?], *Shijie Zhishi*, no. 12 (2003), pp. 22–3.

"Chaoxian Bandao Hewenti Zongheng Tan" [A Broad Discussion of the Korean Peninsula Nuclear Issue], *Guoji Shehui yu Jingji*, no. 9 (1994), pp. 1–5.

"Chaoxian de Hewuqi yu Meiguo de Jingcha Juese" [North Korea's Nuclear Weapons and America's Role as Policeman], *Zhanlue yu Guanli*, no. 5 (2003), pp. 65–77.

Zhang, Ming, "Cidai Weiji dui Dangqian Guoji Huobi Tixi de Chongji" [The Impact of Sub-prime Crisis to International Monetary System], *Shijie Jingji yu Zhengzhi*, no. 6 (2010), pp. 74–80.

"Guoji Huobi Tixi Gaige: Beijing, Yuanyin, Cuoshi ji Zhongguo de Canyu" [International Currency System Reform: Background, Reasons, Measures, and China's Participation], *Guoji Jingji Pinglun*, no. 1 (2010), pp. 114–137.

"Quanqiu Huobi huhuan xianzhuang – gongneng ji guoji huobitixi gaige de qianzai fangxiang" [The Current Situation of Global Currency Swaps - Function and the Potential Direction of International Monetary System Reform], *Guoji Jingji Pinglun*, no. 6 (2012), pp. 65–88.

Zhang, Shengzhang and Li Chunlin, "Gebenhegen Qihou Bianhua Huiyishang Wo Guo Mianlin de Tiaozhang ji Yingdui," [Challenges Faced by Our Country at the Copenhagen Climate Change Meetings and Responses], *Kunming Ligong Daxue Xuebao (Shehui Kexue Ban)*, Vol. 9, no. 11 (2009), pp. 11–16.

Zhao, Huasheng, *Zhongguo de Zhongya Waijiao* (China's Central Asian Diplomacy) (Beijing: Shishi Chubanshi, 2008).

"Zhongya Xingshi Bianhua yu 'Shanghai Hezuo Zuzhi'" [The Changing Situation in Central Asia and the 'Shanghai Cooperation Organization'], *Dongou Zhongya Yanjiu*, no. 6 (2002), pp. 54–9.

"Touxi Eluosi yu Shanghai Hezuo Zuzhi Guanxi" (Analyzing the Relationship between Russia and the Shanghai Cooperation Organization), *Guoji Guanxi Yanjiu*, no. 1 (2011), pp. 15–23.

Zhao, Longgeng, "Shixi Meiguo Zhujun Zhongya Hou de Zhanlue Taishi ji qi dui Woguo Anquan Liyi de Yingxiang" [An Analysis of the Situation after the US Deployment of Troops in Central Asia and Its Implications for China's Security Interests], *Eluosi Zhongya Dongou Yanjiu*, no. 2, (2004), pp. 68–73.

Zheng, Liansheng and Zhang Ming, "Zhongguo Zhengfu Yinggai Qiangli Tuidong Renminbi Jiaru SDR me?" [Should the Chinese Government Strongly Push for the RMB to Enter the SDR?], *Guoji Jinrong*, July 2015, pp. 3–6.

Zheng, Yu, ed., *Dulianti Shinian: Xianzhuang, Wenti, Qianjing* [Ten10 Years of the Commonwealth of Independent States: Current Situation, Problems, and Prospects] (Beijing: Zhongguo Shehui Kexue Chubanshe, 2007).

Zhou, Xiaochuan, *Reform the International Monetary System*, March 23, 2009,: www.bis.org/review/r090402c.pdf.

Zhu, Feng, "Bushi zhengfu de bandao zhengce yu Chaoxian heweiji" [The Bush Administration's Peninsula Policy and the North Korean Nuclear Crisis], *Xiandai Guoji Guanxi*, no. 2 (2003), pp. 1–7.

Zhu, Min, "Shijie Xuyao Zhongguo de Shengyin" [The World Needs China's Voice], *Jingji Huanjing Wang*, October 12, 2009: www.eeo.com.cn/observer/shijiao/2009/12/10/157756.shtml.

"Yanjiu "Weijihou de shijie jingji jinronggeju" de wuge wenti"' [Research the Five Problems of Post-Crisis World Economic and Financial Patterns], *Guoji Jingji Pinglun* (July–August 2009), pp. 25–7.

Zong, Zhangyao, Zhang Bo, Liu Yanyan, and Zhang Yong, "Zhongguo Yingdui Qihou Bianhua yu Qihua Bianhua Waijiao," ["China's Response to Climate Change and Climate Change Diplomacy"], *Zhongguo Ruan Kexue*, no. 11 (2014), pp. 9–16.

Index